PHILOSOPHERS OF NOTHINGNESS

James W. Heisig & John Maraldo, eds., *Rude Awakenings: Zen, the Kyoto School, & the Question of Nationalism* (1995)

Jamie Hubbard & Paul L. Swanson, eds., *Pruning the Bodhi Tree: The Storm over Critical Buddhism* (1997)

Mark R. Mullins, *Christianity Made in Japan: A Study of Indigenous Movements* (1998)

Jamie Hubbard, *Absolute Delusion, Perfect Buddhahood: The Rise and Fall of a Chinese Heresy* (2001)

James W. Heisig, *Philosophers of Nothingness: An Essay on the Kyoto School* (2001)

Philosophers of Nothingness

An Essay on the Kyoto School

James W. Heisig

University of Hawai'i Press
HONOLULU

Originally published in Spanish as *Filósofos de la nada: Un ensayo sobre la escuela de Kioto,* © 2001 Editorial Herder (Barcelona)

Printed in the United States of America

07 06 05 04 03 6 5 4 3 2

Library of Congress Cataloging-in-Publication Data

Heisig, James W.
Philosophers of nothingness: an essay on the Kyoto school / James W. Heisig
p. cm.
ISBN 0-8248-2480-6 (cloth : alk. paper) — ISBN 0-8248-2481-4 (pbk. : alk. paper)
1. Philosophy, Japanese—20th century. 2. Nishida, Kitarō, 1870–1945. 3. Tanabe Hajime, 1885–1962. 4. Nishitani, Keiji, 1900– 5. Nothing (Philosophy)
B5241. H47 2001
181'. 12—dc 2001017133

University of Hawai'i Press books are printed on acid-free paper and meet the guidelines for permanence and durability of the Council on Library Resources.

Camera-ready copy for this book was prepared by the Nanzan Institute for Religion and Culture

Printed by The Maple-Vail Book Manufacturing Group

Contents

Preface to the English Edition

THE IDEA OF WRITING a book about the leading figures of the Kyoto school has been in the back of my mind longer than I care to remember. What kept it from moving forward, more than anything else, was the expectation that someone qualified would soon be taking the project up and perhaps even asking for assistance. As expectations go, it was not unreasonable. There are any number of people well suited to the task, and there were many others like me willing to help out where we could. The years went on, and while the amount of specialized and more narrowly focused research on the Kyoto school increased, the challenge of producing a general overview went unanswered both in Japan and abroad. A number of circumstances then came together that persuaded me to take the matter in hand myself.

In 1999 we invited a young scholar from the Universitat Pompeu Fabra in Barcelona, Raquel Bouso, to join us at the Nanzan Institute for Religion and Culture in Nagoya, Japan, to complete her Spanish translation of Nishitani Keiji's *Religion and Nothingness*. She came accompanied by Professors Amador Vega and Victoria Cirlot, and the four of us collaborated for six intense weeks on the final editing and revision of the work, which was published later that year. I was subsequently offered a visiting professorship at Pompeu Fabra, and the staff of the Nanzan Institute encouraged me to accept the position, offering to take over my duties for the year. A generous grant from the Itō Scholarship Foundation enabled me to purchase the sizable collection of resource materials needed to undertake the work away from Japan. This collection has since been donated in its entirety to Pompeu Fabra, where it will be available to other scholars in Europe interested in the Kyoto school.

So it happened that I came to Barcelona, where ideal working conditions made it possible for me to complete the book you now have in your hands. Despite the simple organization of the chapters, and the style in which I have presented them, I have to admit that the work of condensing the data and ideas often got the better of me. As I look back over the results,

I can still see the tight pleats where pages of writing have been squeezed into a single paragraph, and the seams where whole bolts of material have simply been cut. For a general audience interested in twentieth-century Japanese philosophy, it may be a tight fit; for the more specialized reader already familiar with the subject, I am afraid it may still be too loose.

At least part of the reason for the ambivalence is that the project was tailored to my personal investment in the subject matter. From the outset, I wanted to take the opportunity to sort out what I understood about the Kyoto school from what I only thought I had. In reviewing the notes and translations I had compiled over the years, I soon realized that there was a lot less to lift from them—and indeed from my precious publications on the subject—than I had anticipated. Too much of it was cavalier or misleading. I also realized that there were large amounts of secondary literature that deserved more careful attention, and fairer judgment, than I had given them in the past. In any case, my main concern throughout the body of the text was to make sense, to my own satisfaction, of the three major figures of the Kyoto school, Nishida, Tanabe, and Nishitani. Wherever I could, I found sense in their own explanations or in that of their principal commentators; where I could not find it, I made it. In the notes I have turned the lining inside out to show not only the sources I consulted and my reactions to many of them, but also the tangle of threads and loose ends hidden by the abbreviated accounts and cleaner patterns I have labored to present on the surface.

I had thought at first to wait for reactions to the original Spanish edition of the book before preparing an English translation, reckoning that more criticism and a little distance would make for improving the text. On further reflection, I realized that the most efficient course of action would be to make the rendition while everything was still fresh in my mind. Accordingly, there is very little here that differs from the original Spanish.

Questions of composition and technicalities aside, I remain as convinced as ever that there is a wisdom to be discovered in philosophies of nothingness like that of the Kyoto school. Like all awakening, it comes in sparks, only to be swallowed up again in the ordinary conventionalities of thought. It is when those sparks flicker closer together and for longer periods that the darkness of philosophical jargon begins to yield something of its secret. My only excuse for inflicting a résumé so long and winding as this one has turned out to be is the hope of communicating something of the illumination these philosophers have brought me.

There are so many people to thank, I hardly know where to start. Ueda Shizuteru and Horio Tsutomu were most unselfish in answering my many questions, usually in much more detail than I had asked for. Paul Swanson, in addition to taking over the directorship of the Nanzan Institute, had to put up with my incessant requests for books and articles. Ed Skrzypczak read through the entire text with his usual devotion to detail. And finally, there is that wide and sympathetic community of Kyoto-school scholars around the world, without whose advice and resources at each step of the way this book would be much the poorer. To all of them, my thanks.

James W. Heisig
Barcelona
1 October 2000

Orientation

1

THE KYOTO SCHOOL. The emergence of the Kyoto school marks a watershed in intellectual history. Not only does this group of philosophers represent Japan's first sustained and original contribution to western philosophical thought, they do so from a distinctively eastern perspective. Far from simply reupholstering traditional philosophical questions in an oriental décor, theirs is a disciplined and well-informed challenge to the definition of the history of philosophy itself. The fact that the formative years of this new current of thinking coincided with a period of intense nationalism and militarism in Japan has tended to retard recognition of their achievement both at home and abroad. A countercoincidence of efforts on both sides over the last two decades puts us in a better position today to reassess the Kyoto school and its place in the intellectual history of this world. This book is an account of that reassessment.

The first time the designation "Kyoto school" seems to have appeared in print was in a 1932 newspaper article by Tosaka Jun entitled "The Philosophy of the Kyoto School." His reasons for using the term were two. First, he wanted to draw attention to the fact that the pioneering work of the celebrated Nishida Kitarō (1870–1945), who had retired from active teaching some years previously and moved to Kamakura, was being advanced in new and no less creative form by his principal disciple and Tosaka's own teacher, Tanabe Hajime (1885–1962), who had succeeded Nishida in the chair of philosophy at Kyoto Imperial University. Without in any way belittling the "Nishida school" devoted to "Nishida philosophy" (among whom he singles out Miki Kiyoshi, another young thinker of Marxist leanings, as the brightest star on the horizon), Tosaka felt that these expressions did not do justice to Tanabe or capture the whole of intellectual history in the making. In a companion article he states his case still more strongly:

> In blessing the emergence of the Kyoto school, I mean to say that if Tanabe had not taken up the succession, Nishida philosophy would probably have ended up merely as Nishida philosophy.... But now Nishida philosophy is assured a transmission through the Kyoto school.

His second reason was to exercise what he saw as his "moral duty" to voice a criticism of the approach to philosophy that Nishida had introduced and Tanabe had followed:

> Nishida's philosophy, in a word, represents the most superb *bourgeois philosophy of ideas* in our country if not in the world, ...a fact that perhaps everyone has already surmised.... Though it has been able to treat matters that overstep the phenomenon of consciousness completely, it can only be called *a phenomenology* in the highest degree.

Tosaka's complaint was that in the attempt to undercut the polarity between idealism and materialism, Nishida had sacrificed historical consciousness to his preoccupation with the interiority of self-awareness. This sacrifice lay so close to the core of his philosophical method that, when Tanabe tried to find his own way beyond the polarity by introducing historical praxis and social consciousness into the picture, in the end he, too, was unable to break through the fixation on individual consciousness:

> We might say that Nishida provides the technology for the production of ideas and Tanabe has given the logical method for their marketing.... Nishida-Tanabe philosophy—the philosophy of the Kyoto school—looks to have pretty well summed up the accounts of bourgeois philosophy in Japan.

The tone of Tosaka's comment is respectful but firm in the conviction that the best philosophy Japan had to offer lacked a clear view of the world and was feeding on its own abstractions in the "hothouse" of academia. He was not airing criticisms he had not already discussed in the circles of Nishida's and Tanabe's disciples, and he assumed they were already well known. But he felt it necessary to state publicly that to ignore or undervalue the changes that were taking place in society would be the undoing of any philosophical position, no matter how remarkable the genius of those who upheld it. Despite his youth and beyond his own socialist sympathies, Tosaka knew that there was more at stake than preference for one philosophical method over another. In a few short years his ideas would cost him his academic career and land him in prison, where, still a young man, he would die for his convictions. As for his teachers Nishida and Tanabe, they too were to learn the consequences of carrying their ideas into the turbulent and irrational winds of a political system bent on exerting its military might at all costs.

Exactly who first coined the term *Kyoto school* or when it gained currency is hard to say. In all likelihood it emerged casually from the rather substantial circle of students and professors that had formed around Nishida during his final years at Kyoto and that had continued with Tanabe. By all accounts it was a mixed group, perhaps two dozen in all, who came together in clusters for informal or semiformal discussions on a wide variety of subjects. It was hardly a "school" in any ordinary sense of the term, but rather the kind of spontaneous academic vitality that so often emerges around great thinkers. As the pressures of a special police force set up to monitor ideas dangerous to national unity increased by degrees from the middle to late 1930s, the concentration of brilliant young minds in Kyoto naturally came to draw more and more attention to itself.

Tosaka's appellation had come at just the right time and quickly gained currency in academic and political circles, both left and right. Though his original intentions were quickly forgotten, the name remained. And the more the name was used, the more it tended to flatten out the considerable philosophical differences among those thought to belong to the school. Once the imperial armies of Japan had started gallivanting around Asia, everything changed. Many ideas that had once been right were left, and left right. National and ethnic identity, the rejection of wholesale western-style democracy and culture, the recovery of Asian roots, and so forth, were all usurped by a scrappy set of ideas that advertised itself as a philosophy of "the imperial way." The Marxist left capitulated or remained silent. The old right found their ideas taken over to fatten up the new imperial ideology and its military ambitions. Later historians would look back on these events, with the clearer standards of hindsight, to distinguish right, left, and center wings in the Kyoto school on the basis of how they had responded to the situation politically.

Although checks on freedom of expression within state universities and fear of reprisals dimmed the enthusiasm of many professors and students for association with the Kyoto intellectuals, a small cluster of thinkers struggled to keep the tradition alive. The most outstanding of these thinkers was Nishitani Keiji (1900–1990), a student whom Nishida and Tanabe had recognized from early on as an exceptionally gifted mind, who would eventually go on to develop what he had inherited from his teachers into a philosophy of his own. Less cautious than his teachers, Nishitani brought his considerable learning and youthful idealism to bear on the political ideology of the day, only to be swept along in currents much stronger than he had been prepared for.

It is from these three figures—Nishida, Tanabe, and Nishitani—that the Kyoto school radiates as a philosophical movement. Within that compass a number of minor figures move in and out, depending on whether the focus is strictly philosophical or fixed on the relationship of the circle of Kyoto University intellectuals to the military establishment of Japan during the second world war. More important than the question of who else should be counted a member of the school and on what grounds is the question of how much of that history has to be reconstructed in order to appreciate the thinking of these central figures. This is still a matter of some debate. Those who have made a career of the intellectual history of wartime Japan demand more; those who have focused on the pure philosophy are satisfied with less.

In the pages that follow I will try to strike a balance, but not without first stating my conclusion: *One has, deliberately or otherwise, to ignore the greatest bulk of the writings of these thinkers to arrive at the conclusion that anything approaching or supporting the imperialistic ideology of wartime Japan belongs to the fundamental inspiration of their thought. Insofar as any of them did willingly add support, it may be considered an aberration from their own intellectual goals.*

In large measure the philosophical world of Japan seems to have struck a balance of its own in recent years. By the 1970s the term *Kyoto school* had virtually disappeared from the scene. But then, too, so had interest in the philosophies of Nishida, Tanabe, and Nishitani, except for a small coterie of former disciples and younger students, mainly centered in Kyoto. It is too much to say that the political stigma had uprooted from its native soil Japan's first important philosophical movement, but at least it had some part to play in committing it prematurely to the museum of outdated ideas.

A resurgence of interest in the Kyoto school was stimulated in part by the interest of western philosophers and theologians, not by having worked through their political record, but at least initially by simply ignoring it. As more and more of the writings became available in translation, the intellectual content was brought into clearer relief than it had among scholars of Japan's ideological history. This encouraged a renaissance of interest in Japan. Although focus was originally on Nishida, recently the rediscovery of Tanabe's thought and the first steps toward a comprehensive appreciation of Nishitani's work have emerged as well. Throughout the early years of the restoration of Nishida and Tanabe to grace in contemporary Japanese philosophy, Nishitani was still alive and his presence was a major factor. Not only did he continue up to his last years to welcome visitors from abroad interested in the Kyoto school, but he also continued to lecture around Japan until well into his eighties.

Time has a way of sifting out the incidentals of a philosophy, and in most cases ends up in discarding entire philosophies from collective memory. What time has shown in the case of the Kyoto philosophers is that their thinking offers a fruitful and still vital meeting place for philosophy and religion east and west. As for those intellectual historians who want to dismiss this turn of events from a higher moral ground, the burden of proof that time has done a bad job of it, that those who read the philosophy are likely to be infected with morally unacceptable ideas, rests with them. This burden, it seems to me, has not been borne. On the contrary, the respectable connotation that the name "Kyoto school" enjoys in the west has more or less rubbed off on Japan as well, even if those closest to the center and more conscious of the history, have preferred to speak of Nishida, Tanabe, and Nishitani as creators of distinct but related philosophies. In any case, it is around these three thinkers that I have organized this essay on the Kyoto school.

2 JAPANESE PHILOSOPHY AS WORLD PHILOSOPHY. In the Kyoto school we have the makings of a school of thought able to stand shoulder to shoulder with major schools and currents of philosophy in the west. More than that, it is the *first* philosophical current in Japan of which this can be said. Nishida was the wellspring; of that there can be no question. But, as Tosaka had recognized, Nishida's work alone would not have sufficed to put Japanese thought on the map of world philosophy, even with the help of first-rate disciples. For that it needed the counterfoil of Tanabe's thought and the creative enlargements of Nishitani. It is no accident that the translations of major works of Tanabe and Nishitani catapulted Nishida to a position of prominence abroad that his own writings, already around in translation for over four decades, had not attained for him.

The claim that a new dimension has been added to world philosophy leads us through something of a fog before it clears into the radical declaration that it is. In the broadest dictionary definition of the term *philosophy*, the claim is empty. If virtually any more or less conscious myth or framework of values can qualify as a philosophy, then new philosophies are coming and going around the world all the time, and there is no reason Japan should be any different. Narrowing the term down to refer to a more critical body of thought dealing with ultimate questions, systematically recorded and transmitted, one has to say that Japan has produced its share of such philosophies since the time of the esoteric Buddhist thinker Kūkai in the ninth century.

But if one understands philosophy in its stricter sense as the particular intellectual tradition that began in Athens in the sixth century before the common era, spread through the Greek and the Roman empires, took root in the countries of Europe from the fourth century and in the Americas from the seventeenth, then the claim of Japan's participation takes on a different sense. The line of thinkers from Socrates, Plato, and Aristotle to Aquinas, Descartes, Kant, and James that western history refers to as philosophy in the strict sense of the term has never been broken, spliced, enlarged, or seriously challenged by Asian thought. Rudyard Kipling could never have gotten away with the refrain that east is east and west is west had there been an inclusive notion of philosophy that accepted as an essential ingredient something of the immense intellectual heritage of India, China, Korea, and Japan. It is one thing provisionally to extend the term *philosophy* to traditions of thought in those countries for purposes of comparison, but even this very idea of *comparative* philosophy ends up confirming the separation and covertly supporting the assumption that the only *world* philosophy is philosophy done in the western mold. This is the mold that Nishida, Tanabe, and Nishitani have broken, though the consequences of that rupture have only just begun to affect those engaged in classical western philosophy around the world.

It is no more correct to speak of the Kyoto philosophers as representing eastern philosophy than it is to speak of their use of Zen and Pure Land Buddhism as representing Mahāyāna Buddhism. Let there be no mistake about it: the Kyoto philosophers are eastern and they are Buddhist. But their aim and context is neither eastern nor Buddhist. To see their non-Christian and non-western elements as a kind of oriental spice to enliven certain questions on the menu of western philosophy may be the simplest way to open one's mind to their writings and yet keep them at arm's reach. It also happens to be the way the vast majority of Japanese academics specializing in philosophy have tried to make an original contribution to their field acceptable to the west. In this sense, resistance in Japan to a more encompassing notion of world philosophy has been every bit as strong as, if not stronger than, it is in the west. The step of the Kyoto philosophers onto the forum of world philosophy was by no means as welcome a move at home as one might think.

For Nishida and his colleagues in the Kyoto school there was no way to break through the assumption that the western philosophical tradition must remain the primary domain of western culture except by actually working on a different assumption. They realized that philosophy would always *at least* be western philosophy, and for that reason held themselves responsible for the same general critical awareness of that philosophy as their counterparts in Europe and the Americas. Their contribution would have to be not at the expense of everything philosophy has been, but at its enhancement.

Though they would not have said anything so presumptuous on their own, I have no hesitation in claiming that just as, for example, the way we read Aristotle and Descartes is different after Kant and Hegel, so our reading of Aristotle and Descartes, Kant and Hegel, Heidegger and Nietzsche, should be different after reading Nishida, Tanabe, and Nishitani. To the extent that this is not the case regarding the authors with whose thought they have struggled—and most certainly often it *is* not—it can be said that the Kyoto philosophers have failed to live up to their goals. It is really as simple as that.

There is no single standpoint from which to assess the fruits of their efforts fairly at one swipe. There is no denying the fact that their writings have altered the place of western philosophy in Japan and of Japanese philosophy in the west. On the one hand, they have had, and continue to have, a considerable impact on those among Zen and Pure Land theoreticians, few in numbers though they be, in search of a fresh self-understanding grounded in a wider intellectual perspective. On the other, these thinkers have made the way to eastern philosophy more accessible for a good many westerners who are not yet prepared to think in terms of a world philosophy incorporating east and west. But it is precisely *because* of their commitment to the universal idiom of philosophy, and the success with which they carried it out, that this can be said.

As for their place in the story of world philosophy, my own judgment is that the best that the Kyoto philosophers have to offer sets them squarely on a par with the best western philosophical minds of their time, and in the Japanese context head and shoulders higher. As my critics remind me often enough, I have little cause to applaud my own objectivity in the matter. After all, this is a judgment that comes at the end of more than two decades of dipping in and out of their works when I could have been reading other things. On one conclusion, however, I stand firm. The philosophers of the Kyoto school have given us a world philosophy, one that belongs as rightfully to the inheritance as much as the western philosophies with which they wrestled and from which they drew their inspiration. And, if I be permitted the unkindness of stating what is already implicit in the foregoing, their achievement completely eclipses the scholarly contribution that professional Japanese philosophers specializing in western thinkers have made in the twentieth century.

3 THE BACKGROUND OF WESTERN PHILOSOPHY IN JAPAN.

Looked at from the broader perspective of the history of world philosophy, the story of western philosophy in Japan divides into two with the career of

Nishida. Looked at from within Japan, there is no such watershed, just another landmark along the road. It is worth our while at least to have a look at how western philosophy has been studied in Japan in order to understand why this is so.

The image of the American ships anchoring in the harbors of Japan's capital city of Edo in 1854, determined to pry open the doors of a country that had locked itself off from the world for over two and a half centuries, is not quite accurate. One should think rather of a mother hen pecking at the eggshell to help the chick who has already decided it wants to break out. The Japanese had had enough. They had kept up just enough contact with the outside world to know of the scientific and technological advances of Europe, of the industrial revolution, and of the birth of statehood, and they were anxious to gain access to this new world that had grown up during their isolation.

Their naiveté, of course, left them in a position of weakness, which the western economic and political powers were happy to exploit. The result was that once Japan's government had opened the front door, they found themselves unable to control the pace of change, and that meant forfeiting the leisure of reflecting upon what they wanted and what they did not. The country was flooded not only with new products, foods, clothing, information, and technology but also with the demand for social change that the acceptance of these goods and services forced upon them. What looked to the upholders of traditional Japanese values like an invasion looked to the invaders like just another exercise of the free market. The patterns familiar to Europe and the United States repeated themselves all over again as the forces of industrialization galloped ahead, trampling anything that dared to block the way.

From the start, a number of Japan's more reflective intellectuals knew that they were not equipped to process the whole sea-change that went under the name of "modernization." They saw that there was no immediate way to compete with the obvious superiority of the goods and services being imported from the west. But they also saw that at the end of this forced suspension of judgment—or at least suspension of judgment with any executive power—the Japanese would have to take their destiny in their own hands. The most pressing concern, then, was to prepare the way by securing expertise for themselves in everything the west was pressing on them. "Catch up, overtake!" went the slogan directed at the cooperation of the populace at large.

While the structure of society had been overhauled along western models to serve the purpose, the structure of the government was also gradually transformed from a feudal system to something more or less along the lines of a western nation with the imperial household at the center, at least in name. As the leadership grew more confident, it spread its authority in two very different if not contradictory directions made to look complementary. On the one hand it guided the education system to preserve the traditional values that had been the bulwark of social harmony. Even where these reforms were well thought out, they were shadowed from the first by proponents of the dying feudal order who advocated a rejection of western-style democracy and morals in favor of a doctrine of "Revere the emperor, expel the barbarians!" On the other hand, the government was determined to build itself up militarily to protect its prosperity. "Wealthy country, strong army!" went the slogan aimed at justifying the appropriation of increasing resources to achieve military parity with the outside world.

All of these factors came into play within the space of a single generation, seeding the Japanese soul with the makings of a mass neurosis of preoccupation with its own identity. Thereon hangs the tale of the spiritual environment that twentieth-century Japan inherited and whose symptoms were to provoke not only social upheavals and ideological nationalism in Japan but also to lay the foundations for its modern intellectual history. This, in crude strokes, was the atmosphere in which the Kyoto school philosophers lived and thought.

One of the first steps the Japanese took to catch up with the west was to translate its books—and translate they did, tens of thousands of books on everything from classical literature to medical science. Along with this went the dispatching of young scholars to leading academic centers of the west where they could study the intellectual background of the modern world in the languages of its guiding lights. This was the mood in which the first of the young Japanese, sixty-eight of them between 1862 and 1867, were sent abroad to study and prepare the way for other students.

Among the first to leave was Nishi Amane, who was dispatched to Holland to study law and economics but concentrated his attentions at Leiden on philosophy instead. "In our country there is nothing that deserves to be called philosophy," he wrote home. Though the works he wrote in returning home are only of historical interest today, it was he who is credited as the first to bring western philosophy, as well as a Japanese word for it, to his country.

The wider history of ideas surrounding modernization and the adaptation of western ideas is an extremely rich one, and it is somewhat artificial to try to sort out where western philosophy belongs. It was certainly not the primary concern of most Japanese intellectuals. Some there were, even among those who had studied abroad, that felt the entire move towards academic specialization on the one hand and the construction of general philosophies on the other was an offence to the traditional Japanese idea of learning.

In any case, as the understanding of western philosophy grew throughout the last quarter of the nineteenth century and into the twentieth, it did not flow naturally into the deep channels of indigenous thought. In place of an already existing collective awareness of the distinction between universal truth and vernacular representations of it, philosophy ran headlong into classical Confucian ethics and sectarian religious doctrine. For half a century it streamed broad and shallow over a terrain unprepared for its deeper currents, washing occasionally into the mainstream of Buddhist thought with thinkers like Kiyozawa Manshi and Inoue Enryō or into a systematic ethic with the likes of Fukuzawa Yukichi. For the most part, however, it was seen as no more than an object of curiosity, certainly not as practical as western science or as instructive as western literature.

It was the genius of Nishida and his successors to have first conducted the philosophical tradition of the west into channels dug fresh and to the measure of the modern Japanese mind. The more one understands this story of philosophy's birth in Japan, the more one understands that it did not enjoy a normal childhood. It was denied the natural aging process that produced western philosophy as we know it. Fully twenty-five centuries earlier, the Greeks on the coast of Asia Minor, pressured by the advance of surrounding civilizations, had sought to break free of the confines of a mythical world-view and describe the world and its origins in natural, realistic terms. Within a century there emerged metaphysical principles that crystallized the critique of mythical anthropomorphism into conceptual terms, opening the way to an objective study of nature. This confrontation between the world of the gods beyond and the world of nature here below set an agenda to philosophy that continues to inform vast areas of western culture. Indeed, without it the history of free and critical thought that is the soul of philosophy would not seem to make sense.

The Japanese entered philosophical tradition without that history, standing on the shoulders of post-Kantian preoccupations with epistemology, scientific methodology, and the overcoming of metaphysics. This makes it all the more remarkable that the study of philosophy both ancient and modern should have advanced so quickly to such high levels in Japan's institutions of higher learning, and that in less than two generations they were to produce their first original philosophical school. That the thinkers of this school should have phrased the perennial questions of philosophy on different assumptions is hardly to be wondered at.

4 WORKING ASSUMPTIONS OF THE KYOTO PHILOSOPHERS.

One speaks of the Kyoto philosophers Nishida, Tanabe, and Nishitani as a "school" not only because of their having shared chairs successively at the same university, but because there are fundamental working assumptions they share in common. The differences between the three will perhaps stand out more clearly later if we first lay out some of these assumptions.

In doing so, it should be noted that these assumptions they share are not necessarily held by others in the wider reaches of the "school." By the same token, broadening the definition of the school would oblige us to add other assumptions that were not primary for these three. Thus the elements I will single out here have been extrapolated from the texts of their writings, where not infrequently they work tacitly, and in any case are nowhere laid out as neatly as they are here.

It should also be noted that the Kyoto philosophers approach western thinking *as a whole,* not only all of philosophy but all of religion, science, and literature as well. This gives them the freedom to leap across centuries and across shifts of cultural, economic, and political modes of thought with the ease we are more likely to associate with esoteric traditions than with mainstream philosophical thinking. At least until recently, we should add, this is the same way western philosophy—and indeed eastern thought itself—has tended to treat the intellectual traditions of the Far East. Thus the temptation to rush at once into comparing particular assumptions below with ideas and currents in western intellectual history risks overlooking the way in which the totality of the assumptions demarcates a distinct point of view that is more than a mere sum of its parts. It is true that the thinking of the Kyoto philosophers feeds well into the critique of the transcendental subject and the return to the primacy of experience that has marked twentieth-century philosophy in the west's shift from the nineteenth, and in that sense is more easily understandable. But such points of contact should not obscure the fact that there is nothing in western philosophy that approaches the particular constellation of their thinking. As I will try to show, the assumptions, while not articulated theoretically, do interlace one with the other.

To begin with, there is an important assumption that is *not* shared with western philosophy as a whole: the clear delineation between philosophy and religion. The point is as critical as it is difficult to summarize. I begin with a statement of Takeuchi Yoshinori, the leading disciple of Tanabe, regarding the overcoming of the distinction in reference to Buddhist thought:

> The life of religion includes philosophical thought as its counterpart, a sort of centrifugal force to its own centripetal tendencies. Strictly speaking, Buddhism has nothing like what Saint Paul refers to as the "folly of the cross." This ... has led it in a different direction from western philosophy and religion.... Philosophy has served Buddhism as an inner principle of religion, not as an outside critic.... That is to say, philosophy in Buddhism is not speculation or metaphysical contemplation, but rather a metanoia of thinking, a conversion within reflective thought that signals a return to the authentic self—the no-self of *anātman*.... It is a philosophy that transcends and overcomes the presuppositions of metaphysics.... But how is one to explain this way of doing religious philosophy and reconstruct it in terms suitable to the present world when the very idea of philosophy and metaphysics has been usurped by western models?

For the Kyoto philosophers, thinking either transforms the way we look at the things of life or it is not thinking in the fullest sense of the word. Whether current academic habits distinguish certain modes of thought as religious to distinguish them from the purely philosophical is beside the point. Thinking is, after all, seeing, and seeing *clearly* is the fulfillment of thinking. It is the transformation of awareness of the things of life that erases the need for the distinction between philosophy and religion as distinct modes of thought.

No matter what philosophical problem the Kyoto philosphers come to tackle, in the end it is this "passion for inwardness," as Takeuchi calls it, that wins the day. This is not to deny a level at which the differences between the demands of logic and the attention to the historical texts of philosophy on the one hand, and the rituals, practices, and traditions of religion on the other come into play. But for these thinkers it is the transformation of awareness that justifies specific doctrinal and historical traditions, not the other way around. Hence, insofar as "philosophy" and "religion" refer to *modes of thought,* the terms have nothing to lose and everything to gain by mutual entailment.

Corollary to this is the absence of a presumed antagonism between religion and philosophy on the one hand and Japanese culture on the other. This is a function of the fact that these philosophers understand *culture* here much the same way they understand religion, namely, as something whose essence can be talked about independently of the social institutions in which it is encased. Simply put, this essence is the comprehensive system of values particular to a given social group and by extension the traditional arts believed to embody those values. The wider sociological and anthropological context of culture, which embraces the genesis, transmission, and transformation of the social order of human relationships, work, commerce, entertainment, political power, and so forth, is left out of the picture. As a result of this dimming of the connections between culture and the social order, the former is able to criticize the latter without itself becoming an object of criticism, and the harmony between religion and culture goes unquestioned.

This stands in marked difference to their treatment of western culture—including western culture imported into Japan—where traditional cultural values and present social structures are generally seen together, as they have been in western philosophy and religion at least since the Enlightenment. As a result, the tendency of the Kyoto philosophers to distance religious consciousness from social conscience, a tendency it shares with much of Japanese Buddhism, has helped to stifle the emergence of overriding principles critical of Japanese culture at the same time as they are free to call on their own traditional ascetic and moral values to abet critiques of western culture and society.

At the risk of getting ahead of ourselves, we may note here, that the "authentic self" to which Takeuchi alludes as the goal of religion-philosophy enterprise is less a confession of faith in a fundamental Buddhist teaching of "no-self" than it is a metaphor of their concern with clarity of thought and the transformation of consciousness. The coincidence of terminology is not to be taken lightly, since it does point to a reinterpretation of a classical idea, but neither should it be made to bear the full weight of tradition surrounding the idea of *anātman*.

In this same connection, the Kyoto philosophers have assiduously avoided all reference to psychoanalytical theory, or to any connection between no-self and abnormal or paranormal psychic states. Given the impact the idea of the unconscious mind has had on western philosophy and symbolic theory at the time they were writing, one can only consider this decision to have been a deliberate one, though their motivations are simply not clear from the texts we have at hand. Let me suggest part of the reason.

Japan's intellectual history, like Chinese Buddhism on which it depended so heavily, has lacked the kind of symbolic theory that was essential to the west. As I noted earlier, Japanese concern with philosophical questions did not in any important sense initiate from attempts to demythify the cosmos or to separate the literally true from what is only symbolically true. To put it bluntly, in matters of philosophy and religion *everything* has a double-meaning. To focus on the layers of meaning or metaphoric distortion worked by the particular history of particular psyches—the psychological analysis of mind—is not unimportant, but it ignores the larger question of whether what psychology determines to be the normal, healthy mind is any better suited to see through the self-will and self-attachment that eclipse awareness of reality as it is. In a word, they come at the question from the opposite end: rather than focus on the flaws particular to each individual's private perception of the world, they seek a way through the general flaws that are our common fate as humans. Conversely, by seeing all perception as symbolic, even the perceptions we imagine to be most mechanically reliable and therefore completely literal, they draw attention away from knowing the world with the aim of better manipulating it towards awakening to the world as it is without the interference of utility or other preconceptions.

The omission of discussions of literal truth-claims necessarily entails omission of the entire tradition of logical positivism and analytical philosophy from questions of the transformation of consciousness. Here again, one searches the works of the Kyoto philosophers in vain for a justification. When it comes to the question of the existence of God, their suspensions of judgment can be particularly vexing. The fact is, all three of these philosophers speak regularly of God, not only in reference to the idea as it appears in western philosophy and theology, but apparently simply *of God.* Clearly there is no question of any of them confessing belief in a divine being or beings in the sense in which those terms are normally used, let alone of the God of the Judaeo-Christian tradition. But neither are they simply referring to the God image as it functions in religion or history. No attempt is made to qualify the term as a symbol of ultimate reality or as a metaphysical principle; nothing is said of an objective ontological reality or a subjective fiction. This is one of the most disconcerting aspects of the Kyoto philosophy, but also one of the most significant. In the same way that the concept of the no-self functions as a metaphor for the pursuit of a state of complete awareness, the idea of God appears to serve as a kind of metaphor for the essential oneness of the experience of awareness with reality just as it is, a service it performs precisely as an idea or image functioning in the minds of those who believe in God.

It seems we have drifted away from more or less clear assumptions to a kind of apophatic preference for experiencing without the interference of logical criticism or religious doctrine. This, I mean to argue, is precisely the drift that one meets in the writings of the Kyoto philosophers. If this is indeed the case, then it would seem as if Nishida, Tanabe, and Nishitani have exempted themselves from some of the most serious questions of the history of philosophy, and to have justified the exemption on grounds that can only be called religious. It almost looks as if they get the best of both worlds—to claim that they are being religiously Buddhist when a philosophical criticism hits close to the core, and that they are being philosophically western when a serious objection arises from the Buddhist side. On the whole, I find this objection applies more often to their commentators than it does to the three philosophers themselves. In any case, it is the inevitable risk that comes from straddling worlds the way they do.

If the only measure of whether the work of the Kyoto school can be called a philosophy is what they themselves define philosophy to be, then we are caught in a simple tautology. The only other justification of their achievement as philosophy is that the pursuit of the transformation of awareness on which they have concentrated their efforts is in fact capable of sustaining a self-consistent standpoint that can both enhance those areas of perennial philosophy that touch on the same kind of question, and at the same time revitalize the closed world of their own intellectual tradition through the full weight of philosophical criticism. This is what remains to be shown in the chapters that follow.

5 THE MATTER OF LANGUAGE.

Absent from my account of the working assumptions was any mention of the special quality that the Japanese language brings to philosophy. It is time to address this question briefly before we go any further.

The introduction of philosophical vocabulary in Meiji Japan was a rather haphazard affair. After the initial attempts of Nishi Amane, the first complete dictionary of philosophical terms was prepared under the direction of Inoue Tetsujirō in 1881. Revisions were made regularly as scholars began to specialize in various currents of western thought, leading to the more reliable and comprehensive dictionaries that began to appear around the mid-1950s. Aside from the vocabulary, philosophical writing also had to find its own style, different from the slavishly literal style of Japanese translations of western works in the field. The philosophical idiom was still a wet puddle of clay on the potter's wheel when Nishida began to write, and the samples of finished work filled no more than a short shelf. In creating an original philosophy, he was also creating an original way of writing about it. To a lesser extent the same may be said of Tanabe and Nishitani, though the path that Nishida had cleared left them on much surer ground from the start.

Few questions about the Kyoto school flare up into debate so quickly in Japan as that of language. One of the reasons is that, unlike a great deal of Japanese literature and thought, their writings are almost more accessible to the western philosophical reader in translation than they are to the average Japanese reader in the original. Regarding the difficulty of their Japanese style, I will have more to say in the course of my treatment of each of the three Kyoto philosophers. Here I wish only to deflate the idea that reading them in translation is the major disadvantage that it is often made out to be in philosophical circles.

Nishida, Tanabe, and Nishitani themselves made no claim to a uniquely Japanese mode of thought inaccessible to the outside world, and their translators do not constantly have to apologize to the foreign reader or stuff their texts with footnotes to compensate for everything lost in the rendition to occidental languages. On the contrary, their very reason for working in the philosophical idiom—and adjusting their own language to accommodate it—was that it was a universal idiom. It would have made no sense for them to turn around and claim a particularity for their own Japanese nuances that would have impeded that universality. That said, Japanese academics debating the thought of the Kyoto philosophers in the presence of non-Japanese readers are sorely tempted to make an issue of linguistic impenetrability, while in their absence they are freer to focus on the intellectual content as such. It is a position grounded deeper in emotion than in fact. Still, something must be said of the matter to set it aside, if not once and for all, at least from the concerns of this book.

The structure and literary background of the Japanese idiom represent to the outside world, with the possible exception of China and Korea, a barrier forbidding in the extreme. Aware of this fact, Japanese intellectuals have for the better part of a hundred and twenty-five years assumed the obligation of facilitating communication with the wider world by studying the languages of the west. Working against the enormous obstacles of a schooling system that can only be called dysfunctional insofar as language education is concerned, they have by and large succeeded in meeting this obligation. From the other side, growing numbers of serious students of Japan in the west have succeeded in familiarizing themselves sufficiently with the Japanese language to make contributions to the understanding of the literature and intellectual history which have earned the respect of the Japanese themselves.

Still, the balance of responsibility for the intercourse tilts heavily in the direction of the Japanese contribution, a state of affairs that both sides have come to expect as a matter of course. At the time Nishida and Tanabe were composing their philosophies, the idea would not even have crossed their minds of inviting students of philosophy from the west to study alongside their Japanese counterparts, let alone to participate in formal discussions in Japanese. Instead, as was the pattern since the last decades of the nineteenth century, they encouraged their own students to study abroad under the leading philosophers of Europe and to familiarize themselves with French or German, the philosophical languages of preference of the day. Nishida himself never left Japan, but he sent Tanabe to study in Germany. Nishitani would later follow suit. Tanabe prepared at least one talk in German for a seminar with Husserl during his time in Europe. Neither Nishida nor Tanabe ever became very fluent in a foreign tongue. Nishitani, whose facility with spoken German was better, traveled abroad in the 1960s, addressing audiences in Europe and the United States.

Only after Nishitani's retirement from active teaching in 1963 did the picture begin to change. Trained philosophers and theologians from Europe were studying at Kyoto University under Tanabe's disciple Takeuchi, and they regularly held discussions with Nishitani in Japanese. Translators had begun to commit their skills to rendering the principal works of the Kyoto school thinkers into English and German.

Even though the Kyoto philosophers thought of themselves as participating in the western philosophical tradition, there is no evidence that they ever gave any thought to their works being translated or even accessible to a western audience. This is not to say that they were writing simply with a Japanese audience in mind when they wrote their philosophies proper. Rather, all three seemed to be conscious of the fact that they were forging a new language, in some ways as unfamiliar to the Japanese as it would have been to the westerner in Japanese. None of them wrote the kind of Japanese that defies translation or demands heavy annotation because of its dependence on literary allusion or indirect reference to eastern classical texts. Citations of indigenous poetry are, of course, badly debilitated by translation into any language, just as Chinese poetry often suffers in its Japanese renditions. But this is only rarely a problem in the case of their works. As for the play of language, what we find is no more than a normal dosage, nothing to the extent we find, for example, in Heidegger. Having compared the translations line by line with the originals in my seminars of *Also sprach Zarathustra* and *Varieties of Religious Experience*, I am convinced that my Japanese students who have to content themselves with reading Nietzsche and James in translation lose far more than the westerner who has to read Nishida's *A*

Study of the Good or Nishitani's *Religion and Nothingness* in English. In general, what there is of the esoteric or obscure in their writings is no less unfamiliar to the western reader today than it was to the ordinary Japanese reader of western philosophy at the time the works were written.

The lack of background in the intellectual tradition of the east is not, therefore, a major obstacle to understanding the rather peculiar language of the Kyoto philosophers. Of the three, Nishida is clearly the least indebted to eastern sources, and Nishitani the most. But the advance of scholarship on eastern philosophy was not their concern. On the contrary, in not a few cases their readings of classical texts, including Buddhist materials, can even appear arbitrary to those of a more philological or text-critical bent.

In short, the reader of the works of Nishida, Tanabe, and Nishitani has no need to dread the mystique of the inscrutable oriental mind camouflaged in the complex ambiguities of an oriental idiom. If anything, this is remarkably *less* of a problem with the Kyoto philosophers than it is for the reader of popular Japanese novels. Reliable translations can be approached in the confidence that nothing essential has been forfeited in the rendering. With proper scholarly attention, they can also be criticized for unnecessary ambiguity without fear that a greater familiarity with Japanese would clear up the confusion. None of them was a great stylist in the tradition of James, Bergson, or Nietzsche. All three were capable of writing badly and the faithful translator has to accept that fact.

I realize so bald and apodictic a statement may chafe the sensitivities of those Japanese who are convinced that certain of the writings of these thinkers possess a literary quality that makes them inaccessible to the non-Japanese. After long discussions on this matter with those who know the material much more thoroughly than I, I still have no concrete evidence to persuade me otherwise. On the contrary, I remain more convinced than ever that for the goal of the Kyoto philosophers—a grafting of Japanese thought on world philosophy—to be fulfilled, they *must* be read in translation (not only in the original), and their special vocabulary must be allowed to find a place alongside those of the philosophical giants of the west. True, they have suffered from translations so literal that they are almost meaningless, which is bad enough in any language but redoubled when it comes to putting Japanese into European languages. Still, there is nothing in principle to inhibit good translation of their work.

At the same time, I lay my hand across my mouth when it comes to assessing the views of those Japanese literary critics who have berated the Kyoto philosophers over the years for defacing the natural beauty of their native language in the name of philosophy. I will repeat some of the criticisms in the course of this book, aware that I lack the finesse to do much more than that. The main thing is to recognize that the philosophical styles of Nishida and Tanabe and Nishitani—as different from one another as Kant is from Hegel, and Hegel from Schopenhauer—are very much part of their thought and present as much a special challenge as the ideas they are communicating. This, too, will become clear in the chapters that follow.

6 THE STUDY OF THE KYOTO SCHOOL IN THE WEST.

The study of Kyoto school philosophy in the west has developed in two directions at more or less the same time. On the one hand, it has been studied as a chapter in the history of ideas; on the other, some first steps have been taken to appropriate those ideas into the mainstream of western thinking. In general it can be said that in philosophical circles the former by far outpaces the latter, while in the theological it is the other way around. These are questions that need critical attention in their own right. I content myself with the observation that the numbers of those possessed of both the linguistic skills to read the mass of material not available in translation and the broad background in the history of philosophy needed to appraise it are increasing, and bodes well for the future of both directions.

The first serious attempts by western scholars to approach the thought of the Kyoto school were concentrated on the work of Nishida. Husserl, Heidegger, and Rickert had already heard of Nishida through Tanabe and Nishitani, both of whom had studied in Germany, but did not seem to take him very seriously or to have encouraged their students to do so. In 1940 Robert Schinzinger wrote a German essay for a foreign journal published by Sophia University in Tokyo, *Monumenta Nipponica*, introducing Nishida's thought. He followed three years later with a volume of translations of Nishida's essays, which attracted the attention of others in the German-speaking world.

The first works of the Kyoto philosophers in English began to appear shortly after the end of the war. UNESCO had funded translations of leading contemporary Japanese thinkers, among them D. T. Suzuki, Watsuji Tetsurō, Nishida, and Tanabe. Unfortunately, most of these books were published through a local bookseller and had little readership in Japan and almost no distribution outside of the country. These were followed by other translations in the 1960s, mostly scattered in specialized journals or buried at the end of unpublished dissertations. Many of the first translations were rough and unfaithful, not so much to the surface meaning of the Japanese text as to the philosophical background and sources. Not surprisingly, the main attention they attracted was that of western students of philosophy living in Japan who were anxious to put their hands on whatever they could in their own field. Japanese who had studied abroad also tried their hand at translation into foreign languages, though the results were often unreadable and passed by unnoticed, if indeed they were published at all. In any event, the cumulative effect of these early efforts was to prompt more and better translations.

In 1965 Nishitani took over as chief editor of *The Eastern Buddhist,* a journal published by Ōtani University in Kyoto for which D. T. Suzuki had served as editor during its formative years. From that time until 1999 the journal regularly published translations of and articles about the thought of Nishida, Tanabe, and Nishitani. The high quality of the journal and its philosophical sophistication earned it a respectable readership abroad and served as a major resource for those interested in the Kyoto school and Buddhist philosophy in general.

By the 1970s, young Japanese studying abroad were introducing their foreign professors to the Kyoto school philosophers by summarizing their thinking or attempting comparative studies. About the same time, a journal entitled *Philosophical Studies of Japan* was begun, also with the aid of a grant from UNESCO. Although it was a crude production with a limited distribution, it contained some important translations of works of Nishitani and Tanabe. A small number of translations appeared in the 1980s in the pages of *Monumenta Nipponica* and a monograph series connected with the journal published a book of Nishida's in English translation already in 1970. Although the journal itself enjoyed an international reputation, the monographs were not well distributed and the translation is still hard to come by.

During the 1980s the Kyoto school can be said to have enjoyed its greatest blossoming in the west, a story far too multifaceted to detail here. It is no accident that it coincides with the concentrated decade of teaching that Abe Masao, who studied with Tanabe and who is one of the most enthusiastic proponents of the thought of Nishida and Nishitani, spent in the United States. At the same time, the ascendancy of the Japanese economy and the concerted efforts of the Japanese government to finance instruction in the Japanese language at universities and centers around the world gave additional stimulus to young students interested in eastern philosophy to grapple with the original texts of the Kyoto school.

In Japan, a series of international conferences known as the Kyoto Zen Symposia were organized by Abbot Hirata Seikō of Tenryū-ji temple in Kyoto in collaboration with a team of local scholars headed by Nishitani.

Each year, beginning in 1983, a group of scholars from Japan and from abroad were gathered together to discuss contemporary issues in philosophy and religion. The visible presence of Kyoto school philosophy continued in these conferences after Nishitani's death through the active participation of Ueda Shizuteru, then professor of philosophy at Kyoto University and the most distinguished of Japan's interpreters of Nishida. In addition, deliberate efforts were made to invite academics from Europe and the United States who had distinguished themselves in the study of the Kyoto school. Of the more than 160 papers presented throughout the fifteen years that these symposia were conducted, nearly a third of them were devoted explicitly to the three thinkers being discussed in this book.

In 1980 the Nanzan Institute for Religion and Culture in Nagoya, Japan, held the first postwar conference in Japan with Nishitani and others associated with the Kyoto school, and that same year began publishing English translations of and original works about the school. The brisk sales that these books have enjoyed up to today and the adaptation of several of them for graduate-school courses in the west was only one symbol of an increasing sense of the importance of these philosophers. Translations into German, French, Italian, and Spanish have been slower in coming and the number of dedicated scholars fewer, but the pace has been steady and has resulted in some of the best work available.

Overall it may be said that at present the general ideas of the Kyoto school philosophers are in circulation in the western world and that many of their key ideas have found their way into theological and philosophical discourse. What is more important, a generation of young scholars and critics has arisen to meet these thinkers and to encourage their own students to step on to the forum of ideas that Nishida, Tanabe, and Nishitani have offered to contemporary philosophy.

7 ARRANGEMENT OF THE MATERIAL. The basic framework in which the material of this essay has been laid out is a simple one: a separate chapter devoted to the principal ideas of each of the three major figures of the Kyoto school. The simplicity cloaks a number of choices against approaches I reckoned misleading.

Given my aim of offering an overview of the distinctive perspective that the Kyoto school brings on western philosophy, it seemed to me that drawing out certain perennial questions of philosophy and tracing the respective responses of the Kyoto philosophers to them would yield results more anecdotal than systematic. Although there are any number of specialized studies that do just that, the basic structure of Kyoto philosophy cannot be understood as a commentary on given questions but only as a reframing of the questions from a standpoint all their own.

Given the fact that the three do form a "school" and that this entails a considerable overlap in approach, I made some first attempts to arrange their philosophies into a composite picture, which I thought would help clarify the numerous threads of mutual influence not always apparent in reading their works. It might also, I felt, present a chance to trace their role in changes that took place in the general intellectual scene in Japan at the time each of them was working. I quickly discovered that overlaps in vocabulary and dominant concepts tended to blend important nuances of difference into a surface gloss that did not do justice either to the competing ideological and philosophical ideas of the times or to the the respective contributions each of the three made. Here again, there are scholars who have worked on these questions piecemeal, but what was needed was a clearer backdrop against which to locate these results.

In settling on separate accounts for Nishida, Tanabe, and Nishitani, I began with a strict regime of tracing the development in the thought of each of them. What I found was that the strict pursuit of such a plan would end up in a volume at least half again as long as the one I intended to write. I therefore slackened the framework to concentrate on each of their key ideas, more or less in the order in which they appeared, but freely using later writings to interpret earlier ones without always drawing attention to the fact. At the same time, in the case of ideas more or less shared in common I have taken a fuller exposition in one of the chapters to permit abbreviated mention in the others. Thus, for example, the idea of the "dialectic" that is most developed in Tanabe's thought is passed over more quickly in Nishida and Nishitani, just as "true self" in the chapter on Nishitani and "self-awareness" in that of Nishida are given shorter shrift in the others. The result is that, contrary to appearances, none of the chapters stands independently on its own, but each relies to some extent on the others.

The question of the political thought of the Kyoto school philosophers required special treatment, since it is less the coincidence of ideas than the coincidence of historical circumstances that had to be taken into account. Rather than devote a special chapter to the matter, I have decided to present different aspects of the picture in connection with each of the three philosophers. Accordingly, the general background of Japan is given more attention in connection with Nishida, the critical response to Kyoto school political ideas in the chapter on Tanabe, and the content of political philosophy more in that on Nishitani. While the fuller picture is somewhat bleared in each case by the scatter, I trust that taken together the relevant sections will give some weight to my conclusions on the matter.

The footprints of the texts and many scholars I have followed in composing these pages have all been moved to the notes, where those interested in tracking their way back to the sources should find ample documentation. Only those Sino-Japanese glyphs whose absence would leave some confusion have been given in the notes. Wherever possible, I refer the reader to existing translations of works of the Kyoto philosophers. For the sake of accuracy and consistency, many of the translations have had to be recast. To have noted the changes in each case seemed to me superfluous.

The concluding bibliography aims to be complete only in one respect: it includes all published translations into western languages of the written works of Nishida, Tanabe, and Nishitani that have come to my attention. Otherwise, it contains only those works related to the Kyoto school and its general intellectual background cited in the text and notes, as well as some supplementary material. A comprehensive bibliography on the Kyoto school remains to be done. It was with some regret, and only at the eleventh hour when I realized that the list I had compiled had grown out of all proportion to the rest of the book, that I eliminated about one-half of the Japanese and one-third of the western entries. Even had I left them in, the list would only reflect what I have kept track of over the years and could hardly have claimed to be exhaustive.

There is one glaring omission in these pages that I must acknowledge from the start. The Kyoto philosophers regularly draw on Zen, Pure Land, Kegon, and Tendai Buddhist ideas to explain their reinterpretation of certain fundamental philosophical concepts. Tanabe and Nishitani, in whom this is much more marked than in Nishida, have also written lengthy commentaries on Zen Master Dōgen, and Nishitani has extensive comments on a number of classical Zen texts. To enter even into an introductory explanation of this range of Buddhist ideas would have made this a much longer and less focused book. In addition, certain explanations that would satisfy me would no doubt chill the soul of Buddhist scholars and prejudice the ideas they were meant to enlighten. I have therefore eliminated nearly all excursions into Buddhist thought in order to keep the book within the confines of traditional philosophical thought, since I believe it is *there* that the Kyoto philosophers find their place more than in the circles of Buddhist scholarship.

As seasoned readers of the writings of the Kyoto school philosophers will notice, this is as much a book of conclusions and judgments as it is an introduction. While I have made no attempt to disguise my own interpretations, or differences of interpretation from others, I do not wish them to distract from the broader picture I am trying to paint and have therefore relegated most of this debate to the notes.

Nishida Kitarō
(1870–1945)

8 **NISHIDA'S LIFE AND CAREER.** Nishida Kitarō was born on 19 May 1870 in Ishikawa Prefecture, central Japan. After dropping out of high school over a disagreement with the authorities on educational reforms, he studied independently for and passed the entrance exams to Tokyo's Imperial University as a special student. He graduated in 1894 with a degree in philosophy, having written an optional thesis on Hume's idea of causality, and returned to his home prefecture as an English instructor in a middle-school. To keep alive his interest in philosophy, he studied the posthumous writings on ethics of the British neo-Hegelian, Thomas Green, first with the idea of writing an introductory text on the work and then with the grander scheme of writing a history of ethics from ancient times to the present.

The same resistance to the rigidity of the curriculum and the precedence given to administration over the needs of the students that he had felt as a student resurfaced in him as a teacher. He moved to a high-school position as a teacher of English, German, ethics, psychology, and logic, but already had his goal set on returning to Tokyo as a university lecturer. During these years he began sitting in *zazen* in the Rinzai *(kōan)* tradition under Master Setsumon, apparently at the encouragement of his friend D. T. Suzuki, but did not begin serious practice until 1897 when he attended concentrated sessions at a number of different temples. During the course of that year he was dismissed for disagreements over educational policy with the authorities, and moved to the post of a high-school teacher at his alma mater, the Fourth High School of Yamaguchi Prefecture, where he was named professor in 1899.

Meantime, he kept up his practice of Zen, receiving from his master the lay Buddhist name of Sunshin ("an inch of mind") in 1901. It was during his first deep plunge into *zazen* that he took up writing a journal. In it we find him struggling to strike a balance between the practice of Zen, which he felt put him in touch with "life," and his academic work, which he felt as a personal destiny. He tells himself over and over again there and in his letters, in words that must be familiar to novices of meditation anywhere, that he must not simply use Zen as grist for his scholarly career, and promises to practice Zen "for the rest of my life." As it turns out, he gave up meditation in 1905 and never returned to it. Allusions to Zen appear frequently in his diaries up until 1907, and then disappear. The vestiges of his inner struggle remain, but in the form of a philosophical problem: how to reconcile the intuitive, nonreflective consciousness cultivated in the east with the logical, reflective consciousness cultivated in western philosophy.

The years he spent in Yamaguchi were no doubt formative years for Nishida's career as a philosopher and as a teacher. Among the nicknames his students gave him were Prof. Denken, Prof. Schrecken, and Prof. Diogenes (this latter because of his unkempt appearance). He published a number of pieces on topics such as Hume's idea of causality, the history of British ethics, Thomas Green's *Prolegomenon to Ethics,* and Kant's ethics, and a short piece of five pages on Spinoza's idea of God. In addition to these authors, he was reading Nietzsche, Bradley, Spinoza, and Schleiermacher, among others, and started into William James's *Varieties of Religious Experience.* By the end of the period he would publish in Kyoto University's *Journal of Philosophy* a draft of the ideas that would form the basis of the book that was to launch his career.

Though he had serious intentions to study abroad already from 1903, this was not to be. In 1910, at the age of forty, he was appointed assistant professor of philosophy at Kyoto Imperial University. He had always told people he would wait until he had reached the age of forty before publishing a book, and he kept good his word, publishing in the following year a work he had been drafting and publishing in pieces for nearly four years, *An Inquiry into the Good.*

Meantime, the political situation in Japan was undergoing momentous changes. Five years earlier had seen the outbreak of the Sino-Japanese War, during the course of which he lost his younger brother, who had joined the army. In the same year he became a university teacher, Japan annexed Korea. Within four years the First World War would break out in Europe. His opinions on these events do not appear in his writings, except for a brief flush of youthful patriotism in a memento for his dead brother.

During his first years at Kyoto he wrote a short essay on Shinran and also lectured at Shinshū University (present-day Ōtani University). Aside from two short pieces on Bergson, his interests had turned to epistemological questions and the neo-Kantians. In 1913 he had begun to lecture on Natorp's psychology, and that same year he began to serialize a work entitled *Intuition and Reflection in Self-Awareness* that would take him four years to complete. During these years his lectures reflect his concentration, treating things like the thought of Bolzano, Windelband's outline of the history of philosophy, Kant's first critique, and scientific truth. The same year

When he returns to the same theme again, he evaluates it only in terms of what has survived. It is always the latest stage that holds his attention. So long as he was moving forwards, as he nearly always was, and so long as he had the sense that his work hung together as a whole, which again it almost always did, he was not detained by the need to review the changes that had taken place.

At the same time, what his style camouflages to the first-time reader seems to have been immediately apparent to those who heard him lecture in the classroom: Nishida was always turning ideas around to view them from every angle he could, always looking for connections, always in search of just the right place to set a milestone and the next direction to turn. The more one reads of Nishida, the easier it is to detect this struggle going on and to see that he is less interested in stating conclusions than in making clear the tracks along which his thinking was moving.

Ueda Shizuteru, who has wrestled with the texts as thoroughly as anyone, reflects:

> There are times I just do not understand what he is saying. Even so, at least for me, the feeling that I must go on reading takes over.... Nishida did not write down what he had thought out, he "thinks out as he is writing." He may be compared to a miner deep in a mountain wielding his pick in search of the vein of truth.

Actually, the image of the miner is Nishida's own. What Ueda does not mention is the qualification Nishida adds: "I have always been a miner of ore, but I have never managed to refine it." He was not the first philosophical thinker to work this way, of course, and he himself admitted his "incoherent thinking." The key to Ueda's explanation is that Nishida's attempt to fuse eastern thinking into philosophy obliged him not only to invent new words and meanings for the Japanese language but also to twist grammar to accommodate the lack of homogeneity. The close relationship between western logical thinking and the grammar of western languages is often pointed to as a handicap that Japanese had to contend with from the start. At the same time, Nishida was convinced that he was not working with two philosophies but only one, and that the real way to get to it was through a relentless pursuit of the "depths of ordinary, everyday life."

In any case, any attempt to depict his philosophy as a unified vision gradually worked out over time, or as a logical progression of conclusions from premises is given the lie by the way he actually worked. As Ueda suggests, it is as if the 5,000 pages of Nishida's writings were a single essay that took him a lifetime to write, so that the conclusion of any particular published unit is a mere fiction, soon to turn into the starting point for the next step in the argument. Miki Kiyoshi, who knew Nishida personally and was familiar with how he wrote, has this to say of Nishida's "books":

> His books have a quite different flavor from ordinary ones with their ordered sequence of chapters.... He wrote a series of essays, which accumulated to form a volume.... When he had finished one essay he always immediately registered the feeling that something was missing, and to supplement the lack he proceeded to add another. Like an artist, his work was never done.

Miki notes in the same context that while his ordinary lectures were rather staid and well organized, his special lectures, which were open to students from all departments and were attended by professors as well, showed him at his best and were always packed. "Rather than simply *explain* philosophy to his students he would take them along on his philosophic search." His goal was not so much to instruct them in the thinking of others as to help them catch the "knack" of seeing the world from others' standpoints so that one could find a standpoint of one's own. He complained that the age of simply taking in western culture haphazardly, the same way culture from China had been taken in, was over. To take over any learning, whether science or philosophy, meant not to extract its techniques but to "take in their spirit and digest them."

In a similar vein Nishitani recalls that:

> His lectures were not what one would normally call well organized. His strategy was not to construct a lecture by following a single thread of logical connections and presenting his thought as a unified and well-articulated whole. It was as if all sorts of ideas inside him were jostling against one another and rushing to the exit at the same time. One sentence might not even be completed before another began. This made it altogether impossible to take notes.

He would blow up at the stupidity of students but rarely scolded them. He tended to keep his strong emotions in check, letting his wrath out in his diaries rather than on others. As time went on, Nishida recognized the importance of having disciples, but at the same time his attitude towards his students—those who would become disciples and those who would not—was to encourage them to do their own thinking.

Questions of the flow of Nishida's arguments aside, his written Japanese prompts wildly differing opinions among Japanese readers. In general, there is little enthusiasm for his prose among literary critics, and the prime example is his confrontation with Kobayashi Hideo, who shared with him a number of philosophical concerns. For Kobayashi, Nishida was a "classical example" of the self-righteous scholars who hide behind their ideologies the way bureaucrats hide behind theirs, deadbolting themselves from hard-nosed critics:

> Nishida's solitariness, which is completely incapable of feeling the resistance of these others, has created for us a bizarre system that is neither in Japanese nor, of course, in a foreign language.

These criticisms are leveled right up to the present, and they are familiar to Nishida's translators, who have to cope with the constant repetitions of earlier terms and the introduction of apparently superfluous grammatical phrases—as if he were trying to disguise the intuitive leaps his mind was taking by giving them the semblance of continuity—either by editing them out or by subjecting their own language to similar disfiguration.

Nishida himself did not take well to the slights against his style, but neither is it clear from his published comments or his letters that he understood them entirely. He defends the need to distinguish varieties of written Japanese from literary style, and wonders why certain of his grammatical conventions seem so odd. Nishida himself wrote a small number of light essays in clearer, more refined Japanese on Goethe, calligraphy, and personal reminiscences. These works show more of his personal feelings and avoid the serpentine, complex sentence structures of his philosophical writings.

Looking over the range of opinions on Nishida's style, I conclude that simply to chide him for not having written simpler prose is to ask him to be a different kind of thinker. The discontinuities in his style reflect the creativity of his way of thinking and of his adventure of ideas as a whole, and must be accepted. Only rarely did he write about other philosophers to give an objective presentation of their thought. He wrote about them the way he read them—with a question in mind, sliding over the surface of the text until he came to something he thought useful, at which point he would plunge himself headlong into it.

Given his way of using philosophical texts, had Nishida simply twisted Japanese into the style of the typical translator of western philosophy—a style that has survived up to the present—its weirdness would have been excused as the fault of the foreign material he was working with. Nishida's genius as a writer lies not in his raw literary skills but in the fact that his literary style reflected his attempt to cast bridges between worlds that had been walled off from one another. To read him is to be obliged to the same straddling that defies simple affiliation with either of those worlds. At the same time, if the best of Nishida's commentators today are able to explain his thought in more readable prose without misrepresenting him, it is because the channels of confluence between worlds that Nishida had to dig as he went along are already there from the beginning. His style belongs to history, not to the present, but it belongs to history as something that was ahead of its time.

One final remark is in order. Nishida did not as a rule cite secondary literature, but preferred to mention only primary sources in his work. His diaries give us a somewhat better idea of his reading habits, but it seems clear that he wanted to choose the company with whom he would appear in print, and it was primarily western thinkers of rank. One has to think that much of this was merely an imitation of the convention of those philosophers whose writings he worked with. What is peculiar to Nishida, though, and far from convention, was the fact that he could lift whole phrases and sentences from his reading in order to wrestle with the ideas, often without indicating whom he was citing or from where. During his struggles with neo-Kantian thought this is marked: there are times when one simply does not know if it is Nishida or someone Nishida is citing whose view is being discussed. For the philosophical reader this must be kept in mind when reading Nishida's own work, even in translation, since most translators either have not bothered to track down Nishida's sources or were not aware of what was going on.

10 AN ADVENTURE OF IDEAS. Nishida's adventure of ideas was to make a distinctive Japanese contribution to world philosophy. Before looking at those ideas themselves, it is worthwhile to pause a moment and consider just what this entailed for him, if only to alert the reader to the way his commentators are too often given to collapse that goal to the measure of their own assumptions about the place that Nishida gave that "distinctiveness."

I begin with a statement he made in 1940:

> Must we assume western logic to be the only logic and the eastern way of thinking simply a less-developed form of it?... Willing as I am to recognize western logic as a magnificent systematic development, and intent as I am on studying it first as one type of world logic, I wonder if even western logic is anything more than one special feature of the life of history.... Things like formal, abstract logic will remain the same everywhere, but concrete logic as the form of concrete knowledge cannot be independent of the specific feature of historical life.

What Nishida has in mind here by distinguishing concrete logic from formal logic is basically to draw a line between a more general sense of the principles of discourse on the one hand and attempts to lay out methodological rules that distinguish a good argument from a bad one on the other. It was the former that concerned him primarily.

Nishida did not want simply to contribute to the advance of the study of western philosophy in Japan. For this reason, he never claimed to be an authority on any particular school or thinker of the western philosophical tradition. Nor is he usually credited with such authority, except by the most hagiographic of his devotees. We find nothing in his writings of polemic against the way his contemporaries, east or west, read the works he was reading, nor any attempt to defend his own readings against the received ones. To have set foot in this corner of academia would have distracted him from his grander purpose. Better to be thought a dilettante than to waste his talents on such questions. To put it bluntly, Nishida was confident enough of his ability to assimilate what he was reading not to need the confirmation of experts in the field or to be detained very long by self-doubt. What he aimed at, as Ueda Shizuteru has noted, was the full force of the collision between east and west, like parade floats jostling against one another in a Japanese *matsuri*.

At the same time as he had no pretension to expertise in any branch of western philosophy, he had even less for eastern thought. Here again, he spoke with authority of the east—by which we have always to understand the east as received by Japan and reflected there—once he had established himself as an intellectual, but he never had anything approaching the scholar's knowledge he did of western philosophy.

All of this would seem enough to disqualify him for tenure in the modern academia. Measured by those standards, one would have little trouble disposing of him as a second-rate academic. But if we judge him by the goal *he* set for himself, those criticisms become petty by comparison. To make a distinctively Japanese contribution to world philosophy, he had to do his own original thinking, and he had to do it in a language and logic that would respect the received philosophical tradition at the same time as it shows up its need for what Japan could give it. His novelty had to be philosophical and at the same time non-western, which was itself a novel enough idea. Only then could he expose world philosophy to the hypocrisy of universal aspirations carved in the stone of parochial biases.

Those of his Japanese readers who gloat over his neologisms as having no equivalent in western philosophy and not even any possible translation, which makes them only really intelligible to those who share Nishida's cultural and linguistic background, not only miss the point of his goal, but they they push his ideas in the opposite direction he was headed. Had Nishida thought his ideas were unintelligible to the whole of the philosophical world without teaching them Japanese language and culture first, he would have considered them a failure as far as that goal was concerned. The distinctiveness of the Japanese is only a local value; it is enhanced when its core can be extracted and translated into something of world scope.

When his commentators—even the best of them—cite him in support of their own ethnocentricism, or at least their own privileged position to read him, they are no longer talking about Nishida but about themselves. Of course he knew there was much "concrete knowledge" in Japanese culture and language that he could not turn to the benefit of world philosophy and which would have no place there. But these were secondary. His primary concern was to enhance concrete knowledge beyond Japan, and his philosophy stands without its political and cultural applications.

As we shall see, this grand adventure of ideas was more suited to the logic of self-awareness than it was to political philosophy. Nishida's collapse into Japanism shows up precisely when he sets his goal aside to respond to issues that as an intellectual he was expected to respond to, but that he had nothing of much importance to add to.

Nishida's goal as reflected in the citation above and as I have described it was not his starting point. His initial question was more modest but no less novel: to find a way to introduce the important but radically nonphilosophical language of Zen into the closed world of philosophy; and conversely to use philosophy to find a language to talk about those things that Zen had always insisted were not susceptible to rationalization. For east and west alike, the project was countercultural. On the one hand, the idea of using religious belief or practice as a foundation for philosophy is something the west has resisted vigorously, or at least tried to relegate to the realms of theology. On the other, protagonists of Zen in the east had brandished their irrationalities and paradoxes around like a sword that cut through the presumption of rationalism and protected them from outside criticism. Nishida set out to give a rational foundation to Zen from outside of Zen, and in the process to put to work an indigenous philosophy that was still no more than an infant on all fours.

This motivation was not carried out directly by comparing one set of ideas to another, but it lay clearly in the background of the first of his philosophical ideas: pure experience. Ironically it is the very absence of references to Zen in his writings that shows their importance. As Nishitani remarks:

> For one thing, his thought had taken a turn towards regarding the historical world as the most concrete world, bringing him into touch with a realm of

> meaning not usually included in the world of Zen. For another, he seems to have felt that his thought was philosophical through and through and not to be reduced to Zen and its traditional views.... He once wrote me in a letter that he had differentiated his philosophy from Zen to avoid being misunderstood.

Although he would give up the practice of Zen at age thirty-five after ten years of practice, it was not simply because he did not find it agreed with the ideas he was forging. He never expected that. Nor did he cease to believe that his philosophy continued to be his own appropriation of Zen. He would not have been happy to have his own novel originality accord with ancient Zen such as it was. At the same time, while I should think that he maintained to the last the conviction that his own philosophy was an unfolding of Zen within himself, a new manifestation of the Zen spirit, he does not seem to have encouraged his young disciples, not otherwise drawn to Zen, to take up meditation in order to appreciate his thought. In fact, Nishida is said never to have informed even his closest disciples of his study of Zen until the end of his life.

The "west" whose "philosophy" Nishida was trying to synthesize with the "thought" of the "east": these are no longer the largely univocal terms they were for Nishida when he set out on his adventure. When Miki looked back and claimed that Nishida had "enabled a fusion of eastern intuition with western thinking by what one might call an eastern twist of western logic," he was stating a conviction among Nishida's students that continues to hold force today. The ideas of logic, predication, rationality, self, reflection, and so forth, which he takes as representative and to which he offers his own corrections in many cases, represent only one part of the western philosophical heritage. Gradually he came to see this, and his sweeping generalizations became fewer. It is a mistake—alas, a common mistake—to confuse western philosophy with Nishida's generalizations about western philosophy. To acknowledge his creativity requires that one always keep in mind that one is reading *Nishida's* philosophy, which is based on an impressive but nonetheless limited appreciation of the two worlds he was attempting to wed.

11 THE QUEST OF THE ABSOLUTE.

If we look at Nishida's diaries and letters during the years as a high-school teacher when he was feverishly devouring philosophical books and getting deeper and deeper into Zen meditation, we find a number of short statements about the focal point of his interest. They center on two questions, both of which he received as much from Zen as from his philosophical reading and the intellectual mood of the times: the discovery of the self, and fidelity to life. Typical of the former concern is a letter he wrote to a friend in 1897 in which he explains that for him the most important things were spiritual, and the goal of the spirit was "to dig deeper and deeper into the recesses of the mind to reach the true, authentic self and become one with it." A 1902 diary entry is typical of the latter concern: "In the end, scholarship is for the sake of life. Life comes first; without it scholarship is useless." Although both of these ideas echo in his maiden philosophical voyage of 1911, *An Inquiry into the Good,* they were made to yield center stage to another concern—the attempt to make consciousness into an absolute, unifying principle for all of reality.

Much has been written about this book, and the idea of pure experience, as the starting point or germ of Nishida's thought, and indeed it is just that. It is full of short phrases condensing intuitions and half-ideas that are as arresting to the reader familiar with Nishida's later work as they are confusing to those who do not know it. This was his first book, and he did what many a young author does: he tried to make room for every important idea he had, sacrificing clarity of focus and continuity of argument for breadth of scope. In the context of his later thought and the influence it had on others, it is a classic of Japanese intellectual history. Its success extends beyond its reception at the time. It has come to be revered as a symbol of Japan's parity with the west. The following is typical of comments on the work among Japanese intellectual historians:

> It is valued as Japan's first truly original thinking carried out in the arena of western philosophy. To Japanese in the Meiji era who were subjected to the display of overwhelming intimidation and superiority of western culture, it must have seemed that unless proof could be given of the significance and uniqueness of eastern and Japanese civilization, their country would run the risk of colonization and the loss of its ethnic autonomy. At last, nearly half a century after the Restoration, when the Meiji era was drawing to its close, this book crystallized a way of thinking, solidly footed in western reason, that could bring the blood of the Japanese to a full boil.

Even if we take into account the relatively short history of philosophy in Japan, Nishida's book wobbled when it was published and, by itself, does not walk very far in today's philosophical world, east or west. Although there are no less than six foreign translations of the work, its ideas have had virtually no impact on the philosophical or religious world outside of Japan. It was the daring and giant strides with which it wobbled that made the Japanese philosophical world at the time wake up and take notice, and that gave Nishida the courage of conviction that he was on to something important. As a piece of philosophical thinking, however, it is a classic only in the context of the study of the development of Nishida's thought and the influence it had on others, where it continues to serve as a rich vein of quotable passages.

The irreverence of that claim is not likely to sit well with Nishida's Japanese commentators. For one thing, the central idea of the book, the transcendence of the subject-object dichotomy, still seems to carry the weight of a distinctively eastern critique of western philosophy—or at least of Descartes and the German idealists who continue to be seen as the heart of that philosophy. Be that as it may, the fact is, it was a first attempt, full of ambiguities and unclarities. This is something Nishida seems to have recognized on completing the book better than those of his followers who persist in reading it in the hindsight of his later work.

There are different motivations for this persistence. Abe Masao, for one, simply passes over without question the many inconsistencies and ambiguities in the argument to concentrate on what he sees as the still relevant criticism of the limits of western rationalism. The force of this criticism helps explain the deep impact it had on many young people contemplating a career in philosophy, among them Nishitani, who wrote, "I cannot imagine what my life would have been like, or even what I myself would be like now, had it not been for *An Inquiry into the Good* and the man who wrote it." In any case, Nishida was not so easily convinced by the simplicity of his first arguments or by his appreciation of western philosophy at the time, but would go on to rethink them from a number of different angles.

A second motivation that was only pointed to by the notion of pure experience, but that would thereafter come to eclipse it in his subsequent books, was the motif of awakening to the true self. This is the position Nishitani takes in his argument that the book represents a "complete system of thought" animated by two root problems: how to avoid a subjectivist idealism on the one hand, and on the other, how to introduce the demand for self-transformation into the heart of traditional metaphysics. Nishitani is therefore able to conclude that "Even on its own, *An Inquiry into the Good* is an original *tour de force* that would have assured it a place among other great systems of thought even if Nishida had not developed it further." Nishitani's argument beads suggestive passages from the work onto the thread of his own appropriation of Nishida's thinking, in what can only be called an original piece of thinking on its own. It is hard to think that at the time any of Nishida's readers could have seen what Nishitani did; and for me it is hard to see how even Nishida himself could have.

In any case, at least as far as the notion of pure experience, which has come to be recognized as the central notion of the book, we need to be a little more sanguine. Actually, the idea of pure experience is only mentioned in the opening and shortest of the four parts that make up the book. Although it was the last section to be written, when he drafted it in 1908, Nishida was convinced, as we know from his letters, that it would be possible to construct a whole philosophy beginning from pure experience. As the last chapter he wrote of the book, it had to be consistent with what he had already written and at the same time had to try to wrap everything up with a single unifying principle. Little wonder that it should confuse the reader who begins with it.

Over the next three years he reworked the parts into a whole, but the seams were still very much visible when he had finished. When he was done, he admitted that the opening section on pure experience as the one and only reality presents only the foundations of his thinking, and suggests that the reader return to it after having read the rest of the work, which represents his thinking as such. (He went along with his publisher—who feared such a work by an unknown author would not sell—to allow a title that would point to ethics as the theme of the work.) For his part, when he had finished the book, he set the idea of pure experience aside, never to return to it. Or perhaps more accurately, he allowed it to dissolve into its composite parts. While his concern with locating an absolute principle on which to build a philosophy remained, his first attempt ended up less an achievement than an agenda to direct his work in the years ahead.

12 THE ABSOLUTE AS PURE EXPERIENCE.

The idea of pure experience is not difficult, though it is complicated by the interference of word associations natural to traditional philosophy but alien to Nishida's intentions, and also by a certain unclarity in his own mind. Let us reconstruct Nishida's intention and how he carried it out.

We begin from the assumption that reality is one, and that means it has a single principle that makes it one, or *unifies* it. Nishida never questioned this in his writings. He does not take up at any point the possibility of "other worlds" or consider the possibility that reality might be fundamentally plural. At the same time as reality is a unity, it is not a static unity. It unfolds in time, and this unfolding means that the unity is refracted in a plurality of items that are transient, interrelated, and therefore the relative stuff out of which that single principle maintains a unity.

Now among all of the items of reality that show up in this process, only one completely mirrors the whole. Only one can stand at the cutting edge of the unity as it unfolds, see it happening, and then talk about it. That single item is human consciousness. To *understand consciousness* is therefore to have the best possible paradigm of how reality "works." To *be fully conscious*—or as fully conscious as a human individual can be—is to achieve a unity that mirrors, as if in microcosm, the ultimate principle of reality and mirrors it from within the dynamic unfolding process itself.

So far we have not left the realm of assumption for that of proof. Nishida's way of demonstrating that this is more than a private intuition of his, indeed the only way he could conceive of doing so, was to begin from the most immediate facts of experience and show that nothing other than only such a vision can make sense of them. The immediacy of these facts would have to be such as to show both the unity of individual consciousness and its participation in an unfolding process beyond individual consciousness. In other words, one would have to begin from the experience of full consciousness in which both the oneness and the plurality of the world are manifest. Only this could provide the bedrock fact that argues for an absolute principle at work in everything that is.

It is here that Nishida struck on the idea that would launch his philosophical career and, in one form or another, preoccupy him for the rest of his life: to overstep the subject-object distinction built into our language of experience. Once this step is taken, the logic of it becomes clear, and more and more reasons accumulate to argue its rightness. At this point, we get into something of a linguistic tangle that is made worse by existing translations of *An Inquiry into the Good*. A brief detour should help alert the reader to what is going on in Nishida's prose, and also to make the concepts less esoteric sounding than they typically are.

When we speak of experience we normally think of *someone* experiencing *something*. Linguistic usage does not allow us to say simply "It was experienced" or "I experienced." The term needs a subject and an object. Nishida's idea was to "purify" the term of these demands and talk of experience pure and direct itself, and to make this his absolute principle of reality. This pure and direct experience he calls a "direct seeing of the facts just as they are." Here he is not talking about a particular collection of facts—a liberty that the Japanese term allows him—but about the pure idea of the *factum* of what actually is, without any suggestion of an objectivity apart from the subject; and a pure seeing, but without a subjectivity apart from objects. It must be a pure *empiricum,* without data or meaning of any kind. In his oft cited, but universally mistranslated, passage:

> For some time now I had it in mind to try and explain all of reality in terms of pure experience.... Along the way, I came to think that it is not that there is an individual that has the experience, but that there is an experience that has the individual, that experience is more basic than any distinction individuals bring to it. This made it possible to avoid solipsism, and by taking experience as something active, to harmonize it with transcendental philosophy after Fichte.

By definition the pure empiricum by itself cannot be experienced or cannot experience anything. It just *is*, the principle behind everything that is. At the same time talk of a "direct seeing of the facts just as they are" suggests that the way things are can be experienced and that consciousness can experience it. (The term "direct seeing" is actually the normal Japanese way of translating *Anschauung* or intuition. It is clumsy, and we may dispense with it later, but for now it helps us question the connection with direct experience.) In other words, the same term, *pure experience,* is used to refer to a highly refined conscious phenomenon and at the same time to the absolute foundation of reality. And in both cases it is claimed to transcend the distinction between subject and object. The only possible conclusion would seem to be that all of reality must be a kind of consciousness in which individual consciousness is not only caught up but also can be aware of what is going on at the same time. And this is in fact Nishida's conclusion.

The thesis is as daring as it is ambiguous, but it is not a descriptive statement that can be proved true or false. It is rather a kind of strategy for rephrasing philosophical questions, a kind of heuristic net whose relevance or irrelevance is determined by what its cast drags to the surface and what it lets slip away. *An Inquiry into the Good* by itself is inadequate to answer that question. At best it runs through a short gamut of philosophical questions to suggest that the thesis will in fact work.

The connection of pure experience with the Hegelian Mind working its way to self-consciousness and generating reality along the way is not tendentious. His handful of passing allusions to Hegel, while confirming the point, seem to slight the influence. Nowhere does Nishida directly state a disagreement with the Hegelian model, though there are hints of it in some of his cautious remarks about what "some people say...." The reason seems to be that Nishida simply did not know Hegel that well at the time, and much of what he knew he got indirectly from the neo-Hegelian Thomas Green, whom he had studied for the history of ethics. Given that Hegel was one of the most widely read of philosophers in Japan, Nishida was simply being prudent. In any case, Nishida was not claiming any originality for the idea that consciousness is the sole reality. He was rethinking it. And untrammeled by the opulent speculations of the Hegelian *opus,* he was able to do his thinking fresh and from a different starting point—the point before consciousness decides it is a subject looking at a world of objects.

Allowing free exchange of *pure* experience with what he calls *direct* experience in the rest of the book, we may reconstruct the evolution of this one basic principle into an all-encompassing metaphysic. The first step is to trace the emergence of pure thought or the immediate insight of "intellectual intuition." Nishida begins with the primary fact of pure experience, a unified state of consciousness in which the distinction between a subject who does the experiencing and an object that is experienced has not yet been constellated, and in which there is no prejudice, no judgment, no deliberation, and no intention. To say that this state is unified does not point to any particular form of consciousness that has been achieved but rather to the foundation of all such achievements; it is, we might say, the form of the forms of all states of consciousness.

Both the term and the idea of a conscious state of undifferentiated unity were taken from William James, whose 1904 essays on pure experience had fallen into Nishida's hands while he was drafting his work. James was interested in the fleeting conscious state as such, an observable fact that undoes the "perfectly wanton assumption," as he called it, that all knowing requires an express distinction between the thing and one's own self. He saw it as present in the highest and richest states of lived experience as well as in the consciousness of infants or semi-comatose brain states. In fact, he identifies it with "the immediate flux of life" itself "the sum total of all experiences" that amounts to an Absolute, "a pure experience on an enormous scale."

At this point, Nishida breaks camp with James by making pure experience the foundation not simply of consciousness but of all reality. He does this by combining two claims: that the "unifying" nature of pure experience is not the function of a static order imposed on the flux of experience from without, but a dynamic predisposition to differentiate itself systematically; and that the whole process of differentiation is a kind of consciousness, though not initially one in which the conscious subject is distinguished from the objects of its consciousness. In other words, consciousness works itself around to self-consciousness through the judgment, rational thinking, and intentionality of human consciousness, but neither began there nor, presumably, ends there. The self-consciousness in which this process makes itself patent he calls intellectual intuition, the purest form of thinking.

The link between the dynamism of reality and the consciousness that recognizes it is that both are fundamentally *driven.* If we string together the various contexts in which Nishida uses a word that we may render as "demand" or "need" in reference to reality or consciousness, nearly all of them suggest a kind of innate desire. The translators are not to be blamed for having noticed this—as far as I can tell, *none* of Nishida's commentators has picked up on it. Nishida himself hints at but does not develop a connection between this drivenness and an idea of will or desire more basic than the choice of free will. At this point in his thinking he is more concerned with arguing that willing and knowing are both absorbed in the greater absolute of pure experience, that will is an intentional aspect of all knowing and a defining activity of the self. From there he argues that the truly free will is a kind of dynamism, a "motivation," that sustains the basic unity of consciousness as an activity of the self. Thus he can say that "It is not so much that I give birth to my desires, but that the motivation of reality *is* me"; and later on: "The will is a fundamental unifying activity of consciousness, ...a power of the self." In the years ahead he will take these ideas further to see will, in this broad sense of a fundamental life force, as an absolute principle more fundamental than consciousness, in fact almost a rethinking of the idea of pure experience.

The idea that "reality is the activity of consciousness" and that this active reality is "the only activity and the only reality there is in the universe" differs from Kantian and Hegelian idealisms precisely where it differs from James, namely, that ultimately it is *not* defined as either subjective or as thought. Moreover, its intentionality or telos is not governed from without. The *working* of pure experience is one and the same as what is *being worked on*. The very idea of a starting point or a termination is alien to Nishida's metaphysic. Hence Nishida has no difficulty identifying the natural world and mental phenomena without having to have one emanate from the other. Such oppositions are indication of the fact that the unity of pure experience is "infinitely" active, and does not set up a conflict in which one must be master of the other or reduced to it.

Nishida does not hesitate to call the ground of this infinite activity God, provided we do not reduce God to the "extremely infantile" idea of a "great man that stands outside the universe and controls it." Wherever there is activity in the universe, there is God, and since all activity is at bottom the activity of a nonsubjective, nonobjective unifying consciousness, it is fundamentally good, and "there is nothing that can be called absolutely evil." What is more, since this activity has worked itself out in the form of human consciousness, that human nature is at bottom good and capable of turning back to recognize its ground intuitively. This "deep grasp of life," which at the same time "grasps the true face of God," is what has moved all the great religions throughout history.

Such a sweeping vision raises a great many questions, but this is precisely what Nishida wanted to do. His idea of pure experience, to repeat, was a strategy to redirect the questions of philosophy away from what he saw as the two-world assumptions of western metaphysics on the one hand and the anthropocentric empiricism of science on the other; and to do so in such as way that it would require the complement of eastern philosophy.

Given the variety of functions pure experience has to perform—real, ideal, and intentional—some sorting out of ideas was clearly in order. The novelty of the idea attracted criticism, and Nishida defended himself against it while admitting his own ambiguity of expression. Not the least of his problems was its crowning argument that all of reality can be grounded in a direct intuition, a "self-awareness" in which the knower had transcended the subject-object world. The only way to confirm such an intuition was to achieve it oneself. Nishida all but asks his readers to assume that he had and to take his word for it that they could as well. As he surely realized, this is not a very good argument. A great deal of work remained to be done, and the stimulus to do so came from his reading of the neo-Kantians.

13 THE ABSOLUTE AS WILL.

Already before *An Inquiry into the Good* was finished, Nishida had taken an interest in the neo-Kantians, beginning with the Freiburg thinkers Windelband and Rickert. Initially he saw in them, and also in Husserl, allies in the attempt to "argue the question of theoretical values exclusively from the standpoint of pure experience." This was in fact only an educated guess on his part about that major current of contemporary European philosophy, and turned out to be wrong. A lengthy critique of his first book, written by a young professor specializing in this thought, raised the counterposition of distinguishing value and meaning from the world of actual fact. His equally lengthy answer to these criticisms shows that he took them seriously. That, probably combined with a certain feeling of dissatisfaction with himself for not being *au courrant* of neo-Kantian thinkers, persuaded him that he needed to grapple with the literature at first hand.

And with that he left the blinding sunlight of pure experience for a dark maze of tunnels from which he would emerge only six years later. Aside from a number of essays, later collected into book form, the major production of the period was a serialization of essays eventually rearranged in book form as *Intuition and Reflection in Self-Awareness*, a work that one of its English translators has aptly called "the public diary of a philosophical education." At the end of it he would admit defeat: "I have broken my lance, exhausted my quiver, and capitulated to the enemy camp of mysticism." Thirty years later he would look back at it and even question the wisdom of reprinting it.

There is no reason not to follow Nishida's counsel, but not before registering a certain qualification of his self-deprecating remarks. It is not so much the actual progression of his standpoint—the work begins with seeing immediate experience as self-consciousness and ends with a monism of absolute free will—but its persistent method that would direct Nishida's later thinking. His strategy was to reduce every dualism he met with to some immediately experienced reality that would restore the divisions to an original unity. It is, in this sense, an experiment with the utility of the idea of pure experience for philosophical discourse.

His focus throughout is knowledge of a single, all-encompassing, acting absolute that manifests itself within conscious mind. His starting point is a questioning of the apparently contradictory functions of consciousness that such knowing entails. As *intuition* it needs to be aware of a flowing, continuous reality unbroken by subject or object, and as *reflection* it needs to step outside of the flow of reality to recognize it. One has, if I may impose an image on his project, to be on land and sea at the same time. Without the solid land of the subject thinking about the objective world, knowing simply founders in the ocean of undifferentiated intuition. But without that ocean of reality one can never know reality as it is, only as one thinks about it. Nishida's proposal is to see *self-awareness*, the act in which one becomes both subject and object at the same time, as a raft on which to float out to sea, without sail or rudder, in quest of the absolute. Hence the title of the book.

This raft becomes his world for the duration. From it he tries to see that the differentiations that appear in reflection on the experiential world in the form of oppositions—of fact and value, matter and spirit, self and other, subject and object, knowing and willing, past and future, being and non-being—can be grasped as the same kind of coincidence of opposites that the self's knowing of itself is. To this end he submits himself to the torture of neo-Kantian thought, with Fichte's ideas of the acting self and Bergson's vitalism as a counterpoint. It draws to its close in the rather abrupt return to an idea of will that he had associated in *An Inquiry into the Good* with a fundamental driving force of life.

Here will is made into the absolute principle at the core of the self-conscious self. Self-reflection is always bound by time and must always objectify itself in knowledge, and for this reason can never get to the true self. Will, on the other hand, provided it is understood as the drivenness of life itself and not simply as the exercise of freedom of choice, transcends time at the same time as it is bound to the present reality:

> As unobjectifiable will, as true subject, the self can make the past the present.... Will is absolute reflection, the unifying point of infinite possibilities.... And since it is always concrete, will, in contrast to knowledge, is creative.

Not only is the absolute of will the basis of the self, it is, he suggests, the final principle of reality itself. The mere suggestion of this is enough to bring his voyage to its close without shipwrecking on the rocks of pure objectivity or capsizing into the sea of pure subjectivity. It is rather as if, lying on his back one night, he looked up and saw another dimension beyond land and sea, in the dark and deep abyss of the sky above. To speak of it he turns to the contradictory language of the mystics and the gnostics, to art and religion, to an absolute free will that subsumes within itself not only individual wills but the whole of reality, "an a priori underlying all a priori, an activity underlying all activities."

As an answer to his original search for an absolute, it did not entirely satisfy him, however. If anything, it left him pretty much where *An Inquiry into the Good* had left him—clinging tightly to his philosophical robes but wrapped for the moment in the oceanic embrace of religious sentiments. It is no accident that Bergson appears at the end of this journey, opening the windows once again to the fresh air of "life" that the *Lebensferne* of the neo-Kantians had stifled. But he knew that he had carried out his obligations as a serious student of current philosophical thinking, and that he was free now to use what he had learned to take the leap into a philosophy more suited as a bridge between west and east.

At this point it is best if we focus on the most important ideas of Nishida's mature thought, without paying too much attention to their dating or the development of their interlocking. Many of these ideas can be found as passing but unexplored remarks in these first two books just discussed, but to avoid the common pitfall of reading too much into them, I will not draw any attention to these remarks.

14 SELF-AWARENESS.

The use of the term "self-awareness" to point to something distinct from what western philosophy calls "self-consciousness" only gradually came to force in Nishida's writings. It may be said to be a function of a shift of focus from experience in general to the search for what he called "a standpoint of the self" to deabsolutize the ordinary subjectivity of the ego. This shift was by no means complete by the time he had completed *Intuition and Reflection,* and if he prefers it there to "self-consciousness," it is only because of a general concern with avoiding the creeping psychologism people had seen in *An Inquiry into the Good.*

Nishida had long thought there was something amiss with the preoccupation with the "ego" in modern western philosophy, but at the same time he needed some way to talk about reflexive consciousness. The term "awareness" filled this need. For some years he drew special attention to this self-awareness as the foundation of a "system" of thought and as a "universal" of logic, but as the term moved further and further away from identification with "self-consciousness" and as his idea of the "self" became more clearly distinguished from "ego," this way of speaking receded into the background. In any case, the use of the term that began as a temporary compromise gradually came to take on a character all its own.

The Buddhist overtones that "self-awareness" suggests in English are not necessarily there in the Japanese, though it is one of the many words that Buddhism has appropriated to the purpose. Nishida's position on this is ambivalent, deliberately so, I believe, because he did not want to step into the murky waters of trying to define enlightenment in philosophical language.

To reflect the way in which that special character is carried by an ordinary, colloquial Japanese word without becoming a technical academic term, we generally do better to abbreviate it to simple "awareness" in English. In doing so, we need to remember, however, that we forfeit a double meaning that Nishida found in the character for "self-". On the one hand, it was a person's awareness of one's innermost nature; and on the other, it was an awareness that was not so much accomplished by the person but allowed to take place spontaneously, of itself, and without interference. In other words, *awareness* in Nishida came to carry the combined sense of an *auto-awareness of the self.*

With this in mind, the reader should not expect a definition of awareness in Nishida's thought. It took over from pure experience the function of the core, the goal, and the method of philosophy not by the replacement of one term with another but by a general use that blossomed into a technical term to point to one or the other of these functions. We have arrived at what was for Nishida the heart of the matter: philosophy *is* the transformation of ordinary consciousness into a being aware. If not a definition, then at least we must offer a general description of the role that this being aware played in Nishida's thinking. I will single out four attributes, all of which were already prefigured in his earlier writings. At the same time, as we shall see in laying them out, the tendency to mysticism, for which he had chided himself at the end of his neo-Kantian escapades, is slowly being directed towards the historical world.

First, Nishida's concern as a philosopher was knowing reality at its most basic level. Whether he spoke of it variously as principle, as absolute, or as universal, whether he reasoned about that knowledge inductively or deductively, everything depended on the capacity to know it by firsthand acquaintance. This knowing had to be intuitive in the sense that no one could have intuitions vicariously for another or be aware for another. It was not the sort of knowledge that could accumulate through tradition and be passed on in language, except as the tombstone of a lived experience that had passed away. To know the really real, one had to "see for oneself."

Second, there is no way to step outside of reality in order to know it. The highest form of knowing has to take place from a point at which the knower and the known are one. To know any individual item of reality is, of course, to distinguish it from other items and hence from oneself. To be "aware" of something is to realize that those distinctions are only relative, manifestations of reality at work. The one who is aware can no longer be called "I" in the ordinary sense of the term. In fact, being aware of reality is so unlike being an ordinary I that it can be called the work of the "not-I."

In the third place, compared with the everyday way of thinking, the state of awareness is a flash of timelessness in time, a fleeting sense of a whole in the midst of the fragmentary purposes and ambitions that otherwise drive our lives. It lights up for a moment the insight that at one and the same time "things are as they should be" and "things should be as they are." In this sense, it is the inexhaustible source of all exercise of moral responsibility.

Fourth, the idea of awareness as timeless, nonsubjective, egoless presence that opens up the possibility of a new standpoint for knowing and acting, naturally flows into the recognition of a more authentic, truer self that acts and knows in the state of self-awareness. Whereas self-consciousness points to a field in which the reality is grasped *by* an individual self, self-awareness points to a field in which reality becomes aware of itself *in* the individual self. It is a kind of horizon against which consciousness is set up as only one form, and not the most basic form, of knowing.

At this point we should pause to consider this matter of the "true self" in Nishida's writings, since the currency that term has gained in the meantime, especially when combined with the notion of "awareness," can easily lead to misunderstanding the way Nishida used the term.

Neither "self" nor "true self" were ever technical philosophical terms for Nishida. But he used them both within the context of his technical vocabulary. He did not see the idea of awareness of the true self either as a Buddhist contribution to western philosophy or as corresponding to one or the other western readings of traditional Buddhist ideas—both of which roles they played at the time he was doing his thinking. At most, we can say it was an idea that he had found common to both worlds and that seemed to preserve the core of what philosophy was about. The more Nishida learned of the broader intellectual history of the west, the more he realized that there were cognates to be found in the west for the notion of a self that loses itself in being aware of itself—principally in the mystical tradition—and hence that there was no need to assume its strictly Buddhist quality or adopt a more properly Buddhist vocabulary. It seems fair to characterize his distinction between I and true I as referring to no more than degrees of self-awareness. At the same time, making the knowing, feeling, experiencing self of ordinary consciousness the maidservant of self-awareness meant inverting most of western philosophy as he met it, and this would require that the logic with which he spoke of self-awareness be clearly distinguished from the logic of self-consciousness that he met in western thought.

In his diaries one finds frequent mention of the idea of "self," but it is gratuitous to read anything philosophical into the term on this account. Nearly every occasion of their appearance is associated with one or the other dimension of self-identity. In some cases, they are quite simply the personal struggles of a young man to find his own vocation in life, to struggle against the temptations to dissipation. Sometimes, too, they are simple grammatical references, with no more importance than the "self" in "I myself." At other times they point more directly to concern with continuing to be Japanese in the wave of models of self-identity washing across the culture from the outside world. On a few occasions the term appears in talk of the pursuit of a solid spiritual inner life. But nowhere is there anything like a doctrine or philosophical idea of "self" that we could identify with any particular stream of thought or religious tradition of the day as such.

It is my impression that in his philosophical writings, too, allusions to self or true self are little more than metaphor for one's inner nature that is one with the nature of reality itself, or for the ascent of the subject to an awareness where the ordinary self-centered subject gives way to a more profound principle of identity. Even where the occasional Buddhist term appears in this regard, it is reading too much into it to think that Nishida had really accomplished any kind of Buddhist-philosophical synthesis by using it. It was his disciples, beginning with Nishitani, who developed Nishida's intimations into philosophical ideas and related them to Buddhist ideas.

15 **ACTIVE INTUITION, KNOWING BY BECOMING.** Given the general description of awareness above, we may approach more confidently a new attempt by Nishida to solve the problem he had set out with in *Intuition and Reflection*

If the term "awareness" was allowed to keep its everyday, ordinary flavor, the idea was not. When Nishida decided to integrate a core idea into his philosophy, he did so by introducing a carefully chosen but unmistakable technical term. With each new term, it is as if he were grinding and polishing a lens with which to have another look at the fundamental questions of philosophy. If he found that he could see better with it, he would make a habit of it—at least for as long as he did not find another to replace it. His idea was not simply to replace the borrowed language of pure or direct experience, intuition, ultimate reality, and so forth with more eastern-sounding terms—as some of his predecessors and contemporaries—but to replace the very standpoint from which that language was spoken. For this there had to be a twist to language so that one always knew that one was using habitual terms, both everyday and technical, now from a different perspective.

One of these lenses was what he termed *the standpoint of active intuition.* The idea of a kind of knowing without a knowing subject could not mean a sort of passivity or quietism in which one is lost in a cloud of unknowing. Neither could it be a mere unconscious event. It had to be experienced as a working in which one participates fully aware but without setting oneself up in the position of either passive spectator or active controller of what is wrought. The tack he had taken in *Intuition and Reflection,* namely, to pursue the process of self reflecting on self as a way to overcome the subject-object dichotomy, was set aside, but the problem remained. He still needed a link between actively *thinking about* things and passively *being acquainted* with things as they are. Active intuition was his attempt to theorize about this by looking at the way self and world interact. The go-between would be the relation of each to the body.

He calls it a "standpoint" rather than a "theory," however, because he is not simply concerned with describing a relationship but more with encouraging a new way of seeing the things of life. In terms of the idea itself, it could as well have been called an "intuitive acting" or an "active intuiting," since it is both of these. Nishida settled on the nonverbal, substantive term in order to take advantage of the apparent paradox of calling active what is normally considered passive.

On the face of it, acting and intuiting seem to represent two distinct but equally human ways of relating oneself to the world, roughly corresponding to the subjective and the objective. As a subject, I relate to the world and find my place in it by manipulating it, consuming it, refashioning it, or otherwise acting on it, whether bodily or mentally. As mental action, this is reflection in which the ego seeks to mirror the world, including itself, in itself. Action is a centrifugal movement of self to world. As an object in the world among other objects, I am acted upon passively by what transcends me. This is what I experience physically as the working of need or desire, and what in the mental realm Nishida refers to here as intuition. Whether this intuition be mere sense perception or high artistic inspiration, it is something that occurs to me rather than something I make occur. Intuition is the centripetal movement of world back to self. If intellectual reflection distills the role of the subject as agent, intuition dilutes the subject in order to bring into relief the agency of the world as object.

As is his wont, Nishida sets up the contradiction in order to undercut it. If the self is "a dialectical item in a dialectical world," it cannot view the dialectical elements of the world from without, but must recognize itself as part of the same structure. His idea is that action and intuition, the seer and the seen, can be seen as jointed at the roots in the body, which both sees the world and is the receptacle for the world's making itself seen—so that neither can ever be abstracted from the other. The clue for this is in the idea that the activity of the self is never direct but always involves instrumentality. This is true not only of our physical interventions in the world but also our mental representations of it. Ideas always intend something and as such are instrumental. Nishida pursues his idea of the acting self through the body.

Usually we think of ourselves as at one remove from the instruments we use to manipulate the world. This is only natural, Nishida observes, because we have the freedom to use the instrument or not, whereas the instrument does not enjoy that same freedom to be used or to refuse to be used. This way of thinking carries over to our attitude to our bodies, which serve us as instruments to perceive the world and move around in it. At the same time it defines my place in the world as one thing among other things. If we stop there, we fall into a mind-body dualism of the same sort as the subject-object dualism. Mind can never become body, body can never become mind. Nishida's idea is that body is *not* merely another thing in the world but is at the same time both thing and self. It is the paradigmatic instrument in terms of which all other instruments become "extensions of the body."

Thus the body cannot relate the mind to the world unless it belongs essentially to both. The mere parallelism between mind and body based on the identification of the body with passive sense perception and of the mind with the active reworking of those perceptions into ideas is undercut in the prior identity of self and world in which the self that intuits through acting can never be separated from the world that is acting in all intuition.

In all knowing, there is not only one's active, reflective grasp of things but a passive intuition in which one is grasped by things. The problem is, this ordinary, spontaneous knowing is kept out of reach because of a prior commitment to the idea that one must either be subjective or objective about things, but never both at the same time. Nishida wants a conversion to a new standpoint of awareness in which one sees through the falsehood of this dichotomy. Passive intuition must not overwhelm mental action with the promise of pure objective knowledge of the world, and active intellection must not eclipse the actuality of the objective world with the resignation to its own transcendental predispositions. Rather, a new relationship must be cultivated in which self and world inter-act and inter-intuit each other. Self has to be understood as a subject that is not a non-object, and world has to be understood as an object that is not a non-subject. As Nishida says, one needs to awaken to "a seeing without a seer."

As dense as this idea sounds in condensation, it is not complicated. What keeps it from becoming a sort of mystical union in which self and world simply melt one into the other in the mystery of perception, is the fact that Nishida never really treated self and world as equals. To the end, his primary focus was on knowing, an expansion of awareness, and not on simply letting reality be what it was and do what it did. Granted, at the cosmic level he believed that every increase in awareness was a collaboration with that work of reality; as a thinker he was devoted to *thinking* about things in any case. The difficulty with his idea of active intuition was that, once spoken, there was nothing else to be said about it. As a standpoint, it served to criticize other standpoints, but did not lead him much further. Nonetheless, it did seem to lay to rest the specters of the epistemological problems that had haunted him through his struggles with the neo-Kantians. It also gave him a sort of ontology based on knowing. Active intuition was, in effect, Nishida's definition of "being."

A second lens that Nishida ground in order to see philosophy as self-awareness is what he called *knowing by becoming*. The idea of becoming something as opposed to thinking about it is prefigured in *An Inquiry into the Good:*

> All people believe that there is a fixed, unchanging principle in the universe and that all things are established according to it.... This principle is creative,

> so that we can *become* it and work at one with it, but it is not something we can see as an object of consciousness.

Leaving aside the particular context of these remarks —Nishida is talking about consciousness as the sole reality— the idea of *becoming a thing*, which lay dormant for years, resurrects in a more general use in the sense that one knows and acts upon particular items of the world. This was what Nishida repeatedly called "thinking something by *becoming* it—doing something by *becoming* it."

The idea would have to wait for Nishitani to serve as a clear bridge to Buddhist thinking about the mind-body unity. Nishida used it as a metaphoric expression to draw attention to something that the abstract logic of active intuition tends to obscure, namely, the transformation that takes place in one who intuits actively and acts intuitively. Implied in the idea of thinking and acting by *becoming* what we think and act is the sense that one is more fully aware of self and world in a state where the two are seen as one than in a state where one is allowed to lord it over the other. Such "knowledge" is not susceptible to expression in objective or in subjective terms. Hence its expression aims neither to replace nor simply to supplement the language of subject and objects, but to voice an awareness of the limitations of everything we can know and say because of the dichotomy we set up between self and world. In this sense, it is neither an epistemological principle nor an invitation to mystical intuition. It is an attempt to locate "seeing without a seer" at the requisite foundations of all true knowledge about self and world.

16 **ART AND MORALITY AS SELF-EXPRESSION.** Nishida's idea of active intuition was basically designed, as we noted, to show the correlative interdependence of the activity of mental reflection and the passivity of taking in the world. Not only the layers of meaning contained in the term *intuition* but the idea of *acting* in the world lend themselves to thinking about artistic expression. In Nishida's case, it is not a case of a simple metaphor; artistic creation was itself a direct extension of the notion of "body" that he had set up to mediate the dialectic of active intuition.

His first sustained attempt to tackle the relevance of aesthetics for his idea of active intuition was in a book entitled *Art and Morality*, published in 1923. In it he seeks a common ground for the apparently conflicting ideas of art and morality. He rejected both an idea of *ars gratia artis* that would erase the distinction, and a moralism that would swallow art up in its own concern by seeing it as an enhancement of the interior life of the individual or an expression of ethical judgments about the things of life. From the start he was committed to a correlation of the truth, the good, and the beautiful, and he carried out that commitment by trying to see art and morality as self-expressions of the same vital force at work in the foundations of consciousness—absolute will.

It will be recalled that Nishida had concluded his struggles with neo-Kantian thought in an idea of absolute will. In subsequent essays, mainly in a 1920 collection of essays published as *The Question of Consciousness,* he pursued the connection between consciousness and will further, reviewing a wide range of philosophical and psychological positions, Spinoza, Leibniz, Wundt, and Brentano figuring most prominently in the picture. Unlike that earlier work, Nishida seems to be on top of his material in *Art and Morality,* checking his major philosophical intuitions out and sharpening his own position. The mystical tone of absolute will is all but absent.

Despite the title of the work, the question of aesthetics clearly plays a secondary role to this ongoing concern with the will as a metaphysical principle and unifier of consciousness. The space actually devoted to the process of artistic creation is very small, and the appreciation of actual art left to passing remarks. The connection of will to art may be summarized handily in his own words, which give a good idea of the nature of his "aesthetics" and the complexity of the context in which he located it:

> In actual willing subject and object are united and the "I" finds itself in a context of action. This is what I call the standpoint of absolute will. In the same way, artistic activity is enters into the true reality that is the object of this actual willing. To enter into that reality the whole body must be concentrated into a single force and become a single activity. The truly actual is not found at some point determined by conditions of space and time. Rather it is something that projects consciousness in general inwards, something that lodges within experience itself the infinite forward progress of an ideal. Particular, individual instances of unity only become visible in the never-ending advance of unity. The artist should not think about these things unless he is holding his brush. Only when facing the canvas, brush in hand, does that infinite advance background open up and make it clear how he should paint.

A short essay on Goethe written ten years later, after Nishida's preoccupation with absolute will had subsided and the role of absolute nothingness had come much more to the fore, takes up this final point in much more satisfying fashion. There he declares that art is an expression of beauty, in which the free self transcends time by uncovering eternity in the present moment. By enveloping himself in the reality whose beauty he aims to express, the artist is able to "mirror eternity in eternity," and this effect is able to touch those who view the art and draw them into that same world. Michelangelo's *Schiavi* and Rodin's sculptures are cited as examples of "reliefs hewn out of the marble block of eternity." In more philosophical language he describes its object as realizing a harmony between intuition and reflection—or as he says in this context, between the inner and the outer worlds of the artist. Brush in hand and standing before his canvas, the painter is able to discover the depths of his own personality and at the same time to release control to the expression of an infinite idea. Or again, to cite an earlier example of the art of calligraphy that Nishida himself practiced: "It is a revelation of the free throb of life itself.... As a direct expression of rhythm itself, we may call it the art most immediate to our self."

Once the purely epistemological aspects of active intuition had been set in the broader context of Nishida's distinctively eastern metaphysics, his concern with art tended to crystallize around a discussion of the basic differences between western and eastern art. The basic elements of art discussed above are, as he recognized, universal. The difference between art east and west, Nishida argues, is that the east tends to be more expressive of the space in which the personal element is absorbed, creating the sense of "a voiceless echo reverberating without form and without bounds" in the heart of artist and viewer. The eternal is present in its absence, and the importance of the empty spaces and two-dimensional space, particularly noticeable in much classical Chinese art but also in early Christian art, is crucial. The Greek idea was different. Here the eternal is made visible in a perfection of form and boundaries. This carried on into the Renaissance, where the person came more and more not only into the foreground but also into the expression of particular sentiments and aspirations in the background. He finds this, for example, in Michelangelo's way of making his subject emerge from "the turbulent black flames of a deep abyss."

The same pattern is applied to Goethe's poetry, where the personal appeal is strong, despite the influence of Spinoza's pantheism, where a two-dimensional, formless, timeless *substantia* removes the individual from the picture. Goethe's gift is his ability to create a resonance between the bottomless depths of the human spirit and the bottomless enveloping of the eternal. In Goethe form and spirit become one, and he thus provides a bridge to the east and its pursuit of a peace of mind outside time:

> When history is taken to mean... the eternal now, when past and future are extinguished in the present, everything comes from nowhere and goes to

nowhere, and everything that is, is eternally just what it is. This way of thinking courses in the depths of the civilizations of the east in which we have been raised.

This enveloping "reality" or "eternal now" in which the artist is caught up is here called for the first time absolute nothingness. If we leave these ideas to one side for the moment, without entering into the other examples Nishida's gives or into a criticism of his comparison of east and west, the main point is that Nishida's interest is not in criticizing or classifying particular forms of art but in laying out the metaphysical background. If there is any judgment of what distinguishes good art from bad, it is a function of the degree to which the artist is given over to this background. It is not a question of conscious will aiming to express something transcendent, but of a state of awareness in which the artistic medium takes over, releasing the mind from its subjectivity and reality from its objectivity.

Behind the scenes stands a more general idea of "self-expression" based on his idea of active intuition. Nishida saw the objective world not as a given that can be viewed from without, but always as the self-expression of reality itself. Accordingly, the historical world is not merely the environment for the ascent of individual consciousness to full self-awareness; it is itself part of the process. In seeking to clarify its relation to the world in terms of a common reality at work, consciousness becomes more fully aware of itself than when it simply works on the objective world from the standpoint of the thinking subject. Self-awareness is the highest form of the self-expression of reality precisely because it is able to see through the ordinary idea of a subject looking at the world, to view that common force at work:

> When we submerge ourselves into the depths of self-awareness in active intuition and take the standpoint of a self whose seeing has negated the seer, all things that exist are transformed into a self-awareness and a self-expression. From such a standpoint, what we think of as the "conscious self" is no more than a self that has become visible because it has been expressed.

From such a standpoint, "self-expression," artistic or otherwise, is very different from the usual meaning of the term, according to which an individual inserts one's individuality at the heart of what one is expressing. What reaches expression transcends the individual at the same time as it flows from the deepest, innermost wellsprings of will, beyond the will of everyday ego.

The foundations of morality, Nishida suggests, can be understood from this same standpoint of the self-expression of absolute will. It cannot be based on abstract universal laws but only on an awareness of the impulse of life itself. Where it differs from art is that the goal it serves is not the artistic creation but religion, by which he understands the concrete and disciplined effort to efface the everyday self in its intellectual, affective, and volitional dimensions in order to be free to act in accord with the truth. But like his aesthetics, Nishida's morality is worked out on a metaphysical plane, far from the questions we normally associate with moral activity.

What Nishida expected of himself in the way of a view of morality was certainly not the generation of concrete norms, but neither was it a demarcation of even the most general norms on which to base an ethic. He was concerned with morality as a state of awareness, one that did not really concern itself with the clarification of the formation and deformation of social and individual conscience, let alone the way in which cultural mores generate and color universal principles. All he wanted was to locate the *foundations* for moral action in the structure of consciousness, imitating Kant's question if not his response. He did not disappoint himself.

A history of ethical theories had been the first philosophical project he set himself. That he never finished it, leaving only fragments of that project in *An Inquiry into the Good*, is more than coincidence. And when he came to the neo-Kantians, one of his intentions was to clarify the distinction between fact and value, which led Rickert and Cohen to relate their aesthetics to questions of love and ethics. Here, too, he sidestepped this aspect of their thought and dealt with value strictly in terms of meaning, not of action. *Art and Morality* flows in the same channels. The "ought" is ultimately identified with the real, and this identification is a function of awareness.

The closest he will come to speaking of the need for moral principles generated from this awareness is to say that a concrete ethics based on awareness of the self is something possible and desirable:

> When we are born as individuals in a particular society,... the legal system of that society confronts the I as an external authority that is not to be transgressed.... When we have completely lost respect for the law, we have to look for that authority within ourselves.... A moral motivation that is purely formal and without content cannot give us an objective moral law;... it cannot but land us in subjectivism. True moral conduct, which is an end in itself, in which the inner and the outer are united, requires something objective created from a moral *a priori*.

The objectivity he has in mind is not one that *generates* specific or general imperatives but one that *grounds* them. Nishida likens particular moral ideals in a given society to the way a particular biological species participates in the great flow of life by giving it shape and making it real. Thus, the inner awareness of moral a priori is advanced by being specified in the outer world, but only completed when the self returns to a state in which the external has been re-internalized. Without being detained by the particular details of the externalization, Nishida restores the discovery of the moral law to the self as an "inner environment in which one makes specific the life of spirit."

What the completion of a treatise on artistic intuition with an excursus on morality makes clear is that the level of awareness achieved in authentic artistic expression is not the function of an artistic career but is an "ought" that lies dormant in all ordinary consciousness, waiting to be awakened. The true self is a universal human vocation, the refusal to listen and respond to which is the root of everything evil, untrue, and ugly.

17

ABSOLUTE NOTHINGNESS. The idea of grounding all thought in a single, absolute principle continued to pester Nishida, like a fly buzzing inside his head that he could not swat down. While the terms "pure experience" and "absolute will" had disappeared, the assumption of an absolute beyond subject and object and yet somehow knowable had not. The more he realized that none of his solutions had managed really to dislodge the subject from center stage—in his terms, that a certain "psychologism" still remained—the more acute became the need for a replacement absolute. He sought it in a turn to religion and found it in the idea of nothingness.

The idea of nothingness is tightly braided with the accompanying changes in Nishida's logic, and indeed it is the polysemic use to which he put the idea that adds all the complications for which it is notorious, and which at the same time left it open for further development by others like Tanabe and Nishitani. Still, since this idea, in one or the other variation, is so distinctive of the Kyoto-school philosophers, it is worth trying to abstract the main outlines of Nishida's understanding before providing that fuller context.

Nishida makes it clear that in taking the steps to an ontology of nothingness he is taking on a major supposition of philosophy up until then. "I think that we can distinguish the west to have considered being as the ground of reality, the east to have taken nothingness as its ground." This does not mean that he understood the introduction of the concept of nothingness as a mere paraphrase or mirror-image of the concept of being that had to take on all the traits and functions of the concept it was replacing. It was rather a relativizing of being, which he saw as absolute in western thought, to a greater absolute.

There are suggestive phrases concerning nothingness in *An Inquiry into the Good* that are not inconsistent with the fuller idea Nishida would develop later, but neither are they markedly inconsistent with traditional ontology, in which nothingness is by and large seen as a correlative to being. The reason is that Nishida was not interested in its ontological status at the time. He began using the term as a way of expressing the negation of the self that sets itself up as a subject perceiving the objects of the world. This self had to be "made nothing" so that it could open up into its truer self. The use of this expression, not uncommon in Japanese but unusual in philosophical language, which prefers to speak of simple negation, was clearly deliberate. The allusion to Zen, where meditation on "nothingness" and talk of no-self and no-mind was everywhere in evidence, would not have been lost on his readers. Nishida did not draw it directly, since this was not the context he was speaking in. He did mean, though, as Zen means, that he was not talking about prepositional or rational negation, but about the disciplined effort of dispensing with the bias of seeing oneself as a subject standing in a world of objects.

The step from the use of *nothingness* as an expression of negation to the idea of nothingness as a metaphysical absolute was a large one that did not come directly from Zen, and has by no means been universally accepted in Zen circles. For his part, Nishida did not introduce it as a Zen idea at all, or even as a Buddhist idea. To have done so would have required a greater familiarity with the classical sources, Chinese and Japanese, Taoist and Buddhist, than he was prepared to claim. It was enough for him that the idea was distinctively eastern.

To call it absolute *nothingness* is to say that it does not itself come to be or pass away, and in this sense is opposed to the world of being. To call it *absolute* nothingness—or the "nothingness of the absolute" as he often calls it—is to say that it is beyond encompassing by any phenomenon, individual, event, or relationship in the world. Its absoluteness means precisely that it is not defined as an opposite to anything in the world of being. It is "absolved" of any opposition that could render it relative, so that its only opposition to the world of being is that of an absolute to a relative. Nothingness opposes the world as absolute to relative. The negation of subject and object—or the negation of the self that rests on the subject-object distinction—is in the first instance, relative since it defines itself in opposition to the affirmation of those things. These negations do not become an absolute nothingness until they have been absolved of that defining opposition, that is, until they are seen as a first step in the self-determination of the nothingness of the absolute itself, in which what has been negated in being is again reaffirmed just as it is. In absolute nothingness, as Nishida says, "true negation is a negation of negation."

To call reality itself *absolute nothingness*, then, is to say that all of reality is subject to the dialectic of being and not-being, that the identity of each thing is bound to an absolute contradictoriness. In other words, nothingness not only relativizes the "ground of being," it relativizes any model of co-existence or harmony that sublates, transcends, debilitates, or otherwise obscures that contrariness. At the same time, it is to say that the ascent of nothingness to self-awareness in human consciousness, "to see being itself directly as nothingness," is both the place at which the self can directly intuit itself and the place at which the absolute becomes most fully real.

From early attempts to describe the idea of nothingness as a kind of "infinite idea" intuited at the depths of the self, it grew into a metaphysical principle proper. Nishida calls it "the universal of universals," by which he means to name it the highest principle of reality and that which relativizes all other universals of thought. The identity of the individual is a coincidence of two limiting principles: its own activity (self-determination of the individual) and the objective fact of being one among many (the determination of the universal). Although time can be understood as a dynamic shaping of the world as determinations of individuality and of universality, time does not account for either of these, nor does either for the other. Their ground must lie in a self-actualizing totality that is absolute relative to all determinations, be they of the individual or of the many. It must be like a timelessness in time, an eternal now.

Consciousness does not stand outside the world to watch all of this going on from a privileged position. Like all other items of being, it is self-determining and determined by the universal. In respect to time, too, consciousness belongs among the items of the world of being: it both *is a process* (insofar as it occurs in the flow of time) and *is not a process* (insofar as it is located on the permanent ground of nothingness). As with all things, so with human consciousness, it is absolute nothingness that creates a place for self-identity to take place, a place that neither the historical world of time nor consciousness itself can create. Once this place has been established as the ultimate horizon, Nishida is able to return to time and see it not only as belonging to the world of relative being but also as a "self-determination" of absolute nothingness in the historical world. That is to say, in the very contradiction of the idea of the present moment as continuous with the past and discontinuous towards the future, the absolute of nothingness is manifest. And at the same time, Nishida can return to consciousness and see that its achievement of true self-awareness does not stop at simply being conscious of reality as the activity of nothingness, but recognizes this self-actualizing as expressed paradigmatically in the unity of the awakened self itself.

18 IDENTITY AND OPPOSITION.

In *An Inquiry into the Good* Nishida had spoken of a *given unity* in reality that exists prior to the mind's carving it up into a dualism of subject and object in order to render it intelligible. In time, he was to shift his idiom to speak of the real as a *self-identity*. There is not a great shift in content, only in emphasis. His choice of terms is significant, however. Rejecting the idea of a principle of individuation as he found it in western philosophy—that which gives a thing its identity, based on the idea of an underlying substance in things—Nishida suggests that the true identity of the individual only emerges through a co-existence of opposites. The device of establishing identity through contradiction is more than a means of criticizing the way we identify items in the world with the language or ideas we have fashioned to take them out of their native environments and make a home for them in thinking. This element is certainly there, but it is not the most important for Nishida. In the same way that his idea of nothingness reached beyond logic and into ontology, so, too, self-identity is meant to take over the role that *substantia* or *hypokeimenon* has played in traditional philosophy since Aristotle. Hence it is a *self*-identity in the double sense noted earlier: it is spontaneous and it has to do with the true nature of things.

The introduction of a principle of individuation based on opposition is not meant to imply a dualism of absolute principles in the world or innate in the nature of the individual items of the world. Neither is it meant to simply relativize the opposites from a higher standpoint or locate them in a dialectical process where the opposition is eventually dissolved. The only true unity or unifying principle, Nishida saw, was one that allowed individuals, just as they are, to stand in opposition to one another as *absolute* contradictories. Only in this way can their true identity be known:

> As Hegel has stated, reality is contradiction, and the deeper the contradiction, the more we can think of it as true reality. For the more profound and spontaneous internal unity becomes, the more it includes contradiction within itself.

As with everything in Nishida's philosophy, so here, too, all questions of logic and metaphysics had to answer to the fundamental question of illuminating the self. It was not a matter of finding a standpoint from which to "transcend" opposition but rather of bringing it down to a problem of consciousness, a standpoint of "transdescendence" as he called it. In this sense, the final paradigm for the union of opposites in reality lay not in the cosmos but in the self-awareness of the individual.

The notion of totality as a coincidence or harmonizing of opposites was one Nishida was familiar with from western philosophy, where it has a long and pluriform history. The principle oppositions that first drove Nishida to introduce a similar idea into his own philosophy, as we see in a rather late essay on the subject, were that between subject and object and between the past and the future. He first spoke of a "constellation of self-contradictions," and then changed it to the clumsier but distinctive term "the self-identity of absolute contradictories." Once he had worked the idea out, he applied it to any number of oppositions and did not hesitate to cite analogous ideas from the history of philosophy and mystical thought to clarify his meaning. The most common function of the idea, however, is one that is not accompanied by the formula as such but that shows up in the increased use of grammatical expressions combining affirmation and negation.

For Nishida true self-identity does not take the form "A is A" but that of a unity of contradictories, so that, as we have just seen, "the more self-contradictory the opposites are, the more it is a self-identity." There is no question here of offending the principle of non-contradiction, but of relativizing it as unsuited to the task of talking about reality. In other words, Nishida does not say "A is not-A" but rather something like "A-*in*-not-A is A." The matter merits a closer look lest it be too quickly dismissed as a piece of oriental mumbo-jumbo, as it not uncommonly is. In fact, it is rather simple to understand.

The copulative –*in*- translates a Chinese character of notorious ambiguity (usually pronounced *soku* in Japanese). Its meanings include "i.e.", "at the same time", "and also", "or", "forthwith," and "as such." The common ingredient is the connecting of two items or attributes, the second of which is attached to the first as a matter of course. The character by itself does not say *is* in the sense of the opposite of *is not,* and therefore cannot be said to engage the law of non-contradiction as such. There is therefore nothing linguistic to prevent Nishida from using it to join elements, like "A" and "not-A," that in ordinary logical language would be a contradiction.

Nishida does not draw attention to the logic of *soku* explicitly until his last essay, at which time he puts it in the context of Buddhist logic and his own idea of inverse correspondence, which we will take up separately. For now it is enough to note that the *soku* joining contradictories does not point to the same relationship that ordinary logics have no choice but to force into the formula "A is not B." He has no intention of dispensing with the rules of grammar "A is not not-A" and "B is not-A," which are implied in the distinction between *is* and *is not.* If he did, he would have to give up arguing sensibly altogether. What he means to say is rather something like this: "A is not just A, and not-A is not just not-A; neither are the two simply different aspects of one and the same thing; A is A and not-A is not-A, but neither of them are real unless each belongs to the other just as it is." And the reason he says this is that it allows him to say that "A transforms B and B transforms A" in virtue of "something common to both."

At this point a certain confusion enters the picture when we realize that what Nishida calls "contradictories" are often closer to what we might call "contraries" or "correlatives." Affirmation-in-negation, continuity-in-discontinuity, being-in-nothingness, and subjective-in-objective are, rightly speaking, copulations of contradictories. They cannot co-exist in the same thing at the same time without offending the rules of logical discourse. Self-in-other, death-in-life, past-in-future, one-in-many, on the other hand, are not so obviously contradictory since they are readily understood to share a common basis—human encounter, creativity, will, totality, or what have you. To say that there is an affirmation that is *at the same time and just as it is* a negation, or that there is a connection that is *at the same time and just as it is* a disconnection, is to talk nonsense. But to speak of the identity of the self as entailing the other, of life entailing death, is to see these terms as correlatives, requiring one another and a common medium (or universal) to be understood. This is the way dialectical logic proceeds, and there is nothing logically "contradictory" about it.

The question is, which of these was Nishida opting for? Surprisingly enough, it seems to have been the former. While he does talk of the historical world as a dialectical process already from his early writings, his own idea of absolute nothingness as the ultimate explanation of why things are and why they are what they are, required a different logical formulation. Hegel's conviction that being and consciousness are ultimately identical, the one evolving out of the other, lay at the root of his dialectic. It also allowed Hegel to take the step—whether necessary or not, that is another question—of going beyond mere dialectical mediation to seeing logical contradiction as an expression of this evolution in action.

There is some of this in Nishida. In particular, his idea of affirmation-in-negation is cut of the same cloth as Hegel's idea that a negation clarifies the meaning of an affirmation. The difference is that Nishida was not bent on seeing a dialectic at work in particular historical events the way Hegel was, nor did he conclude that *all* contradiction, whether in categories of thought or in social movement, is simply the manifestation of a deeper unity that gives them their reality. The examples he chose were chosen for one of two motives: either they enlightened the way consciousness falls into and overcomes the subject-object dichotomy, or they pointed to the basic contradiction between being and nothingness. The way he carries this out is epistemological in the first instance, ontological in the second.

Epistemologically, the language of absolute contradictories joined together draws attention to the limitations of language and logical forms to express the full meaning of conscious experience. As a subject I take the *things* of the world as objects. I am interested in "what" a thing is, and language and logic help me to distinguish it both from any interference of my own and from other things. But when I shift my attention to the fact "that" things are experienced, I must take leave of my disinterested objectivity to account for the way in which the meanings accruing to the experience because of affect, will, memory, prejudice, and so forth all intermingle in my "knowing" what a thing is. Similarly, the "that" of experience requires that I take into account the relationship that any particular thing has with the other things that judgments of its "what" abstract from. Straightforward judgments of affirmation and relationship break down. If the experience as such can be said to have an identity that includes both the experiencer and the experienced, then its identity overflows the rules of language.

To say that language is inadequate is not to say that formulating the identity of that "that" as a self-identity of absolute contradictories does any better than, say, poetic or artistic expression in which things are allowed to run together without concern for affirmation or negation, continuity or discontinuity. The reason for the formula has to be sought elsewhere.

The second, ontological motive is grounded on the metaphysical principle that if every relative thing that *is,* at the same time located on an absolute foundation of a *nothingness,* then its identity is *automatically* a coincidence of the relative and the absolute. Here we see the crux of the formulation of an absolute identity of absolute contradictories: self-identity is not an enhancement of an item of reality or an attribute, but merely a way of stating that the fact that things have an identity of their own at all is not due to something internal to them—a substantial principle—but is based on the location of the relative world of being in an absolute of nothingness.

These two motivations are not parallel but concurrent. When we see contradictories and contraries coinciding in the world of being, we see how consciousness and language have trouble putting up with the raw facts of experience as they present themselves to us, and at the same time we see them as a microcosm of the ultimate dialectic of being and nothingness. In the end, the logical form of the self-identity of absolute contradictories is another version of the prototype of human consciousness reflecting the way the real is.

19 THE HISTORICAL WORLD. The place Nishida gave to history is one of the weakest points of his thought, and the lack will be glaring when he turns to questions of political philosophy. As his position is not argued at length, it has to be reassembled from his remarks about time and allusions to history scattered throughout his works.

Nishida generally refers to history in terms of what he calls "the historical world." The use of the term is telling. His final concern is not so much with the events whose unfolding gives us our concrete idea of history as a flow of *time,* as with the metaphysical *place* of history. The historical world can then be seen as a whole that can be relativized by locating it in a wider context of what it "expresses," namely the self-actualization of absolute nothingness. This is not an intuitive leap he takes all at once; it is arrived at by patiently setting up the idea of the history of the world of being that has to be broken through to its truer foundations.

The historical world is distinguished by an ongoing transition "from the done to the doing," that is, "from what has been finished to what is still in-the-making." But Nishida sees this not from the viewpoint of the cumulative results—for example, as the advance and decline of civilizations, cultures, technologies, and the like—but from the viewpoint of individual consciousness caught in the grip of time, straddling the past and the future. Concreteness is supplied by means of what he calls "the historical body," which basically extends the idea of the body we saw earlier as mediating between consciousness and the world in active intuition to make it the mediator of history. This works in two directions. It means that the body gives concreteness to historical life, and that the historical world gives the body an arena in which to work. In the end, the historical body is a means to enhance self-awareness or, as Nishida says, "to ground the self in the depths of the body." These two opposing functions of the body are experienced as a struggle between the determinations of the concrete environment in which one is placed and the desire to be free of those determinations—to move beyond what has been created to create something of one's own.

In this binding the historical world to human consciousness, Nishida subsumes the history of the natural world, which is not of itself conscious of the process, into the personal search of the self for higher meaning. Awareness of the present moment, accordingly, is given privilege of place in history, as a kind of dialectical middle-ground between the facts of the past and the possibilities of the future. The form that time seems to give to history is only the surface of an underlying formlessness, an absolute nothingness expressing itself in the world and recognized in an awareness of the self that has overcome ordinary ego-consciousness. This is what I understand him to mean when he claims that the historical world, like time in general, is "a determination that is at the same time a negation of determination."

Nishida does not, therefore, see the contradiction of past and present as overcome in the forward advance of history only to be regenerated in new form. For him, the basic question of the philosophy of history is how to unify these contradictions of time and how to unify all the beings caught up in them—that is, how to give history its self-identity "as an absolute contradiction of the one and the many"—and the only way to respond to that question is to transcend temporality. He is not so much concerned with any sense in which past and present can be said to co-exist in current events, as with locating the point of the eternal now that discloses the true identity of time and history. In this way, the temporality of time is relocated in the present, the locus of a more basic process of self-determination going on. This is how I understand him when he said that the self-awareness of the present is "a contradictory self-identity of time and space."

In this way, Nishida is able to "locate" the historical world in its metaphysical ground, at the same time as he preserves the temporality of the historical world not as a feature inherent in the things of the world but only as a perceived relationship between what things have been and what they are becoming. The essential nature of history is not to be sought in the flow of events in time but in the ground of everything in nothingness.

This view of time and history fits hand in glove with his idea of knowing things just as they are by *becoming* them. The locus at which such true knowing takes place is at the ground of their history, not in the temporality of their own becoming. Thus when he claims that one needs to *become* a bamboo in order to *know* one, he is talking about knowing the inner nature of the bamboo, not its historicity. To break with the attachment of consciousness to the subject-object distinction, he has to abstract from the fact that things and the minds that know them have a history. In other words, what one might learn from a bamboo by *raising* one from a sprout to a full-grown plant is relative knowing by a historical subject of a historical object.

Nishida's focus was on the eternal now of the bamboo that can be intuited only by forsaking time for a locus outside of time. The assumption was that once one had seen the world from this locus, one would be able to look at the world of historical becoming with renewed and deeper insight. But this was a step that Nishida seems to have had trouble negotiating with any success.

From the foregoing, it would seem as if Nishida had floated himself fairly high above the historical world as we normally conceive of it. In fact, however, he tied a rope around his ankle and moored the other end to concrete history at a most peculiar spot, namely the living tradition of Japanese culture. We will leave details of his remarks for later. For now, it is the historical framework in which he cast those reflections that concerns us.

The gap that Nishida had left between the metaphysical ground of the historical world in absolute nothingness and the actual events that make up that world as we live in it, was too great to bridge in a single bound. The number of questions that arise in shifting the focus from self-awareness to the analysis of the structures of historical change, as Nishida was surely aware, was too many to handle all at once. At the same time, the demand for rootedness in the present did not allow the luxury of a studied pace. Nishida's response was to leap over the gap and throw himself directly into a very generalized comparison of ideas of history east and west in the hopes of carrying something of his thought into the previously unfamiliar realms of social conscience.

The Greeks, he said, had viewed historical time as a shadow cast by eternal ideas that flowed into the present from the past. Christianity has broken with that idea by orienting history to the eschaton, so that the present always flowed ahead towards the future. Japan's eastern culture does neither. It is focused on a symbiosis of past and future in the here-and-now that allows time to flow in both directions. In this sense, its image of history subsumes the dialectical opposites of Greek and Christian culture.

Even granted that all three cultures have developed a plurality of views of history, as referring to a general cultural mode of thought the idea is interesting enough. And as part of his general adventure of ideas, introducing eastern ideas into western philosophy at the point where the latter ceases to describe reality as it is experienced, we would in fact expect some such statement. But what we also expect is that it be made as a statement about modes of thought, and therefore at the same level of abstraction as the rest of his philosophy. Instead, the best he can manage is the suggestion that "the point of contact between cultures east and west is to be sought in Japan." For the rest, his talk of the concrete world is bound to the cultural structures of Japan, and *only* Japan. The living world of history, in short, is identified with questions of the living Japanese spirit, the emperor-system, the national polity, the role of Japanese culture in Asia, and so forth. Allusions to western philosophy in this context are restricted to remarks on how they do not capture the essence of the oriental mind. In doing this, Nishida lands himself in a frame of discourse that seems to allow his philosophy to stand as a justification for the concrete, historical reality of the country at that time. This was to prove an unfortunate step. And it is a step aggravated by the fact that the moral question, otherwise highly abstract in his thought, shows up here in an unexpected specificity, identifying the state as the primary "moral reality." We will look at this step presently. For now something should be said about the abstractness of his attention to the moral.

In principle, Nishida's nothingness does not have the other-worldly nature of the transcendent God, but in moral matters ends up more removed from the historical world than the Christian metaphysic, a problem that Tanabe and Nishitani would later struggle with more directly. The fault lies not in the idea of absolute nothingness as such, but with his view of history and the consequent dehistoricization of morality in his philosophy proper, as we saw earlier.

Nishida sees a fundamental contradiction of form and content at the heart of the moral self. On the one hand, we have the moral ideal to be strived for—the form—and on the other, the reality of one's own imperfection—the content. The more one is aware of one's own imperfection, the more brightly does the ideal glow. This prompts a kind of rupture in the self that open up into religious consciousness. In Nishida's thought, this contradiction is relativized by seeing the moral anguish, and the self that suffers it, caught up in an absolute where there is no good or evil, no sin or ideal—only nothingness. This is, for Nishida, the core of the experience of "salvation." In this way, the core of morality is shifted away from evil in the world to the consciousness of evil in the self. And with it, the imperfections of the world are left to history to sort out.

The context of these remarks is one of the few instances in which Nishida strings together examples from Zen to illustrate what he is talking about, reconfirming the fact that moral responsibility towards concrete evil in history has long been the Achilles' heel of Zen. My point is not to fault Nishida for not having had another focus to his philosophy than the one he had. I wish only to indicate that one should not expect much in the way of insight on problems of history and morality from Nishida. At the same time I register surprise that he should have dipped into the political arena of the day, armed with a philosophy whose focus was clearly on the expansion of consciousness into self-awareness and not on sorting out the root causes of injustice and prejudice, as one would expect from a political philosopher.

20 THE LOGIC OF LOCUS. Nishida's first treatise on the logic of locus appeared in 1926. The idea, unlike any other, was like a magnet that drew to itself all his other ideas and increased its pull, if not its clarity of definition, to the end of his work. Clearly, it was this idea, more than any single work, that was Nishida's crowning achievement.

The idea itself is not complicated, nor is it new. He had spoken of a "locus of will" already from 1919 and other uses of the term appear in *Art and Morality.* Though in none of these cases does he attach a technical meaning to it, it has the ring of the idea of a "field" in physics, even if Nishida's word is different. What is clear is that it did not refer to either time or space but only to the abstract "point" at which an activity "takes place."

In any case, when Nishida did take it up as his own term it was to signal a comprehensive way of reorganizing his thinking. Up to that point, the organization of his philosophy tended to revolve around a particular metaphysical absolute (pure experience, will, or nothingness), an ideal form of consciousness (active intuition or self-awareness), or a combination of the two (self-identity in absolute contradiction). The logic of locus changes all that. It does not point to a particular ideal or principle or activity, but rather to a general scheme for "locating" all of these things. He speaks of the discovery as helping him to

> grasp something that had long been lying at the bottom of my thinking, a shift from Fichte's kind of voluntarism to a sort of intuitionism, but one that gave intuition a different orientation and content from former intuitionism. My aim is to think not along the lines of something based on the intuition of a unity in subject and object, but to see the working of all things that exist as shadows reflecting the self within a self that has nullified itself, a kind of seeing without a seer into the bottom of all things.

What Nishida is suggesting here turns the image of Plato's cave on its head. Rather than see freedom from illusion as leaving the half-light of self-opinionated self-enclosed ignorance, where the world can only appear as shadows dancing on the wall, for the bright sunlight of reality where things can be known as they are, Nishida wants to find a standpoint in which the knowing subject, standing foursquare in the sunlight of the real, objective world, can be seen as itself an illusion to be broken through only by negating the self and seeing everything moving around in the world as shadows of the true, awakened self. It is not the search for a standpoint from which to see the things of the world clearly so as to confirm or refute the truth of our ideas about them but a replacement of that standpoint of the clear-seeing subject over against clearly-seen objects by a standpoint from which the self can find the truth about itself mirrored in all things just as they are. The logic of locus, we might say, is an attempt to explain the process of the one standpoint opening up into the other, to *dislocate* the ordinary self from its apparently fixed abode on a landscape of subjects and objects and to *relocate* it in its true landscape, which, like the background in oriental painting, is an absolute nothingness.

The logic of locus can be said to have occurred to Nishida in the inverse order in which he presents it. It begins from an insight into a final resting place for the true self, but is explained almost as if in a process of spiritual ascent. In the illumination of the aware self, the I of ordinary knowing is a kind of fictional center of conscious activity. All empirical knowing, Nishida writes, begins in the more basic sense of something "becoming consciousness to me." It is not that there is first an established I that looks out over the world, as one item in the world among other items, and grasps it in perception and judgment. Rather, the I belongs from the start to the whole experiential field. It is not a kind of organizational, central "point" in consciousness, but is the "event" of coming to awareness. When I say "the thought occurred to me" we are closer to the facts than when we say, "I had a thought." It is not that I am aware or that consciousness belongs to me, but that awareness is me, and I belong to consciousness.

This puts the I in a rather ambiguous, if not contradictory position. If the I is indeed nothing other than the self-awareness of an experience, then it must be affirmed. At the same time, since the I of itself does not have any meaning, it must be denied. Here we have the prototype of the logic of identity in contradiction that we discussed above. The I is I because at the same time it is not-I. It is, we might say, an "I-*in*-not-I." The important thing is not the mode of expression, but the fact that it signals a warning that whenever one speaks of the knowing subject one is abstracting, from one point of view, part of a wider event that, from another point of view, requires the negation of that abstracted I.

Since the sense of the I is derived from the state of self-awareness and not its prime mover, it is possible to speak of awareness as extending outside of the individual I to include the self-awareness of the world itself, as we noted above in speaking of the relationship between subjective awareness and the self-determination of absolute nothingness. Like Hegel, Nishida breaks from Kant by seeing the "thing in itself" not as the hidden mystery of reality that the prestructured subject can only approach asymptotically but never reach, but rather as a fact of reality part of whose dynamic consists in structuring the subject. In any case, given the secondary nature of the I, it is more accurate to speak of the I not as a preexisting entity but as a locus of activity.

On a model of concentric circles, Nishida takes a series of steps that lead from the imperial I, standing in judgment over the phenomenal world of form and matter, to an I humbled by reflection on its own workings and the limitations of language, to an I disillusioned with its own subjectivity by awakening to itself as the object of the things it knows, to a true I aware of itself as an instance of the self-awareness of reality: to an absolute nothingness manifest in the immediate experience of the world as it is. The world is affirmed radically only when it is located against this final background. At this point, self-awareness is no longer defined vis-à-vis being but vis-à-vis nothingness.

In Nishida's words, this process ends with one being "immersed in the bottom of consciousness itself." It is a conversion of the ordinary ego into a nothing to become what Nishida calls, taking over a Kantian term to his own purposes, "consciousness in general." Nishida thus depicts the locus of nothingness not only as a background but as a background against which everything in the foreground reappears in its clearest relief. His own formulation is recondite in the extreme:

> What is general transdescends downwards to the bottom of the general, what is immanent transdescends to the bottom of what is immanent, and the locus towards the bottom of locus.

Here again we see Nishida making consciousness the prototype for ontology in general. The locus of the subjects and objects is logical predication, the locus of logical predication is consciousness, and the locus of consciousness is the true self in full awareness, at which point the world of being reappears against the background of its own final locus, nothingness. He refers to this as a progression "from a working to a seeing" (which he also took as the title of the volume in which he first worked out his logic of locus in detail). It is a process that questions the reflective work of trying to know reality by rearranging the objects of the world in propositional judgments, rejects the apparent absoluteness of the working ego as relative, and finally brings one to insight into that which underlies the world and our work in it. This insight brightens up the ordinary locus of the ego so that one can see through it and look into the abyss of the true absolute of nothingness, dark and impenetrable to the light of the ego.

Earlier Nishida had tried to define the culmination of being nothingness by means of the idea of active intuition. Now he recognizes that all being is a "being located," and that this location is only finite. It is itself a locus within a locus that is really not a locus at all but an infinite horizon: absolute nothingness. It must be called *absolute* not only because it is not "located" like all things in the world of being and consciousness, but also because all knowledge achieved at any other locus is relative to the awareness that that knowledge itself finds its native ground in nothingness.

Nishida found the image of God as the circle whose center is everywhere and whose center nowhere—an originally gnostic-alchemical idea that he discovered in Cusanus—suited to express the final locus of absolute nothingness in which his logic ends. Each concrete reality of consciousness is circumscribed as a world that turns out to be no more than a microcosm of a wider world, and so on until it reaches the macrocosm of self-awareness, which is then seen to be a point opening infinitely in all directions on the locus of all loci, or absolute nothingness. Everything thus straddles two contradictory locations: it *is* in the world of being and it *is* in the world of nothingness. The straddling is its self-identity, a union of opposites.

21 SUBJECT, PREDICATE, AND UNIVERSAL.

The clue to reading Nishida's texts on the logic of locus lies in seeing how he takes the dialectic of active intuition between the idea of the subject as mental reflection and the object as the world that is intuited, and rethinks it in terms of the relationships among the grammatical subject and predicate in the judgments that come from the collaboration of the active self and the intuited world.

Perhaps the best place to begin is with his idea of the universal. Basically, it can be said that Nishida uses the idea of the universal in three senses. First is its ordinary logical sense of an attribute or relationship that is shared by individuals, allowing them to be grouped as a class. This is no more than a rational taxonomy we need to talk sense. Second, he uses it to refer to a potentiality that is actualized in individuals. Here the insinuation is more metaphysical, namely that the concrete things we find in the world are limited in what they can become, and by identifying these limitations we know something of how the world is constructed. In neither case does Nishida claim that the universal is "actual" or "existing" until it is embodied in some individual in the temporal world. At this level it is only in a metaphorical sense that we can speak of the universal determining the individual by providing it with a particular quality or attribute, and the individual determining the universal by providing it with actuality in the world.

But there is a third sense of the universal, derived from these two, that Nishida found more stimulating: the idea of the universal as determining itself. Here the universal is seen as something real and functioning to give the individual items of the world shape. Simply put, if every real thing is concrete and determined it is because it is the expression of a greater reality taking shape, and this greater reality is the universal. The identity of an individual, its self-determination, is at the same time the manifestation of the self-identity of the universal determining itself through the individual.

The question then becomes how to relate these two self-determinations and the fact that they are not continually conflicting with one another. The terminology of self-determination had been present in Nishida's writings from early on. It was only in the formulation of his logic of locus that he was able to clarify this basic conundrum at its core.

Combining the idea of an active, self-determining universal at work behind historical time, with the more properly logical senses mentioned earlier, and given the general outlines of the logic of locus, another idea suggests itself. Just as there are classes within classes (the class of red tulips in the class of tulips in the class of flowers in the class of plants, and so forth), so there can be self-determining universals that are embraced by greater self-determining universals. In fact, we saw that Nishida refers to history, society, and the individual all as forms of self-determination. And if there is a class of all classes—namely things that are real—then there must be a universal of all universals—an ultimate reality that determines everything in the process of determining itself. The transition from one to the other was what he attempted to capture in his logic of locus, locating universals within universals, and finally locating everything in absolute nothingness.

This was Nishida's basic vision of how the reality "works" to be what it is and how it works to appear as it appears to the human consciousness that sees it. The logic of locus thus provides a bridge between the working to the seeing that is at the same time a bridge between the intuition of reality just as it is and the logical judgment that constitutes rational reflection on that intuition.

His language can seem hopelessly matted at times, but with the basic ideas in hand it is possible to comb out the snarls to get a sense of what he means. A typically difficult passage can serve as an example:

> Individuals can be thought of as the self-determination of a universal. But more than that, the individual itself can be seen as a universal that determines itself. For in concrete logic the individual is a universal, the subject is a predicate. Everything real has this kind of logical structure. In this sense, dialectical unity can be considered to possess in itself its own identity, to be a self-identity.

In Aristotelian logic, Nishida notes, the idea of an underlying substance that gives individuals their identity is expressed by saying that there is something in "the subject that cannot become a predicate." Of the tulip I can say that it is red or blue, that it is wilted or fresh, growing in a field or standing alone in a vase. These are all attributes of the tulip, but the tulip itself cannot become an attribute of anything else. This self-identity is therefore ambivalent towards the universal. It determines it and at the same time remains determined by it, always subservient to the wider classes of which it is an instance. Hence, even though the subject that cannot become a predicate is thought to be the solid substance of which the world is made, "in the traditional form of judgment, the predicate that cannot become a subject is thought to be more wide-reaching than the subject."

Nishida turns this on its head, suggesting that we need a logic that makes room for a subject to become a predicate, and for the universal predicate to become the final subject. Because if we do not, then the whole idea of individuals determining themselves and in the process being the self-determination of something else falls on its face. He goes on:

> For something to possess its own identity does not mean that it is just that one thing, that it is just a subject that cannot become a predicate. If it were, it would be no more than an asymptote or a center without a radius—in a word, there would be no single point at which to take hold of it. To be identical with itself, in addition to being a subject that cannot be a predicate it must be a predicate of itself, the individual must determine itself in the manner of predication. Or put the other way around, the predicate becomes the subject so that subject determines itself in predication.

Obviously subjects cannot become predicates in normal judgments, or grammar would collapse in the contradiction of not having anything to talk about, just attributes with nothing to attach them to. Nishida does not deny this. What he means to say, as we alluded to earlier, is that the locus of normal judgments, where universals are applied to fixed things in order to classify them, does not put us in touch with what is *really* going on in reality. We need to transcend that logic to a standpoint where that whole logic itself can be predicated of another activity closer to reality. This place is the locus of consciousness, which is not a simple mirror of reality but a way of grasping reality and working on it. To see an individual item of the world as located in consciousness in this sense is to see its identity not as an independent substance but as dependent on a consciousness that predicates of things their identity. The "subject" that we call the conscious individual therefore makes predicates of those "subjects" we call individuals. In Nishida's terms, the conscious subject is the universal of those logical subjects, and this is *its* identity.

What is more, insofar as consciousness can catch itself in the act of working rationally, its self-identity is more fully its own doing than the self-identity of the tulip. Not only can it attribute self-identity to the things it intuits outside of itself (that is, making them subjects of predication), but it can make those judgments a subject of predication. This is the essence of self-consciousness in which the subject ("this tulip") of which something is predicated ("it is red") can itself be seen as a predicate of consciousness. By seeing itself at work, self-consciousness identifies itself—it is an individual that determines itself and *knows* that it is doing so. This is not just the self-consciousness of a self reflecting on itself, but a self that is *aware* of itself as the medium within which individuals are given their identity. It is not just a self-enclosed unity but a locus in which the world achieves a kind of unity. It is, in his terms, a "dialectical universal," in the sense that it provides the environment or "locus" for the universals of judgment and concrete individuals to interact in such a way that they become real. It is the *noesis* of the *noema*.

But we have not yet finished, or rather if we were to finish here the universal would be a kind of subjective consciousness, landing us in an idealism, if not a solipsism, in which the absolute principle of all reality would be the thinking subject. Nishida takes a further step to relativize this universal to a still higher universal. One again, we return to his text and proceed patiently:

> This is not true self-identity, since it retains everywhere the sense of being one more "thing." True self-identity cannot be thought of either as a simple universal (subject) or a simple individuality (predicate). It must be something that can be thought to be a straight line and a circle at the same time—that is, an absolute nothingness.

If consciousness is able to give things their identity, then it can be said to be the universal locus of those things. At the same time, since it exists only where embodied in individuals of whom it is attributed, it cannot be the universal locus of its own identity. *Self*-consciousness is therefore inherently contradictory and asymptotic, like a mirror reflecting a mirror, or a circular straight line. The only locus on which this final and absolute contradiction of consciousness can be overcome to yield an identity is that of a self-consciousness without a self, a seeing without a seer, an awareness that is both spontaneous and self-determining of everything that is—in other words, a location of the self in absolute nothingness. In one sense this nothingness can be seen as a negation of being, in the same way that any class that envelops another class is at the same time a negation of the ultimacy of what it envelops. But absolute nothingness is not only a negation of the ultimacy of the context of consciousness. It is itself the last of all the contexts, the class of all classes, the "universal of all universals" as Nishida says. Thus, it is both an absolute and a nothingness—a predicate that can never become a subject.

The introduction of the grammatical subject and predicate into the works increases geometrically the number of ways in which the idea of the self-determination of the universal can be paraphrased. One can almost open Nishida at random in essays written after his introduction of the logic of locus and within a few pages come a new jumble of the ingredients. At the same time, in a rather tortured fashion, it helps to relate his idea of self-awareness as a seeing without a seer to the idea of this seeing as in fact an absolute nothingness expressing itself in the historical world of being, giving things their individual identities and rational thought its rightful place in the scheme of things.

22 **SELF AND OTHER.** In the theory of active intuition, it will be recalled, the body was presented as the meeting point of self and world, while the problem of other selves was left out. Clearly the notion of body, or active intuition for that matter, was not sufficient to capture this important ingredient of the relation between self and world: the fact that there are other centers of awareness, in interaction with which there is something to know about one's own self. The logic of locus helped to raise the issue and to fit it into Nishida's overall philosophy.

Self-awareness, in the sense of a consciousness of the true identity of the individual person, cannot be set up in simple opposition to other persons, since this would reintroduce the subject-object dichotomy through the back door. There must be a sense of self-identity in which self and other are no longer two. The ideas of an identity-in-opposition and an ultimate locus of absolute nothingness allowed Nishida to find this sense.

"What is this self of ours? What is the real world in which that self is born, in which it works, and in which it dies?" Nishida's question goes deeper than that of the relationship between self and world that he had tackled with his notion of active intuition. Now it turns to the identity, or locus, of the items of the relationship themselves. The common ground of self and world will no longer be simply reality mediated by body but reality as the locus of absolute nothingness.

This question is taken up in a 1932 book called *I and You,* which is best read as a continuation of an essay completed four months earlier under the title "Love of Self, Love of the Other, and the Dialectic." From the start it is clear that Nishida's approach will be highly abstract, the reason being that his concern was not a reflection on interpersonal encounter and its philosophical implications but simply a way to find a place for it in his logic of locus. It leaves no other tracks in the way of a rethinking or the addition of a neologism, but is absorbed back into the general category of religious love that was the source of the question. Indeed, the idea of love as a manifestation of absolute nothingness that can only take place between persons drops so unexpectedly into Nishida's writings and is then absorbed back into familiar categories so soon and almost without trace in later writings, that it is hard to think of the I-you relationship as a philosophical question Nishida struggled much with. New editions of the work in Japan and foreign translations have drawn fresh attention to the work, which nevertheless remains more an application of his thinking than an advance of it.

For Nishida only a radically self-negated I can encounter the world as it is. But if the I and the world belong to the universal of "being" as its subjective (self-conscious) and objective (phenomenal) poles, respectively, then every encounter with the phenomena of the world—including the encounter with other subjects—ends up reinforcing the I. Therefore only a universal of nothingness in which the subject-object dichotomy has been restored to unity can allow for a truly self-aware encounter with the world. The consequences of this shift from being to nothingness for the encounter between self and other are mainly three.

First, since the final, all-encompassing locus of reality for Nishida is nothingness, any quality of being that adheres to events, processes, or individuals, or to the categories of thought used to express these, and that is further presumed to point to something "ultimate," must be relocated against a wider horizon in which the item in question shows itself to be secondary or derivative. Further, since the ultimate structure of nothingness as it presents itself to consciousness is that of a "self-identity of absolute contraries," any relationship of individuals based on a "being with" or "encounter" that mitigates the absolute otherness of one to the other is based on a mental fiction of "unity in being."

To see reality as ultimately an absolute nothingness means that no relationship is exempt from the dialectic of coming to be and passing away. All continuity is relative to a radical discontinuity. When Nishida says that "Each individual is an individual only in opposition to another individual," he is not making a metaphysical claim about all existence as co-existence, and certainly is not opting for any sort of personalism that sees the interpersonal encounter as the prototype of all reality. For Nishida, the option for radical personalism in any form is excluded precisely because the fulfillment of the I is located in the transformation to non-I. He means that the very idea of an individual as *being* requires that it *not be* another individual being and yet that it define itself in terms of the other that it is not. If there is anything like a general atmosphere that surrounds and pervades this interplay of being and not being, of affirmation and negation, of birth and death, it is best characterized as something other than just the sum of all the moving parts or a lowest common denominator—namely as nothingness rather than as being.

Secondly, when Nishida speaks of a locus of absolute nothingness, he is referring to something very different from a common ground on which human individuals can meet and mutually enhance the quality of their lives. Not that he fails to recognize the importance of such a common ground, as we shall see later. His concern is rather to place the coming to awareness, the crowning achievement of the world of becoming, in the picture. He does so by challenging the primacy given to the idea of the disciplined intellect reasoning about the world. As we have seen, for Nishida, the field of subjects dealing with objects, whatever the level of achievement, is a small and artificial circle drawn within a wider field of immediate experience in which there is no distinction between subjects and objects.

Third, the history of the relationship is purged of the normal sense of the "development" of a relationship and abstracted to an awareness of the Eternal Now breaking into history. Using a distinction described above, Nishida introduces history into the encounter of self and other in terms of a transition from *noemic* consciousness (focused on objects or the process of objects advancing along a temporal continuum from the past to the future), to a *noetic* consciousness (focused on consciousness as an activity of reality determining itself apart from that continuum). The idea of reversing the determination of time by introducing an "eternal now" that acts on the present from the future, a deliberate confrontation with the philosophies of

Bergson and Hegel, figures predominantly in the text from the opening paragraphs of *I and You*, as a carryover from his previous essay:

> To think of reality determining itself does not mean thinking in terms of a continuity in which one point progresses to another or gives rise to another, but of a discontinuous continuity in which each moment passes away, a life through death. To think in these terms does not mean conceiving of nothingness as something in the background that has the farthest reaches of being as its object and determines it, but as something that transcends and envelops this kind of determination altogether—as a nothingness that determines itself by enveloping being, the result of which is that being becomes visible.

The strategy is not unexpected, given the overall direction of Nishida's thinking. Sooner or later he is bound to break through any event in the historical world to the final, circumferenceless circle, the locus of absolute nothingness in which all contact of consciousness with reality, all our attempts to express its ultimate structure, every encounter with reality, whether between one self and another self or between a self and inanimate objects, is negated and then restored, one by one, in a conscious affirmation of the phenomenal world just as it is.

In the exercise of the logic of locus, then, there can be nothing absolute in the interpersonal relationship itself—no matter who the partners happen to be—because self and other always relate to each other as absolute contradictories. By this he means "absolutely independent and absolutely bound" to each other. Only in this way can the self-negation of the I be accomplished radically and at the same time open to a reality beyond the personalism of one's self and other selves. The absolute has to be located elsewhere. Nor can the *contrariness* between self and other ever be reduced to a mere *paradox* or logical *contradiction* attributed to the limitations of conscious knowing or the transcendence of one of the partners. For Nishida the structure of reality cannot be described on the model of a dialogue between persons, any more than nothingness can be reduced to the affirmation or negation of a mere quality shared in common by beings. The eternal now that breaks through time in the encounter of an I and a you never becomes for Nishida an Eternal Thou.

From the opening pages of *I and You*, it is clear that the defining activity of personhood is self-reflection, a dialogue between I and I, and that this is the locus for the encounter of I and you. The fruit of that dialogue is meaning, which is not something inherent in things merely because of their being, but something that simply needs to be recognized by a subject as an objective fact. Meaning must be an activity of reality itself, and therefore the unity of consciousness from one day to the next that allows for the constellation of meaning in the flow of actual events must ultimately be the particularization of a universal in which there is no distinction between that which expresses and that which is expressed—namely, the universal of nothingness:

> Each element that goes into this constellation of meaning is an expression of the individual consciousness. The true significance of conscious unity lies in the fact that the expresser and the expressed are one and the same. The I is in dialogue with the I within the mind.... The I of yesterday and the I of today exist in the world of expression, just as I and you do.... All individuals must somehow be conceived of as determinations of a universal... and by the same token, the individual must determine the universal.... The meaning of the individual and the universal must consist of a dialectical determination between the two—not a universal of being determining the individual, but a universal of nothingness in which determination takes place without anything doing the determining.

In the dense prose from which I have extracted the above comment lies the basic structure of Nishida's argument. The initial impression that the I-you relationship looks to be no more than a secondary, derivative function of self-reflection on the field of absolute nothingness, is confirmed again and again. The encounter of an I with a you is simply one instance of the I en route to its own negation in self-awareness of nothingness:

> What we think of as transcending the self always confronts us in one of three modes: (1) as a thing, (2) as a you, or (3) as a transcendent I.... The personal self awareness that sees an absolute other within the self includes these three confrontations.

To speak of self seeing itself in itself means that the self sees an absolute other, but this other is not a you but only the self itself recognized through the you. What unites seer and seen, what determines without anything doing the determining is the universal of nothingness in which all personality, and therefore also all personal encounter, has been abolished.

23 LOVE AND RESPONSIBILITY.

Given the logical pattern at work in Nishida's idea of the I-you relationship, it is hardly surprising that until the concluding pages of *I and You* when Nishida turns his attention to love, no particular attention is drawn to the affective element in the

I-you relationship. Even in "Love of Self, Love of the Other, and the Dialectic," the I-you (or more often, the I-other) refers principally to the basic unit of human society; not even in the perfection of love does it rise to the stature of religious or personal sentiment. In the end, as we saw above, the I-you is no more than a stage in self-awareness, the stage in which one awakens to the fact of social existence:

> What defines I as I defines you as you. Both are born in the same environment and both are extensions of the same universal there.... The individual is born in society; social consciousness in some sense precedes individual consciousness.

The intimation that society is somehow a permanent foundation for relationships and obligations crucial to the awakening of the self is, however, set aside. Instead, the I that breaks free of the subject-object relationship to the world must also break free of the I-you relationship in the external social order in order to reclaim it in the inner recesses of self-awareness. And this awareness of the other entails a depersonalized I encountering a deobjectified other, a seeing without seer or seen. Both the I and the other are enhanced reciprocally in the encounter, but the question of any resultant enhancement of the social foundation in which that encounter takes place is overshadowed by the fact that the primary enhancement for the I is its conversion to a non-I. And the non-I affirms everything it touches by negating its own attachment to being, both the natural and the human worlds.

Even apart from the question of the social dimension, why it should be that the idea of "knowing by becoming" is not applied here is something of a mystery. It would have introduced the possibility of extending the I-you relationship to the inanimate world, and hence to a discovery of true self through nature. The closest Nishida comes to this is to affirm the absolute otherness as something discovered within the self:

> As a direct contact between one person and another, the I knowing a you or the you knowing an I, must take the form of direct intuition. This is not, as we are accustomed to think in the classical form of intuition, artistic intuition, a matter of directly uniting with an object, but of recognizing oneself as harboring in the recesses of interiority an absolute other and turning to that other to see it as absolute other, not to unite with it.

Mention of enhancing the other and of social consciousness leads to love and the ethical responsibility of the self. But Nishida's clearest statements about love appear in contrast with the failure of love: Love is not a satisfaction of personal desire. It does not turn the other into an object. Love discovers the self by negating the self. It does not value an other in terms of what lies outside the other. It is not rational but spontaneous. It is not longing but sacrifice. One cannot love oneself without loving others. His most direct descriptions are set in a language of dialectics that paraphrases classical expressions about love. Note his following description of Christian agape:

> By seeing the absolute other in the recesses of my own inwardness—that is, by seeing there a you—I am I. To think in these terms, or what I call "the self-awareness of absolute nothingness," entails love. This is what I understand Christian agape to be.... It is not human love but divine love; it is not the ascent of the person to God but the descent of God to the person.... As Augustine says, I am I because God loves me, I am truly I because of God's love.... We become persons by loving our neighbor as ourselves in imitation of the divine agape.

It is not clear whether the Christian idea of the selfless love of God for humanity is being used to paraphrase the idea of the self-awareness of absolute nothingness or the other way around, nor what one idea has to contribute to the other. In any case, Nishida makes the claim that this loving self-awareness of absolute nothingness discloses an "infinite responsibility" of a historically situated I towards a historical you. To take this claim at face value—that is, to accept it as more than a link in a logical argument—is to raise an important question, since the evidence in his own writings seems to point in the opposite direction, away from responsibility to the concrete demands of history.

There is no question that Nishida sees love as a function of the sense of responsibility generated in the I-you encounter, in that "true self-awareness must be social." And this means that the distinction between I and you must be preserved:

> There is no responsibility as long as the you that is seen at the bottom of the self is thought of as the self. Only when I am I in virtue of the you I harbor at my depths do I recover an infinite responsibility at the bottom of my existence itself. This you cannot be a universal, abstract you or the recognition of a particular object as a simple historical fact.... The genuine "ought" is only conceivable in recognizing the other as a historical you within the historically conditioned situation of the I.

The self of Nishida's self-awareness thus relates to the world and to the you as a kind of no-self, which is said to give itself more fully to the other because it is grounded in a nothingness rather than in being. But no other criteria are given for judging this self-giving. It remains locked up within the self's ascent to self-awareness. For all his attempts to insist that he is talking in concrete terms, the concreteness is located not in a call to reform one's values or to exercise them in action, but in an increase of self-awareness.

As far as I am able to judge from Nishida's work, the consequences of his position come down to this: the non-I that emerges from the self-awareness of absolute nothingness looks for all the world to be a highly cultivated form of ataraxia, a self-transcendence of which the highest good consists of its inability to be moved by either good or evil. This was in fact the position that we shall see Tanabe takes towards Nishida. If there is a counterposition to be found, it will have to be sought in Nishida's political philosophy, as the concrete ethical dimension is missing from his treatment of the interpersonal.

24 JAPANESE CULTURE, WORLD CULTURE. Allusions to Japanese culture and the culture of the east were common in Nishida's writings from the first, and were further nuanced through his comparison of artistic and poetic forms east and west, some of which we mentioned above. But it is not until 1934 that he broaches the idea that the philosophical ideas he has worked out may be rooted in culture as such and are not simply transcendental insights seeking confirmation in cultural expression.

The context of his remarks is an attempt to lay out a cultural typology that will trace differences in classical culture east and west to the differences in their metaphysics. He summarizes his starting point handily:

> From a metaphysical standpoint, then, how do we distinguish the forms of culture east and west from one another? I believe we can distinguish the west as having taken being as the ground of reality and the east as having taken nothing as its ground. Or, we might say, the one looked to form, the other to the formless.

In terms of the distinction between philosophies of being and of nothingness, Nishida is quick to qualify this generalization on a number of counts, recognizing elements of nothingness in negative theology and even in modern science. In terms of the distinction between east and west, he also recognizes the chiaroscuro of cultures like those of ancient India and modern-day Russia.

The idea of eastern culture as grounded in the "formless" begins from a generalized comparison of China and Japan on the one hand, and Greece and Rome on the other. This leads to his quick sketch of Japanese culture as one that prefers immanence to transcendence, the here-and-now to the eternal, emotion to intellection, family bonds to general law and order, the formlessness of time to the solid geometry of space. And all of this precisely because it is a culture based on absolute nothingness, whose radical negation of any other reality than the reality we are in is at the same time the most radical affirmation of that reality just as it is, in all its ephemeral immediacy.

In suggesting a direct relation between philosophical ideas of reality and underlying culture-specific modes of thought, Nishida would seem to risk relativizing his understanding of the absolute. If reality as nothingness and reality as being were functions of cultural difference, then even his idea that culture can be seen as one expression of the greater story of consciousness actively intuiting the world (or what he can now call the "self-determination of the historical world located in absolute nothingness") would have to find some ground beyond culture to justify itself as a more accurate rendering of how reality works than an idea of history based on being as the absolute.

Nishida did not in fact ask this question of himself, though he certainly would have known it from his reading of the Freiburg neo-Kantians. The answer can, I think, be inferred from the conclusion to which his comparison leads him. What the plurality of cultures share in common is that they are all particular embodiments of "a self-awareness of the world of historical reality." That particularity, he insists, must be preserved through a dialectic in which each one defines itself in terms of the larger world, and the larger world defines itself in terms of each one. "A true world culture takes shape," he argues, "by each developing itself through the mediation of the same world," not by fusing them into one or by each developing along the lines of its own particularity.

These words can be read as an *apologia* for his own adventure of ideas, for without some such idea of the world, his philosophy could never have taken shape. Those who read Nishida as implying the superiority of Japanese culture from the fact that he used his own metaphysic of nothingness as a model to understand what culture is and how a plurality of cultures interact to form a single world, assume what Nishida could never have assumed: that his philosophy is primarily part of the intellectual and spiritual patrimony of Japan.

Already in a short article written in 1917 he noted with displeasure those resigned to the fact that "just as we cannot truly understand western culture, so there are things in the morality and art of our people that those from other countries cannot possibly understand." To have accepted such a premise from the start would have undercut everything he was trying to do. What cannot be understood—and there *are* such things, he realized—

should be discovered to be such in the trying, not assumed on the basis of the prevalent prejudices. Nishida's was from start to finish a world philosophy precisely because he believed he could understand the west, and the west him. And this in turn emboldened him to criticize western philosophy for thinking it could continue to do without the east. In his phrase, if the uniqueness of a culture is not seen as part of a larger unity of the human community, if, in the face of pressures from dominant cultures, it simply sets itself up as something unique, it becomes merely idiosyncratic. His own concern with philosophy, he says, should form part of a wider cultural effort:

> I want us rather to go on developing a characteristic culture of our own, one that becomes more and more Japanese; and along with this, I want us to become an indispensable ingredient in world culture.... I want to see the greatness and depths of the spirit behind the culture of Japan.... In Nietzsche's words, "I love those who want to create out of themselves what goes beyond themselves, and in this way get to the bottom of things."

Nishida's philosophy of nothingness has no meaning simply from within the context of Japan. His treatment of culture needs to be read not only as a confirmation of that philosophy but also as a confirmation of the motivations that led him to it.

Given Nishida's philosophical temperament and standpoint as we have outlined it above, it is not surprising to find him weaving his comments on concrete historical cultures together with his customary, highly abstract philosophical formulas, and in the process reinforcing those formulas. What would be surprising, and entirely out of character, would be for him to do the opposite and try to rethink his philosophical ideas in terms of a particular historical culture and in the process reinforce that cultural form. Yet this is precisely what he was asked to do. Unfortunately, he accepted the request, and the results have haunted Nishida's image ever since.

In 1935, Nishida was approached by the Ministry of Education to join Watsuji, Tanabe, and others on a special committee to reform education and academia. He knew that pressures against liberal thought had been building up for several years through a number of attempts to silence criticism, and had met with so little resistance that they grew stronger and stronger and were beginning to surface boldly within the government itself. In private he had not hesitated to call this whole trend "fascist," but he was convinced that it would burn itself out, and that meantime it was best not to put his head on the block by inviting a clash. Still, against his better judgment he attended the first meeting; he found its leaders so narrowminded and dogmatic in aims that he gave up on it. Two months later the government fell to a military coup.

Nishida's views, like those of most of the ordinary people of Japan, were that this was a disastrous turn of events, and that the fault lay with those in power for having courted the military so naively. His plan of spending a quite retirement writing, and the hopes that reason would win out, were both thrown to the winds. Still, hoping against hope, he limited his comments to his private letters to those he trusted. Two years later, in August of 1937, the military launched an invasion against China.

Meantime, the grip on academia and the educational system grew tighter and freedom of thought and expression was being erased in the name of national unity. At the same time the ministry was trying to secure as much support for its policies as it could by luring more and more intellectuals into its special committees for "reform." Nishida accepted the offer to address one of these groups on the subject of "Scholarship."

He knew full well that he was being asked to use his position and his distinctive ideas to justify the status quo. But he thought he could engage those who were trying to use him and perhaps win the attention of those among them who genuinely wanted to restore some measure of sanity to the madness in evidence on all sides. Inexperienced in matters of state, and with no clear model to follow, he believed it his duty to raise a voice of common reason, and he believed that if he did it prudently he could help free people from thinking in the clichés of the official propaganda. On nearly every count his belief was mistaken. Still, with the critical conscience of the philosopher as his guide, he took up the prevailing idiom and engaged in what Ueda Shizuteru has called "a tug-of-war over words." He had some inkling of what he was getting into, as a letter to one of his former students shows:

> When we say "world," they hear "cosmopolitan" and when we say "universally" they think we are talking about the abstract generalities of science. They just take words out of context and use them as ammunition for their own attacks.

From the start, it was a battle he could not, and did not, win. For one thing, it was not about choosing one's words carefully and then making sure they were heard by the right ears at all. When he had taken the initiative to write letters to leading politicians calling for restraint, he had no impact at all. For another, he thought he could go it alone, without any political base, largely because those that existed seemed to him to lack intellectual coherence. When he was invited to share his thoughts as part of a larger program not within his control, his instincts should have told him to stay away.

If we look at that talk, we find that he begins where his previous essay on the subject of culture had ended, namely at an idealistic plea for Japanese tradition to find its identity in the context of making a contribution to world culture. He probably should have stopped there. What he *intended* to emphasize by repeating those arguments—the appeal for solid scholarship and critical thinking, and for a mutual fecundation of philosophy and politics—was not nearly as important as the emphasis he *in fact* communicated: support for the cultivation of "the Japanese spirit" as containing "truths that are equal to if not superior to anything found in the west."

Nishida's carefully chosen words were no match for the symbolic reality of the context in which he spoke them. He spoke at a microphone in Tokyo's Hibiya Park and shared the stage with the Minister of Education, the first to speak. Of course, there were those in the government and military who read him attentively and saw him as a threat, but his was the kind of critical voice that the *Realpolitik* ultimately had no trouble absorbing into its own agenda. Even though he complained later in a letter that he would never again take part in such "street theater," the deeper symbolism of the event seems to have eluded him.

25 THE TURN TO POLITICAL PHILOSOPHY.

Nishida's passing reference to the need for a relationship between politics and philosophy seems to have created the expectation, both in his own mind and in the minds of the keepers of the official ideology, that he would add this dimension, so far lacking, to his own thought. In the past, he had gone right from the *idea* of the concrete world of history into religion and the arms of the all-encompassing, passing over concerns with moral principles or the social structure. For the same reason he did not develop his thought in either of these areas, he should not have stepped into the realm of political philosophy without them. Whatever his motives, they are not clear from the texts or from the personal letters and diaries he left behind. I leave it to others, who have a better understanding of the psychology of writing under circumstances like those in Japan at the time, to divine just what those motives might have been. I mean only to conclude that his ventures into ideas on nation, constitution, imperial monarchy, and polity, far from raising high the sails on the adventure of ideas that had driven his thought until then, dragged like a weighty anchor.

At this point, we should back up for a moment and put events in a somewhat larger perspective, to understand where Nishida's attempts at a political philosophy came from.

From the time Nishida began his professional career as a teacher to the end of his life, Japan seemed to be either at war or preparing for war. The Meiji ideal of bringing Japan shoulder to shoulder with the rest of the world by "enriching the country and strengthening the military" had succeeded by the 1890s to the point where she was ready to expand her presence among her Asian neighbors. The wars with China of 1894 to 1895 and with Russia in 1904 and 1905 were aggressions with just this aim, and were largely successful, with Korea, Manchuria, China, and the area around the Yellow Sea the site of Japanese victories. Payment of the costs for holding on to its winnings, and the conduit of raw materials they supplied to the islands of Japan, had to be secured structurally, which meant that the military presence in the government had to remain strong. In addition, patriotic societies, some of them secret, worked in the background to insure that Japan would remain *primus inter pares* among its neighbors, that the victors of conflicts in Europe would ratify its actions, and that the ordinary people would believe that this was all being done as part of their imperial right and duty. The Manchurian Incident of 1931 tested the power of the army to work conspiracies contravening official diplomatic policies of the central government, and even to ignore the reprimands of the League of Nations, which wanted to halt what it saw as a dangerous precedent.

Still the fighting went on, especially in northern China, where it broke out into full-scale campaigns in 1937 at Marco Polo Bridge outside Beijing, without the central government making any formal declaration of war. These campaigns continued until 1945. While the army was carrying out these escapades abroad, the justification at home was centered on a euphemistic ideal that emerged in the 1930s of a "new order in eastern Asia," one of "co-existence and co-prosperity" that would at last put an end to the imperialistic order that the west had devised in the nineteenth century. This ideal was popularized, moreover, as a preservation of the "ancient order" of Japan. The divinity of the emperor, the uniqueness of the national polity, the mission of the race and to share its cultural patrimony with foreign lands—all these ingredients were concocted into a thin gruel of a worldview that was fed into the education system and into the intellectual world for recognition and enrichment, at the same time as its was monitored by special forces.

Resistance was weak among the intellectuals, who generally preferred the safety of scholarly specialization. The war was at a distance, and despite the casualties that individual families would suffer, there was little base of popular support for questioning its rightness. The ethic taught in the school, and capsulated in the 1937 publication of the *Principles of the National Polity,* had contributed greatly to the scarcity of critical voices. Individuals were made to believe that they were "essentially not beings isolated from the state, but each has his allotted share as forming part of the state," and have their identity in a harmonious "body of people, under the emperor, of one blood and one mind." Anything that countermanded this was an affront to the traditional spirit of Japan.

The pact with Germany against international communism in 1936 gave Japan leverage against the increasing threat of the Russians, and eventually culminated in a pact of nonagression. With Nazi victory in Europe seeming all but certain in 1940, a tripartite pact with Germany and Italy was signed. At the same time, under the banner of the creation of a Greater East Asia Co-Prosperity Sphere, but at the risk of engaging western powers that still had colonies in southeast Asia, Japan turned south to get the raw materials it needed to keep its wartime economy going. When diplomatic efforts failed, and with shortages critical, Japan launched out on the Pacific War that was to be its last.

At home, the rhetoric focused on saving Asia from the colonial powers and creating a new world order in which all could prosper and in which the ethical values of Japan would be poured into the foundations of a new "spiritual essence" for which the "materialism of the west" would be no match. In no time at all, the impact was felt on the ordinary Japanese: first the economic hardships of sustaining the campaigns abroad, and then the experience of seeing Japan itself become a battlefield. The whole project, doomed from the start, eventually collapsed with Japan's defeat in August 1945.

This, in the boldest of strokes, was the Japan in which Nishida carried out his adventure of bringing a Japanese contribution to world philosophy. Telescoping a half century of events into a few paragraphs makes it seem almost unthinkable that one could philosophize through it all and not create a political philosophy. Yet it was not until the eleventh hour that Nishida took the step of trying to make up for the absence of ideas that, during the daytime of his career, were no more than a nuisance.

In 1938, already ten years retired from active teaching, he agreed to present a series of three talks on "The Question of Japanese Culture" at Kyoto University. The event was intended to symbolize a reaction against the attempts of the government and military ideologues to arm the educational system of the country against the western world and its values by propagating its simple-minded evangel of Japanese traditionalism. The lectures were arranged by a philosophy professor, Amano Teiyū, who earlier that year had been attacked, under a new law regulating the public views of government employees, for criticizing the educational system as reducing training in rational thinking to no more than fixed military drills. The book in which these ideas were expressed was banned from reprint, in exchange for which he kept his post. The lectures were a kind of retort, and Nishida was enthusiastic about taking part, against the advice of those who cautioned prudence. The lectures were written up into a little book that sold 40,000 on its publication. Clearly, Nishida's was a voice of some authority for a great many people.

The lectures carry on some of the themes from his earlier sorties into typologies of thought east and west. The conclusion of his final lecture is the same, an "original culture" joining people east and west:

> Does not a comparison enable a mutual complementarity that clarifies the depth and breadth of human culture itself? ... It is not a question of the east developing to the point that it can absorb the west, or vice-versa. East and west do not stand completely apart one from the other, but are like two branches on the same tree.

These ideas, as vague as they are, were more suited to his philosophical thinking up to that point than they were to the foundations of a political philosophy applicable to the politics of the day. Yet in rewriting the piece, he concludes by taking a step in just that direction. All in all, it is no more than a short trip. The most noticeable thing is that in the space of a few short pages he broadens his base of highly-charged vocabulary beyond "Japanese spirit" to include "national polity," "ethnic conflicts," "imperialism," "imperial succession," and "ethics." As an argument, aside from the occasional phrase from his mainline philosophy that rubs off its effect on the text, it is no more than an outline. The style is straightforward and, though the ideas fly by quickly one after the other, the sentences are not complicated by his usual grammatical acrobatics.

The world, he says, has already become a single environment, and the whole of humanity is caught up in the crisis of how to handle the fact. The ethnic struggles going on, far from being meaningless, are the sign of the birth of a new culture. A simple balance of power is not enough to insure peace; a "new historical life" has to be born. The very things that cause nations to struggle with one another, including the battle over natural resources and the struggle of the colonized for independence, can also lay the foundation for a restoration of peaceful relations in the one world. The process must include social reform, not only an improvement of relationships between one individual and another. Environment and subject complement each other by negating each other.

In terms of ethics, he sees a shift from the horizontal to the vertical. The horizontal ethic, culminating in Kant, the Enlightenment, and the French Revolution, was rational and opened to all; the vertical is centered on an imperialistic view of the human, exemplified in nineteenth-century Europe, that is at work in Europe today. Hegel saw absolute spirit as a common ground of "subjectivity" to keep nations from falling into imperialism. But this was only the western model. Nishida suggests that the model at the root of oriental culture, namely that of a self-creating world that relativizes subjectivity, can lead to a true union of the opposites of subject and environment. Within this process, ethnic groups—and the great individuals who arise to represent them—need to be seen as an opposing plurality making a one. A direct face-off between groups is self-destructive. Only the creation of a unity allows individuals within them to flourish. As a nation, the ethnic group becomes a kind of "moral subject." And since humans are essentially a social and historical creativity, the aim of moral praxis is not the mere execution of duties towards the "ought" of the nation, but a "service" towards its moral energy.

I have paraphrased his comments in such a way as to focus on phrases that echo ideas he had before, but at the same time to indicate the way in which he threw himself into the thick of the dominant vocabulary of the day. Once he had taken this step, the excitement of new applications for his ideas seems to have taken over. The fact that his ideas were *not* condemned but rather elicited invitations from moderate voices among the powers that be for him to continue on in this vein, emboldened him to do just that. But the further he stepped into the bog, the more his philosophical argumentation deteriorated into a mere application of his abstract logic to juggling ideas that deserved much greater care, even apart from the political situation of the day, than he gave them.

The closer Nishida gets to a political philosophy, the more his weaknesses show up. We see a glimpse of this in his cultural typology. As long as he is talking about the philosophical side of western culture, he is on sure footing. But when he begins to compare the psychology and everyday cultural modes of thought of what he knows from his own upbringing with one that he knows principally from having read philosophical texts, he is making the same methodological mistake the ideologues he intended to oppose were making, and indeed the same mistakes that western typologies generated from a similar ignorance of the east were making at the time.

A knowledge of cultural modes of thought is only one of the requisites of political philosophy. But he built his rudiments of a political philosophy by combining the actual situation of the world, and particularly Japan's position in the world, with a logic based on history as a self-determination of reality. The intervening variables—in short, most of what makes up the foundations of a political philosophy—were skipped over. It is not that this *could not* have been done with Nishida's thinking, and indeed some commentators have bent over backwards to patch ideas together from throughout his writings to take a stab at it. It is that it *should not* have been done under the pressure of an ideological debate whose parameters were not of his own choosing. Indeed, Nishida himself lamented that it was "a crude collection of things that struck me," and that he "hated cudgeling his brain on such stupid stuff" in order to avoid phrasing that would anger the enemies of free thought who had their eye on him.

26 RUDIMENTS OF A POLITICAL PHILOSOPHY.

That Nishida continued to develop these ideas in the direction of a political philosophy cannot be explained simply as a continued reaction against the deleterious effects of the war on freedom of thought. The justification for that repression lay in an ideology that put the unity of the Japanese people under the emperor first, and the development of individual conscience and thought second. But these were the very questions he skirted around cautiously, once again allowing his voice to lend support to the very thing he most detested. If it was indeed a tug of war, it was so slack that most of his readers would not have noticed it, and his opponents at the other end of the rope were not budged so much as an inch.

Regarding the morality of war and peace itself, Nishida never pronounced a philosophical opinion. It was part of life, a cruel part and filled with absurdities, but nonetheless a part. At the death of his younger brother in the Sino-Japanese War in 1904, Nishida concluded a memento in the newspaper with a tribute to his brother as a good soldier and a flush of pride that his death was not in vain. His words are not much different from those of any citizen convinced of the righteousness of their nation's war effort:

> If one thinks that as a result of this war the forces of our country have been expanded in eastern Asia, and that the bodies of the fallen have become the cornerstone of a new empire, one can hardly bear the feeling of excitement it brings.

Seven months later, when the news of the fall of Port Arthur reached Japan, he wrote in his diary, in classical Chinese imitating the Zen phrases cited in the entry of the day before: "A joy beyond control! The triumph of brave and loyal lads of the north. The whole city is ringing bells and beating drums to celebrate." Three days later, fed up with the celebrations that were interrupting his Zen meditation, he complained in his diary about how inconsiderate people are, "not giving a thought to how many lives were sacrificed and what a long haul still lies ahead."

Born in a country at war and lacking any reason to oppose it outright, he was more resigned to its reality, occasionally in his private correspondence blaming its excesses on those controlling the implements of war. To the last he wished that national identity were more based on a "higher spiritual plane rather than on military might," but he never made a philosophical problem of it. Even the mention made earlier of "ethnic struggles" amounts to no more than another instance of how opposites work dialectically on each other to bring about a new identity.

In 1936 Miki tried to answer the question of what Nishida understood the nation to be by noting that it is a question "he has not argued in any detail." Extrapolating from the logic of locus, Miki reckons that "Nishida seems to see the nation as a kind of particular society," subservient to a larger "scheme of the world" as the locus of the self-expression of an absolute, so that in it "individuals forever maintain their independence of society even though they are determined by it." As it turns out, this was not a bad guess, but Miki could not have foreseen, and certainly would not have approved, of the way in which Nishida worked it out.

In a 1941 essay on "The Question of the *Raison d'État*" Nishida relates individual, ethnic group, and national polity as a series of ever wider classes, the larger subsuming the opposition in the smaller into a kind of unity. In theory, this allows for a variety of races to co-exist in the same polity, but he does not dare apply this to Japan, a particularly tender issue for the racial purists. In fact, as we will see presently, he accepts the principle of ethnic unity as the foundation of the idea of the country as a single "family." In any case, at each level, the absolute opposition is relativized by a higher unity, which then sets itself up as an absolute, only to be further relativized by the next higher level. This idea of relative absolutes culminating in a final absolute is more or less of a kind with his general logic.

Now the highest political unit, the family of the nation, is itself a particular historical configuration that stands in opposition to other unities of the same sort, thus necessitating a still higher class to subsume them. This is what Nishida calls the one world in which the plurality of states, each one relatively absolute towards the oppositions that it subsumes, are unified. This is a world still in the making, which means that the opposition among nations is a clash of opposites. In such circumstances, the absoluteness of the Japanese state can only promote that higher unity if it is itself a true unity that protects the co-existence of opposites within its own unity. As we noted, Nishida jumps over the questions of ethnic groups to focus on the position of individuals within the absolute state.

The absolute that insures the identity of individuals in the Japanese state is none other than the emperor. Nishida accepted the structure of the country set up in the Meiji period, with the restoration of the emperor to a position of administrative authority over the country, as a given. Along with this, he accepted as a cultural given the symbolism of an unbroken line of imperial succession grounded in ancient Shinto myths. The imperial family protected Japan, he suggests, from revolutions from one absolutizing principle to another that would tear the country apart. Competing clans, "subjective principles," found in the emperor a common point of "revival" that was at the same time a rejuvenation, "a step ahead into a new world, as the Meiji Restoration exemplifies best of all."

Applying the terminology of his idea of the locus of the historical world as transcending time, he describes the imperial family as a stable point of reference in the midst of the vagaries of history, providing a principle of continuity that the mere passage of time or the progress of civilization cannot. By locating the present in this historical line of succession, he has no trouble accepting the current idea of the emperor and the people of Japan as one big family:

> The imperial household is the alpha and omega of the world. The quintessence of our polity as a nation is the imperial family. It is the center from which all living, breathing development proceeds, the self-determination of an absolute present, embracing the past and the future.... It is said to be like a family, and I agree with that. This is the beauty and strength of our polity. There is no other example of a single ethnic group, from the beginning of history up to the present, unfolding like a family in the way our nation has.... Nowhere else than in Japan has a view of national polity developed along the lines of a state-*in*-morality.

In 1941 Nishida was invited to give a New Year's lecture to the emperor. In it he recasts his general idea of the spiritual life of a people transcending time while the world around them is changing, through interaction with other cultures, from a local environment to a worldwide one. He refers to this process of change as a "nationalism" and defines it as meaning "not that each country should turn back in on itself, but that each should take its proper place in the world." He ends with a carefully worded paraphrase of his idea of the imperial family as the bearer of the founding spirit of Japan that insures a harmony between the totality and the individual.

Despite rejection of the idea of the *Japanese nation* extending its own center to absorb other nations, he does hold that the *Japanese spirit* has a special mission to lead the other countries of Asia, through political and economic initiatives, to take new shape in conjunction with one another. Rather than set itself up as one moral subject vying with others for the absolute control, it should become the locus for a new order that transcends this polarization of "subjects" one against the other. Thus, while rejecting the idea of imperialism (the Japanese word uses a term suggesting a western emperor, different from that used to refer to its own emperor) and ethnic self-interests, Nishida is still convinced that Japan can gather other nations into its spirit to the advantage of all. What keeps this process "moral" is that it is the self-expression of a wider historical life and not just the self-expression of national interests.

The gap between this idea and that of an Asian sphere of co-prosperity that the government was advocating (all other rationales for its military escapades having failed to convince the international community) was too small to have bothered the ordinary reader. The result was that the criticisms of the official ideology largely fell between the cracks, as indeed they continue to do to this day for many western readers who rush through the text the way one can rush through an ideological tract. One has to assume that Nishida did not realize that the idea of the East Asian Co-Prosperity Sphere was a smokescreen for a plan to secure the natural resources needed to run the war machine. In either case, he served its purposes. As the Greek proverb says, one takes on the stature of the beast one chooses to wrestle with. I don't think there is any denying that Nishida's tracts on the Japanese spirit and the national polity did just that and not, as he would have intended, tame the beast.

The assessment of his disciples and later historians are mixed, with opposing opinions each presenting its own reading of more or less the same documents. Having worked through the literature several years ago and again in the preparation of this book, and having studied further his responses to overtures from the government and military for collaboration, I do not see the point of adding yet another resume of the spectrum of opinion. Neither is there an opinion I feel comfortable enough to ratify.

The issue, it seems to me, is not whether Nishida lent validity to the question of the identity of the Japanese spirit at a time when it was being used to justify military aggressions. Of course he did. Nor is the issue whether his idea of the nation shared with the ideological propaganda of the day important assumptions about the imperial household and the special mission of the Japanese people vis-à-vis the other peoples of Asia. Of course it did. The question is whether his political philosophy flows naturally from the fundamental inspirations of his philosophy or was a distraction from that inspiration. I believe it was the latter, and that the hybrid style of his political philosophizing mirrors that fact.

Nishida's philosophy was not the roar of a great intellectual beast sinking its teeth into the political questions of the day. It was a labyrinth of insights and counterinsights that was best suited to detached philosophical speculation, making their way circuitously, detached from all questions of immediate practicality, better suited to inviting reflection than to countermanding the prevailing propaganda of the day. The inner recesses of the mind seeking full awareness by denying the self was the arena of his thought about history. If such a philosophy was politically irrelevant, this was not a weakness to be corrected by throwing it out into the public forum of political ideologies jostling against each other for the control of the popular imagination. The results, I conclude, are not significant either for the development of his ideas nor for the history of political philosophy as such; and if he is to be faulted for anything, it is for the failure to realize that ignorance of his own limitations was a kind of complicity.

27 RELIGION, GOD, AND INVERSE CORRELATION. At some point, Nishida shook the dust of the journey into political philosophy from his sandals and returned to what he knew best. In the dusk of his years, Nishida looked back over his work and made one last attempt to comprehend the whole. He wrote as Japan was under bombardment from the Allied Forces and ordinary life was deteriorating rapidly. He wrote to Hisamatsu Shin'ichi:

> I put myself in the mind of Hegel writing his *Phenomenology* with the cannons of Napoleon exploding in the background, writing with the thought that I could die any day now.... I have just now put together my general views on religion in an essay I have called "The Logic of Locus and a Religious Worldview."

Nishida was too much a creature of his philosophical style to give us a tidy summary. What he did was to give *himself* a summary. Without being privy to his previous thinking, however, large sections of the essay are in effect unintelligible. As always he no sooner starts summarizing than his characteristic intuitive leaps take him in new directions. Rather than tie up the loose ends of his thinking, as he may have intended it to, it wraps everything up in a *furoshiki*—the way he must have each day for years when he set off for the university, tossing pencils and papers and books in and joining the corners of the cloth into a knot for carrying. The *furoshiki* here is religion.

Nishida had taught courses on religion proper in his first years at Kyoto University, and again at the end of his teaching career, and remnants of his lecture notes indicate that he took up religious topics with some frequency in other courses as well. His lecture notes from his first course in 1913 on religion give a good idea of how well versed he was in the field as it was known at the time. In addition to philosophical works, he read some of the major works in anthropology, history, and psychology of religion. Religion in general had remained an interest for him, but he had never written up his own views on the subject for publication. While we can read his last essay against the background of these notes and his scattered comments, it is a little hazardous to try to present anything systematic.

It is fitting, and surely Nishida recognized the coincidence, that his last essay should deal with the same questions that conclude the book that had launched him on his philosophical career, and that closed the book on his years of struggle with neo-Kantianism. With his political and culture philosophy to one side, he returns to concern with the highest absolutes: God, Amida, Buddha, absolute nothingness.

Although this last essay introduces explicitly Buddhist ideas in connection with the absolute, the model for the connection remains, as it had always been, the idea of God. Nishida's idea of God was formed the way most westerners form theirs: he began with the received image and simply painted out the parts he didn't like and painted in what he felt was missing. He did not approach God as a "western construct" *per se*, unsuited to Japanese temperament or modes of thought. This is the cause of some confusion, since there are certain liberties he takes with the notion that take him beyond the limits of western theism. But the confusion is not necessarily Nishida's, since what he writes about God is really of a piece with his general attitude to western philosophy; it confounds only when separated from that context.

Nishida's God did not transcend the world. From the beginning, as we saw in the concluding section of *An Inquiry into the Good*, religion "is something the self requires," and God is very much part of experienced reality. God's absoluteness did not consist in independence from the world but in being absolutely related to it. God was in no sense an ontological reality *sui generis* but a cipher of the dynamism of the life of the world. At the same time, this relationship to the world was not a personal one. In fact, it has not even the modicum of the personal we found in his idea of the I-you relationship. Like the I-you, the relationship to God is subservient to the ascent of the individual to true self-awareness. Thus God becomes for Nishida a supreme expression of the awareness—without a subject, without an object—that consciousness can attain. God is a function of human interiority:

> We are connected to God at our origins, because we are created beings. As ourselves creators in a world where the opposites unite, where the contradictions of past and future co-exist in the present... we touch the absolute. It is just that we are not aware of it. But by looking back deeply into the recesses of our own self-contradiction, we reach the absolute. It is an unconditional surrender to God.

There are other hints of an identification of God with the true self. For example, Nishida speaks of the self discovering itself by seeing the things of the world as its "shadows." The connection with the Buddhist idea of the true essence of the self as an innate but unrealized "Buddha-nature" is easy to draw, but it is also an idea that has analogies to the discovery of God in creation scattered through western tradition, both philosophical and literary.

At the same time, God is not to be identified outright with the true self of the individual, any more than the true self was for Nishida the absolute principle of reality; neither is to be identified with nothingness as the absolute principle of reality. God is always and forever an expression of a relationship between the individual and reality. God belongs irrevocably to the world of being, which is why Nishida has no trouble referring to God as "the absolute of being." As an absolute that is not the highest absolute, it must combine within itself contradictories, in this case being and the self-negation of being. These contradictions appear in God's kenotic act, whose origins are in the act of creation and whose fulfillment is in the incarnate act of love that is Christ:

> Beneath the emergence of the individual, the personal self, there lies the self-negation of the absolute. The true absolute does not simply absolve itself of all relatives. It must always and everywhere contain self-negation within itself, and through relation to this absolute self-negation define itself as an absolute that is an affirmation-*in*-negation.

Here again, he is not speaking ontologically but attempting to interpret ontologies of God as a metaphor of how consciousness reaches identity: God can no longer exist apart from consciousness that relates to God than a metaphor can exist without language. In the end, we might say, the idea of God was not so much a philosophical idea that had to be given a place alongside other ideas, but an invitation to preserve the whole dimension of religious sentiment in his account of experienced reality. The idea of God works for Nishida much the way the great and inexhaustibly intelligible perennial symbols of human civilization have worked, eliciting participation in the opposites that they crystallize.

In a sense, God may be said to be paradigmatic of the idea of the union of opposites more than the I-you relationship, though a God rarely met in the thought of the west. For Nishida, God cannot transcend the relative world or he would therefore be relative to it. Rather, the relative world must somehow represent a self-negation of God. He justifies this understanding of God by appeal to the theological notion of the *kenōsis* of God in Christ:

> A God who is simply self-sufficient in a transcendent way is not the true God. It must have a kenotic aspect that is everywhere present. A truly dialectic God will be one that is at all times transcendent as it is immanent and immanent as it is transcendent. This is what makes a true absolute. It is said that God created the world out of love. Then God's absolute love has to be something essential to God as an absolute self-negation, not as an *opus ad extra.*

This idea of God, which is also evident in his final essay, affected the way Nishida understood religion, namely in its ahistorical, diachronic dimension. The historicity of God, like that of religion, stems from the fact that it arises from human reflection on our actual situation in the world and grows as we pursue that reflection. This is why he can claim that his idea of God is "neither theism nor deism, neither spiritualism nor naturalism; it is historical."

We should note here that not only was Nishida not concerned with promoting any form of institutional affiliation, he was also not interested in promoting a noninstitutional form of religion. He simply does not concern himself with how religious practice requires a particular tradition of rituals and symbols to function. Although his final essay cites passages from Buddhist and Christian scriptures, the religion he seeks is something that transcends these particular patrimonies. From the start religiosity for him was not a function of doctrinal knowledge. I cite an early book review from 1898:

> For me, what makes religion to be religion is not a matter of what kind of creed or ritual it has, but of the individual leaving the finite world to enter into the higher realm of the infinite. It is an extremely variable activity of becoming united, without necessarily knowing it at the time, with what philosophy calls the "absolute." Call it feeling or even intuition, religion is get-

> ting to where life is: Buddhism speaks of liberation, Christianity speaks of salvation.... For me, knowledge is completely unnecessary for religion. By nature religion does not need to coincide with true knowledge.... Knowledge can easily distinguish true doctrine from false because it is shallow. Religion has a hard time discriminating the two because it is true.

Later he will go still further to distance his idea of religion from dependence on ethics and the concern with salvation, seeing these as products of religion rather than its source:

> Religion does not ignore the standpoint of morality. On the contrary, the true standpoint of morality is even based on religion. But this does not mean that one enters religion through the medium of moral deeds.... In our day it is sometimes thought that the goal of religion is the salvation of the individual..., but this is based on ignorance of the true nature of religion. Religion is not a matter of individual peace of mind.

His study of religion as religion was like his empiricism in that it skips over the concrete world of synchronic history, armed only with an *idea* of that world, to get directly to God, which was in fact a real world for him in much the same way that intuition, reflection, and self-awareness were real. God was never merely an idea, but always an experienced relationship. In this sense, too, it is less like absolute nothingness than like the living expression of absolute nothingness that one can only know by becoming.

Nishida crowned this treatment of God as relationship with a new idea introduced in his final essay, that of *inverse correspondence.* In logical terms, it is an extension of his idea of identity as the function of opposition, so that the stronger the opposition, the more deeply rooted the identity. The model of the application of this idea to religion is already present in his earlier remarks about how the sinner is the one who is most conscious of the moral ideal because the contradiction is constellated in him, and that "the more one is an individual the more one is confronted with the transcendent." He repeats that idea here in connection with Shinran's teachings, but goes further to include the relationship between the human and the divine. His aim is to challenge the idea of a direct correspondence between human imperfection and divine perfection.

The God of Nishida is not the inverted image of human impotence projected on to an omnipotence in the skies, as critics of religion since Nietzsche and Feuerbach were fond of saying. As a union of opposites, God represents the task of human consciousness itself. In traditional theology, the closer religious consciousness tries to draw to God, the more one's own finitude comes to the fore and inhibits knowing the divine, except as the divine chooses to reveal itself. Nishida's proposal is that the deeper the consciousness of one's own finitude, the closer does one draw to the core of divinity itself—namely to the awareness of finitude as negated by that which embraces it without limits and affirms it, just as it is. God can save human beings from their finitude because God's nature is kenotic, a consummate constellation of both being and nothingness.

As I have tried to show, Nishida's is not so much a systematic philosophy as a philosophizing about a few basic questions. In a sense, his thought goes around in circles, ever wider circles, but in circles nonetheless. There are no great turning points or ruptures, and this gives a kind of artificiality to attempts to distinguish "stages" in Nishida's thought or to lay his ideas out in straight lines. In this regard, I cannot deny a certain impatience with those who try to use Nishida's ideas as molds into which to pour particular philosophical problems in order to acquire an eastern slant on them. I am convinced that either one goes around in circles with Nishida or one ends up wondering what all the fuss over his thought is about. Reading Nishida is always greater and more exciting than learning how to manipulate his technical vocabulary.

Still, there would be no Kyoto-school philosophy, and probably far less interest in Nishida aside from those specializing in the intellectual history of Japan, were it not for the original thinking his ideas stimulated in his disciples. Only in knowing them do we get an appreciation of the full force of his philosophizing. It is to the first of the principal disciples, Tanabe Hajime, that we turn next.

Tanabe Hajime
(1885–1962)

28 TANABE'S LIFE AND CAREER. Tanabe Hajime was born in Tokyo on 3 February 1885. He entered the department of natural sciences at Imperial University of Tokyo in 1904, specializing in mathematics. The following year he switched to philosophy, recalling in later years that he did not think he had it in him to be a mathematician. After graduating in 1908 he took up a post as a teacher of English at a middle school, later transferring to the school where his father was principal.

His philosophical career began in 1913 at Tōhoku Imperial University, where he was appointed lecturer in the department of natural sciences. In his lectures during those first years he concentrated on the fundamental problems of science, basing himself on German texts. His first writings, among them a book on the philosophy of science published in 1915, shows that he had kept much of his interest in mathematics and logic. Like many a young student of philosophy of his day, he was drawn to the currents of neo-Kantian thought that were dominant in Germany at the time. Given his interests in science and mathematics, it was natural for him to be more attracted to the circle of thinkers in Marburg around Paul Gerhard Natorp and Hermann Cohen, who were laying the groundwork for a theory of knowledge that would bring philosophy and the natural sciences closer together. Nevertheless, he was convinced—and wrote as much in a 1915 essay—that the work of Heinrich Rickert of the competing Freiburg school, who was interested in the human sciences and in understanding the role of value-systems and the place of a scientific worldview in general culture, was a necessary balance, and that only a combination of the two approaches would satisfy.

In any case, although he had already finished his formal study, he hoped to familiarize himself at first hand with the intellectual environment in Europe in order to complete a grand project he had set himself: a rethinking of Kant's transcendental logic in the light of Husserl's phenomenology, Bergson's vitalism, and the ideas of his brilliant senior colleague in Kyoto, Nishida Kitarō. Natorp had already retired but Cohen was still active, and Marburg seemed a natural choice.

Cohen's death in 1918 cast a cloud over those hopes, but within a year things had changed completely with the invitation by Nishida to take up the post of assistant professor of philosophy at Kyoto Imperial University. Nishida, who had himself just surfaced after four tortured years of struggle with neo-Kantian thought, had heard of the young Tanabe and saw promise in his writings. Tanabe was ecstatic at having been singled out, and even more pleased to learn that Nishida would support his plan to study in Europe.

In 1922, with a grant from Japan's Ministry of Education, Tanabe left for Berlin, where he worked for a year under the Austrian Kant scholar Alois Riehl, a neo-Kantian interested in showing the relevance of Kant to scientific positivism. Riehl advised him to study further with Rickert in Heidelberg, but Tanabe moved instead to Freiburg to work in the shadow of Husserl. With the end of the First World War, the winds that had once billowed full in the sails of neo-Kantian thought had died down to a breeze, and Tanabe was not about to put himself through what Nishida had gone through if there was an alternative that would satisfy his demand for a philosophy alert to the demands of science. Phenomenology held out just such promise, and the fact that it was an attempt to break free of the radical subjectivity of the neo-Kantians that had kept Nishida in its grip for so many years must have made it all the more appealing.

In 1923, while in Freiburg, he was invited to Husserl's home to address a small gathering. Although the impression he left is reported to have been favorable, Husserl seems to have taken over in midstream and left the young Japanese philosopher, already fumbling with the German language, to one side. Husserl made clear his hopes that Tanabe would be a bridge for the phenomenological movement to the east. Tanabe would have none of it. Disenchanted, he turned his attention instead to the younger Martin Heidegger, who had just been appointed professor at Marburg with the help of Husserl, and in whose "phenomenology of life" he recognized an orientation sympathetic to his own interests. The two became friends and Heidegger tutored him privately in German philosophy.

When Tanabe returned to Japan in 1924, anxious to continue his own work, he was immediately saddled with a request from Nishida to prepare a memorial lecture in celebration of the two-hundredth anniversary of Kant's birth. In preparing that lecture, which focused on Kant's teleology, he made a clean break from what he saw as the epistemological muddle of the neo-Kantians and the abstract dogmatism of German idealism. Soon thereafter, in the course of two years of lectures on Fichte and Schelling his interest in Hegel was piqued. He devoted two years to the *Encyclopedia* followed by thirteen years spent on the *Phenomenology of Spirit*. During these years he came to see the importance of the element of dialectic in Hegel and to adjust his own thinking in line with it. From this grew his own original contribution to Kyoto-school philosophy.

In 1927 Tanabe was named full professor and the following year Nishida retired, leaving the chair to him. Tanabe rose to the challenge of the position with great outward intensity and even greater inner turmoil. Students noticed a nervous edge to the usual earnestness of his lecture. The scattered streaks of gray in his hair spread visibly. It was far less the prestige of the appointment than the lingering presence of the absent Nishida that was weighing on him. In January of 1930 Nishida published his *System of the Self-awareness of the Universal*, and Tanabe took the occasion to publish in May a critical essay fitted out with the ambiguous title "Looking Up to Nishida's Teachings." Nishida found it a "heartless" affront and was incensed. Thus was provoked the confrontation with his mentor that was to prove a turning point in the advance of his own philosophical position.

What began as no more than a slight crease in Tanabe's esteem for his mentor ended up as a yawning chasm of discord that neither was able to bridge. They grew further and further apart until they could not suffer each other's company, and in fact could hardly read each other's writings without misunderstanding. This is not to say that they did not continue to learn from their differences, and even to sharpen their own views as a result, but only that their personal relations had deteriorated to the point that those who counted them both as their teachers were helpless to do more than look sadly on as their empathy toward each other worsened more and more.

Many of the reports concerning the bad blood between Tanabe and Nishida are contained in essays written while Nishida was still alive, which tells us that it was common knowledge and that somehow his students expected him to set things right. With Nishida's death in 1945, Tanabe did not, as one would have expected, compose a memorial piece. His reflections are missing in major collections of reminiscences. One hesitates to call it an act of vengeance, but so vehement was the division that when the first edition of Nishida's *Complete Works* was published, Nishida's correspondence with Tanabe (over one hundred letters in all) was omitted. Pressures from the academic community had the letters instated in a later edition.

Though he had contemplated resigning during the difficult times of the war years, Tanabe held out until age sixty, retiring from Kyoto University in 1945, at which point he was named professor emeritus. For reasons of health he moved to the relative isolation of a small mountain cottage in Kita-Karuizawa, Gunma Prefecture, where he had been accustomed to spending his summers. There he and his wife Chiyo spent the last six years of their life together. It was from there that he would put the finishing touches on his existing philosophy, issue a call for a metanoesis of the Japanese people, and work out his final thoughts—a philosophy of death. Conditions there, which were pleasant enough in the summer, were harsh in the winter. With temperatures falling as low as –20°C, the bitter mountain winds would easily find their way into the simple wood structure.

In 1952 he traveled to Tokyo to receive the cultural order of merit from the government, the only philosopher since Nishida to receive it. Other than that, he did not leave his retreat. He is reported to have said that he could not stand the sight of the foreign occupation forces monitoring Japan's politics and the wretched condition into which Japanese morality and arts had fallen after defeat. More than that, he added, "I can only feel my part in the responsibility for having led Japan to the pitiable fate it is in today, and the more I feel it, the more I lose the right to die a peaceful death on my tatami mats."

While in retirement he continued to write and held occasional seminars and lectures in one of the two cottages of his villa, and to receive visitors, among them Nishitani, who is said to have spent long hours in discussion with his former teacher. The death of his wife in 1951, after thirty-five years of marriage, left a large gap in his life and turned his thoughts away from the dialectics of the living historical world to the dialectics of death. His increasing interest in religion included attention to the Christian idea of the *communio sanctorum* in which the life and relationships that are transformed into death are again transformed back into life.

In 1957 he was recommended by Heidegger for an honorary doctorate at the University of Freiburg, which he received in absentia due to his age and failing health. Tanabe entered hospital in 1961 suffering from a softening of the brain and died there on 29 April the following year at the age of seventy-seven. His gravestone, which rests outside of his mountain cottage, is plain and unadorned, as befits the life he led, and carries only the phrase *My search is for truth, and it alone.*

29 TANABE'S PHILOSOPHICAL STYLE.

For the most part, Tanabe's philosophical prose is ponderous and lacking in rhetorical flourish. His sentences are long and winding yet crafted with mathematical precision. At his best, he makes his way from one thought to the next in short, studied strides, with a great deal of repetition but little ambiguity of expression. At his worst, he concentrates earlier complex arguments into almost unreadable density. His frequent concatenation of abstract terms tend to grate on the Japanese reader not already familiar with western philosophical style, but the clarity of his conjunctions makes translating him into western languages relatively easy, even when the content is too obtuse to understand. It comes as no surprise that he refused all offers to write light, topical pieces. He was a philosopher, and anything else was mere distraction.

At the same time, he was a voracious reader and his own interests were remarkably wide ranging. As one student recalls, they used to refer to him as "the trawler," because while others would angle in the philosophical pond one fish at a time, he would drag the bottom and sweep up everything at once. But he was careful, and his style of writing reflects the way he himself worked with the philosophical texts that he decided were to be of importance for him. As a rule, he preferred to read the original texts with little reference to secondary literature, which gave him a certain liberty of interpretation. In the seminars and lectures he held on Hegel's *Phenomenology of the Spirit* in the 1930s he used the original German, and there is little doubt that the pain he took with explaining the material to his students left its mark on his own writing.

Tanabe was a popular teacher during his years at Kyoto, the halls where he lectured often filled to overflowing with students and professors. He took preparation of his classes seriously, and his students recall him as the only one to lecture without notes. To this end he normally refused all visitors the day before. He would stalk back and forth as he talked, "like a lion roaming restlessly about in its cage," as one of his students recalls. At the same time he was strict. He welcomed questions, however naïve, but was slow to suffer triviality, caricature, sarcasm, and simple cleverness. He never smiled in the presence of his students and commanded an almost terrified respect from them inside the classroom and out. Even in the company of his peers he was not given to banter and joviality.

At the same time, he is remembered as one of the rare teachers of his day who would often admit in front of his students that his thinking was still on the way and that he did not know the answers to some of their questions or what the consequences of his own thinking were. In philosophical discussion he would use all his skills without distinction before students and professors alike. As Takeuchi recalls,

> The nature of his philosophical dialogue may be compared to a lion concentrating all its energies on its prey, even if it is only a rabbit. At times we novices would be struck a painful blow, but we know that it was motivated by our teacher's love of philosophy, waiting for us to recover before he would attack again.

If Tanabe was demanding of others, he was more demanding of himself. Already from his university days he is remembered as serious and aloof. He lived a stern and ascetic lifestyle. Over the thirty years that he spent in Kyoto he assiduously avoided sightseeing and excursions, "fleeing the world as if it were a virus."

Once Tanabe had laid the foundations for his own philosophical standpoint with the dialectics of absolute mediation, his work had an intensity of focus. Everything from then on was connected to that position—filling it out, clarifying, enhancing. But the growth was organic and the stages we discover in hindsight were passed through naturally by Tanabe himself. Only his metanoetics seemed to him to represent a major change of position, though as we shall see it was not so great a change at all.

As a philosopher, Tanabe was nothing if not a system-builder. Wrestling with classical issues in philosophy, keeping *au courant* of the latest intellectual developments, and applying insights to concrete problems were not enough for him. He needed a grand scheme into which all the things of life could be translated. Once he had put his formal education behind him and decided to shake free of the imposing shadow of Nishida, he set out to do just that. With the creativity of the architect he sketched out the blueprints of his Gothic philosophical cathedral line by line—annexing, tearing down, elaborating, but always with the whole in mind so that each part reflected it and yet added something. Master architect though he was, he worked to scale, at one remove from the tools and materials needed to realize what he had sketched out on the drawing board. And should part of his blueprint prove disastrous in the practice, that only sent him back to the drawing board. Not even his later radical critique of reason was able to challenge his conviction that philosophy must be a systematic and all-inclusive representation of reality. It simply meant it had to be buttressed from the outside to keep it from caving in.

When it comes to laying out his main ideas and contributions in résumé, there is no choice at times, as was the case with Nishida, but to overlay earlier ideas with later ones. And this in spite of the fact that his crowning idea, the logic of the specific, led him in a direction that he later repented of publicly. But it was a repentance of a very general nature, tempered by the insistence that he had been misunderstood and with no apparent attempt to locate the point at which his thought had taken a wrong turn. Tanabe's flirtations with nationalism need to be read differently from Nishida's. For almost no one reads Tanabe's lapses—or even his judgment that it was only his silence and lack of action that was his downfall—the way he himself does. In the presentation that follows, I will try to show that his thought does present a total structure from beginning to end, and that his political deviation resulted from a failure to examine his own premises and to heed his own warnings.

30 **PURE EXPERIENCE, OBJECTIVE KNOWLEDGE, MORALITY.** From early on, it was clear that Tanabe would head in a direction different from that of Nishida. Indeed, it was precisely his different perspective on the idea of pure experience that had drawn Nishida's attention to him.

Tanabe's first essay, "On Thetic Judgment," was a short piece that gathered up the main ideas he had presented in his graduation thesis. It was published in 1910 in the *Journal of Philosophy*, a year before Nishida's *Study of the Good* would appear, but was based on the idea of pure experience as Nishida had outlined it in the pages of that same journal. What interested Tanabe in the idea of pure experience was how the subject-object dichotomy was generated from it. His argument is that it is the objective element that first appears, announcing its existence as necessary in the form of a judgment in which the subject does not appear at all, namely the prescriptive or "thetic" judgment. The basis of all objective knowledge, he says, is that *esse est percipi,* which cannot lead to subjective idealism because it does not initially posit an ego.

This last point is significant because it would steer him away from Nishida's focus on consciousness. While Nishida focused on the subjective element in art, literature, and religion, Tanabe headed out in the direction of objective knowledge—including objective idealism—that would keep mathematics and the sciences within the realms of philosophy. He considered the idea of pure experience to be in accord with the basic Kantian position that knowledge is not simply the representation of an objective world to a perceiving subject but a unity constructed in consciousness. But he felt that focusing too exclusively on either the construction or the consciousness did not do justice to the idea of pure experience.

The route by which Tanabe came to clarify this focus was far from straight. His writings during the years before his period of study in Germany show him shifting from one foot to the other in search of a clear philosophical agenda. The more he read of neo-Kantian thought, the more he was of two minds about it. The Marburg school seemed to him too fixated on logicism as a way to bridge the gap between philosophy and the natural sciences, and missed out on the human sciences. This was compensated by Freiburg-school thinkers, who preferred to speak of the construction of worldviews grounded in values. But since by nature "the natural sciences and the human sciences both tend to objectify pure experience," they also tended to forget it. The clearest indication to him of this was the downgrading of the place of human freedom in a philosophy of science on the neo-Kantian model.

This theme shows up in his first book, *The Natural Sciences Today.* Turning his attention directly onto the scientific worldview itself, Tanabe argues that the remarkable achievements of science in manipulating the natural world tended to exempt it from the value judgments proper to the human sciences. The idea of moral freedom, he argued, would serve as the meeting point at which all approaches to objective knowledge could enrich one another and without which they could never find a way back to original, pure experience. A short essay on "Moral Freedom," published the following year while he was preparing his second book on *An Outline of the Sciences* (and that at the same time as a series of articles on mathematics), adds this important question to Tanabe's philosophical agenda.

Like Kant, Tanabe accepted that freedom is not a given fact, but an ideal that belongs to the world of value and not the world of being. And he ends his essay on just this note. But he also indicates that it will not do to dispose of free will by shuffling it off to an inner subjective realm where it gets cut off from the objective world ruled by the law of cause-and-effect. We have forgotten how important it is, he insists, "from time to time to take leave of the dogmatism and biases we see in science for a wider standpoint from which to focus our gaze on the self." He ends his book on this note:

> If the method of the natural sciences is taken as the only way to look at human life..., religion becomes delusion, morality becomes a utility, and art becomes a mechanism for pleasing our natural impulses, leaving no room to understand the true meaning of religion, morality, and art. If, on the other hand, one looks at things from the standpoint of ideals, one looks at the science as embodying the results of the ideal of "truth," in addition to which are other ideals like good, beauty, integrity, and so on, then we have to say that morality, art, and religion each share the same foundations as science.... It is up to the various domains of philosophy, based on a phenomenology that seeks out the truth of intuitions, to show the way to understand these foundations. This is the task I set myself for future work.

For a brief spell he did in fact turn away from Kant and the neo-Kantians toward nineteenth-century German idealism and the thought of Fichte, Schelling, and Hegel for an idea of consciousness in general that would be consistent both with his interest in objective knowledge and the preservation of freedom. The strongest attraction at this time seems to have been to Fichte. In particular, he was drawn to the idea of rejecting the static transcendent unity of the pure Kantian subject in favor of an active ego that constitutes itself in its interaction with the world. At roughly the same time as Nishida was struggling with Fichte, as Tanabe would have known, he was trying to appropriate Fichte's idea of selfhood as not one substantial *datum* among the other data of the world but itself as much a *captum* as the objective world—that is, as an act-fact or *Tathandlung*.

It was not until he had returned from study abroad that he would face the question of morality and free will head-on. On the boat returning from study in Germany, Tanabe pored over Kant's three critiques to prepare himself for the essay Nishida had requested of him. It was to turn him in an unexpected direction, away from epistemology and toward the pursuit of a worldview. He recalls his sentiments:

> I felt resonate within me that same demand for a philosophy of worldviews that had swelled in the German philosophical world during the First World War.... My first work on returning was to write on Kant's teleology.... By what I can only call a twist of fate, it ended up a turning point for me from critique to worldview, from mathematics, physics, and the natural sciences to the history of human society.

The line is not quite as direct nor the causes so reliant on fate as Tanabe has it, but at least brief mention should be made of the contents of this carefully argued essay.

Tanabe focuses on what he sees as the unsatisfactory notion of teleology in Kant's critique of practical reason. Tanabe sorts out three kinds of teleology in that third critique that he tries to synthesize under the rubric of "a dialectics of will." First is a formal, logical teleology whereby the structure of the mind predisposes us to move inductively from particular laws to universal laws so as to make a systematic whole. Second, there is an internal teleology required to explain purposiveness in living organisms and in nature as a whole, a teleology that is not explainable through mechanical principles of natural science. Third, he introduces what he calls a "teleology of self-awareness" to mediate dialectically the gap that Kant had left between the laws of nature and the free will of the moral subject. This teleology belongs to neither nature nor free will but to the realm of culture and history, which do not belong as such to reflective reason but stand against it. "In the same sense in which freedom is a constructive principle of morality, a teleology of self-awareness is a constructive principle of history."

Insofar as morality and free will are essential to philosophical critique, the question of teleology is unavoidable, and this, observes Tanabe, in turn requires attention to religion. It will not do to see all of this as merely another analogy for the innate structure of the rational mind. The demands of reason itself require filling out from a standpoint of moral praxis in which the transformation of consciousness and the transformation of the historical world are brought into the picture.

The only indications Tanabe gives of what the telos of moral action might be are strictly formal, based on a general principle of dialectic, according to which the self loses itself in the other for the sake of a goal outside of the self. His notion of morality is not yet fitted out with any more concrete goal other than to say that it is a creative act of freedom in which the forfeiture of self for other is objectified in culture and history. Still, we have here the ingredients for the first major step that Tanabe would take toward establishing his own philosophical standpoint.

31 PURE RELATIONSHIP, ABSOLUTE MEDIATION.

When Nishida introduced his logic of locus in 1926 in the attempt to relate absolute nothingness more closely to the goal of awareness, Tanabe did not follow suit. Instead he began to work out an idea of "absolute mediation" distilled from his careful reading of Hegel. In a 1930 essay openly critical of the senior Nishida, he presented his idea as an alternative way to incorporate the idea of absolute nothingness into philosophy.

As we have seen, the more Tanabe tried to work from Nishida's perspective of awareness grounded in pure and immediate experience (or in its more recent formulation, active intuition), the more he realized it did not fit him as a starting point for philosophy. In addition to his interests in laying the ground for an objective knowledge that would bring science into philosophy, he had never been drawn to the practice of Zen as Nishida had, nor did he draw inspiration from the kind of poetic utterances that Nishida used to talk about experience or intuition. He fully shared his mentor's conviction of the philosopher's task as increasing awareness and ridding the mind of the clichés in which it is used to think. But the appeal of the scientific method and the language of mathematics, coupled with an inveterate impatience with the stupidity he saw at work in the political arena, needed surer footing for his thinking to advance. He found this in the idea that all reality is interrelated, and all of the events of the world are a dialectic of that interrelatedness.

If this reorientation of his thinking was prompted by the philosophical texts with which he was working in his lectures, it was solidified by his deliberate fall from grace as the crown prince of Nishida's philosophy. One can hardly fail to note the irony in the fact that the most important personal relationship of his philosophical career soured just when Tanabe was offering its mirror-image in an idea of the primacy of relationship—an idea with roots as deep in early Buddhism as Nishida's pure experience was in the Zen tradition—worked out in dialectical tension. Tanabe does not seem to have noticed the coincidence.

The first step in Tanabe's idea of a dialectic of absolute mediation was not very different from Hegel's, or for that matter from Nishida's logic of locus. His study of Kant and the neo-Kantians had left him deeply dissatisfied on several counts. His instincts told him that the individuality of particular beings that make up the real world cannot be accounted for by virtue of some numinous essence or thing-in-itselfness that is permanently obscured from view by biases built into the structure of mind. Even if the base of the critique of mind is broadened to include the conventions of language and social structure, the assumption of an underlying but inaccessible substance to things seemed misguided, and when applied to the mind itself, viciously circular. It also infringed, and did so without sufficient reason, on the foundational Buddhist ideas of the nonsubstantiality of things and the self on the one hand, and the co-arising of all things on the other. On every count Hegel's starting point—that each individual is what it is and does what it does by virtue of relationship with other individuals—was more promising.

If the primary fact of individuality, then, was to be explained in terms of the relationship between one thing and another, the paradigmatic example of this lay in the awakening of the conscious self through consciousness of an other that is not the self. By denying its identity with an other, the self not only affirms its own individuality but at the same time affirms the dependency of that individuality on the relationship with the other that it is not. The self-sufficiency of the notion of substance is too obviously a fiction to serve as the basis for what makes a thing the individual that it is. The essence of the individual items that make up the world can only be grasped as a function of their radical relativity to other things around them. Each thing, and hence also each individual consciousness, is at one and the same time its own self and an other to every other thing with which it interacts, and apart from this interaction nothing exists.

The model is Hegel's but his explanation adds to this echoes of Nishida's concern that philosophical logic reach beyond grammatical form and rules of thinking to keep us in mind of the fact that there is, after all, an actual experiential world we are trying to explain, and that the mind that is trying to explain it is part of it. When Tanabe speaks of the essential identity of the individual as a "self-*in*-other," he means to include not only relationships among conscious human beings but among all objects in the material world, as well as among the whole range of customs, institutions, and social structures in which the historical world entangles us. And when he speaks of the dialectic this entails as an "affirmation-*in*-negation" he means to insist that no statement of pure affirmation or pure negation about the way the world is, is complete without its opposite.

But simply to say that things or persons or institutions are what they are because they are not other things, or that things are related to one another by not being one another, is almost banal in its self-evidence. The crucial point is that these very relationships are always and ever mediated by other relationships. Nothing on its own relates to anything else directly, but always through the agency of other relationships. And nothing in reality is exempt from this pattern, not even the reason that mediates this realization. This was the nature of an irreversible insight from which Tanabe would never retreat. Still, there was a long and twisting road ahead as what was basically one abstract model replacing another strove to have something concrete to say about this mutually dependent, absolutely mediated reality we live in.

32 **A REINTERPRETATION OF ABSOLUTE NOTHINGNESS.** At the time Nishida was studying philosophy, and indeed throughout his career, one of the major problems inherited from the nineteenth century was that of the conflict between the individual and society. As his students and contemporaries caught in the maelstrom of Marxist thought complained to him often enough, the issue was begged, not settled, by focusing concrete attention on the awakening of the individual and reducing history to some general notion of historicity. The younger Tanabe, who had not yet worked out a clear philosophical position of his own, was quick to register the significance of the criticism. The first use to which he put his new idea of a dialectics of absolute mediation was that of a wedge to pry open the ideas of absolute nothingness and self-awareness he had inherited from Nishida—ideas whose crucial importance for philosophy he never questioned—to the historical world. For Tanabe, awakening to a transhistorical, universal absolute nothingness must be seen as a "differential" fact within a wider historical-relative reality, whereas for Nishida absolute nothingness was the

principle of the entire system and as such was thought of from the start as an "integral" whole in terms of which relative things are systematized.

The shift from pure experience to absolute will, brought about by his experiment with a "dialectics of will" in his essay on Kant, shows up in his attention to the role of will in moral praxis. While the influence of Nishida's attention to "knowing by becoming" as the foundation for morality is clear, it was only natural that Tanabe would not stop there but go on now to ask whether the totality of particular correlations among things, persons, and institutions pointed to a grander, universal dialectic working itself out in time; and whether that could relate to absolute nothingness.

From even the short account given above, it should be clear that Tanabe's view of history itself as dialectic—that is to say, as a process in which the giving-and-taking of identities among individuals constitutes a comprehensive drama of conflict, resolution, and new conflict—was sympathetic to Hegel. In broad terms he agreed with the idea that as individuals and the social structures they build up among themselves live and die through time, it is not only particular relationships that are changing shape from one moment to the next or one age to the next, but history itself that is working out its own identity.

What is important to note here is that he did not take the further step that Hegel did, namely the leap to a providential, if somewhat cunning, rationality at work behind history. This would have required the notion of an absolute self transcending history, since there is no reason without a rational subject. Either this self would be a true absolute and hence exempted from the universal law of absolute mediation, giving identity to others but not receiving it in return; or it would be an absolute only relative to our history, partaking in a parallel history, in which case it would require a realm of other selves also transcending our actual history to form its own dialectic, thus raising the question of a still higher absolute and hence an infinite regress. In either case, it was unacceptable. If mediation is an absolute principle, then there can be nothing beyond it that mediates it; it must be an in-mediate fact. History must therefore be an all-encompassing unity, a single story of selves and others coming into being and passing away in relationship with one another. To talk of the world of being as a whole would be to talk about reality in-the-making. Just as nothing that exists is unmediated, so nothing that exists is not in the process of becoming. If there is teleology in history, it must be *in* history, not beyond it.

From the start, Tanabe was wary not only of submitting the individual will to a transcendent will but also of submerging it in an ineluctable advance of pure historical necessity. For this reason, it was not only Hegel's idealism that he rejected but the alternative of a Marxist-oriented dialectical materialism as well. Like many of his age, he read this as contradicting the free will of the individual, a step he firmly rejected. Thus, while he maintained a certain sympathy towards Marx, he did not see the point in replacing the rule of providence over the conscious subject with the rule of social institutions, no matter how good those institutions happen to be.

Numerous early comments on the position of the state vis-à-vis the individual scattered throughout his writings confirm our suspicion that Tanabe's adoption of the dialectic was headed in a direction quite different from that of either the Hegelian or the Marxist recipes. What is more, the fact that so avid a reader as he never bothered to base his views regarding Marxism on a serious study of Marx's works, and that he seems to have maintained to the end his initial impressions that its economic theory and data were simply a "secondary means" to enhance what were fundamentally philosophical ideas, makes it clear that socialist thought never worked more than a marginal stimulus on his own thinking.

At the same time as he resisted the diminution of the subject in history, Tanabe was not prepared to see conscious awareness (or its pure form of "immediate experience" in which the subject-object dichotomy falls away) as a sufficient consciousness of history—as he thought Nishida had done. What then is left to account for the unfolding of history? What is it that is working itself out in time through the interplay of relationships whose paradigm is that between the concrete subject and the social order? Is history's "dialectic" an ultimately meaningless hydraulics of energy flowing back and forth between self and other to give each its identity by negating the other, or is there some telos corresponding to the myth of a divine providence making its will concrete in history? The answer, he concluded, lay in reclaiming the Buddhist notion of nothingness, which Nishida had already elevated to the status of an absolute, as a kind of anti-telos.

For Tanabe absolute nothingness, even if viewed as a transcendent locus with Nishida, is not an unmediated universal, a supreme class embracing all beings but itself lacking in differentiation. That would make it the equivalent of the totality of being and return it to the realm of being. It does not *belong* to being, but at the same time its activity is only *manifest* in the world of being, refracted, for example, in the ethical activities of self-negating praxis. As Tanabe understood it, absolute nothingness had to serve at least to function as a mirror image of the Judaeo-Christian God of Being in the sense that it would provide a transcendental unity to history, but without being assigned the role of providing a final telos as in Hegel's philosophy.

As an absolute *nothingness,* the idea was not merely a shorthand for an apophasia or aphasia of reason in the face of ultimate reality; it was also a rejection of the absoluteness of the concept of being itself, and hence of its suitableness as a ground for correlatives to stand on in order to identify and determine each other:

> To imagine an absolute apart from this historical mediation, a being that transcends and encompasses relatives, is to end up either in the submersion of the autonomous individual in the vile equality of pantheism, or in the dominion of the unmediated, selective divine will of theism.... Both tendencies are undeniably present in Hegel.... The basic and unfortunate underlying mistake of Hegel is the positing of an unmediated, absolute being beyond the transcendental unity of dialectical nothingness, locating it outside the working of nothingness as self-identical being, and entrusting it to a heretical logic of substance.

As *absolute*, nothingness must be universally at work in all the relationships that make up the dialectics of history and it must be unmediated. It cannot be a self, a totality of selves, or a higher self, since the self requires an other, and the absolute by definition is absolved of all interrelationship and dialectic with others. There can be no unchanging Entity or unchanging substrate of Being giving a telos to the dialectical world of being. Only an absolute (that is, a non-mediated) nothingness (that is, a non-being-ness) can provide a unifying telos to history.

However far Tanabe's thought wandered into history and later into religion, he never questioned the primacy of the concept of nothingness in the philosophical venture. To cite from a late work:

> All science needs to take some entity or other as its object of study. The point of contact is always in being, not in nothing. The discipline that has to do with nothingness is philosophy. Religion encounters nothingness and overcomes it in faith, art in feeling; but it is only philosophy that deals with nothingness in knowing from the academic standpoint. Since Aristotle metaphysics has been defined as the study of existence as such, of being itself; but if being is something that can only be known concretely through the mediation of nothingness, it is more fitting that we should define philosophy in terms of nothingness, paradoxical as this may look at first.

At this point in his thinking, it is clear that absolute nothingness is a kind of dynamic, almost a kind of *élan vital*, that keeps the dialectic of interrelatedness going. But Tanabe does not yet make clear just what difference this makes to philosophical argument. What is clear is that human consciousness enjoyed the privileged capacity to realize what was going on, and that this capacity was the ground for moral action. Given our innate impatience with the frustration of personal desires in the larger order of things, the awareness of what history is makes no difference without the capacity to distinguish between what *is* going on and *should be* going on. "It is in morality," he write, "that we find philosophy's vital immediacy."

At least initially, therefore, the new interpretation of absolute nothingness did less to clarify the content of the telos of history than to ask the question of how human will can best share in its vitality. The answer begins with a critique of how will errs by not consulting its reason, a critique that led him to his logic of the specific. Later we shall see how the notion of absolute nothingness gets new depth when enriched by the idea of Other-power in Pure Land Buddhism.

33 THE ORIGINS OF THE LOGIC OF THE SPECIFIC.

With the reformulation of the idea of absolute nothingness, Tanabe's dialectic of absolute mediation had next to come to terms with its own abstractness and distance from the actual historical world. As he himself admitted, "my past bias towards abstraction stems from a flaw in my speculative powers." He sought an answer in a new logic, the logic of the specific.

Tanabe's expressed reasons for introducing a new logic, in which he did not include any mention of a confrontation with the logic of locus of Nishida, were two. First, he said, was a practical concern with "seeking out rational grounds to the controls imposed by the society as a nation on its individual members." Second was what he felt as the need to revise general logic in the strict sense of the word. The ordering of these two purposes is deliberate. Tanabe did not first work out a logic and then apply it to problems in the historical world. At the same time, we must not be too hasty to conclude, in the light of later events, that he had simply worked out a logic to justify a political position towards the Japanese state that he had already decided on by the mid-1930s.

Allusions to the first concern with the role of the state as a limit on the individual were already present in his earlier writings, but had not figured in his idea of absolute mediation or in his grounding of history in absolute nothingness. Already in 1922, for example, years before Japan's military buildup and at the height of Taishō liberalism and its positive mood of democracy, Tanabe had published such remarks in an essay on "The Notion of Culture." In it he accepted socialism's critique of bourgeois culturism and its idea of democracy, but at the same time rejected what he saw as its wholesale dismissal of the philosophic enterprise. His aim was a kind of social democracy that would preserve the best of both viewpoints. He stressed the development of an "ethnic state" as Japan's "duty" to the international community of nations. He expressed there his disappointment with what he called Taishō "culturism," by which he understood the worship of high culture from abroad and the attempt to emulate it. The root of the problem, as he saw it, lay in a rush from a stress on the individual to humanity as a whole organized in the form of western democracy but "ignoring respect for the race and forgetting the important significance of the nation." What was needed was a new philosophical ideal distinct from that of western states.

It was against the backdrop of this general critical approach to the Japanese saeculum that Tanabe had been rethinking Hegel's idea of the concrete universal and objective spirit as a way to work the notion of absolute nothingness into history. As he worked out his own dialectic of absolute mediation grounded in absolute nothingness, it struck Tanabe that the reason that the rules of logic are not useful for clarifying moral issues in the historical world is that they are structurally designed *not* to. Nishida's critique of logic based on subject and predicate had helped to explain why logic could not get at what was going on in the process of coming to awareness. It had shown how the concatenation of relations between universals and particulars in the realm of pure logic failed to do justice to pure experience. But it had not bridged the gap between awareness and the way social institutions of civil society affect our modes of thought.

The immediate catalyst for the proposal of a new logic did not come, as we might expect, from the neo-Kantians, where the concern with the effect of social values on philosophical and scientific worldviews was already very much present. In fact, Tanabe does not really cite them in this context at all. Rather it came from a reading of Bergson set against the backdrop of the increasing tensions in Japan's current political situation at the time. Tanabe had already known Bergson's work, though it seems more indirectly through Nishida's writing than from any reading of his own. When a copy of Bergson's *Two Sources of Morality and Religion*, which came out in 1932, fell into Tanabe's hands, he immediately recognized in it his own concerns with the historical conditions of a religious worldview and an ethic.

Drawing on Durkheim's sociology to distinguish between the "open" and "closed" society, and adding his own distinction between "dynamic" and "static" religion, Bergson tried to show how the option for the former over the latter was a matter of crucial importance for philosophical thought. Tanabe was led to see two important facts about Japan: first, that its engagements in Asia were grounded on the ideology of an ethnically based, totemically sealed clan mentality of the closed society, which would prohibit it from joining the great open societies of the world; and second, that the truly open society is not merely a function of intellectual conversion but must draw on and transform the same instinctual drives and innate sense of obligation to the group that is at work in the closed society.

The obvious, and simplest, solution would have been to follow Bergson and encourage an openness of the individual mind to the whole human community without being bound by the constraints of one's particular tribal unit, and to rely on religion to provide the necessary motivation in the form of universal love. But Tanabe took a different tact by overlaying his dialectic on Bergson's distinctions. He saw ethics as by nature tending to close a society in on itself and religion as by nature opening it up to universal human concerns, and argued that a mutual mediation of the two would supply each with what was wanting. The first and most important task, accordingly, was to make the nature of tribal bias as transparent as possible in order to allow it to be replaced by the rationality of the open society. To achieve that transparency, he had to identify the formal parameters of the logic that individuals in society use to think their thoughts and to exercise their moral obligations, in order thereby to clarify the difference in rational content between the open and the closed society.

When Tanabe first broached these ideas in a lengthy 1934 essay on "The Logic of Social Existence," it was clear that he was caught in a question that would occupy his attention for some time to come. It was the first time he used the phrase "logic of the specific," which he understood in both a critical and a constructive sense. Unlike the dialectic of absolute mediation, the logic of the specific was meant to tackle "logic" in the classical sense of the term. That is, it was an attempt to describe the circumstances under which inferences were drawn and which determined what constituted evidence and self-evidence and what did not. In this way, Tanabe felt it would be possible to determine what it was that an "ethnic society" did to close itself and the minds of its members, and keep them closed, and also what means were at its disposal to open them up again and keep them open. He was convinced that between the concrete, living individual and the universal, ideal human community that Bergson had set up in opposition, there was another dimension, largely unconscious and irrational, at work. This is what he called the realm of the specific.

Unlike the Kantian categories, which were transcendental, the ethnic society filtered the way reason processed the interplay between the actual and the ideal in the midst of history. But like the transcendental categories, its workings were invisible to the workaday mind, protecting the closure of society from the compelling reasons for opening up. He saw examples of this in the Nazi ideology of *Blut und Boden* and in Heidegger's search for German uniqueness, both of which he criticized. It is also clear that he meant to include Japan in his critique. The closed mentality of contemporary Japan that showed up in its culturism (and to a limited extent, also in its growing militarism) constituted his clearest concrete example.

Although we seem to be much more embedded in time and history than we are with Nishida's logic of locus, in fact Tanabe's argument remained largely formal. Little effort was made to refer the critique to the problem that prompted the idea in the first place, namely the irrational habits of thought that made Japan a closed society. The mere *possibility* of the existence of such an irrational logic seems to have satisfied him at this juncture. Nevertheless, at the theoretical level, the texts leave little doubt that Tanabe was very much aware of the irrational limitations that his own "specific" society imposed on the thought of its members.

Before we see just how he did apply his logic concretely, we need first to get a more general picture of what it encompassed. We can do this by distinguishing four steps in the logic.

34 **THE SPECIFIC AND THE SOCIOCULTURAL WORLD.** The logic of the specific begins in a shift from the formal, syllogistic function of species to an ontological role in the dialectic of absolute mediation. The first step in Tanabe's reinterpretation of the notion of the specific is to dislodge the concept of species from its obligation to formal logic, where it served as a mere category of classification pinched between the universal and the individual. This entails two things.

First, as Hegel had shown, when the dimension of history is brought into the picture, the two-valued logic of the grammatical syllogism gives way to a dialectic in which negation and affirmation work incessantly to make the world, and our understanding of it, over and over again. In place of reliance only on the principle of non-contradiction, Tanabe followed suit with the proposal that logic be grounded on a principle of absolute mediation. Tanabe concludes:

> The logic of the specific is a dialectical logic, ...both a logic and a denial of logic. The self-contradiction of existence and the reversibility of affirmation-*in*-negation and negation-*in*-affirmation cannot be expressed, still less, described, in terms of a logic that takes the laws of identity and non-contra-

> diction as fundamental principles.... Existence destroys and transcends the logic of identity....

The reference to the denial of logic is Tanabe's way of insisting that the logic of the specific is always a logic *of* an evolving reality, a way of seeing that only makes sense when it is engaged in seeing.

Second, in making absolute mediation a logical principle more fundamental and fairer to reality than the principle of non-contradiction, Tanabe does not merely mean that reality is full of contradictions that require a continual give-and-take among our ideas about it, but also that the mediation that propels history through time as an interrelated totality itself belongs to reality. It was at this point that he struck on the idea of reinvigorating the syllogistic function of "species" as a link that joins the universal or genus and the individual (the "Socrates is a man" that enables "all men will die" to be applied to the individual case as "Socrates will die"). This formal mediating function, he thought, might be extended beyond the abstract proposition to point to the actual ontological reality of many individuals participating severally in a common, generic universal.

In speaking of a universal "one" and the individuals that make up the "many," the role traditionally given to the specific was merely ancillary. On the one hand, it served as a way to group the many into units smaller than the universal one. On the other, it helped break up the immensity of the one into units larger than the mere individual. The reason the category had been so confined, Tanabe argues, was that the specific lacked the ontological possibilities of the universal and the individual. True parity for the specific would require that it be seen as something fully real, in fact that which gives the universal and the individual its historical reality.

In short, Tanabe felt that the method of classification traditional to philosophy had tended to focus attention on individuals and universals (or genera) to the neglect of the intervening subclasses (or species). Such classification may aid in locating the one in the many, but it tends to engender expectation of theories that see the many as somehow derivative of or emanating from the one, or that see the interplay of concrete reality and abstract ideals as descriptive of the real world.

The consequences for his own earlier formulation of the dialectics of absolute mediation are obvious. Without the concreteness of the historical world, he saw, the idea that mediation is as real as the real things that interact with each other sounds more like a rhetorical flourish than a critical statement. There is no reason at all why dialectical language should be less liable to read its own biases into the phenomenal world than static, two-valued logic is. This criticism, which the reader of Hegel's richly experiential and historical *Phenomenology* and *Philosophy of Right* can hardly avoid lodging against the dry and ethereal *Logic*, did not escape Tanabe. As a result, he could not propose his principle of absolute mediation as a logic—that is, as a way of seeing reality—without first mooring it in the immediacy of temporal-historical process. This brings us back to the goal he had set himself with his new logic, namely the opening of the closed society.

In order to play the role of the guarantor of concreteness, the specificity of the specific had itself to be both synchronic and diachronic: it had to refer to a particular epoch but also refer to what unfolds across epochs. In other words, the epoch-specificity of culture and society needed to stand a middle ground between the universal history of the human race and the individual history of men and women. Moreover, like the Christian Hegel, but unlike Nishida whose logic of locus frequently opened out into Buddhist metaphors of the wider natural world, Tanabe's logic of the specific seems to have assumed that the primary sense of history was that of human history. Unlike Nishida's logic of locus, which always seemed to tilt history in the direction of the self-awareness of the individual, Tanabe's logic would aim directly at praxis and its moral implications. All of these assumptions combined in Tanabe's decision, the second step in his logic: the immediate historical reality of the specific is none other than the sociocultural substratum of particular races, the mode of thought of the "ethnic society," which initially presents itself as "closed" but which is open to transformation.

For Tanabe, this opened a new agenda for his philosophical thinking and brought it face to face with the major problem of the day, the identity of Japanese society vis-à-vis the rest of the world. In the background of his first essay on the logic of the specific one can hardly fail to hear the echoes of the contemporary clamor among intellectuals for greater attention to concrete social praxis. Tanabe was aware that he was about something very contemporary, and he even takes a moment to pardon Hegel for having lived at an age where he would know no better. For his part, Tanabe was convinced that the closure or opening of Japanese society could not be a matter of indifference to a logic that had moved from the purely formal to the realm of ontology.

We cannot overlook the political situation in Japan at the time Tanabe was framing his logic of the specific. Critical reflection on social structures had to contend with military escapades abroad and a growing totalitarianism at home. In that mood, the technical language of the Kyoto philosophers, as perhaps the major philosophical force in Japan at the time, lost its innocence and even the most abstract notions were overlaid with meanings often far from their authors' intent. That Tanabe chose to deal with questions coinciding with the practical, moral, and religious dimensions of the state philosophy of the day only drew more attention to his writings.

For Tanabe, the logic that keeps a society closed is one that fuses the individual and the specific and thus closes the way to a universal. On the other hand, a logic that opens a society is not brought about by individual minds intuiting universal ideals but by a dialectical opposition of the individual and the specific wherein each enriches the other and opens it to something greater. In identifying the specific as the ethnic society, therefore, he had at the same time to clarify the logical structure of its closure. The root causes of the closure cannot rest in culture or ethnicity themselves, since without them there would be no society at all, closed *or* open. Neither can they lie ultimately in any particular form of social organization or institution, since these are always in a state of flux. Rather, the causes for closure must be sought in the fundamental irrationality of the specific itself.

Tanabe's point is every bit as serious as it sounds. The task of philosophy is to help reason rise above the sociocultural conditions in which it has no choice but to work. Either that, or it has to capitulate to irrationality. Reason and awareness are not bound to social conditions the way unreason and unconsciousness are. The individual mind must find a way to see through the biases that culture and society impose on thought, to grasp a telos deeper than the surface traditions and fashions that drive a society from one generation to the next. And more than that, once it has seen *through* the specificity it must return to see *again* so that it can exercise moral judgment over the direction of society. The philosophical question is not exhausted by rising above the ethnic society or living in isolation from it —the very fact that we are educated in the habits of language and food and clothing make this a pipe dream—but by bringing reason to bear on it.

If there is a fundamental irrationality at the heart of human society that it is our ambivalent duty as free, conscious individuals to overcome, there is also a kind of nonrationality that we have to respect. That is to say, if the specificity of social existence is both a spur to our innate drive to salvation from ignorance and a guarantee that we shall never be saved from it, then we are victims of a cruel and irrevocable law of existence. The only way Tanabe could escape the aporia was to see the nonrational dimension of the specific as pointing beyond itself to a religious dimension.

This brings us to the third step in the logic: the ultimate foundation of specificity is not the being of historical relativity, but absolute nothingness. This step is brought out clearly in his attempt to introduce existentialist ideas of Heidegger and Jaspers, and to relate them to the religious transformation that he saw culminating in the awareness and praxis of absolute nothingness. The cornerstone of his thought he shared with others of the Kyoto school, and it comes simply to this: the immediate reality of the human as a thinking social being, does not ultimately rest on any higher state or form of being but on an absolute nothingness that at once embraces and penetrates the inherent contradictions and relative nothingness at the limits of being. In Tanabe's case, nothingness became the "subject" of the absolute mediation at work in the world of being. As such it was the principle behind the conversion of individuals only because it was also the principle behind the transformation of the sociocultural specificity that gives individuality its immediacy. His language is dense, but clear:

> Insofar as nothingness is nothingness, it is incapable of functioning on its own. Being can function only because it is *not* nothingness.... The individual is mediated by nothingness through a self-negating mediation of the specific in which the being of the specific functions as a nothingness-*in*-being, thus making the individual a being-*in*-nothingness.

In the logic of the specific, then, absolute nothingness appears primarily as the religious dimension to social existence. Tanabe rejected as mere "bias" Bergson's idea that religion is of necessity mystical. For him, religion was always a cooperative *via salvationis* in which the self-awakening of the individual could never be authentic without an accompanying overflow into the moral sphere of social praxis. Even the *via mystica* was always a *via specifica* trod in the midst of the concrete human community. This was the way in which he worked the religious dimension into his understanding of the nation. Furthermore, at least from the time of his logic of the specific, he was consistent in his claim that the function of religion is one of absolute negation.

Religion negates the nation in both a practical and an ontological sense. Practically, it is a way of salvation from the specific, which Tanabe marks with either the Buddhist term for "unconditional acceptance" or his own version "absolute acceptance." Ontologically, it negates not only the nation, but all immediate forms of sociocultural specificity, as well as the self-subsistent being of individuals and the existence of the human race as a universal. In negating all the affirmations of morality, reason, and power that function through the concrete mediation of the individual, the specific, and the generic in human social existence, the negation of religion is an *absolute negation.* As *negation,* it is not so much a denial of the fact of mediation as a denial of the affirmation that the mediation that binds society together is actually the work of the members who make it up. As *absolute,* the negation prevents the practical working out of salvation from being identified with particular structures; this would land the state in some form of theocracy, which for Tanabe was no more than an absolutizing of the specific.

35 THE SPECIFIC AND THE NATION.

These three steps—the ontologizing of the specific, the structure of the closure of the ethnic society, and the religious grounding in absolute nothingness—represent the core of the logic of the specific. There was one more step he took, a step whose consequences would lead him down a path he would later regret.

Although the freedom of the Japanese language to omit distinction between singulars and plurals, together with Tanabe's own failure to give concrete examples, leaves a certain ambiguity; nevertheless, there seems little doubt that the logic of the specific was aimed primarily at the situation in Japan. The immediate problem for Tanabe was how to introduce a process of conversion to a more "open" society. This was the stimulus behind his quest for locating a rational foundation for social existence. On the basis of what we have already seen, we might expect him to diagnose at the lowest level what goes on when the individual and the specific combine to shut out the universal, to study the particular modes of thought this gives rise to, and thus to shed more light on the closure of a society. Instead, throughout the years in which the logic of the specific took shape, roughly 1934 to 1941, Tanabe chose to focus his attention on the highest level of the rationalization of social existence—the modern nation.

Tanabe's concerns with the social situation in Japan at the time are not reason enough for introducing the nation into the logic of the specific. One has to suppose that there are two other factors at work. First, there is the general intellectual concern of his day, inherited from the Meiji period, with establishing the identity of Japan as a nation. The countries of the west, since the time of the French Revolution, had felt the importance of a national identity, which included not only external elements like a national flag and anthem, but also national literature, a *Volkspsychologie*, an interest in local folklore, and so forth. Japan was simply following suit. Second, and not unrelated to this, is the exalted place that Hegel gave to the state in his philosophy. Given Tanabe's commitment to a dialectic of history, there was no way around the question. Somehow the nation was bound to find a place in Tanabe's philosophical standpoint.

At the same time, the logical consistency for the step is not hard to see. The specific, as immediate a reality as it appears to be in the closed society, is really only immediate to the unreflective mind. When the individual takes a critical position against the specific ethnic or racial society, the dialectic between the two comes to consciousness. As long as the interplay remains conscious, it can lead to a mutual transformation without either conquering or silencing the other. For this, neither side can remain an "immediate" reality. Not only can there be no return to the naïveté of the closed society, but the individual cannot simply assume a cosmopolitan position floating freely above the world of the specific. Rather, the specific is "generalized" by becoming rationalized; and at the same time culture, morality, law, and the ideals that underlie them, work as universals to transform a society only by becoming actual in history. Tanabe saw no other way for this dialectic to function than through making the nation a focus of moral reflection and action.

The inclusion of an idea of the nation was not only obvious, he felt, but fit well into the way his thought was developing. If absolute nothingness is not bound by the world of becoming and yet is "at work" in some sense wider than as a rational cement to hold beings together in mutual mediation, that is to say, if in any sense absolute nothingness is engaged in the unfolding of history, then there must be some way to speak of it as incarnating itself in time. Obviously this incarnation cannot take place immediately in individual subjectivity, since this would elevate consciousness beyond the law of absolute mediation. But neither can the Absolute embody itself immediately in the collective memory and modes of thought of a specific race or culture, since this would do away with the very thing whose transformation makes up the advance of history. Nor again is the universal human race a suitable locus for the Absolute to make itself manifest in historical form, since it is no more than an abstract ideal. The one remaining reality that qualified as a blend of the real and the ideal made concrete in time and history was the nation.

Here Tanabe made a crucial step. In a 1939 essay on "The Logic of National Existence" he suggests a view of history as a higher-level dialectic embracing other dialectical relationships. On the one side of this higher dialectic is the relationship between the individual and the specific ethnic, sociocultural environment; the interplay between the two accounts for the concrete relativity of history. On the other side is the nation, which is relative vis-à-vis other nations but absolute vis-à-vis the dialectic of individual and specific. History is thus the interplay of the relationship among nations, each of which is absolute relative to the individuals and the specific social environments they mediate. The nation is thus what he calls a "relative absolute" or "an actualization of the absolute" in the relative world. In this way, the absolute of nothingness is manifest in history at the level of the highest dialectic in the world of being, which has nothing higher to mediate it, namely the nation.

Already from the very first essay in which he introduced the logic of the specific, it is clear that Tanabe would not only see the nation as the embodiment of the specific but as a necessary condition for salvation from the irrationality of the specific and an opening to the ultimate ground of reality. As a relative absolute, it would be the direct mediation to the absolute as such:

> In the sense in which the nation achieves unified form as an absolutely mediated unity of the specific and the individual in religion, the nation is the only absolute thing on earth.

In contrast to so-called primitive or totemic societies, where the individual is absorbed into the group's will to preserve and disseminate its life and being, the modern European nation is built on the Enlightenment ideal of shifting the accent from the group's "will to life" to the "will to reason and morality" of the individuals as the political atoms that make it up. Tanabe saw the nation's essence to consist in a "will to authority" that brings a kind of molecular, rational unity to the whole. Accepting Hegel's idea that "membership in the nation is the highest duty of the individual," Tanabe adds that the essence of being a nation consists in opening up what ethnic specificity had closed, or as he puts it, "elevating its individuals to the status of universal individuals."

In other words, the mere idea of race is able to mediate the dialectic between the universal human race and the concrete individual only in the form of irrational conditions for thought. It is not able to function historically in any other capacity. But when raised to the level of the nation, the individuals of a race are able to bring those irrationalities to light in the course of interacting with other nations, and at the same time to enlighten the irrationalities of other racial groups. This is the sense in which Tanabe reckoned it absolute: it lifts the single race above its relativity to the point that it can function in history as a whole. In this sense it is the mediator of the telos of absolute nothingness in time and space.

In this way, the opening up of society comes to be considered for Tanabe the moral vocation of the nation, whereas Bergson had stepped over the nation to introduce humanity as the generic universal that elevates individuals beyond their instincts and specific societies beyond their self-enclosure. Without the nation, he felt, there was no way to mediate in concrete history the salutary effect of abstract ideas like "human society," "human race," or "world community" on the immediate, specific substrate of ethnic groups. At the same time, without preserving the abstractness of these ideals, like a kind of permanent protestant principle, there was no way to prevent particular nations from simply inflicting their own cultural specificity on others in the name of universal humanity.

Admittedly, Tanabe saw the immediate reality of the specific as only a provisional form given to the social dimension of human existence. Still, he could not conceive of any reformation or transformation taking place outside the concrete structures of particular nations. Thus, opening the closed society required seeing it not only as a nation but also as only *one* nation among many others in the human community. The concrete execution of such an opening of the modes of thought of the ethnic society requires individual will grounded in something larger than itself: "Through service to the nation and submission to the orders of the nation, moral autonomy does not disappear but is rather made possible." Conversely, should a society turn in on itself in totalitarianism and oppression, morality requires that the individual resist it and lead it back to its true destiny as one among the multiple societies that make up universal humanity.

These ideas were maintained consistently throughout his writings on the idea of the nation. In one of his last pieces on the subject, "The Morality of the Nation," published in *Chūōkōron* in 1941, the same year that saw the first of the famous discussions on *The World-Historical Standpoint and Japan* that we will take up later in the book, we read:

> In order for the state to make itself concrete through the mediation of its individual members, it has to give rise to the autonomy of the individual and at the same time unify that autonomy to itself.... Only in a self-conscious autonomy of coexistence in a universal order with other nations, can the nation express its absoluteness.

Tanabe claims that it was his dissatisfaction with Nishida's intuition of a direct and basic unity between the contradictories of individual and human race that drove him back closer to the realities of history and to see the nation as

> *from without* as partaking in mutual cooperation and mutual respect among the various countries united at the level of genus; *within*, fulfilling the desires of each individual; and *within and without*, mediating fulfillment and cooperation and love in the individual.

To base a nation only on racial or cultural specificity, he repeats, is to risk leading it into communism or totemism. Only in the intercommunion of specific states can the human community truly become a concrete reality. In other words, the logic of the specific as such did not lead to the conclusion that the national polity of Japan should be seen either as an alternative ideal to that of the human community or as occupying a central role in that community. Nonetheless, it was to just such a conclusion that he took his new logic. To see this in context, we need to return to the political situation at the time and Tanabe's involvement in it.

36 AN AMBIVALENT NATIONALISM. In September of 1931 Japan's colonial army in Southern Manchuria, impatient with the indecision of their government back home, unilaterally attacked the Chinese garrison in Mukden. Within fifteen months they had assumed control of Manchuria. The aggression not only widened the rift between Japan and China, it also prompted the Russians to a military buildup in Siberia and brought the Japanese government general censure from the nations of the world. This in turn further hardened the extremist elements within Japan in their resolve for military hegemony in Eastern Asia. Step by step they began to tighten their grip on the country's resources, material as well as intellectual.

Tanabe's first direct confrontation with the fascism of the Shōwa period came in 1933 when the government intervened to call for the dismissal of a professor of law, Takigawa Yukitoki, for supposedly dangerous remarks against the state. Tanabe led a small contingency in the Faculty of Letters to oppose the interference as being against academic freedom. The *Chūōkōron* brought the details to the public eye, and by October Iwanami Shigeo had published the account in book form. Given the widespread attention the incident attracted, even though Tanabe had not imposed his own views to any extreme extent, his involvement seems to have aroused the displeasure of Nishida, who also turned down Iwanami's offer for support, fearing to endanger the university as a whole for just this one case. In any event, the affair led Tanabe to seek a philosophical explanation for what takes place when the state exercises its will against the individual.

Two years later, in 1935, Tanabe voiced public opposition against the Ministry of Education's drive to isolate Japanese culture from the west, and the following year argued his case in print in the context of a more pointed assault on the emerging militaristic ideology and a defense of the need for western science. Tanabe is reported to have said that he felt his life was on the line for his remarks. Though this may have overstated the facts, his comments did elicit sharp, *ad hominem,* and immediate accusations of infamy from Minoda Muneki in the pages of *The Japan Principle*, an ultra-rightist magazine founded to defend the emperor system against the inroads of

Marxism and western democracy. Among other things, Tanabe was suspected of providing support to the Marxist revolution. The following month, the magazine printed a similar attack by Matsuda Fukumatsu. Nishida encouraged him not to reply, but once again Tanabe refused the advice and sent his reply to the magazine, where it was printed in May of the following year. In it he stressed the peril of Japan's isolating its intellectual culture from the scientific progress of the rest of the world.

At this same time, we should note, on reading a piece in a German newspaper reporting a speech of Heidegger, who had just joined hands with the Nazis, Tanabe penned a short article entitled "A Philosophy of Crisis or a Crisis of Philosophy?" in which he roundly criticized his former friend for having allowed his philosophy to bow to its destiny of subservience to the state:

> As a philosophy of freedom, German idealism surpassed Greek ontology. It is odd that in the attempt to champion the racial significance of German academia, Heidegger should not take this seriously.... Philosophy cannot, as he thinks, simply resign itself to fate and serve the nation.

The piece, dated 5 September 1933, was published in a leading newspaper of Japan the following month. Whether or not he communicated these sentiments in some other manner directly to Heidegger is not clear. In fact, the only thing we know of his direct contact with Nazi Germany is that in 1941, upon hearing that Jaspers and his wife were in danger from the Nazi persecution, Tanabe intervened with others to secure their safety, an event for which Jaspers expressed his eternal gratitude in a letter some years later.

In any case, within two years Tanabe's philosophical reflections had turned seriously to the question of the state. He was still convinced that a simple stress on subjectivity would not do to assure individual freedom. Something had to be done to locate the reality of the state in the rational scheme of things, and his logic of the specific seemed to offer the right tools.

Meantime, Japan's army was launching the first stages of its fifteen-year campaign in Asia. It was only three months before the incident at Marco Polo Bridge, which triggered all-out war between China and Japan, that he had published his theory of the racially unified society as a specific substratum that mediates the relationship between particular individuals and the universal ideals of the human community. In the first of these essays, published in 1936, he makes the cryptic statement, typical of the ambivalence that would characterize his position throughout most of the war: "Religion does not simply negate war; it clearly ought to excite humanitarians to national questions." Three years later, in 1939, when Japan's writers and intellectuals were still reeling from the loss of freedom of expression, Tanabe applied his new logic to argue that the Japanese nation, with the emperor at its head, has the status of a divine, salvific presence in the world.

Although there is nothing overtly nationalistic at the core logic of the specific as we described it earlier, it was becoming clear how, with a twist here or there, it could serve the purposes of a fascist ideology. Unfortunately, it was Tanabe himself who provided those twists. I left them out of the account above only in order to highlight how really nonessential they are to his basic inspiration, and to concur in Tanabe's later view that the value of the logic of the specific was not erased by the distortions to which it had led. In order to appraise just how far Tanabe was responsible for these distortions, we cannot rely merely on his own assessment, however. We have to let the texts speak for themselves.

What the texts tell us is that however much Tanabe insisted that his idea of the nation as a relative absolute does not imply any particular form of government or even any particular ideal of social structure, he could not avoid reference to participation in politics in general, and eventually reference to participation in the politics of Japan's wartime government. Looking back on these events after the war, he claimed that this is precisely what he did *not* mean by his new logic. We can take Tanabe at his word only on the assumption that he did not really mean what he wrote. His later writings seem to me to support just such a conclusion.

As incurably rationalist as Tanabe was, he was hardly free of the kind of culture-specific and epoch-specific irrationalities his logic of the specific wanted to bring to light. In the same way that Kant hammered out his transcendental categories unaware of the limitations of Newtonian physics, which he considered an absolute for reason, so, too, Tanabe accepted the ideas of race and nation as the absolute categories of the specific in history. The point of his transference of this absoluteness to the emperor in the case of Japan was precisely to lift the nation beyond identification with any particular political party or faction of the military. It is not the emperor as such that he thought absolute, nor even the imperial see. Rather, the emperor is the *symbol* of the absoluteness of the nation. For it is always the nation as such and not any particular symbol that is the condition for the possibility of overcoming the bane of racial specificity. In this regard, Tanabe was in fact misunderstood, though the blame does not lie entirely with his readers, as we shall see.

In fact it was here that he took a step that was fatal but really unnecessary, if not outright inconsistent with the principles of his logic: he raises the "relative absolute" of his own historical nation above others. Later he would try to backpedal and claim that this elevation was true only for the Japanese, and that even they had misunderstood it to give them a right to lord it over other nations. But the step had been made, and it was made in full public view.

To give one of the most concrete examples of this step, Tanabe argues that the Japanese nation cannot base its morality on principles imported from the Judaeo-Christian myth of the west but must turn to its own indigenous Buddhist roots. In place of a moral ideal incarnated in the person of Jesus, he recommends an eastern ethic that sees the nation as the embodiment, or *nirmāṇakāya*, of the Buddha in history. In the process, we see him leap to a startling conclusion in an uncharacteristic breach of logic:

> My philosophy of the state may be said to possess a structure that radicalizes the dialectical truth of Christianity by liberating it, as it were, from the confines of myth and by putting the nation in the place of Christ.... Such a comparison, I think, helps better explain what I mean by asserting that our nation is the supreme archetype of existence and that, as a union of objective spirit and absolute spirit, it manifests the absolute as a Buddha-embodiment.

There are no formal, rational grounds in Tanabe's thought to warrant the conclusion that the Japanese nation so viewed deserved a place of honor as a "supreme archetype" in the larger scheme of things or that service to the emperor is the ideal way for Japan to become an "open" society. According to his own logic, the community of the human race is to be made up of a community of nations that have found a way to transcend their specificity without transcending time and culture. Each nation may come about as an instance of the generic universal, but nothing in the logic of the specific allows any one instance to become an archetype for the others. It is as if Tanabe were quoting himself out of context.

Nishida, for his part, found all of this disconcerting in the extreme, not the least of all because Tanabe was still encasing his views in the language of the ongoing battle with him. In 1940 Nishida is reported to have snapped to a common friend, "This Tanabe stuff is completely fascist!" Be that as it may, in publishing his views, sound though many of them may be in the abstract, Tanabe let loose a brood of ideas that seemed to flock right into the nests of the ultranationalists in a way that Nishida's thought never explicitly did. This seems to have confused Tanabe himself. At the time that Tanabe was framing the core essays of his logic of the specific, Nishida was arguing that the mutual determination of the individual and the world was manifest biologically in a specific race and that this in turn, through the contractual relationship among individuals and between the individual and the race, forms the *Gesellschaft* into a civil society. Moreover, Nishida had stated clearly that "we become concrete personalities through the state," and further hints that each species is a kind of world, and that under certain conditions these specific worlds cross swords with each other. He even described the state as the concrete form of the ethical substance in which each individual can fulfill himself. Nothing Tanabe could say criticizing Nishida's goal of the harmonious fusion in the state of the many in the one as having effectively eliminated the basis for resistance against the state seemed to matter to Nishida or those in his circle.

Rather than retreat to the realm of the abstract where he was at home, Tanabe aggravated the situation in 1943 by addressing in print students on their way to the front. Tanabe told his readers that they all knew the day that was upon them would come, and that "this late hour is not the time to waver over the problem of life and death." He pauses for a moment to consider the wider significance of the government's unprecedented enlistment of hundreds of thousands of students, insisting that refinement of thought and cultivation of the arts are also "indispensable elements in all-out war." But bowing to necessity—and without a thought to his earlier criticisms of Heidegger for having done the same—he sets the question aside and instead encourages the young recruits to enter the army as representatives of Japan's intelligentsia. I quote from the core of the piece because it contrasts so sharply with the style Tanabe is better known for:

> War today, as all-out war, is not exhausted in mere fighting in the narrow sense of the term. It is hard to expect final victory without engaging intelligence and technology through and through. Moreover, in order to demonstrate positively the results of the fighting, there is a need to back up with deep thinking and high insight both the benevolent improvement of culture for the local races involved as well as the moralization of the everyday life of those engaged with the war effort. This has become for us common sense....
>
> But to ward off misunderstanding, I ask you to pay particular attention to this: I am not saying you should enlist in the army with the aim of intellectualizing the army. I am only encouraging your self-awareness by speaking of the natural and inevitable results....
>
> First you are to learn the spirit of the Imperial Army, ...which is none other than the quintessential flowering of the spirit of the nation. To take up the spirit of Japan as a member of the armed forces is the gateway by which a Japanese becomes a Japanese.... Aware of your heavy responsibility as military cadets, take the lead in breaking through the pass between life and death. Actualize the spirit of the Imperial Army, which sees that living or dying is only for the sake of the Sovereign.... In this way, by serving the honorable calling of the Sovereign as the one whose person brings together God and

> country, you will share in the creation of the eternal life of the state. Is this not truly the highest glory?

At the time the question was rhetorical for Tanabe.

37 CRITIQUES OF TANABE'S NATIONALISM. A small resistance of thinkers, Marxist as well as Christians, were quick to identify Tanabe's new "logic" as cut from the same cloth as the rhetoric of the ultranationalist government. Once the war was lost and the government disgraced, the ranks of the critics swelled liberally, and the same ideological fever that had sent the country blindly to the battlefields was turned mercilessly against the errant intellectuals who had supposedly given substance to many of the slogans of mass deception. Leading scholars of the Kyoto school were relieved of their posts as part of a wider purge. Tanabe, who had already retired five months before the end of the war in 1945, was labeled a "racist," a "Nazi," and a "fascist."

Already during the war, charges of militarism had been raised. In a 1942 book entitled *State and Religion*, Nanbara Shigeru linked Tanabe's logic of the specific with the racism of the Nazis. Speaking with a courage that led Ienaga Saburō to speak of him as "our pride for having protected the smoldering wick of conscience in the Japanese academic world," Nanbara ended his book with a direct attack on Tanabe, whom he singles out by name for having put Japanese philosophy at the service of the quest for the "uniqueness" of the Japanese spirit. Though Nanbara's is not an especially sophisticated argument, it is a good indication of how those opposed to the wartime aggressions read the writings of the Kyoto philosophers.

In particular, Nanbara sees the ideas of absolute nothingness and absolute dialectic as "marred by the attempt to revitalize the historical content of eastern culture on the basis of racial awareness." In Tanabe's reliance on Buddhism, in particular Zen, "religion, philosophy, and the state are united in a way different from the west." For Nanbara, Tanabe's notion of the "absolute society," which distills species and individual, through a process of mutual negation, into a nation that makes concrete the generic universal, amounts to a simple "faith in the nation" based on a "belief in dialectics":

> "Absolute nothingness" is elevated to the status of a supreme faith, the source into which all things flow back through the self-negation of the individual.

The chief stumbling block for Nanbara, as a Christian, lay in the fact that Tanabe tried to explain the nation as the incarnation of the absolute in time, in effect conceding it the role that Hegel had given to Christ. Not only does this eliminate the *ought* from history (which Nanbara, like others of Tanabe's critics, attributed to his Hegelian leanings), but it also does away with the critical distance between reality and our perceptions of it. For Nanbara, Kantian dualism was preferable in that it maintained the transcendence of the divine order over the human. His sensitivities are further offended by Tanabe's attempt to twist the dialectic of the Christian myth of incarnation to the point that the Japanese nation would be a mediator of salvation in the world order, thus reducing the idea of God to a logical negation:

> In such an eastern pantheism, the race is elevated even higher than it is in Nazism, and the rationalizations for the spirituality of "race" and "nation" are debased still further. Given the way the idea of the racial state is thriving today and the religious foundations have weakened, what a broad and profound foundation such an idea offers compared with the Nazi ideal of the totalitarian state!

The fact that Nanbara's attack was not limited to Tanabe's logic of the specific was not lost on the Kyoto-school philosophers. In reviewing the book some months after it came out, Nishitani Keiji recognized it as one of the most important religious works of the year, but criticized it for "leaving one feeling alienated from historical realities." The problem for Nishitani lay not in the distance that Nanbara had set up between the religiously ideal and the politically actual, but in what he saw as its "general failure to take into account the subjective element," in its failure to point to just who—or what—is supposed to bear the burden of history. Clearly this was not a task for "humanity" as such. Nanbara's critique of Tanabe is passed over without comment.

As for Tanabe himself, he seems to have been deeply touched by the explicit attack. In a later essay on the logic of the specific, he alludes to the critique and thanks its author, without alluding to the contents or to Nanbara's closing plea for saving the true universality of Christianity so that it can help Japan find its place in the world.

More severe criticisms, it comes as no surprise, issued from the Marxist quarter, where the clash of ideologies was at its rudest and most inflexible. If the dialectic of absolute mediation gradually became a kind of tacit assumption for Tanabe, the socialist critique of the state-individual relationship through an analysis of class struggle and control of the means of production was no less a tacit assumption for Japan's Marxists. But there is more at work here than a simple disagreement over principles. Tanabe had attempted a rather feeble critique of socialist philosophy that failed to convince the Marxists but that had some influence in the prestigious circles of philosophy and may have contributed to the persecution of philosophers sympathetic to Marxist thought during the war. The counterattack that Yamada Munemutsu represents needs to be read, at least in part, as retaliation for those events.

While the war was still in progress, Yamada Munemutsu, then a student in Kyoto's Department of Philosophy, was given special permission from the munitions factory where he had been mobilized to work, to attend Tanabe's "Metanoetics" lectures. Looking back over his notes at the time, he finds that he was not convinced by Tanabe's assertion that his only failure was a failure of strength. Yamada felt there were problems in the philosophy itself that kept its epistemology from facing social realities head on. In his book-length critique, however, Yamada does not take his own point seriously—or even mention the notes he took at the time. All nuance is eclipsed by his conviction that Tanabe was not just philosophically incomplete but also politically fascist.

Yamada basically accepts the idea of a shift from the liberalism and individualism—or "culturism"—of the Taishō era to the social awareness and politicization of the Shōwa period. He finds taints of Nishida's culturism in Miki Kiyoshi's humanism and humanistics, in Kōyama Iwao's study of cultural patterns, in Kimura Motomori's expressionism, in Tanigawa Tetsuzō's cultural theory, and the like. In contrast, the core of Tanabe's critique of Nishida, he felt, lay in his rejection of this culturism. Simply put, the racism of Tanabe's logic of the specific was a natural result of his having been "born and baptized" in bourgeois society. Instead of establishing a link between the universal and the particular as Nishida had done, Tanabe's stress on the nation as the "specificity" through which transformation actually takes place in the historical process provoked a conflict between the two thinkers. This conflict in turn added fuel to the rise of the militaristic ideology that lay behind the Manchurian Incident of 1931, the military coup of 1936, the Sino-Japanese War of 1937, and eventually the Pacific War that began with the attack on Pearl Harbor.

Yamada does not provide very much detail as to just how these connections are made, but assures us that Tanabe's logic was more appealing to the militaristic ideologues than Nishida's idea of the "self-determination of history," which kept the reality of history from being identified with any particular nation. On the positive side, Tanabe's position cut closer to the bone and mobilized the Kyoto school as a whole to come to terms with what was going on. Unfortunately, they accepted the standpoint of Japanism and a nationalism based on the emperor system as a platform from which to resist militarism to the right and Marxism to the left. In Yamada's view, within this commonly accepted nationalism,

> Tanabe stood at the right, seeking a more classical interpretation of the state, while Miki and Nishida himself stood at the left, aiming at limiting the nation. At the initial stage, the centrist faction was made up of Mutai, Kōsaka, and Shimomura, followed by Yanagida later and perhaps Kimura. Still later, Kōsaka, Nishitani, and Kōyama shifted over to the right to advance a philosophy of all-out war, while Shimomura preserved rationalism in the "overcoming Modernity" discussions, and after the war Mutai and Yanagida gradually stepped over into socialism.

As Yamada sees it, Miki tried to limit nationalism through a kind of globalism, and Nishida, agreeing with him but more in direct response to Tanabe, worked on a logic of the historical process in conjunction with the centrists Mutai, Shimomura, and Kimura. As Konoe Fumimaro, who presided over Japan's transformation into a "national defense state," steered the ship of state closer and closer to the Pacific War, the relations among the three factions changed shape:

> Aggravations between Nishida and Miki brought about a change in the Kyoto school as a whole, with the centrists shifting to the right. Miki's comments on current events dried up while those in the center who had turned right—Kōsaka, Nishitani, and Kōyama—spoke out on current events. Nishida, as if one possessed, argued various particular points from the fundamental standpoint of the self and came out with one philosophical collection after the other. Miki sunk into a logic concerned with the power of ideas.

Determined to keep Tanabe at the opposite extreme from Nishida, Yamada does his best to shift the blame for the fate of Nishida's theory of "moral energy" to disciples who had misunderstood their teacher's aim of limiting the state. No such slack is given for Tanabe, who is made to stand alone at the far right.

There is far too much to sort out here without a careful look at the writings and records of the time, but what is clear is that Yamada gradually leaves his sources as he tries to draw the bigger picture. He returns to the texts with Tanabe's *Metanoetics*, which he sets aside summarily as a "supermetaphysics" fabricated by someone caught in a pinch between his ideal of the nation and the stubborn realities of nationalism at work. For Yamada, it seems to have been no more than the final, parting gesture of the right wing of the Kyoto school as it strides off haughtily into complete philosophical irrelevance.

38 CRITIQUES OF TANABE'S POLITICAL NAÏVETÉ. A second sort of criticism, no less severe, was intent on showing Tanabe simply to have been incompetent to pass judgment on matters of state. A certain abstractness and distance from the real world in Tanabe's thinking and lifestyle, the argument goes, not only made his ideas easy prey for political ideologues but also clouded Tanabe's own perception of the events going on around him. Umehara Takeshi offers himself as a representative of those who felt themselves cheated by the philosophers at Kyoto—first herded off to war and then brought back to the pure heights of speculation as if nothing had happened.

Umehara recalls in retrospect that the Kyoto philosophers filled a need for many of the young students of his generation. After the Manchurian Incident, it was only a matter of time before the whole country would be at war. All the efforts made at sitting in Zen meditation and studying existential philosophy were supposed to help them find a standpoint beyond life and death, but none of this was any match for the raw anxiety of young students facing the prospect of being sent to war. Only a philosophy that could prepare them to die for a cause would do, and eventually this was what their teachers gave them.

Umehara places himself among the philosophy students of the time who knew too much of modern thought to be taken in by the official "imperial philosophy" and for whom the idea of the emperor as a living absolute divinity beyond criticism was the "supreme insult" to their intelligence. At the same time, Nishida and Tanabe were a "godlike presence" that lent credibility to what their principal disciples were saying in class. For example, the recondite and mystical philosophy of Nishitani, as difficult as it was to understand, at least succeeded in communicating that the moral thing to do was to sacrifice the self to the fascist state.

Not without a certain animus of regret, Umehara admits that the Kyoto philosophy of a "world-historical standpoint" offered an answer to the question that he and others like him had at the time. Indeed, after the war he returned to study under the very people who had forged that philosophy—until an edict from the Occupation Forces that had them purged—and who continued to advance its truth in spite of the circumstances of Japan's defeat at the hands of the west. At the time, Tanabe and Nishida remained the chief gods in the Kyoto pantheon, and every attempt to correct or advance their philosophy was based on the assumption of continuity with their absolute dialectic. Umehara, on whom much of Tanabe's subtlety was admittedly lost, describes his position as a barren middle ground between existentialism and Marxism that forfeits the very elements it is trying to relate dialectically:

> Existential philosophy is the standpoint of the individual. But the individual that is not mediated by the specific—that is, by society—is abstract and without concrete actuality. Thus existential philosophy must be mediated negatively by society. At the same time, Marxism is a standpoint centered on society and fails adequately to establish the individual. But a society that does not create free individuals is an evil universal, and therefore socialism must be mediated negatively by the individual.

Aside from the fact that Umehara is content to wrap Nishida's logic of absolute self-identity in the same bundle, this is not an inaccurate picture of Tanabe's position as far as it goes. In any case, the abstractness of it all was too much for Umehara, who found himself longing for something closer to his own lingering preoccupation with the problem of death that he carried back with him from the war. The appearance of Tanabe's *Philosophy as Metanoetics*, not to mention the apparent idol-worship that surrounded its somber call for religious conversion, far from righting the wrong that Tanabe's philosophy had done, in the end did little more for Umehara than gloss over the naïveté of its engagement with history.

Contrasting sharply with Umehara's self-serving criticism is the accusation of Tanabe by the Tokyo philosopher Katō Shūichi, in more objective but no less damning language, of a simplicity unsuited to the seriousness of the questions he was dealing with. In fact, Katō summarily lumps the rationalist Kyoto philosophers together with the irrational "romanticists" of the age as offering support from opposite quarters for the Japanese invasion of China and the Pacific War.

For Katō, Tanabe was at home discoursing on the pure abstractions of logic, but "when he spoke of the meaning of Japan in world history, it was pure nonsense." Thus, when Tanabe applied his logic of the specific to the actual political situation and referred to the emperor as Japan's symbolic way of transcending totalitarianism; or again, when he credited service to the emperor with breaking Japan out of the closed, tribal society and into the wider human community, Katō sees him as simply out of touch with the events that were transpiring around him.

Tanabe did realize, of course, that proof of these applications of his logic of the specific could not come from within the logic itself but would have to rest on objective fact. Tanabe's version of what constitutes such evidence, Katō concludes, amounts to this: "The majority of the people today are of one mind about retaining national polity through continuing the emperor system." For Katō, not only was the idea of retaining the unity of the state through its identification with the emperor "pure fantasy," but Tanabe should have seen that the "majority" of which he spoke was no less a fantasy, planted in the minds of people by a half century of education since the Meiji period. He concludes that both during the war and after, Tanabe was out of touch with the real world. His words cut with a bitter air of sarcasm:

> Tanabe's logic is a technique for justifying the ideas of the "majority of the people" in a given age. With no other interpretation of reality than "the majority of the people," the experience of reality is no more than so much barbershop banter. It begins with a Sanba-like experience of "the world of the baths," followed by dialectics, and then by the unity of opposites in nothingness. Tanabe's philosophy, in a word, is a philosophy of dialectical bath-talk. Taking a dialectics from the west and the baths from the Edo period, it united east and west in nothingness. On one hand, it appeals only to the head; on the other it appeals to raw and earthy sentiments. The result is a unity of body and spirit in the self-unity of absolute contradictories.

Passing over the introduction of Nishida's vocabulary into the discussion, what is clear is that this does not qualify as imperialism of the usual political sort, nor does Katō claim that it does. But neither does it qualify as the sort of reasoning that political philosophy expects. The simple fact for Katō is that Tanabe remained aloof from the facts, seeing them from the distant mists of the philosopher's podium, where, the implication is, the simple facts of life could not oblige him to review his assumptions.

Perhaps the most sympathetic of Tanabe's critics is Ienaga Saburō, whose thoroughgoing study argues that Tanabe's relationship with nationalism alternated between resistance and cooperation, until in the end the pattern was broken in a final act of repentance. Ienaga's mustering of the facts on the one hand, and his decision to suspend judgment on the accuracy of Tanabe's various philosophical critiques on the other, lead him to reject a simple conclusion. This alone sets him apart from most of Tanabe's other critics.

Laying out before him the full range of the texts of Tanabe, Ienaga's conclusions bear citing at length to conclude our account of Tanabe's critics:

> Acknowledging the rationality of the state, Tanabe did not oppose the current state head-on. He did not step forward and fight to stop its policies. For this reason, he does not deserve to be included in the small number of those who, from a variety of intellectual persuasions, risked the little they had in wartime and continued to resist. But at least in the early stages of the fifteen

> years of war and from within the sacred precincts of academia, Tanabe did show courage to the point of publicly issuing a severe criticism, limited though it was, against the state authority run wild.
>
> ....
>
> Tanabe's philosophy in 1935, seen as the wartime thought of an intellectual, shines out proudly, as rightly it should, but there is another side to the picture that cannot be forgotten. Subjectively sincere though he was, there is an objective tragedy to Tanabe that cannot escape severe criticism.
>
> ....
>
> Beginning with a resistance that tried to correct, from within, a military policy that was heading blindly down the path to extreme irrationalism and inhumanity, by and large his efforts did not prevent him from cooperating in such a way as to justify philosophically the very things he was set against.

In the end, the ambivalence of Ienaga's verdict seems to rest on two factors. On the one hand, at the time the logic of the specific was being formed, the political drive to reinforce national unity was already a fact to be reckoned with. No simple cause-and-effect relationship can be drawn from one to the other. On the other, the strongest opponents to Japan's military adventures looked at weaker, compromising opponents, and of course at *ex post facto* critics, as collaborators. Given the courage it took the former to speak out, one hesitates to dismiss their judgment too quickly.

39 RESPONSE TO THE CRITICISMS.

To understand the extent of Tanabe's repentance, we first need to see the extent to which he did not repent but merely "clarified" or "enhanced" previous positions.

Tanabe did not take well to the criticisms of nationalism and totalitarianism that reached him. The accusations understandably hurt him, as it did others in the Kyoto school. As early as 1937 he composed a first defense of the logic of the specific in which he addresses the criticisms in a general fashion:

> My view, which at first glance appears to be no more than an extreme nationalism, is in no way simply and directly an irrational totalitarianism or racialism. Rather, it is like a "self-sacrifice"-*in*-"self-realization" or a unity-*in*-freedom whose aim is to build up the nation in the form of a subjective realization of the whole through the spontaneous cooperation of each member.

In fairness to Tanabe, it must be said that, for all his attention to the nation as a way of opening up a closed society, he had never denied his initial position that the nation shares with the ethnic closed society that essential and permanent presence of *nonrationality* that is the mark of the specific. It is quite another matter whether and to what extent he applied that insight to the political situation at the time or conveniently ignored it, but this is not a question he puts himself in hindsight. In the attempt to preserve the soundness of the pure theory of the logic of the specific, it was enough for him to cite his own earlier ideas together with certain adjustments that might protect it from the previous excesses, without mentioning those excesses.

We see this clearly in an essay on "The Dialectic of the Logic of the Specific," in which he speaks of the period just before the virtual blackout of philosophical publications he maintained between 1941 and 1946:

> During the years 1934 and 1940 I pursued a study of a dialectic logic that I called the "logic of the specific" and by means of which I tried to explain logically the concrete structure of the society of the nation. My motive was to take up the philosophical question of racialism that was emerging at the time. Together with a critique of the liberalism that had come to dominate us at the time, I rejected a so-called totalitarianism based on a simple racialism. Mediating by mutual negation the race that formed the substrate of the latter and the individual that was the subject of the former, I took a standpoint of absolute mediation as substrate-*in*-subject, subject-*in*-substrate and thought to discover a rational foundation for the nation as a practical unity of the real and the ideal.

Leaving aside the technicalities, the passage makes it clear that Tanabe wants to present himself as an enemy of nationalism or racialism from the start, and that for reasons grounded in his logic of the specific. What he fails to mention is that his logic had undergone a rather important shift as a result of the war experience. Where before he had characterized the state in Buddhist terms as an "absolute incarnation," he now refers to it as a "republic" whose ultimate purpose is to serve not its members as a principle of unity, but as what Buddhist doctrine calls an "expedient means" for a higher religious end. In the end, he had to find a way to distance himself from the identification of the nation as the salvation of the realm of the specific.

The key to this step appears in an invigorated contrast between the positive and negative dimensions of the specific. Negatively, as before, the specificity of the sociocultural substratum is said to limit the individual, closing off the will to moral action in the name of ideals coming from outside of the ethnic group. Its totality is nonrational, opposing all who oppose it with the aim of mediating it through rational reflection, presenting itself as superior precisely because it is immediate and unreflected reality. Positively, however, it is also now said to be the foundation for culture, which arises among the members of a society through a process of education. In this sense, the unreflected immediacy of the specific society is transfigured into a conscious and mutual mediation among its individuals. In place of earlier emphasis on the nation in contrast to the oppressive tendencies of a merely ethnic or racial identity, the positive dimension reemerges in the context of a moral culture somehow seen to be superior to, though not exclusive of, political obligations to the nation. His claim is that people concentrated on the *extensive* side of the specific—namely, its definition as a particular racial class—and ignored the *intensive* aspect, which is that it is the necessary locus of all change in history and the condition for the possibility of redemption from ignorance and self-will. He gives two reasons for insisting that the specific be included to mediate the way between universal ideals and particular individuals:

> In the first place, the society of a nation, by opposing the individual, binds and limits the individual through its authority. In its specific customs and laws it embodies specificities which can be attested to neither by the appeal to individual conscience nor in the light of the universal principles of humanity.... I could not help considering its reality as something that I could neither deny nor idealize. It is a dynamic reality that has the power of opposing and negating my will.
>
> In the second place... it is the ground wherein the basis of my own life is to be found. If necessary, my existence should be sacrificed to it. The species is not only a reality that transcends my own existence. Insofar as I of myself am converted into the mediation of absolute nothingness through the negation of myself, the species also thereby loses its nature of opposition to me....

If there is rationality in the sociocultural specificity that mediates a relationship between universal humanity and individual human beings, it would not do to chalk this up to the mere fact that nations exist with particular governments. Rational attempts to create government and to rule by moral or religious ideals were always for Tanabe an imposition of human reason, not the working of an ineluctable law of nature. The interplay between the individual and society was simply too varied, too vital, to be fully rationalized. Quite the contrary, as the living soul of a people, the specific substratum that bound a people together into a sociocultural unit was not only *irrational* in the sense of being unreasonable or imperfectly reflected, it was also *nonrational* in the sense of posing immediate limits to reason.

Tanabe never compromised his abiding distrust of the tendency of the specific toward herd thinking, collective superstition, and simply sloppy thinking. Nothing in his writings backs down from his belief in the irrevocable inhumanity of simple blind obedience to habits of thought inherited in the structures of language or cultural mores. Never one to honor common sense unduly, Tanabe located the tendency to think badly in the group and the overcoming of that tendency in private discipline. This was part of the original sense of the word *specificity* in his first essays on the subject, and appeared again in redoubled force in the *Metanoetics*, where he announced that the irrationality of the specific was something he had personally "suffered" and hence hard to explain to those who lacked the experience of wartime Japan. The disenchantment at waking up to one's own inability to critique collective patterns of thought taking shape in one's own time is, of course, a common enough experience, and belongs as much to the victors of the war as to the defeated.

At the same time, revaluing the nonrationality of the specific seems to have drawn his attention to elements in vernacular wisdom and common sense that limit our attempts to be rational and give them a practical and objective raison d'être in time and space that mere private reflection cannot. No doubt old age and the approach of death aided this positive appreciation of the nonrational side of the specific substratum. Together, if it is not out of place for me to say so, they help us to understand the unaccustomed tinge of piety one runs across in his later work.

In late writings the religious meaning of mediation gets stronger and clearer in proportion as the nationalistic side pales and fades into the background. Specific society, insofar as it closes itself off from the community of other specific societies, is seen as the self-alienation of the generic unity of absolute nothingness. Religiously, the specific is the locus for the enlightened engagement in the world, where absolute nothingness works to save the members of a society through mutual love and cooperation. "As the mediator of the totality of nothingness in the world of being, the individual becomes nothing and thereby becomes the expedient means for mutual instruction and salvation."

But the role of religion in working for the self-awareness of generic unity is not only to bind the individuals within a specific society together but to open them to the wider world outside of their own community. In the same way that Tanabe adopts the Christian symbol of the *communio sanctorum* to speak of the relations among awakened individuals, there is at least a hint that he had the Christian idea of the specific "local church" in mind when speaking of the religious dimension of the nation in relation to the ideal "universal church" of the entire human family. In this scheme the nation loses the character of simple "immediacy" that Tanabe had given it earlier and in its place becomes simply an "expedient means" for working out a salvation that draws one across specific boundaries.

In spite of this reorientation of the logic of the specific, and despite his insistence that "culture worship... is a symptom of the decadence of a culture," it is surprising to see that Tanabe never recanted his earlier attempts to elevate the Japanese emperor religiously to the status of "avatar of absolute nothingness." At the height of Japan's transformation into a military state, Tanabe envisioned the emperor rising up symbolically out of the nation of mutually mediated beings to represent the higher reality in whose power all beings are ultimately joined one to another. His motives for repeating this idea, substantially unchanged, as late as 1947 are hard to fathom. At most we can say that as Tanabe's religious reflections drove his logic of the specific further and further away from the idea of the nation, they also overshadowed his curious attachment to finding a place of honor for the emperor in the logic.

We may note a passage from a 1946 essay on "The Urgent Task of Political Philosophy," which appeared just two months after *Metanoetics*, to show how Tanabe clung to the monarchical model as the guarantee of political unity in a social democracy:

> The emperor is the embodiment of the ideal of the unity of the people as a whole. Only nothingness is able to unify things that stand in opposition; simple being cannot do it. The absolute inviolability of the emperor is a function of transcendent nothingness. Thus understood, the symbolic presence of the emperor should be seen as the principle that unifies through absolute negation both democracy and the opposition that it contains.

At the same time, he accepts the demand of the west that the emperor acknowledge, to the people of Japan and to other countries, responsibility for the war, and does one better. He calls for a symbolic gesture of unity with the people—he did not dare to call it a metanoesis, though that is what he had in mind—that would show the emperor's share in their suffering:

> It would be a good thing for the emperor to embrace a state of poverty as a symbol of absolute emptiness.... The truth of the gospel, that he who seeks to have his life will lose it, and he who loses his life will find it, is the very heart of the dialectic in which being and having are nothing and emptiness is everything. Is it out of place for a subject to suggest such an insight to his sovereign?

As we will see presently, Tanabe would in fact take steps to reach the emperor more directly.

From the hindsight of the historian, the logic of the specific may be said to have opened a new stage in Tanabe's thought after the war, bridging his early interest in the dialectic and his later turn to religion. But to Tanabe himself, it was anything but a bridge. It was a groping in the dark for an answer to the spirit of the age, an answer that could not rest on the assurance that it was leading him just where he wanted to go. In the end, it did not. Still, Tanabe's postwar writings on the logic of the specific show that he did not accept the possibility that something had gone wrong in the logic itself. They did, however, reorient the manifestation of absolute nothingness away from the nation and closer to a nonpolitical, Buddhist-Christian "compassion-*in*-love." At no time did he repudiate the logical status he had given the nation as a universal relative to other universals, but neither did he explicitly look to it any longer as a concrete realization of the ethical substance of history. Because he did not address this question directly in his self-criticism, the reorientation meant less of an advance for the logic of the specific itself than a retreat back into a safer level of abstraction, leaving him free to concentrate on more personal, existential questions. That religion occupied his principal attentions in his declining years and that he withdrew into virtual isolation to do his writing is hardly to be wondered at.

40 REPENTANCE. In a public act of repentance issued during the final stages of the Pacific War, Tanabe acknowledged his lack of strength to speak out against what he knew in his heart was wrong. In his crowning philosophical work, *Philosophy as Metanoetics,* he called for a complete overhaul of the notion of philosophy, which had betrayed itself in opting for expedience over truth. To his critics, this eleventh hour call for a "metanoia" to purge philosophy of its tainted innocence was viewed as courageous only in the sense that a dive from a burning ship can still be an act of courage for one who cannot swim. And indeed, one looks through that work in vain for any admission of guilt for particular actions or statements he had made. But we may point to two such instances of self-criticism in order to place that work in a better perspective.

The first took the form of one last attempt at practical action, where his refusal to part with former ideas takes a curious turn. In 1945 Tanabe, already retired to the mountains of Karuizawa, wrote what was to be his last letter to Nishida. In it he laid bare his genuine concern for the future of Japan and the emperor system. Given his idea of the emperor as a symbol of absolute nothingness on the one hand and the difficult conditions that had fallen on the population at large on the other, Tanabe proposed that initiatives be taken before the arrival of the occupying forces to ward off the impending deposition. Concretely, he suggested that the emperor publicly renounce all possessions associated with his position and return them, in the form of a salvific offering, to the Japanese people. In so doing the emperor would embody the Buddhist principle of nothingness—"without a single thing"—and perhaps prevail on the west to leave the emperor system intact.

In highly formal prose, Tanabe asked Nishida for permission to communicate his plan to the emperor as representing Nishida's own views. His letter reads in part:

> The danger our nation finds itself in today is unlike anything in the past, and like you I am most anxious about it. There is no need repeating that without clear thinking nothing can save us. I am an old and powerless man in a weak frame, and as always full of my own opinions. But I cannot repress the hope that perhaps there is something in those opinions that might help to save the country. Once I have expressed them to you and heard your criticisms, if there be something of truth to be had in my plan, I would like to ask your power to help see it realized....
>
> With your kind leave, I would like whatever you find useful to be presented to Prime Minister Konoe, and from there have it brought to Takamatsu no Miya [the emperor's younger brother] for handing over to the emperor. Under normal circumstances, such a request would be unreasonable, but the anxieties of the moment make time of the essence. I am convinced that whatever may come of it all, there is something here of service to the emperor and the nation, and that steps should be taken to pursue its realization. I know this is asking a great deal, but I would be grateful if you would give this matter your serious consideration.

Kōyama Iwao, who in the main agreed with Tanabe's idea, went to Tokyo in June of 1945 to start the process. He first consulted with Yabe Teiji, whose diary mentions the visit by Kōyama. Apparently there was a consensus, as later entries in the diary speak of the need for "extreme steps for the very foundations of a genuine national community," of the "fatal error of separation of the imperial household from the people if the future of Japan's group unity is to be saved," and of "the unthinkability of overlooking confidence in the nation's internal system and the moral strength of the Japanese race."

In the end, there was no time to put the plan into action and it came to naught, although Tanabe's views on the emperor system were eventually communicated directly to the emperor by the minister of education.

Actually, the idea of having Nishida collaborate in his plan was doomed from the start, as there was talk among certain military officials of having both him and Konoe arrested. In his reply to Tanabe of 20 May Nishida wrote (in friendlier prose) his agreement that "there is no other way for the imperial household to get out of the situation," indicating at the same time that he was aware of the danger to his own person. As for Konoe, Nishida remarked that he considered him a man of "sufficient insight" but lacking the clout to do anything in the present circumstances. The rest of the politicians he dismissed as "awfully weak." A month later Nishida died.

A second example appears in a 1956 essay titled "Memories of Kyoto." In it Tanabe takes the same phrase that he used to close his remarks to the students being shipped off to war, "highest glory," and uses it to describe the teacher who is able to embrace in the classroom a great number of students "burning with the love of truth." The connection between the two, which rather leaps out at one today, was probably lost on most of his readers at the time. The content of the article leaves little doubt that it was more than coincidence.

Tanabe admits that his own experience of the highest glory had not been without hardships. The perennial task of philosophy does not consist in transmitting accumulated knowledge but in reassuring the love of truth. This demands a special relationship of mutual criticism between teacher and student for which reason and not rank provides the basis. He thinks back to the waves of socialist thought that had beat against the walls of academia and fired the imagination of Japan's young intellectuals, admitting that for him personally it had been a test of his commitment to philosophy.

In this context, Tanabe acknowledges his sympathy for the theoretical consistency of socialist thought and its demand for social justice, and even concedes that to some extent it answered the demand for a philosophy of social justice. What he resisted, he says, was the introduction of politics into the philosophy classroom, not to mention that "reactionary thinking" and irrationalism that were used against those like himself who resisted reducing everything to class struggle. With the Manchurian Incident in 1931, things grew still more complicated. On the one hand, the intellectual confrontation with socialist thinking grew more intense; on the other, the government began to step up its monitoring of teaching at public universities. Together, these two forces threatened the existence of the rational forum that philosophy depends on. In these circumstances, Tanabe says that he opted to focus on classical German philosophical texts and not to take up the vital political issues of the day, in order the better to face the basic existential questions of philosophy. Looking back at this decision he writes:

> In the face of the gradually worsening pressures of the Second World War, and the ever-increasing strict control of thought, I was too faint-hearted to resist positively, and more or less had no choice but to be swept up in the tide of the times. On this point I cannot reproach myself deeply enough.

The thought of the students rushing to the battlefields, some of them to die there under the banner of a "blind militarism," leaves him, he says, with "a strong sense of regret for my own responsibility. I can only hang my head low and confess my sin." Here again, the connection to his earlier harangue is clear.

The conclusion one would expect Tanabe to draw, that he was wrong about keeping politics out of the classroom, or at least naive to think that it was possible, is not drawn. I have yet to find a passage in his works where it is. His call for a metanoesis in philosophy does not challenge this fundamental point, but rather shifts the accent to religious consciousness. The oversight is telling.

41 PHILOSOPHIZING THE REPENTANCE.

With *Philosophy as Metanoetics* repentance is transformed into a philosophical method. The work is not an attempt on Tanabe's part to redress anything he himself had done or not done, thought or not thought, but a lamentation on the philosophical enterprise itself and a call for its general reform. There are three factors in play here.

First was the disaster of the war and the closing of the Japanese mind to critical reflection, which required nothing less than a repentance by the whole nation. Second was the poverty and cowardice of philosophy in the face of this closure. After nearly three generations of what was thought to be a pursuit of wisdom, the philosophical community found itself mute in the face of mass self-deception. The desire not to know had completely overwhelmed the desire to know, and philosophers had hardly even lifted a pen to monitor the process, let alone object strenuously against it. Had the Japanese missed the soul of philosophy entirely? Or had it sold that soul in order to lose itself in the safety of academia? Third was his own private weakness of heart. Tanabe clearly felt a keen sense of embarrassment at his own complicity, and the sense of moral duty runs through the pages of his book as much as an attempt to salvage his philosophy does.

Now the only way to pose these questions in a way that philosophy can answer them, he felt, was through a radical transformation of perspective concerning the task of philosophy—not so much new ideas as a new way of seeing. All combined, this gives us the double-entendre of what he called metanoesis: a change of heart and a rethinking of thinking itself. Of course, it needs to be read against the background of the tangle of political ideas in which the logic of the specific had been caught up. But more than that, it is a major philosophical work in its own right and, as I said, Tanabe's crowning achievement.

After the surrender of 1945, many of Japan's writers broke their pens in shame. Others reupholstered their memory to find a consistency in their ideas that never was there. Some even doctored their collected works to hide the stains. In such a mood, the idea that the Kyoto philosophers had made the best of an oppressive situation, that against impossible odds they had tried to encourage more moderate elements, could hardly get a fair hearing. To some extent, the *Metanoetics* did. Granted it did little to answer the direct criticisms against Tanabe himself or the other Kyoto philosophers, it does seem to have attracted considerable sympathy in both philosophical and religious circles. As noted earlier, Tanabe's distance from Nishida throughout the fifteen years of war, though in no way related to their respective views on the war or Japanese nationalism, prevented his ideas from being cited to back up any political position of Nishida or his closest disciples. There is, for instance, not even a hint of his logic of the specific in the *Chūōkōron* discussions. No doubt this fact, too, though entirely circumstantial, had a role to play in the enthusiastic reception of the *Metanoetics.*

This may not have been entirely to Tanabe's advantage. Takeuchi Yoshinori laments the extent to which the circumstances of the book's emergence "overshadowed its true origins and caused it to be absorbed into the general atmosphere of mass appeals for national repentance being generated by opportunistic politicians." For, all things considered, the *Metanoetics* is a supremely nonpolitical book. Even when it tilts towards the concrete in "despising the shamelessness of the leaders primarily responsible for the defeat who are now urging the entire nation to repentance" and expressing a belief in "the collective responsibility of the nation," its call is for a religious change of heart, not for a reform of social institutions.

Tanabe's personal crisis of belief in his own vocation as a philosopher had brewed during the five-year silence he imposed on himself, during which time he foundered in indecision over whether to confront the government over its war policies or to find a way to cooperate in saving the nation from its impending disaster. He found himself, we might say, in the position of what William James had called a "live, forced, momentous option." Not to decide was already a decision. He knew that when he took up his pen he would risk saying things he would regret later, or being used for purposes he had not intended. Not even the strongest of his philosophical convictions had shown him a way out of his dilemma. As the situation in the country deteriorated and freedom of expression was more and more suppressed, he contemplated giving up his post as a teacher of philosophy altogether.

At some point he realized, in what can only be called a kind of religious experience, that he was too full of himself. He spoke of it in the closing days of the war, to a hall filled with students in what Takeuchi recalls as a tense atmosphere. I cite from the opening lines of that first lecture, which was to become his long and moving Preface to the *Metanoetics:*

> My own indecision, it seemed to me, disqualified me as a philosopher and university professor. I spent my days wrestling with questions and doubts like this from within and without, until I had been quite driven to the point of exhaustion and in my despair concluded that I was not fit to engage in the sublime task of philosophy.
>
> At that moment something astonishing happened. In the midst of my distress I let go and surrendered myself humbly to my own inability. I was suddenly brought to new insight! My penitent confession—metanoesis—unexpectedly threw me back on my own interiority and away from things external. There was no longer any question of my teaching and correcting others under the circumstances—I who could not deliver myself to do the correct thing. The only thing for me to do in the situation was to resign myself honestly to my weakness, to examine my own inner self with humility, and to explore the depths of my powerlessness and lack of freedom. Would not this mean a new task to take the place of the philosophical task that had previously engaged me? Little matter whether it be called "philosophy" or not: I had already come to realize my own incompetence as a philosopher. What mattered was that I was being confronted at the moment with an intellectual task and ought to do my best to pursue it.

In principle, all the ingredients of the metanoetics were already present in the reams of material he had published: the primacy of self-awareness, trust in the working of absolute nothingness, the letting go of self, the need to put reason at the service of morality. All that was needed was a catalyst to crystallize these ideas into a viable standpoint.

The stimulus came not from his accustomed reading of philosophy but from a student of his whom we mentioned earlier, Takeuchi Yoshinori. Takeuchi had seen that the heart of Tanabe's idea of absolute nothingness in history was very much consistent with the Shin Buddhist notion of Other-power. He wrote this up in a little book, a copy of which he presented to his teacher in 1941. Tanabe concurred, feeling he had found a way to extricate himself from the tangle in which he was caught. Not only would this lead to *Philosophy as Metanoetics*, it would alter his vocabulary and redirect the focus of all his later work as well.

The logic of the specific would have ended in a dead end without the *Metanoetics*. Yet as we noted earlier, the idea of metanoetics gave his logic "a new and deeper basis," not a radical restructuring. Even the ultimate ideal of the metanoetics, an "existential community" through collective repentance, does not depart far from his original idea of the nation. If there was any vacancy left by the emperor, who does not figure in the scheme of the metanoetics at all, it was more than filled by the religious figures of Shinran and Jesus, in whom Tanabe recognized true religious "cosmopolitans" rising above the epoch-specific conditions of their origins.

The opposite is not the case. The central argument of the book, a thoroughgoing critique of the way reason functions in history, presented in the form of a series of confrontations with the western philosophers who had been most influential in the formation of his own thought in the past, stands on its own without the logic of the specific. In it we see Tanabe in a new position. On the one hand, he is clearly retreating from the world and taking his misunderstood ideas with him. On the other, he is throwing himself back into the world with which he is most familiar with a spirit of criticism and confrontation that has never been stronger. For not only is he lodging criticisms against particular ideas of particular authors, he is engaging the whole philosophical enterprise itself. Tanabe was convinced that he had found an Archimedean point outside the world of philosophical tradition from which to dislodge that world and set it spinning in a new orbit. As he says, his aim is nothing less than to construct "a philosophy that is not a philosophy."

The result is a masterpiece of philosophical thought that shows Tanabe at his very best like nothing before and nothing since.

42 THE LOGIC OF ABSOLUTE CRITIQUE.

The work as a whole may be said to circle around the reform of philosophy elliptically, as if on a double pivot: the limits of reason and the force of Other-power. In the same way that the ellipsis needs both its pivots at the same time, so does Tanabe's argument. For the sake of brevity, I shall treat the two separately here.

The first aim is constellated in what he calls "the logic of absolute critique." The logic of the specific had shown up the irrationality at the basis of all historical praxis. The *Metanoetics* takes a leap beyond that to show the irrational core at the heart of all philosophical thought, including that which criticizes the irrationality of social existence. In the same way that the absoluteness of nothingness has to lie outside of the world of being, the absoluteness of the critique of reason cannot come from within reason itself but only from without. Given Tanabe's rejection of a transhistorical divinity, the without can only be the absolute nothingness at the ground of history, which is encountered not in pure thought but at the point where pure thought reaches its limits—in the expression that he repeats several times throughout the book, at the point where reason "blooms seven times and wilts eight":

> What the absolute critique of reason aims to do is not to provide a safety net for the criticizing subject by assuming a criticism that lies beyond all criticism, but rather to expose the entirety of reason to rigorous criticism and thus to a self-shattering. The critique of reason cannot avoid leading reason to absolute critique.... Pure self-identity is possible only for the absolute. Insofar as reason forgets its standpoint of finitude and relativity, and erroneously presumes itself to be absolute, it is destined to fall into absolute contradiction and disruption.

The model for the critique is Hegel's critique of Kant and Kierkegaard's critique of Hegel, to which Tanabe adds a corrective of his own. Kant's trust in the autonomy of reason and his attempt to apply it universally fails, Tanabe concurs with Hegel, in that it did not critique its own critical standpoint. It can only land in antinomies that it is incapable of resolving and chalk them up to the structure of the mind from which we have no relief as human beings. Tanabe's reasons are not only Hegel's. For Kant, to question criticism would be to question the whole purpose of philosophical venture itself. For Tanabe, the purpose of philosophy was not criticism but awakening, for which critique was just one of the ingredients needed.

Tanabe also follows Hegel in introducing dialectics into logic and religion into dialectics. His idea of the radical imperfection of the human condition and its need for transformation by something transcendent leads to a position of "reconciliation with destiny through love," which in turn becomes the touchstone of Tanabe's metanoetics. But this step needs the corrective of what Kierkegaard calls the conversion of the individual to religious existence that cannot be accounted for by the working of universal reason. What Kierkegaard misses in his ascent from the aesthetic to the ethical to the religious, according to Tanabe, is the return to care for the world of other selves. The individual's love of God and God's love of the individual must be completed in our love of one another.

If all of this sounds like rather ordinary Christian theology, it is only because in abbreviating the ideas I have eliminated both the full range and rigor of Tanabe's argument. Also missing is the crucial ingredient of entrusting the will to absolute nothingness, which he saw as necessary for the Christian symbolism to satisfy the demands of the absolute critique. The logic of absolute critique is applied not only to critical reason and history, but also to free will, which he now understands as a "will to nothingness." Just as reason cannot grasp nothingness without turning it into being, neither can it grasp the freedom of will by deducing it from the intuition of a moral law. Like Kant, who saw that belief in God is inferred from free will and not the other way around, so Tanabe cannot ground freedom in an absolute being. But unlike Kant, who reasoned freedom to be the ontological ground of the moral law, Tanabe locates freedom in the same no-ground *(Ab-grund)* as belief in an absolute being, that is, in an absolute nothingness experienced in metanoesis:

> It is not being but nothingness that provides a foundation in the human for freedom.... Nothingness is not something to which immediate experience can attest; whatever can be experienced immediately, or intuited in objective terms, belongs to being, not to nothingness. To suppose therefore that freedom is capable of being grasped in an act of comprehensive intuition is tantamount to turning it into being and thus depriving it of its essential nature as nothingness.

The idea of absolute nothingness thus comes into its own here not simply as a deduction but as something that *encounters* one like a force beyond. Although this is the starting point of the *Metanoetics*, the method of argument is properly philosophical. Beginning with a fresh look at Hegel's *Phenomenology* and an appreciation of Kierkegaard's criticisms of its rationalism, he grapples with Heidegger, Kant, Schelling, Pascal, Nietzsche, and Eckhart, as well as with Zen master Dōgen. One by one he takes up the thinkers that had influenced his thinking, in each case driving their use of reason to the point of despair at which it must let go of itself—or as he says, making use of the Christian terminology, die in order to resurrect. In this way each philosophical argument is brought back again and again to the theme of metanoesis.

I will not even attempt to summarize the range of ideas he brings under the axe of his absolute critique. It is a dense book that defies abbreviation. There are whole pages that will be almost unintelligible without some knowledge of his earlier positions, and even then the introduction of subtle shifts of emphasis requires more attention than any but a student of Tanabe's thought is likely to give it. But the deliberate and carefully-worded arguments are important less for any systematic philosophical content they contain—the logic of absolute critique never amounted to the consistent philosophical standpoint for Tanabe that absolute mediation or the logic of the specific had—than for the fact that they are surrounded on all sides by an air of religiosity. The effect is so unlike Tanabe's early writing, and so often so incidental to the argument he is pursuing, that one has always the sense that he is indeed aiming at a philosophy that refuses simply to be philosophy.

Throughout the book he refers to his philosophical partners—or at least many of them—as "saints and sages" who have understood philosophy in the normal sense of an awakening to the autonomy and power of reason. It is a path he walked once but can no longer:

> The experience of my past philosophical life has brought me to realize my own inability and the impotence of any philosophy based on self-power. I have no philosophy whatsoever on which to rely. I now find that the rational philosophy from which I had always been able to extract an understanding of the rational forces permeating history, and through which I could deal rigorously with reality without going astray, has left me.

Against this, he now postures as one of the "sinful and ignorant" unlike the "saints and sages in communion with the divine."

There seems to be a little irony in this latter statement insofar as it assumes that there are others who *can* rely on traditional philosophy in a responsible way, while at the same time carrying out a critique of reason that in effect makes ignorant sinners out of all the philosophers he had previously emulated. On the one hand, he wants to confess his debility as a philosopher as something peculiar to him; on the other, he wants to praise those who have engaged in philosophy with greater moral strength than he. The conclusion, that any well-intentioned thinker would come to the same position eventually, is left unspoken in the text.

This irresolution reflects an ambivalence in Tanabe's own state of mind. To begin with, while composing the book he began with the idea that it would be his duty to "participate in the task of leading... our people as a whole to engage in repentance." At he got deeper into it, his focus returned to the philosophical readership, though he always held out the hope that his philosophy would somehow serve that original purpose. At the same time, recognizing that his own failure was in some sense his own fault and not that of philosophy, he begins to focus more on the actual philosophers as individuals and to assess their level of self-awareness from their writings. His judgments take on a different tone, as if he is looking at them as if in a mirror, trying to detect something deep in himself that went wrong, some potential that had gone untapped.

To give one example, we might cite his remarks on Nietzsche, in whom he struggles to find a harbinger of his idea of absolute critique. But then he pauses in what can only be called a sigh of lament for his own lack of awareness of the full reach of the philosophical quest:

> The egoism that lies directly on the surface of Nietzsche's will to power is actually nothing more than a disguise. Though the mask be that of a devil, the reality is that of a sage. Herein lies the secret of Nietzsche's Dionysus: on the outside we see a strong and heroic figure who does not shrink even from a religion of Satan; but on the inside, beneath the exterior garments, lies the heart of a sage overflowing with infinite love.... I should like to interpret him as a saint who rejected debilitating sympathies to preach a strengthening evangel of suffering and overcoming....

Even Pascal, whose views he considers the precise antithesis of his metanoetics, he excuses on the grounds that it would be unmetanoetic to treat a holy sage any differently:

> This is in no way to cast doubt on the authenticity of his faith or to accuse his thought of being shallow. Nothing could be further from the spirit of metanoetics. Quite the contrary, it seems to me that Pascal was such a pure and noble spirit by nature that he would have never felt the inner impulse to metanoetics. Metanoetics is the way of the ordinary and the foolish, not that of the holy sage....

One has the sense of Tanabe bending over backwards to disrobe himself of the image of the confrontational, hard-nosed critic who treated ideas in the abstract, apart from the thinkers who had them. For the absolute critique is aimed at the hubris of reason, not at reasonable people, and it is prompted withal by the pursuit of virtue in the philosophical act itself.

Despite the highly personal tone of the book, Tanabe's inner religious life remains a mystery. What we can say, it seems to me, is that Tanabe saw in the abstractions of philosophy a defence behind which to safeguard his private life and feelings from public view, and yet from whose privileged position he could address the modern soul directly. Even the repeated referral to himself with the words "sinful and ignorant as I am" so rarely touches down on the solid ground of particular historical fact that the reader cannot but slide over the phrase after a while. Since I find it hard to imagine that

Tanabe himself was not aware of this as he was writing, I can only conclude that he had taken what was originally a genuinely personal sentiment and turned it into the mask of an Everyman so that his readers might gradually be led to think "sinful and ignorant as *we are*," and be drawn into the same experiment of life-and-resurrection through Other-power that Tanabe himself was conducting. In this way, far from being an asbestos cloak that protected his inward self from catching fire from outer critiques, the outer mask begins to take on the glow of a religious conviction burning within.

43 **RELIGIOUS ACT, RELIGIOUS WITNESS.** The great and ineluctable philosophical paradox of the *Metanoetics*, that only reason can ultimately persuade reason of its own debilities, is overcome by the addition of—or rather, attention to—the religious dimension. It is not a matter of turning philosophy into a "religious philosophy" or religion into "philosophical religion," but of recovering the original ground at which the two rely on each other, a kind of philosophy-*in*-religion. As we noted, the key here is the enhancement of the notion of absolute nothingness. There are three new elements interwoven here: absolute nothingness as Other-power; its manifestation as a nothingness-*in*-love through the self-negation of the absolute; and its relation to Amida Buddha and the Pure Land.

In order not to draw absolute nothingness into the world of objective being so that it can become an object of faith, Tanabe transforms the idea of faith into surrender to something that is *not* being and cannot therefore become an object of conscious intuition. This *something*, as we have already noted, is not a thing but a power that can only be experienced as a force that disrupts the subject-object duality of reason, and only from there deduced as the power that mediates everything that happens in the world of being and becoming. Any association with a concrete object of faith must begin from this premise and not from the premise of an object pre-existing our faith in it.

At first sight the idea of an object of faith defined by its non-being seems radically to demythify all the metaphors of faith and religious experience. To say that the object of desire does not exist before it is desired (as Kant does in his idea of the "good will") redraws the distinction between religious faith and simple superstition. It means that the true object of faith is one that cannot be grasped or manipulated as an image that points literally or symbolically to some particular object among other objects in the world of being. It can *only be imagined* and has no power apart from the imagining.

In order to apply this to western notions of God, the focus has to shift from God as a subject who reigns supreme over the realm of being to a self-emptying divinity who is manifest only in the self-negating act of love. Whereas previously the working of absolute nothingness was apparent in the mere fact of absolute mediation of the world of being, from this point on Tanabe will describe it as nothingness-*in*-love. As absolute power it does not exercise its will directly on relative beings but is only manifest indirectly:

> A God who is love is an existence that forever reduces itself to nothing and totally gives itself to the other. In that sense, it is an existence that has nothingness as its principle and does not directly act out of its own will.

This indirect manifestation appears wherever relative beings negate themselves in the act of love. Self-emptying *is* God's activity in the world of being. God's only reality is the continued "negation and transformation—that is, conversion—of everything relative." Tanabe uses the image of a divine net cast over the world of being to replace the idea of faith as an individual's personal relationship with God:

> The relationship between God and me is not enough to explain the role of the divine net. It is absolutely necessary that we ourselves become nodes in the net and play our part in the divine love that embraces and encompasses all relative beings—in other words, that we assume a joint responsibility. This is why the love of God entails a love of neighbor.

The model Tanabe takes of a religion that complements philosophy is drawn from the *Kyōgyōshinshō* written by Shinran, the thirteenth-century founder of True Pure Land Buddhism, a work revered as scripture but at the same time, as Tanabe laments, shackled by sectarianism. There are two major ideas he takes from this work, or perhaps better, reads out of it. For as it turns out, taken together these ideas confirm "the mediating role linking ethical reason inseparably to religion," a phrase that echoes the earlier influence of Bergson on his logic of the specific. But here, rather than talk of historical praxis as he had before, Tanabe uses the Buddhist terms *gyō* and *shō* to highlight the difference between the awakening of the primal religious act and the response of ethical behavior.

Gyō is the religious act in which the sinful and ignorant fool comes to trust in the Other-power of Amida Buddha. Taking heart in Shinran's conviction that it is first and foremost the *bonbu,* the ordinary fool, who is saved, Tanabe is quick to see the connection to the Socratic virtue of knowing that one does not know. He sees the *daimon* of Socrates as a warning against trust in one's own powers of reason and a call to abandon oneself in metanoesis. But what was only implicit in Socrates becomes explicit in Shinran, namely the "Great Act of genuine religious practice based on Other-power, through which the self, cast into the abyss of death, is immediately restored once again to life." The pursuit of the absolute critique of reason is such a religious act. It is, we might say, the philosophical equivalent of the *nenbutsu,* or practice of invoking the name of the Buddha in complete trust that leads to salvation.

But this act is incomplete if it remains in the inner recesses of mind. It must be confirmed in the form of outward witness, *shō,* to the power of transforming love. This witness supplies the ethical component of metanoesis. Drawing again on Pure Land teachings, Tanabe asserts that whatever merit there is to ethical activity is all due to the great compassion of Other-power. Unlike the mysticism of Meister Eckhart and the Zen of Master Dōgen, which Tanabe sees as caught in a circle of the awakening of the self to its inherent Buddha-nature, Pure Land faith is based on awakening to an absolute Other. Again reflecting his distance from Nishida, he speaks of Zen as "continuous, self-identical, and in-itself," while Pure Land is "disjunctive, discontinuous, and for-itself." He found Zen *kōan* sympathetic to his own absolute critique, but argued that, in the end, it substitutes what Kierkegaard had called "the aesthetic" for "the religious." Tanabe's point was not to set up Zen and Pure Land as an either/or choice, but to show how the two complement each other, contrary to popular opinion.

The meritorious work of compassion *(ekō)* works in two mutually related directions, a kind of ascent-*in*-descent, *egressus est regressus.* The first phase of "going to the Pure Land," or *ōsō,* consists in awakening to one's own inability to save oneself and abandonment to the saving power from Amida Buddha. The second phase, that of "returning from the Pure Land to this world" *(gensō)* is the return to this world to work for the salvation of others. Both of these are direct actions only in the sense that in them self-power is "transferred" to Other-power:

> We can see an essential logic at work here insofar as saving oneself means performing an act of absolute self-negation that is only brought fully to consciousness when one can sacrifice one's own self compassionately for the sake of others.

The symbol of this transformation of consciousness is the bodhisattva Dharmākara, the embodiment of the Buddha as a relative being lighting up the way to faith through self-discipline and religious practice.

Whereas Shinran saw the *gensō* as the true prerogative of the Buddha alone, Tanabe reads the Dharmākara myth as pointing to *gensō* as a task for all individuals to complete. Naturally, this did not settle well with Pure Land orthodoxy, but then again that was not his intention. Similarly, his appropriation of the story of the death and resurrection of Jesus as a symbol of a universal human possibility—actually a rather old and familiar pattern in western Christianity—is not an attempt to offer a competing theology but to garner the philosophical truth in religious doctrine and thus liberate it from the confines of orthodox believers.

Although this pattern is repeated consistently throughout the *Metanoetics*, it is not used as the foundation for ethical principles. In the return to the world, witness is said to "produce knowledge" but no specific content is given to this knowledge. Rather, Tanabe is content to speak of the religious ground without which any ethical principles remain locked in either the irrationality of social conventions or the rationalism of philosophical reflection. The ethical "ought" is no longer based on an "imperative" or "ideal" in Kant's sense but rather on a participation in a greater reality. All moral action becomes a kind of "action of no action." The very concepts of ethics are emptied of their rational content to become *upāya*, expedient means to "mediate the mutual transformation of being and nothingness." And whereas formerly the question of the telos of the working of absolute nothingness in the world of being and becoming was left vague and undefined, it is now given new meaning: the building up, through love, of a peaceful world, a *communio sanctorum* on earth.

44 **SELF AND SELF-AWARENESS.**

The religious tenor of the *Metanoetics* sets the tone for Tanabe's late work in retirement. Even when he returned to his interest in science, carrying on what Takeuchi has called his "lifelong guerrilla warfare" against the inflated claims of natural science, he did so in a religious mood. The "progress" gained through an accumulation of knowledge, he saw, was ultimately no more than the working out of the innate methodological fragmentation of science itself, impeding a true synthesis of knowledge. Tanabe welcomed the contradictions that the new physics was uncovering at its own foundations, and suggested that they be read as an existential *kōan* on which science as a whole would do well to meditate. In this way, the metanoetic spirit of his later writings is apparent in his attempt to define the goal of philosophy as to insert itself into both science and religion so that the two might unite and cooperate in promoting love and peaceful collaboration among the peoples of the earth.

Although Tanabe did not fully abandon the attempt to reshape his logic of the specific, this concern was nudged to the periphery so that another idea that had been on the periphery could replace it: that of self-awareness. The concern with inheriting the great religious wealth of Buddhism and Christianity that we find in his late writings had nothing to do with affiliation or participation in any institutional form of religion, nor with applying religious doctrine to the reform of particular social institutions. His focus had clearly moved to the self that has died to itself and risen in the power of absolute nothingness. He gave no particular name to this position nor did he attempt to fit it out with its own "logic." But a glance at the way the notion of the self functioned in his earlier thought makes the shift transparent.

Along with the idea of absolute nothingness, Tanabe had inherited from Nishida the importance of coming to awareness, though he developed it in a different direction. His early writing, as we saw in the essay on Kant, clearly placed a premium on the transformation of individual consciousness, but it took him a long and circuitous route before he would return to this position. It is not until after his *Metanoetics* that the full religious dimension of the idea emerges, when ideas that had lain latent in his thought come to full bloom.

Nishitani, who had studied under both Nishida and Tanabe and who was the chief editor of Tanabe's *Complete Works,* contrasts the positions of his two teachers regarding the question of the self this way:

> While Tanabe's philosophy pivots around action or praxis... Nishida's philosophy pivots around self-awareness.... Now these two standpoints are by and large the same in that they represent a standpoint of a *self that is not a self* turning on the same axis of absolute nothingness.

Though it would take Tanabe some time to get to the point that Nishitani describes, when he did, we find remarks on the subject throughout his works that one could easily mistake for Nishida's own, as in the following:

> The problems of philosophy arise from our awareness of a deep life. Even Greek philosophy, which is said to have arisen in wonder, in fact came from the intelligent Greeks' own self-awareness of life.... Philosophy is nothing other than a self-aware expression of life.

We find Tanabe saying more or less the same thing in early writings up until the time of his first steps towards a new logic, as in the following from a 1925 essay on "The Logic of the Specific and the World Scheme":

> Life and logic do not exist apart from one another. It is only their correlative identity that exists concretely. When we focus on the aspect of immediacy, we speak of life, and when we focus on the aspect of mediation, we call it logic. Just as there is no logic apart from life, so there can be no life of philosophical self-awareness apart from logic. Logic is the logic of life, and the self-awareness of life is the self-awareness of logic.

Before he could make his way back to these early ideas, however, Tanabe would first distance his idea of the self from that of Nishida. The hints of a difference show up already in the concluding sections of his essay, completed the year before, on "Kant's Teleology," where he refers to the "dialectics of will" as "a finality of self-awareness" and offers it as "a common principle weaving history, religion, and morality into an indivisible relationship with one another." As Nishitani points out, this was to prove a separation point from Nishida, who saw participation in history as basically a "seeing." While Tanabe's concern with praxis in the historical world will not eclipse entirely the conviction that the job of philosophy is to clear up consciousness, it is not until his *Metanoetics* that he returns to state with renewed vigor that the proper goals of philosophy are "reflection on what is ultimate and radical self-awareness." In the intervening years, the idea of awareness based on negation of the self will bow to the demands of his concerns with historical praxis.

In his essay on Kant just mentioned, it is not a universal "moral law within" that grounds practical judgment but absolute nothingness, the self-awareness of which gives a kind of ultimate telos to moral judgment. On the surface, this is fully consistent with Nishida's thought, and yet there is a subtle subjectivism here at cross-purposes to Nishida. In the attempt to shift the universal of practical judgment from a *datum* to a *captum*, and at the same time to maintain absolute nothingness as the ultimate fact of reality, both the consciousness that creates meaning and the self-awareness of a necessary finality in the creative process that drives it to its deeper ground beyond being, seem to set the knowing subject up as a relative being that confronts the world and absolute nothingness as its objects. Consequently, the true self—a term that does not in any case figure as prominently in Tanabe as it had in Nishida—works primarily as a moral *ideal* to be brought into being and not as a "deep reality" that need only be awakened to. It is not surprising, therefore, to find Tanabe criticizing Nishida in 1930 for "the hubris of having turned the self into a God" and philosophy into religion.

Tanabe himself was aware of the latent subject-object dichotomy in his thinking and in a 1931 collection of essays entitled *Hegel's Philosophy and the Dialectic* (a portion of which was published in a volume commemorating the centennial of Hegel's death), he tried to make adjustments. Dissatisfied with the crudeness of his former "dialectic" he quickly came to replace what he saw as the equally vacuous notion of absolute knowledge that crowned Hegel's system with "a self-awareness of praxis," again grounded in an absolute nothingness beyond being. Under the influence of Heidegger, he dubbed his reinterpretation of Hegel an "ethico-religious existential dialectic" wherein the enlightened state of self-awareness works an absolute negation on both matter and ideas.

Relative now to the absolute nothingness beyond being, Tanabe's idea of the self was no longer that of a knowing subject facing a world of objects but of a self of praxis *in* the world and yet enlightened to the ultimacy of absolute nothingness. The shift from the moral subject he had forged in his critique of Kant was considerable but still inadequate. Compared with Nishida's logic of locus, which was framed during the very years that Tanabe was immersed in his reading of Hegel, Tanabe's dialectics seemed to lean in the same direction of defining the self in terms of creative seeing—which, however, he called a praxis instead of following Nishida's designation of it as a poesis—rather than in that of a passive knowing. Yet it was still the object of the praxis, the historical world, and not absolute nothingness that gave the self the concreteness he demanded of it. In a word, the idea of affirming the self by negating the *individuality* of the self vis-à-vis a larger historical whole is clear; the idea of affirming a true self by negating the *being* of the self vis-à-vis the nothingness of the absolute is not. Absolute nothingness remained an asymptotic ideal towards which the historical self aims. It was only with the logic of the specific that Tanabe would find a way to include the ideas of "absolute nothingness" and "self-awareness" in the realms of the historically conditioned.

Whereas Nishida had, at least in theory, taken the idea of a "true self" in the wider sense to include the true essence of things in nature, Tanabe restricted his attentions to the realm of the human. On the one hand, he felt that Nishida had oversimplified the way from the ordinary self to the true self, reckoning it to be a matter for *privatized* self-awareness. On the other, he felt the lack of sufficient attention to the moral element through overemphasis on a trans-subjective self. Tanabe's counter-tendency to relativize absolute nothingness to historical praxis and to define the true self as a goal to be striven for rather than as a reality to be awakened to was, of course, already present in germ in his earlier studies of Kant and Hegel. His logic of the specific brought this tendency, as we have seen, to full flower.

Tanabe's idea of the self was, not surprisingly, infected with the ambivalent nationalism of which we spoke above. In a series of articles written in

1939 under the title "The Logic of National Existence," he melded a critique of Nishida's idea of "the self-identity of absolute contradictories" with the following kind of statements:

> The act of self-denial in which individuals sacrifice themselves for the sake of the nation turns out to be an affirmation of existence. Because the nation to which the individual has been sacrificed bears within itself the source of life of the individual, it is not merely a matter of sacrificing oneself for the other. Quite the contrary, *it is a restoration of the self to the true self.* This is why self-negation is turned to self-affirmation and the whole unites with the individual. The free autonomy of ethics is not extinguished in service to the nation and in submission to its orders, but rather made possible thereby.

This tone continues all the way up until 1943. Almost immediately before his turn to metanoetics, we find him writing in an essay entitled "Life and Death":

> In time of crisis country and individual are one; the people dedicate themselves out of necessity to the country. To distance oneself from one's country means at the same time to destroy the self itself.... On this standpoint, the self does not live and die, but is put to death and restored to life through God or the absolute.

The spirit of personal repentance at work in *Philosophy as Metanoetics* does not seem significantly to have altered the structure of his dialectical understanding of the self. What has changed is the focus: concrete history, which had once provided the central locus for the praxis whereby the self dies to itself to be reborn and where the ideal of the true self takes shape, is displaced to the periphery to make room for self-awareness of the finitude of all historical praxis. This belongs to the double negation of the metanoesis. On the one hand, it is a repentance of one's personal failings; on the other, it is a confrontation with and rejection of the radical evil that lies beneath those personal failings in the depth of human existence itself. This rejection is not something that can be achieved by one's own power, since that power is infected with radical evil. It can only come about through trust in the absolute nothingness that encompasses human existence on all sides. Thus the transformation of the metanoesis is a death-*in*-resurrection of the self.

In the context of Tanabe's idea of metanoetics, the "self" of "self that is not a self" is the particular individual that has broken free of everyday modes of thought and action to attain to insight into the fundamental human condition of finiteness and to engage in repentance for its deluded moral behavior. Given his failure to develop the notion of the true self beyond the abstract point of a moral ideal, once this self-negating dimension of the dialectic of self-awareness (the recognition of the self-power of the relative being) has been achieved, Tanabe has nowhere to go next but to appeal to an equally autonomous "other" to invert this negation and affirm a new self, a "self that is not a self" (a self reliant on the Other-power of absolute nothingness). In retaining the importance of the transformed self, he concurs with Nishida but departs from Pure Land doctrine. At the same time, he differs from Nishida's idea of self-awareness, in which the self does not become something else from its everyday self but only becomes aware of a different mode of being. As Nishitani remarks, "*ontically* so to speak, it remains the same even though its *ontological* ground has shifted."

In his last essay, Nishida himself makes the point still more clearly, his references to Tanabe ("people") having become by this time as indirect as Tanabe's to him:

> The question of religion lies not in what our self *should be* as an acting being, but in the question of *what kind of existence* the self has.... People have frequently attempted to ground the religious demand merely from the standpoint of the imperfection of the self that wanders into error. But merely from such a perspective of error the religious consciousness does not emerge.... Moreover, to err religiously is not to err in the purposes of the self, but concerning the place where the self truly exists. Even in regard to morality, the true religious mind does not emerge merely from the powerlessness of the self in regard to the moral good objectively conceived, no matter how acute the feeling is, as long as there lies at the bottom of this moral sentiment the self-confidence of moral power. Though it is generally called metanoia, it is merely remorse over the evil of the self, but self-power still remains.

Tanabe countered by rejecting Nishida's paradoxical formation of a "continuity of discontinuity" to solve the problem of the continuance through time of a true self within the ever-changing everyday self. And he did so precisely because it seems to him to eliminate the radical forfeiture of the actual self that he saw as the beginning of self-awareness:

> Self-awareness is not the introversion into itself of a self continuing in existence. There can be no turn inward for a self that continues identical with itself. Self-awareness is brought about when the self takes leave of this position and destroys and erases itself.

With Tanabe, then, it is the deluded self, the sinner filled with the darkness of ignorance *(avidyā)* and passion, that is the self's true countenance, both ontically and ontologically. Awakening to the ineluctable finiteness of human autonomy can only lead to an experience of the self as *not a self*—

that is, as a self that can no longer rely on the self-power that defines it as self. To realize the ideal of a *self* that is not a self requires an Other-power, the awakening to which does not dispose of the self's finiteness and yet somehow reaffirms its existence and its relation to other relative beings.

Where Nishida's "true self" pointed to an original state of awareness that can be cultivated by transcending the work of discriminating consciousness and the realm of being that it constitutes, Tanabe's ideal self is cultivated through an awareness of a radical relativity and the futility of reliance on its own powers. For each, the "self that is not a self" rests on absolute nothingness. For Nishida, nothingness is experienced as a seeing in which world and subject are one—defining each other, creating each other, erasing each other. For Tanabe, in the end, it is experienced as an absolute mediation in which all relationships between the subject and the world, between one subject and another, are seen to belong to a history whose rhythms transcend those of our own willful praxis.

45 A SYNTHESIS OF RELIGIONS. After his first full-fledged experiment with Shin Buddhist categories in *Philosophy as Metanoetics*, Tanabe's attention remained focused for the rest of his life on developing a "philosophy that is not a philosophy." The absolute critique he considered to have been more or less accomplished in that book. What remained was to clarify the transition from philosophy to religion.

Tanabe had always drawn the line between the two bolder than Nishida had done, never to separate them but only to keep their tasks distinct. Indeed, as we saw in discussing his logic of the specific, religion was always in some sense a fulfillment of philosophy for him. The connection remained a rather abstract one for him, however, with the result that he tended to absorb religion into philosophy, as we see in a lengthy 1939 commentary on Dōgen's *Shōbōgenzō*. The work concludes where it began, in the assumption that philosophy differs from religion in that philosophy reaches the ultimate through the mediation of religion whereas religion reaches it directly. But in his actual attempt to locate the core of direct Zen experience and allow it to mediate reality to philosophical understanding, he ended up—as D. T. Suzuki observed—doing the opposite, trying to squeeze Zen out of his philosophy rather than the other way around.

To some extent the *Metanoetics* corrected this and restored religion to a position of being able to criticize philosophy. Perhaps his clearest statement of where he intended to take philosophy in his late years appears in a serpentine sentence in the final supplement on religion to his *Introduction to Philosophy* of 1951:

> Religion by nature does not, like philosophy, pursue the relationship between relatives from the side of the relative until in the end it arrives at the absolute, but immediately and from the outset entails a process in which the relative is acted on by the absolute—in religious language, receives revelation, or, put the other way around, a process in which the absolute itself reveals itself, that is to say, *makes itself apparent* to the relative—and through that process assumes a standpoint from which the relationship between the absolute and the relative does not proceed, as it does in philosophy, through thinking and rational argument but is directly and with certainty disclosed to us.

The tone of the remarks makes it clear that he sees religion as pointing to a defect in philosophy, namely, that it does not end in an awakening to reality. And in fact, what takes place in his thinking after the *Metanoetics* is precisely that the orientation of philosophy itself comes to embrace that of religion, so that philosophy is no longer directed simply *toward* the absolute but includes movement *from* the absolute to the relative. It is wrong, he judged, to think that religion is simply tacked on to the philosophical pursuit. It has transformed it.

In other words, his understanding of the implications for philosophy of the idea of the self-awareness of absolute nothingness had at last broadened to the full reach of Nishida's understanding, different though the results were. In general, Tanabe seems to have felt the shadow of Nishida lift and a greater affinity in old age to the most important philosophical influence of his life.

During the composition of the *Metanoetics* Tanabe's eyes were opened to Christianity in a way they had never been before. His 1948 book, *The Dialectics of Christianity*, carries this a step further. As he writes there, Christianity is in need of a "second reformation" because the lifeblood of the original experience that had once enlivened it had dried up and left only an empty shell. This shell could in turn become the seed of a new Christianity, but to do so, Jesus' preaching of the Kingdom of God would have to replace the soteriology of St. Paul, keeping only the idea, in demythified form, of the death and resurrection of the individual in Christ. The reformation itself was something that would have to take place within Christianity itself, under the full weight of its tradition, not in the heads of philosophers or the free-thinking imaginations of non-Christians. But its effects would reach much broader, allowing it to be appropriated by well-meaning people everywhere. What he meant by appropriation was not any form of official affiliation with the faith, but a creative symbiosis with Buddhism, and even Marxism, which was the dream of Tanabe's late years.

Leaving aside questions of the validity of Tanabe's interpretations of the world religions he sought to synthesize, the main contours of his project become apparent in the structure of his next book, *Existenz, Love, and Praxis.* From this point on, what had already been implicit in earlier writings becomes clearer, namely, that Tanabe felt an affinity for Christianity so great that at times it was greater than that he felt for Buddhism. It is in this sense that he had remarked in the final pages of *The Dialectics of Christianity* that he considered himself a *werdender Christ.* Earlier it was the commitment of Christianity to mediate itself through moral engagement with history that had attracted him, and in fact we see this repeated in his application of Jesus' teaching on repentance to a religious view of society in that same book. But in general it was Jesus the teacher of love and rebirth through dying to self, who appealed to Tanabe, not the moral teacher or the resurrected, eternal Christ of Pauline theology. Be that as it may, his aim was not to make a comparative study of the relative merits of various religions or theological positions, but to find a religious position that would synthesize what is best in Zen, Pure Land, and Christianity.

His hope of a unified religious philosophy combining these three seemed, curiously, to bracket his insistence on the specific as the immediate mediator of historical experience and understanding. It is almost as if he had swung to the opposite extreme from identifying the nation as the supreme form of historical specificity. While there he had glossed over the irrationalities of religion in the specific in order to stress its salvific dimension, here he practically ignores the specific altogether in order to focus on the rational dimension of the religions he wants to synthesize.

His omission of Shinto from the picture, striking to us today who view it as a religion proper to Japan, is not hard to understand. For one thing, his interest was in the doctrinal content of historical religions, not in their ritual or myths. Lacking such a clear doctrine or studied interpretation of its founding myths, Shinto fell wide of the reach of his project. Along with this one cannot discount the fact that Shinto had been expropriated by the state to serve its military ideology, which in effect had raised it beyond the reach of rational critique. Tanabe was not about to tangle himself in the question of what meaning Shinto might have freed from that recent history.

The synthesis that Tanabe had in mind was not based on the fact that all religions have a common source, and certainly not that phenomenologically they showed common, archetypal patterns. But if all things in the world and in consciousness mediate one another, if by nature they collaborate, sympathetically or agonistically, in one another's identity, then obviously the same should hold true of religion. Insofar as he understood religion as a function of self-awareness, it was enough for him to draw attention to the points of sympathetic contact, the touchstone of sympathy being their ability to enhance awareness of Existenz, love, and praxis. What the consequences of this contact might mean for the purity of tradition of any particular religion or the development of its doctrine simply did not concern him. It was only the consequences for the self seeking to appropriate in awareness the truth of the historical religions that occupied him.

The reason Tanabe chose Existenz, love, and praxis as the meeting point for religions is that they represented to him the necessary conditions for the religious self-awareness to which the historical religions have finally to answer. Existenz represents an awakening to the element of human finiteness that characterizes the self as it is (the self in-itself). Love represents an awakening to the mediating work of the power of absolute nothingness that affirms the self in its freedom to be other than it is (the self for-itself). Praxis represents the enlightened action of the self that has let go of itself and hence begun to realize its potential (the self in-itself and for-itself). Together these three ingredients make up the final aim of the philosophical task, and make it clear that the "philosophy that is not a philosophy" is so called because it is a "deliberately religious" philosophy.

Behind this description, it may be observed, one sees a tripartite model of finitude, mediation of Other-power, and life-*in*-death that had been developed in the *Metanoetics* and is repeated so often in Tanabe's late work in any number of different forms of paraphrase. For example, we see it at work in his idea of "turning to logic what there is of myth" in religion. This includes not only the Pure Land myth of the bodhisattva Dharmākara, but also the Christian myth of the *kenōsis* or self-emptying of God in the historical Jesus. The dialectic common to both of them is one of self-descent (annihilating the self) and self-ascent (reaffirming the self), or of death-*in*-life and life-*in*-death. In each case, the religious person, "the subject of sin," dies the death of despair over its own finiteness and is restored to life through an absolute conversion to the infinite power of absolute nothingness, God or Other-power.

A second pattern, based on the idea of nothingness-*in*-love from the *Metanoetics,* evolved in the form of a triunity of God-*in*-love, love of God, and love of neighbor, *God* being freely replaced with *nothingness* as the occasion demanded. This appears commonly in his late works as a way to salvage his earlier goal of combining socialism and democracy to form a social structure in which Japan can commit itself positively to sociohistorical praxis and promote the cause of peace throughout the world. In an essay entitled "Christianity, Marxism, and Japanese Buddhism," Tanabe describes his understanding of the content of religious self-awareness as just this sort of nothingness-*in*-love that mediates the whole of our existence as relative beings.

What survives of his interest in Marxism is the religious dimension. He had long felt that there was a kind of spiritual eschatology in Marx's thinking that Marx himself never let surface. Now he sees that the socialist ideals of solidarity among people and the liberation of religion from superstition can serve his dialectics of love. Concretely, philosophers form themselves into a kind of "classless class" to help Marxists see the positive role of religion as liberating people from the selfish preoccupation with their own salvation on the one hand, and on the other to represent to capitalist self-interests the scientific and theoretical social value of Marx's ideas. This class functions like a kind of "specific society," but unlike the ethnic race, which is the source of the irrational, closed society, it would be free of the attachment to race and aimed at opening up society to the wider world. While he saw that this may seem to dilute the notion of the specific by making it apply to any grouping whatsoever, it is in fact a necessary step to show that the individual need not confront the specific alone to mediate the universal, but can do so in communion with other like-minded individuals.

46 A DIALECTICS OF DEATH. In his very latest writings, we see Tanabe's reform of philosophy not only incorporating the religious dimension more basically but also turning back to restore to philosophy the breadth of scope he had denied it previously. He had always thought it in the nature of philosophy "to try to think about reality in such a way as to leave nothing of reality out of the picture." Still, there were two elements he had neglected, aesthetics and a philosophy of life. These come together only at the end of his life with his turn to what he called the dialectics of death.

Already from his days in Germany, we will recall, he had been attracted to Heidegger's idea of a "phenomenology of life" and had every intention to follow up on it after returning to Japan. In fact he did not, but in an ironic twist he comes back to it in old age through a critique of Heidegger in order to advance his own alternative—a philosophy of death.

In the final section of *Existenz, Love, and Praxis* Tanabe takes a first step towards converting philosophy to the Socratic ideal of "practicing death." Taking examples from the life of Jesus and the Zen samurai ideal, he shows how the death—or final negation—of the self in which one "lets go" of the self or removes it from the world of life and being to "make it nothing" turns out to be a mediation (a skillful means, *hōben*) for coming to the affirmation of a new life. In this way he brings together strands from his earlier writing to develop a dialectic of death-*in*-life and life-*in*-death that becomes the final touchstone of religious self-awareness.

Without abandoning his final goal of a universal love that synthesizes Christian love and Buddhist compassion, he rethinks love in terms of death. Zen Buddhism is given a special role to play in this reconsideration:

> If there is any philosophy that can save us today, it can only be a dialectics of death. This is my suspicion. Is not the way to pry open the dead-end to which western thinking leads none other than the eastern thinking of Zen?

The idea of death-and-resurrection he had applied in the *Metanoetics* is, of course, present here, as is his final vision in that book of a *communio sanctorum*. But both these ideas were like half-filled vessels completed only by his own experience of facing death—first the passing of his wife in 1951 and then his years of living and writing with her image in mind. "In his dialogue with his deceased wife," Nishitani recalls, "it is as if Tanabe felt a world open up in which the realm of life and the realm of death interpenetrate." The task of philosophy broadens to unite the world of the living and the world of the dead.

His most important essay on the philosophy of death is framed as a contrast with Heidegger's "ontology of life." Death, he claims, is more than the gloomy shadow that contingency casts over the things of life—which Tanabe sees as particularly real today, given the threat of nuclear holocaust—but this is where Heidegger stops. It is that, of course, indeed it is the clearest "representative of our exposure to contingency." But death is not something that comes into life from the outside. It is, rather, the other side of life and needs to be remembered as such for the two to mutually convert one another. Otherwise the fact of impermanency ends in mere nihility. Metaphysically, the "dialectical conversion" he has in mind is nothingness-*in*-love, the activity of absolute nothingness. It is not deduced as a principle from the fact of the relativity of being. Nor is it a mere heuristic invention, as Kant had seen immortality to be, believed in because it helps us focus on the business of life. The conversion has to be "practical," something that entails the awakening of the individual at the very point that one's trust in life experiences collapses. Tanabe speaks of this conversion as a "frustration-*in*-breakthrough," that is, as something that opens up from the very midst of confrontation with one's limits. He calls it an epiphany of absolute nothingness in the world, drawing us beyond frustrations and death to a rebirth in new life. The practice of this dialectics of death is therefore an "existentially collaborative awakening to death-and-resurrection."

Tanabe continued to work Christian vocabulary freely into his arguments, but one should note two important qualifications here. First, insofar as the Christian God is absolute being, it is also a principle of life believed to envelop absolute nothingness. As a result, "Christianity cannot be expected to take a radically dialectical stance towards death." Second, he viewed the death and resurrection of Jesus always in a nontheological, demythified sense. He recognized, of course, that belief in death-and-resurrection has been central to Christianity ever since Saint Paul. But he makes it clear that it is not for him a question of a metaphysical statement about a direct and objective experience undergone by the person who dies, but a mythical representation of something indirectly experienced by the living.

In this regard, he speaks of the practice of death as a collaboration of the living with the dead: "bound to the dead in love, the living work through them." He calls this collaboration a "radicalization of absolute nothingness" and a "sympathetic crossing of paths" that takes place in self-awareness. He likens it not only to the Christian idea of the *communio sanctorum* but also to the Mahāyāna way of the bodhisattva. Even as he tries to distance himself from the transcendent God of Christianity, one can hardly fail to recognize the echoes of the Pauline hymn of divine *kenōsis* in the background of Tanabe's paraphrase of the bodhisattva ideal:

> While preserving the condition of being able to become a Buddha, of his own he puts own powers in abeyance and does not rise to those heights but stops at a state lower than a Buddha, takes his place among all living beings, and thereby gives himself over to the salvation of them all.

Elsewhere he even expands this idea of personal renunciation for the salvation of others to cosmic proportions along the lines of Leibniz's idea of monads, removing all traces of a pre-established harmony and replacing it with the Kegon Buddhist idea of harmonious collaboration expressed in terms of a "collaborative realization of the love that symbolizes absolute nothingness."

It is in the midst of his efforts to turn philosophical thinking around the relationship between love and death that he attempted to introduce the aesthetic dimension through a book-length commentary on Stéphane Mallarmé's posthumously published experimental poem, "Un coup de dés jamais n'abolira le hazard." Ten years earlier, in 1951, he had written a still longer work on Paul Valéry, in whose blend of aesthetics and social philosophy he had found himself in strong agreement. It was through reading Valéry's appreciation of Mallarmé's poem in the course of preparing that work that his interest was first drawn to it. Tanabe's own commentary would turn out to be the last writing he completed before he died.

The poem's play on the idea of contingency and the abyss that it opens up fits well his own ideas, as he explains in detail. But what is new in Tanabe's treatment is the idea that the beauty of symbolic language can do something that neither philosophical nor scientific language can, and does this precisely in eclipsing the centrality of meaning. He understood the poems of the symbolists to share with philosophy the aim of a "negative mediation of science" in pursuit of what is more ultimate than scientific knowledge. Accordingly, he read them as metaphysical, but as a metaphysics "viewed from the standpoint of religious awakening." At the same time, he found the distinction of the symbolists between "everyday language" and "pure language" to his liking, and saw the "alchemy of words" of the poet as coming closer to expressing spiritual sentiments—particularly the dialectics of death—than the dense obscurities of the transcendentalists. More than that, he argued that the power of symbols is that they bring nothingness out of being and draw being into nothingness, and thus serve the dialectics of death as an idiom of negation of being (the ascent of *ōsō*) and at the same time the reaffirmation of being (the descent of *gensō*). This power of the symbol he contrasts with mere "expressions" or "signs" whose focus is life and yet which miss the whole of reality by presenting only a part, either drawing out the nihility of existence or turning nothingness into an idol that eclipses the world of being.

Given developments in symbolic theory at the time Tanabe was writing, his results are not very remarkable, nor his language very precise. Still, this seems to be the only place that any of the Kyoto philosophers takes up the question of the function of mythical and symbolic language in a way that does not simply absorb it into their existing categories. For that reason alone, it merits mention, if not further commentary.

In 1972, ten years after Tanabe's death, the celebrated theologian and astute commentator on Nishida's philosophy, Takizawa Katsumi, noted that the logic of the specific and the dialectic of absolute mediation had been completely forgotten, that not even in Kyoto did one hear talk any longer of Tanabe and his philosophy. His own suggestion is that Tanabe's lean towards nationalism and totalitarianism is at fault. Still, he concludes:

> But anyone who takes the trouble to plow through his prose will realize that the aims of that philosophy and the sentiments of that philosopher disclose an unexpected depth and touch on the most fundamental questions of our own day.

Had there been no clash with Nishida by a disciple of Tanabe's intellectual stature, it is arguable that there would be no Kyoto school as it is known today, and knowledge of Nishida's thought would not be as advanced in the west as it is. This is so not only because of Tanabe's own writings but because of the position in which they put the leading disciple of the next generation, Nishitani Keiji, who could not follow Nishida without coming to grips with Tanabe's critiques and unique contributions.

Nishitani Keiji
(1900–1990)

47 NISHITANI'S LIFE AND CAREER. Nishitani Keiji was born on 27 February 1900 in a small town in Ishikawa Prefecture on the Japan Sea. He did most of his pre-university schooling in Tokyo, where he lived alone with his mother after the death of his father when he was fourteen. Ill from the same tuberculosis that had killed his father, he failed the physical examination on his first attempt to enter the prestigious Daiichi High School. Since he had the highest grades in his class, the humiliation of this weighed heavily on him. After a period of recuperation on the northern island of Hokkaidō at age seventeen, he waited the year out to try again, and this time passed the examination. While waiting, he took some comfort from the novels of Natsume Sōseki, where his attention was caught by references to the Zen state of mind. This led him to reading what he could find on Zen, where he met the writings of D. T. Suzuki.

Once in high school, he found himself liberated from concern over grades and read widely outside of the official curriculum. The works of Dostoevsky, Nietzsche, Ibsen, Emerson, Carlyle, and Strindberg, as well as the Bible and St. Francis of Assisi, were among the books that captured his young imagination. During these years he chanced on a copy of Nishida's *Thought and Experience* in a bookstore and this piqued his interest in philosophy. As graduation approached he had to face a choice on a future career. Though on track to enter Tokyo Imperial University's law department and from there proceed along to the higher echelons of a government post, he had no interest in this. Three choices lay before him: to enter a Zen temple and become a monk, to pursue his interest in philosophy, or to join a newly-begun utopian community called "New Town" founded by the literary figure Mushanokōji Saneatsu. He chose to read philosophy in Kyoto under Nishida, completing the course with a thesis on Schelling, a work so dense that legend has it Tanabe himself had to read it twice.

After graduation in 1924 he taught philosophy at local high schools for eight years, and in 1928 assumed an adjunct lectureship at Kyoto's Ōtani University, which he retained until 1935. During this time he kept up his interest in Schelling by composing a number of essays and by translating two of his works into Japanese, *An Essay on Human Freedom* and *Philosophy and Religion.* Already at this time he showed a wide-ranging interest in a number of philosophical questions, publishing essays in leading philosophical journals on such topics as Kant's aesthetics, idealism, religious feeling, the history of mystical thought, and Plotinus. In 1932 he was appointed lecturer at Kyoto University, the same year that his *History of Mysticism* was published, establishing his reputation in academic circles. Three years later he was promoted to associate professor. During these years his publications focused for two years on Aristotle and then turned to philosophical anthropology under the influence of Dilthey's ideas. The majority of his work, however, focused on religion and the religious dimension of existentialism.

Though he took well to philosophy, it did not entirely satisfy him, and he found his interest in Zen revived. Four years after arriving in Kyoto, in 1936, he traveled to Kamakura with a letter of introduction from D. T. Suzuki to practice Zen under Furukawa Gyōdō at Engaku-ji, but returned after a week to be with his wife for the birth of their second child. In the following year he took up practice at the temple of Shōkoku-ji under Yamazaki Taikō, since it was close to his home. It was then, for the first time, that he says he understood what Nishida means by "direct experience." He continued his practice with Yamazaki for twenty-four years, interrupted only by the two years he spent studying abroad. In 1943 he was given the layman's name of Keisei, "voice of the valley stream." Zen became a permanent feature of his life, though not initially of his academic interest. Rather, it was a matter, as he liked to say, of a balance between reason and letting go of reason, of "thinking and then sitting, sitting and then thinking."

At the age of thirty-seven he received a scholarship from the Ministry of Education to study abroad under Henri Bergson, but the aged philosopher's failing health made this impossible and Nishitani was allowed to go to the University of Freiburg instead, where he spent two years studying under Martin Heidegger, who was lecturing on Nietzsche at the time. While there Nishitani himself prepared and delivered a talk on Nietzsche's *Zarathustra* and Meister Eckhart. On returning he wrote long essays comparing Japan to modern Europe and on German mysticism. Regarding these latter, as he would later recall, he was convinced at the time that "in the mystics the confluence and union of religion and philosophy reached a high point."

With the war in Japan in full swing, Nishitani, as a bright light among the young thinkers of the Kyoto circle, was drawn into questions of political ideology, even as he pursued his interests in religious questions. He did not resist, hoping—as his teachers Nishida and Tanabe encouraged him to hope—that his ideas would add something important to the small chorus of voices resisting the irrationalities of the prevalent ideology. A voracious reader, he was at his best when determined to appropriate what he read into his own inner existential questions. The detour into questions about the cultural, ethnic, and historical identity of contemporary Japan, even where not directly political, were determined by an ideological context outside that inner quest, and seemed to distance him from his native gifts. Ironically, Nishitani is at his most abstract and unappropriated—and I would add at his least perceptive—when he is dealing with public or social issues.

Like Tanabe, and unlike Nishida, he had tried to think out the foundations of a political philosophy from early on, as an essential part of philosophical reflection. His first extended attempt at a philosophical position, a volume he called *A Philosophy of Elemental Subjectivity,* shows him weaving all the main elements of a position together from an epistemological foundation. But his heart and soul were not in the most political of the sections of it, and one senses a certain relief when he was finally able to shake free of these questions.

At the age of forty-three he assumed the principal chair of religion. Not unlike others of his day, he had difficulties with the wartime Ministry of Education, and it was not until two years later, thanks in part to the intervention of Nishida, that he was awarded the doctoral degree with a thesis entitled "Prolegomenon to a Philosophy of Religion." In December 1946, after the defeat in the war, he was obliged to take a leave of absence from the university, and the following July was designated "unsuitable" for teaching by the Occupation authorities. Relieved of his position in the university, he was banned from holding any public position on the grounds of having supported the wartime government. He intensified his practice of Zen, which seems to have given him added strength to accept the affront silently and with tranquility, though not without considerable distress. It was a difficult time for him, and his wife, who would watch him spending whole afternoons watching lizards in the yard, was afraid he would crack under the pain. Still, it was during those years that he produced some of his finest works, including *A Study of Aristotle, God and Absolute Nothingness,* and *Nihilism,* all acknowledged by Tanabe at the time to have been "masterpieces."

Nishitani wrote later complaining of unjust treatment at the hands of the ideologues. "During the war he had been slapped on the left cheek and after the war on the right." Still, the stigma the Occupation forces intended did not have the crippling effect one might imagine, both because the purge itself was so haphazard and viewed with the same distaste as the presence of the foreign army itself, and because Nishitani took it as an opportunity to rethink his philosophical vocation. In doing so, he turned his back resolutely from then on against all invitations to draw practical social conscience into philosophical and religious ideas, preferring to think about the insight of the individual rather than the reform of the social order.

He remained in Kyoto and continued to write, expanding his interests in religion and mysticism to include criticisms of the scientific standpoint that opposed these interests. He did not attempt to defend himself directly against the charges for his expulsion, but two years later published a small book on *Religion, Politics, and Culture.* His main concern at this time lay in the question of nihilism and how to overcome it. The first of a series of important essays on Nishida and Tanabe, not to be completed for another thirty-five years when they were later gathered into a separate volume, shows that at the same time he was trying consciously to appropriate what he had learned from his teachers. These two foci were to set the tone for his mature work.

Five years after being relieved of his teaching post, at the age of fifty-two, Nishida was reinstated in the same chair of religion he had been made to vacate. Six years later, in 1958, he was moved to a chair in the history of philosophy, ceding his former chair to the younger Takeuchi Yoshinori. While continuing his existentialist approach to religion, he also kept up an interest in a wide variety of cultural issues, as well as a critique and appreciation of Japanese spirituality. The touchstone for his broadening the notion of religion seemed to be the relationship of these questions to Zen and what he had begun to call his "standpoint of emptiness." Soon after his reinstatement, he was asked to write an essay on the topic "What is Religion?" One essay led to another, and the results were published in 1961 under the name of the title essay. This was Nishitani's masterpiece, and its publication in English as *Religion and Nothingness* in 1982 by Jan Van Bragt, a Belgian philosopher who had studied under Nishitani after completing a doctoral dissertation on Hegel, marks an important milestone in the introduction of the Kyoto philosophers to the West.

Nishitani retired from Kyoto University in 1963 and, as is customary for retirees in good health, accepted a post as professor at Ōtani University in Kyoto where he had first begun his university teaching. The following year he was named professor emeritus of Kyoto University and was invited to Hamburg as a visiting professor. In fact, Nishitani had kept considerable contact with foreign philosophers, with a solid, if somewhat halting, command of spoken German and English. Living in Kyoto he was more accessible than either Nishida or Tanabe had made themselves in retirement, and he was also more comfortable with public lecturing and with debate with serious scholars from Japan and abroad. Moreover, he was a popular contributor to roundtable discussions, and several volumes have appeared of his conversations with leading intellectuals of Japan.

In 1965 he was asked to serve as chief editor of *The Eastern Buddhist*, a journal begun by D. T. Suzuki and published at Ōtani University. Between 1964 and 1972 he traveled abroad to the United States and Europe on several occasions to address international conferences and deliver special lectures. In 1970 he was awarded the Second Order of the Sacred Treasure, and in 1972, the highest award of the Goethe Medal from the Goethe Institute. In 1982 he was given the Award for Culture Merit. Other awards for scholarly achievement followed.

In 1971 he retired from his professorship at Ōtani University, but continued to teach there as an adjunct professor. He was named president of the Conference on Religion in Modern Society that same year, and retained the post until just before his death. His *Collected Works*, in twenty-six volumes, began appearing in 1986 and were completed in 1995. He died in 1990 at his home in Kyoto, and on that very day was awarded the Senior Grade of the Fourth Court rank, Second Order of the Sacred Treasure. The posthumous Buddhist name he was given at his funeral was based on his Zen name: The layman called the Voice of the Valley Stream, coming from the west and resounding in emptiness.

Nishitani's personal library was donated in its entirety to Ōtani University, where a special collection has been set up in his honor. It is composed of nearly 1,000 volumes of works in western languages and 4,100 in Japanese.

48 NISHITANI'S PHILOSOPHICAL STYLE. Nishitani's mature style, as it has come to the west in translation, shows a buoyancy of expression, a liberal use of the Zen tradition, and a gift for concrete examples that make it stylistically Nishida's and Tanabe's superior. His is the sort of originality that shows up not only in major innovations of thought but also in a making intelligible and tangible much of what his predecessors had left in the abstract. Without Nishitani's genuine feel for the heart of the philosophical problems that Nishida and Tanabe were dealing with, and for their relationship with the fundamental problems of the age, I have no hesitation in saying that the term "Kyoto School" would have little of the currency it now enjoys.

That said, it took his style some time to reach its best, and even then he was still capable of writing prose as dense and difficult as Nishida's. In a roundtable discussion held in 1942 the literary critic Kobayashi Hideo, while having high praise for the clarity of Bergson's prose, pointed an accusing finger at the young Nishitani as typical of Japanese philosophers' unintelligible prose. This was the same Kobayashi who, we recall, had referred to Nishida's writing as "weird." Neither a nationalist nor an enemy of western philosophy, Kobayashi simply loved his language and wanted it to be treated with the same respect with which other countries treated their language. In his words, Nishitani's essays "lacked the sensuality that the Japanese bring to their language," and indeed the style of philosophers in general "give the impression of total indifference to the lot that has fallen them of having to write in Japanese."

Nishitani's response was one of a timid recognition of the problem, followed by a defense of the project he had inherited from Nishida and Tanabe:

> Since we have mainly studied western philosophy, the kind of philosophy we are doing at present has never been done in the east.... It is extremely difficult to stand within this stream from the west and express our thoughts in traditional Japanese. We could force that language on our thinking, but then we would not be understood. It is only natural that we express ourselves by making new words in Japanese.... We have no giants like Pascal or Nietzsche in our ranks, and the fact that the ground is not yet ready for such persons to appear seems to me to be the joint responsibility of literature and philosophy together.

I cite the words at length because the laying of these foundations is what Nishitani himself tried to do in bringing Zen poetry, religion, literature, and philosophy all together in his work. It was not simply the *topics* that interested him, but the *style* proper to each of these topics. In this regard, too, he is the stylistic superior of Nishida and Tanabe. When he counterpoints the song of the cicada with the silence of the rocks, when he contrasts the lies of mechanization and the truthfulness of the natural world, when he depicts Francis of Assisi feeling the cross of the cauterizing iron on his eye like the gentle caress of a mother's hand, his words show an affinity with what they point to that engages the reader.

His arguments do not proceed along a straight line, and indeed at times seem to be going around in circles, but not in the ordinary sense of the word. It is as if Nishitani were making his way up a circular staircase, where at each elevation the perspective broadens beyond the "first sight" so that the relative importance of the items in view need to be adjusted again and again. Even so, it is not an ascent to a final summit of "second sight," but an ascent that is itself circular, descending back to the starting point of everyday experience, which is seen to have been illumined by the insights accumulated during the circumambulation. Independently of the matter being discussed, this way of argumentation lies at the core of Nishitani's philosophy as an exercise in awakening. He was an enthusiastic debater both with his teachers—he remarks in an aside once that he never debated with anyone as much as with Tanabe—and his own students. This is probably why, in late years, he is said to have disliked having his writings published to be read by people he did not know. His greatest fulfillment was thinking in conversation with small groups of students.

Nishitani did not share with Nishida and Tanabe the preoccupation with building a consistent and full philosophical system. His interest was rather with finding a "standpoint" from which he could enlighten a broader range of topics, or perhaps more correctly, with *creating* that standpoint by grappling with them. He wrote essays on classical authors like Aristotle, Plotinus, Augustine, Eckhart, Boehme, Descartes, Kant, Schelling, Hegel, Nietzsche, Dostoevsky, Bergson, and Heidegger, and was one of the pioneers of the translation of classics of western thought into Japanese, including works of Schelling and Kierkegaard. He drew on Asian classics from Buddhism, Taoism, and Confucianism and gave original interpretations of a number of Christian scriptural themes.

One cannot read Nishitani the way one reads Nishida or Tanabe. He was not struggling to define and redefine his working concepts, or to present any kind of a body of thought in the ordinary sense of the word. His is an accumulation of insight. Whatever the particular insights he had along the way, it was the continual uncovering of the sense of things just as they are, and the exposure of what we do to block ourselves from seeing them, that was his focus. He was always looking for the same thing, and once he found it, he went out to look for it again. The breadth of his interests was the opposite of the dilettante; the lack of specialization the opposite of the popularizer. He wanted only to see, nothing more. And while he was generally tolerant of those pursuing philosophy as a career or a field of expertise, he refused to be drawn into their world. I have seen this time and again. Those who knew him better and longer attest to it also.

Nishitani was aware of the overtly religious quality of his writing, much more than Nishida's was but close to the later Tanabe's. He also felt that this would affect his acceptance abroad, where religious questions are more assiduously separated from the philosophical and quickly aligned with the theological. He felt a closer affinity with the existentialists—Kierkegaard, Sartre, Heidegger, Jaspers, in the main—and the mystics—principally Eckhart—for their insistence on the appropriation of insight, than with scholars of religion, Buddhalogists, or theologians who aimed at a greater objectivity toward their subject matter. This affinity is reflected in the way his own philosophical style evolved from the purely theoretical to the ever more radically internalized theoretical.

As a person, Nishitani is remembered by those who knew him as magnanimous but possessed of an inner strength and an uncanny ability to strike at the heart of the matter in discussion. Ueda Shizuteru recalls after nearly forty-five years in his presence, "It was almost as if he were breathing a different air from those around him." Mutō Kazuo, known as one of the major disciples of Tanabe, called him "the finest, most remarkable teacher I have ever encountered upon this earth."

When Nishitani delivered an address, he would often carry with him no more than the corner of an envelope or a matchbook on which he had written his notes, and then proceed to wind his way slowly into the subject matter. The impression was of someone speaking from rich resources within, and no doubt it was that. But in going through the papers he left behind, it was discovered that those notes he carried with him were simply the final distillation of several sets of notes for a particular talk that typically begin with a bundle of papers, are condensed to a few pages, then to a single page, and finally to a couple of lines. It is not surprising, therefore, to find his published lectures—which comprise no less than eleven of the twenty-six volumes of his *Collected Writings*—reading as well organized as they do.

I have avoided the customary carving of the careers of Nishida and Tanabe into stages because I felt it more important to concentrate on recurrent themes as far as I could. In the case of Nishitani, no one has yet studied his opus as a whole, let alone stage it. In any case, to impose a structure on a thinking as organic as Nishitani's was, even if only for purposes of résumé, risks obscuring what is most distinctive about it. As before, we can focus on specific motifs, several of them signaled by a distinctive vocabulary. With the exception of his excursus into political ideology, we can describe these motifs with a minimum of attention to their dating or locating them in the development of his ideas.

One further caveat is in order. As the years passed Nishitani dealt more and more with Buddhist themes. Unlike his dealings with western philosophers, which can be referred to without further ado, the Buddhist concepts need considerable background to understand; and all the more so because here, too, Nishitani is reinterpreting and rereading in a way that does not always coincide with received scholarship. In the framework of this book, I will not make those digressions but take his Buddhist generalizations at face value and with the simplest of résumé.

49 **A STARTING POINT IN NIHILISM.** Jaspers says that philosophy begins—where Aristotle and Plato had seen it to begin—in wonder at existence and the desire to know, is clarified by doubt, and is confronted with the finitude of human existence itself. Nishitani saw things the exact reverse. As a child of his age, he saw that the only route to philosophy was one that began in a nihilistic despair over the human condition, passed on to doubt over all of existence, and only then ascended to the wonder of emptiness. This pattern is present already in the essay he wrote on Nietzsche and Eckhart while with Heidegger in Germany, in which he sees that nihilistic despair is overcome not from without but from within nihilism itself, at its depths.

Behind these ideas lay the story of a troubled youth who seemed to have constellated in his person the anxieties of the age:

> My life as a young man can be described in a single phrase: it was a period absolutely without hope.... My life at the time lay entirely in the grips of nihility and despair.... My decision, then, to study philosophy was in fact—melodramatic as it might sound—a matter of life and death.

Whatever other motivations may have been at work in Nishitani's first dabbling in philosophy, the way it disciplined his existential questions, sharpening and deepening them, is what kept him there throughout his life. Indeed, the deeper he got into his study of the German idealists and the western mystics, the more he began to suffer from a psychological condition that he described as "a great void inside of myself." The more his thinking matured, the more distance he felt from life, "like a fly bumping up against a windowpane but unable to get through," or like a person watching a blizzard from behind a window, unable to feel the bite of the snow and wind on his face. For a period he seems to have questioned the whole validity of philosophy and the academic life as such. It is not that the dark halls of academia had cut him off from the fresh air and bright sunshine of the real world, but that the artificial light and comfortable environment of the university shut him off from the great darkness and anxiety that awaited outside.

As he regained his footing, with the aid of Zen meditation, he did not simply return to the same philosophical themes but went on to rephrase them to include the experience of the "bottom dropping out from under one" and the "conversion" of this experience from a negation of life to its reaffirmation. This led to his work on elemental subjectivity and to his reappropriation of the mystics, to which we will turn presently. Indeed, the idea of finding a place to stand in full awareness of the bottom having dropped out of the ordinary standpoint of religion or philosophy was to remain a permanent feature of all of his philosophy from that point on, eclipsed though it was for a brief period by his interest in political philosophy.

Part of the cause of the attraction to nihilistic thinking that cannot be discounted was the general malaise of the loss of identity among Japanese intellectuals, who distanced themselves from the common people and the "native ground of traditional culture" to lose themselves in western ideas that could not provide them with an identity either. The "I" became, as he says, ephemeral. During the early years of the war, he was convinced that the ordinary Japanese still carried in their hearts the traditional spirit, if only it could be reawakened for society at large. After the war, he grew pessimistic in this matter, and this view remained with him for some time to come, as reflected in comments he made at a 1958 roundtable discussion:

> Religion is impotent in Japan. We don't even have a serious atheism. In Europe, every deviation from tradition has to come to terms with tradition or at least runs up against it. This seems to explain the tendency to interiority or introspection that makes people into thinking people. In Japan… ties with tradition have been cut; the burden of having to come to terms with what lies behind us has gone and in its place only a vacuum remains.

Wonder does not provoke questions of despair, but questions of despair, if lived through, do provoke a restoration of wonder. Jaspers's viewpoint seems to fall in line with the fact that the fall from grace in the Christian myth is preceded by an original state of paradisal bliss and followed by revelations of the divine in history. Pathos is surrounded by wonder. Nishitani's cultural background provided no such assumption. One is tempted to think that, at the same time as he falls into a long line of philosophers of the west, he draws the inspiration for his nihilism rather from the Buddhism of the East. But this is not the case either. By nihilism he does not mean the mere confronting the meaninglessness of life to overcome it by appeal to some religious tradition or outside philosophical system. It is rather confronting the religious and ethical answers to this meaninglessness and rejecting them. It pronounces with Nietzsche "God is dead," and from that point on begins to deepen. "My basic task, simply put, was to overcome nihilism by passing through it."

The history behind these words was one of personal despair, combined with a reading of Dostoevsky's novels and of Nietzsche, whose *Thus Spoke Zarathustra* he once told me he had carried around with him in his school years "like a bible," and to which were added his struggles with the dark, pessimistic side of Schelling's philosophy. Unlike Nishida and Tanabe, whose philosophical starting points may be associated with a certain cluster of ideas or a distinctively philosophical ideal, Nishitani began in despair, nihility, and negativity. To this extent his philosophy mirrors language in having more to say about the dark side of life than the bright, as storytellers have long known. In this sense, his starting point was not his own but something close to the human condition itself. But it was first his own. More than his early struggles with the meaning of life, he saw his whole career as a promising young teacher of philosophy wrenched out from under him when he was in his prime. These were the conditions in which his earlier confrontations with nihilism were brought to a head. Either he passed through these events in a deliberate and self-conscious form, with all the reflective tools he had at his disposal, or they would defeat him.

50 ELEMENTAL SUBJECTIVITY.

Nishitani's first book, published in 1940 under the title *A Philosophy of Elemental Subjectivity,* is actually a collection of ten essays previously published, and shows the typical disjunction of such collections. What is interesting is that, rather than follow the order of their appearance, he rearranges them, with the section on "Religion and Culture" at the opening, a choice that symbolizes the direction his thought was moving in already at this early date.

Here we find a first clear expression of what Nishitani understands the nature of religion to be: the awareness of elemental subjectivity. The term *subjectivity,* which Nishitani introduced into philosophy through his translation of Kierkegaard, fills the role that western languages give to the reflexive pronoun by making it a noun: selfhood, the self, the ego. Later he will use the term sparingly, though grammar forces us to continue using the noun forms to describe what he means by self and ego.

By calling subjectivity *elemental* he means something different from *fundamental;* in fact, he means something completely *without foundation* in outside authority, divine law, or faith. This subjectivity is the autonomous reason of the modern world, which he sees containing a contradiction as well as the dialectic structure to overcome that contradiction. While the form this takes in the modern world is different, the basic pattern of the contradiction was something he had already recognized in the western mystical tradition:

> The awareness that says "I am I" senses on the one hand a *transcendent* freedom and self-existence that not even God can rob me of.... On the other hand, "I am I" signals an egoism: one is closed up in oneself, in the isolation

> of being someone particular. And in this isolation lies the possibility for mooring *free choice* for good or evil.

Here Nishitani is as much voicing his own views and experience as he is saying something about mystical thought. In any event, it is just this contradiction that is the goal of his proposed philosophy of elemental subjectivity. The breakthrough comes in realizing that the ground of one's freedom and transcendence that seems to be all one's own, is not solid ground at all, but an isolation from life itself and a form of self-deception. And with that the very bottom seems to drop out of the self. This is the standpoint, he tells us, he tries to make his own, similarly to the way Nietzsche and Eckhart had tried.

Without following his argument through all its twists and turns, not to mention the convoluted vocabulary he was given to in his early thinking, the overcoming of the contradiction of elemental subjectivity is achieved by awakening to the "elemental naturalness" of life itself. As the "bottom drops out" of the ego, a new subjectivity emerges, naturally and of itself, which is the fountainhead of religious wisdom, rational understanding, and a natural life—and with this new subjectivity, the possibility of a critique of culture, history, and religion.

This latter theme forms the basis of a 1937 essay on "Religion, History, and Culture," in which he tries to submit culture and history to a religious critique. By "culture" he means the culture of autonomy that characterizes the modern world (the "culturism" that we recall Tanabe had criticized more than two decades earlier), particularly as it infects religious consciousness. Similarly, by history he understands a historical understanding of religion that shows up in an eschatological view of time, and that takes the form of fideism or an opposition between faith and reason. In other words, culture and history represent the domains of reason and faith respectively, whose contradiction religion overcomes in what he now calls "a standpoint of absolute nothingness" in which the truly elemental and the truly subjective coalesce. He characterizes the standpoint this way:

> (1) Absolute nothingness opposes all things by absolute negation, both ego and its egoity, humanity and its human-centeredness.... (2) That it is nothingness and not being signifies that elemental subjectivity can appear as egoless.... It is the nothingness that Eckhart called the "ground" of God in "godhead" in which God is my ground and I am the ground of God. It is the standpoint of an elemental and subjective unity of God-centeredness-*in*-human-centeredness and vice-versa.... (3) As a standpoint that unites the elemental and the subjective..., only through this absolute nothingness can one be stripped subjectively of autonomous reason.

Historical faith, Nishitani asserts, negates the autonomy of reason as something relative, only to turn around and make itself absolute instead; just as the autonomous reason of modern culture negates the debilitating effects of faith on reason in order to set itself up as absolute. Neither of these negations is absolute, but only relative to that which they are trying to overthrow. It is the breakthrough—the term is drawn from his extended treatment of Eckhart—of these relative negations into absolute nothingness that makes possible true elemental subjectivity.

The key here is the idea of the "naturalness" out of which a new subjectivity emerges. The source of this naturalness is life itself, to which the categories of freedom/dependency, good/evil, reasonable/unreasonable that we usually associate with human consciousness of the world of being do not apply. Nor do the ordinary categories of religion and faith. The restoration of subjectivity from its source means a return to this life in a nothingness beyond being, in a godhead beyond God.

At the same time, this life does not lie in another world beyond this one. It is found on what Nishitani calls, using the Buddhist term for life beyond death, the "other shore" of this very world; or in a paraphrase of Nishida's description of reality as pure experience, a "pure practice." This practice discloses itself as the love innate in life itself. In the process of a conversion to elemental subjectivity beyond ego, religion shows us "the other face" of God, different from that of the just lawgiver, the face of indiscriminate love:

> On the far shore of justice, of good and evil, there is a standpoint indifferent to value judgments. It is the standpoint of absolute love, of the nothingness of the godhead, a standpoint at which a no-self that has left behind its ground appears. Just as the godhead surpasses God as person, and just as non-ego surpasses the self as "person," so does this "love" transcend the personal.... It is what the mystics called "the naturalness of God."

In these lines we see condensed a theme that Nishitani will enrich for the next two decades and orchestrate as a major motif in his magnum opus, *Religion and Nothingness.* We also get a glimpse at how Nishitani took it as a permanent task to appropriate the notion of God into his thinking.

51 A PHILOSOPHY FOR NATIONALISM.

Whereas Nishida had tried to squeeze a political philosophy out of an abstract metaphysic and only ended up breathing life into the idols he wanted to topple, Nishitani did create a political philosophy, the principal statement of which was a

1941 book entitled *View of the World, View of the Nation.* He knew that he was doing something novel. In his late years he confided in a letter that his book "was the first book that attempted to analyze from a philosophic point of view the historical reality of the time in terms of world politics—and of Japan as a country seen from that same perspective." What he did not know at the time he was writing his work was that as a result he would be drawn into discussions of nationalist topics that would contradict, and contradict mightily, the naïve idealism that had drawn him into political philosophy in the first place.

The initial motivations for turning to this area were his own, and did not come in response to any outside request. Three months after beginning his study abroad in Germany, full-scale hostilities broke out between China and Japan. He chanced upon a newspaper article in the local Berlin press which said that "the stage of history was shifting to the Pacific" and that "the spotlight was on Japan." Though having no more than the ordinary interest in history and politics, he said, the fact of reading this while abroad caused a shock:

> While most Germans looked on the event as unavoidable, given the combination of the political attitude of China at the time and the overpopulation of Japan and the deficiency in natural resources, many of my countrymen just stood aloof or criticized it from the grandstands.... In letters from Japan I learned that while the newspaper boys were running the streets screaming out the headlines, the intellectuals just took it all in with a cool eye.

For his part, as a scholar of religion and philosophy he could not stand by while his view of the world was being challenged, and particularly not as he saw how his German colleagues were debating the issues. Though doubting he was the right one to take up the question, he felt that he could contribute something. He carried these thoughts back with him to Japan, and almost immediately began to frame his thoughts.

We might note that during this time he penned a short commentary on Hitler's *Mein Kampf* in which he points out the grave danger of combining "brutality" and "idealism" with a "totalitarian" view of the nation that sacrifices religion, the arts, and indeed all of intellectual tradition to the aim of preserving a particular race to the neglect of humanity.

View of the World, View of the Nation is a short but dense book, with a carefully structured argument. He begins by laying out a number of current ideas in political philosophy that challenge the liberalist idea of the state as a "legal" subject. The trend towards increased politicization and control, which other western historians of his time were writing about as a phenomenon in western nations, seemed to him an inevitable counterreaction to liberalism. From a fatalistic (he would have said at the time "realistic"), almost Hegelian, height, he sees the battle between state authority and individual freedom as the necessary preparation for a new form of freedom: "a direct synthesis of thoroughgoing control by the nation and thoroughgoing freedom... is the fundamental requirement of a modern nation."

It is the interplay of these two poles that take up the bulk of his book. He handles it philosophically by speaking of the orientation towards state control as "substrate" and the orientation towards individual freedom as "subjectivity." The essence of the nation is to control by "substrating" the individuals in a ground of common unity. The essence of individual freedom is to appropriate this control consciously and thereby to "subjectivize" the state. This latter, he insists, is not a mere absolutism that swallows up freedoms or a liberalism that isolates the individual from the state. His earlier criticisms of Hitler notwithstanding, he then adds:

> For example, movements manifest in mottos like "One million, one mind" or "Ein Volk, ein Reich, ein Führer" are the perfection of the movement of a national community in which the self is shaped all the way to the level of the nation. Here the nation (and hence the community) reflects its will in the interiority of the individual and thereby raises its own unity to a higher plane, while individuals recognize the will of the community (and hence also their own will) within the will of the nation and awaken to the nation within themselves.

Despite his repudiations of totalitarianism in any form, by reducing the freedom of the individual to the freedom to appropriate the controls of the state, Nishitani is clearly tottering on the edge of a justification of just that. As his argument proceeds, however, it is clear that this is not an ordinary nationalism, and that it could be perceived as dangerous by the militarists in power.

The idea he advanced, and which was in fact considered a threat by the ideologues at the time, was that the subjectivization of the nation's essence included an awakening to something that those preoccupied with maintaining the control of the modern state miss: the realization in the minds of its free citizenry of the nation's inner drive to open to the wider world. This latent "globality" as he called it was necessary to overcome the idea of the modern liberal nation without collapsing into totalitarianism. He called it a "leap from the subjectivity of a national *ego* to that of a national *non-ego*." But it is only possible if individuals see that current forms of the state are at a turning point in history, and see that this transitional time is also a spiritual task of the individual who needs to undergo a transformation of perspective, one that stretches the horizon of "being in the world" beyond national boundaries.

> Just as the individual ego manifests itself in its true form at the point of self-negation or no-self,... so, too, the nation attains its true form when it has transcended its ordinary mode of being and has discovered a new mode of being centered on self-negation.

Nations can perform this spiritual task only through their individual citizens. The "standpoint of absolute nothingness" that is required to negate the self, to transcend history in order to be fully within it, remains the task of the individual. But it is not the individual locked into the preservation of private freedoms, but an individual in which "the age of global history as such comes to awareness of itself as a single body, as a spiritual totality."

From such a standpoint, he argued, the dark side of the state, its tendency to revert to its "natural, authoritarian roots," could be replaced with a resurgence of a more "intense naturalness" in the form of a "moral energy" to help the nation transcend its present form. Since he was writing a political philosophy, however, and not a religious tract, he needed to come to terms with the ruling ideology. He did this by taking up the *Principles of the National Polity* that the Ministry of Education had issued in 1936 as a handbook for ethical training, though without mentioning it by name, and argued his case in that vocabulary. The connections were not lost on the ideologues who attacked him, he says, for having claimed that the nation should abandon its self-identity.

The spiritual task, while individual, is not chosen in the first place by the individual but is presented by history, which he saw at the dawn of a new age in which the current order was breaking down. The ancient empires organized on the principle of conquest—a universality that did not allow for a plurality of individuals—had collapsed to make way for the modern state that camouflaged its Eurocentricism under the fiction of a plurality of individual nations that did not allow for a universality. This world is now at its end:

> That the world no longer has a specific center and therefore a defined periphery but has numerous geographical centers represents the simplest and yet the most universal impetus for a new world order.... It is the expression of the most profound movement in world history, the appearance of the ultimate foundations of world necessity.

The "specific center" that could no longer organize the world was Europe, and the plurality of centers that he saw as capable of doing so was "a community of individual nations made up of a plurality of self-sufficient and distinct spheres striving for unity." This order, however, was to be held in place not by a simple totality of all nations but by blocs of nations forming a plurality of unities. On this basis he justified the Japanese drive to become the center of a new East Asian order as a necessary defence against the vestiges of a former Eurocentric colonialization. Japan has a special role here because of its clear "mark of superiority" among the other nations of eastern Asia in the strength of its culture and spirituality; this strength will enable it to live through the chaotic limbo of living between two worlds, the one passing away and the one coming to be.

The danger that this "promotion of the Japanese spirit in the world at large" (he uses the same words as the slogan being touted by military sympathizers in the mid-1930s) would end up simply imposing what is specifically Japan on other nations, he felt, could be overcome by the cultivation of a new "ethos" whose model he found in late-Edo and early-Meiji Japan, where religious belief was tied to religious devotion to the emperor and patriotism. He argues that this ethos arises from a distinctive fusion of practice and insight long cultivated in the east, engaging tradition rather than setting it aside as the scientific rationalism of the west does. It is at once "the pride of Japanese culture" and a stimulus to other countries to take pride in their own cultural achievements.

The implication here is that religion has a role to play in politics, and in the final chapter of the book he says in so many words that "the concentration of all life and culture in the life of the nation" is something good for the nation and for religion itself. Although he qualifies his enthusiasm with a reminder that the heart of religion belongs to the individual and therefore cannot be made to coincide with public life, still, insofar as the fundamental task of religion is the overcoming of the private ego, "there is a healthy relationship between religion and politics at the point where the return to the 'public' takes place through an obliteration of the 'private'."

He goes a step further to argue that traditional mythology has a role to play, despite the attempts of modern rationalism to relegate it to a relic of the past by expropriating it entirely into the realm of academic study. At the same time he is concerned about efforts in Japan's native Shinto to move from "myth into history," a danger we will recall that Nishida also objected to. To do so is to put it on the same plane as the irrational tendency towards a racial ethics based on *Blut und Boden* or towards political totalitarianism. Nishitani saw both of these as a kind of historicized mythology meant to counter the rationalizing of morality that leads to philosophies of a "morality of universal human nature" and to the imposition of political theories of liberalism and democracy.

Insofar as religious institutions produce doctrines they become objects of learning, Nishitani argues, but at the same time they create a certain imperceptible but deep gap between religion and the religious demands of ordinary people, which weakens the doctrine. Religion needs to mediate its doctrine through a positive concern with ethics, though always in a relationship of negation-*in*-affirmation, since religion as such by nature transcends both ethics and doctrine and is, in the end, "the only force that can eradicate the deepest roots of our self-centered ego."

He concludes his book with a statement that Christianity and Buddhism share the magnanimous ideal of a subjectivity of non-ego:

> If we can repossess and preserve this great heart in the midst of the growing tribulations of the present, it may become the core of a religious doctrine directed to our age. In its education system the nation teaches learning and expounds morality. These things are necessary for the life of a nation, but they also depend on religion not simply turning its back on that necessity but going on, from its own standpoint, to supplement them with its own teaching about this great heart.

During the war Nishitani was aware of the social implications of his work as never before. He knew that his remarks on Shinto and globality within the nation were scrutinized by the powers that be as well as those opposed to those powers. The special police watched his house; the army was suspicious; the Marxists were unhappy. His interest in world philosophy—something that had all along been obvious and easy to defend on intellectual grounds—had become a social issue. The very notion of a *world*view was suspect of blasphemy against the land of the gods. The idea that Japan belonged to a larger world was rejected in the program of militaristic education of the day. Aware that the young were reading their books, Nishitani and others of the Kyoto circle published in specialized journals, and by 1943 and 1944 were avoiding mainline publishers altogether.

52 **HISTORICAL NECESSITY.** In September 1939, Nishida, then in retirement in Kamakura, was paid a visit by Captain Takagi Sōkichi, an officer in the research division of the secretariat of the Department of the Navy. The purpose of the visit was to request the support of academics of the "Kyoto school" in helping the Navy stem the escapades of the Army,

which was headed for a war with the United States that it could not win. Recognizing the hollowness of the ruling slogans of "all the world under one roof," and "East-Asian Coprosperity Sphere," he broached the subject by asking for advice regarding what intellectual and political ideals might be employed to give these slogans a richer sense, one that would appeal to Japan's Asian neighbors and at the same time draw on both the traditions of the east and the philosophy and science of the west. As Nishida had already cooperated, though not full-heartedly, with a previous attempt of the Navy to set up a discussion group of intellectuals, he felt confident of support.

He was not mistaken. Nishida advised him to talk to Kōsaka Iwao but to be sure to go through Tanabe, who was the central figure in Kyoto at the time. Takagi did just that, and found them both enthusiastic about the plan. Nishida gave his approval by letter and the faculty at Kyoto approved Kōsaka's appointment as an attaché to the Department of the Navy and gave its approval to cooperation by Nishitani, Kōsaka Masaaki, and Suzuki Shigetaka (a historian who would also take part in the discussions on overcoming modernity) in the project. None of these decisions was made public to avoid drawing the attention of the Army.

This was actually part of a larger project of Takagi's to set up a "brain trust" of intellectuals on whom the Navy could count for support against the Army. While he was at work on this, the Kyoto participants met to discuss what the form and focus of their contribution would be. Frequent visits were also made to Kamakura to ask Nishida for advice. It was not until more than two years after that first visit to Nishida that preparations were ready for the first of what have come to be known as the *Chūōkōron* discussions, after the name of the journal in which they would be published. It took place in November of 1941, less than two weeks before the declaration of the Greater East Asian War. The following discussions were held in March and November of 1942.

The first printing of 15,000 copies, which bore the title *A World-Historical Standpoint and Japan,* sold out in no time and had to be reprinted. The press hailed it as an open-minded debate and young intellectuals were drawn to it. The Army was not pleased at the reaction it caused and railed against its "ivory-towered speculations that risked reducing the Empire to simply one more category of world history." They pressured the government to ban any further reprints and to put a stop to the "Kyoto school" interventions in the war cause.

The initial enthusiasm with which it was received underwent a complete about-face after the war, when it was condemned across the board as part of the general campaign of fascist propaganda. Even many of the same persons who had read carefully between the lines for the veiled criticisms of the Army and who had privately gloated over the reaction of the ultranationalists, were content with dismissing the surface of the text—a habit of thinking that was in fact rather common among those who hopped on the postwar bandwagons to condemn anyone and anything that had led Japan to its sorry fate. Within ten years some historians were throwing around wild claims that the young scholars of the *Chūōkōron* discussions had forged an "imperialistic philosophy" that had "rationalized ultranationalism with ideas taken from the philosophy of Nishida and Tanabe, and led the people of Japan towards war."

Calmer assessments of the discussions tend to focus on a naïveté shared by the participants and the most fanatic of their postwar critics regarding the contribution the Kyoto intellectuals had made, and to argue that attempts to pour the history of a country at war into the mold of an already formulated philosophy of absolute nothingness at most end up "stumbling into endorsement" and in any case can hardly be expected to respond to the concrete issues involved. "What kind of logic would it take after all," asks Takeuchi Yoshimi, "in order for thinking to act effectively on reality? No one was able to discover such a logic during the war, and no one has been able to discover one since." Nonetheless, as important as the context of the remarks and the currency of the vocabulary is to the text, there are any number of points at which the text speaks strongly enough for itself, and I will draw them out lest the judgment of Nishitani's nationalism look completely fabricated.

In Nishitani's contribution, there is less novelty in his ideas than there is in his attempt to argue that they in fact matter to the situation at hand. But the leap from a theoretical political philosophy to a practical one is by no means a simple matter, and certainly not as simple as Nishitani tried to make it. His strategy, shared by the others, was to offer an alternative history to the Japan-centered view being force-fed to the nation—"like frogs in a well" as Nishitani said—as a matter of governmental policy. By taking the high ground of world history, it was felt, events could be seen in context. This was the focus of the first discussion. In the second and third, this was applied to the morality of the East Asian coprosperity sphere and then to the idea of all-out war itself.

If there was any doubt of the nationalistic side of Nishitani's political philosophy up to that time, these doubts are fairly well laid to rest by reading the way the proceedings turn after the outbreak of the Pacific War. This is reflected in a preface to the published volume, bearing the signature of the four participants, which aggravates any attempt to excuse him entirely from such sentiments:

> The quintessence of our esteemed national polity was exalted more and more in the face of hardship, as it faced hardships with honor, and the dignified mien of the Imperial Army at land and at sea moved the hearts and minds of the world.... We were deeply impressed by the great beneficence of the empire and privately consoled that our discussions had hit the mark as well as it did.... At bottom there was something on which we stood in full mutual agreement: the world-historical standpoint of Japan.

There is nothing out of the ordinary in this rhetoric understood as the patriotic sentiment of a people at war. But since it was precisely the ideas upholding that popular sentiment that they were questioning, and doing so in a deliberately "scholarly" manner, one cannot justify this collapse into pure sentimentalism except that they were speaking tongue-in-cheek, a justification no one has seriously offered. One has to assume their sentiment belonged to an unreflected side of their thought.

This assumption is borne out by the discussions themselves. While it is true that they wanted to distance themselves from the government ideologies, both by avoiding mention of things like the Shinto mythology of the sacred foundation of Japan and by widening the stage of history to see Japan as only one of the players on it, they were doing so not in order to see the war effort as a dishonor but to place its honorable intentions in a more worthy philosophical setting.

They accomplished this philosophically by arguing that Japan had become a "world-historical race" not of its own choosing but as a matter of necessity. The question is whether it will assume its role consciously or simply be led along blindly by fate. If the former, then it needs to combine a sense of history wide enough to recognize that such necessities do in fact occur—"a deeper grasp of the great workings going on in the flow of history"—with a subjective awareness practical enough, constructive enough, to create the new world order that historical necessity is in fact now calling for.

On this latter point, notice the progression of the argument in the following of Nishitani's interventions:

> Viewed in terms of an I-you relation, Europe's position towards the problem of Asia has been one of an exclusive "I." This is why European consciousness is now in crisis, while Japan is simply looking to a new world order....
>
> The idea that only the Aryan race is *kulturschaffend* while the Japanese are at the lower level of the *kulturtragend* is a good indication of the feeling of superiority... of the Europeans at large....

> For Europe, in addition to German history and British history there was also European history—a world history—that begins from Egypt and Greece.... Is not the most important thing to cultivate the same kind of historical outlook for an East Asian history that comprises Japan, the Korean states, China, and the rest as one world?

Taken out of context, these remarks would seem to harmonize quite well with the official government ideology. It is the qualifications I have left out, namely the repeated appeal to Japan to act with the demands of world history taking precedence over self-interest, that drew the ire of the rightists and the Army against the published volume. This ire was symbolized in the speech of a ranking member of the Army calling for the Kyoto school philosophers to be rounded up with the Koreans and the American and British prisoners of war and bayoneted. Hard as it may seem to think of the comments that will follow in the coming pages as counterproductive to the war effort, we have no choice but to accept the fact that this is precisely how they were perceived by those at the helm of power.

53 MORAL ENERGY AND ALL-OUT WAR. Nishitani argues in the second of the *Chūōkōron* discussions that accomplishing a unity in Asia as Europe had done for the west will call for a *moralische Energie* based on an idea of nationalism and racialism strong enough to stand up to democracy, and that only Japan is up to the task. It was Nishitani who introduced the term into the discussions, though it was not until the second discussion, with the war uppermost in everyone's mind, that he tried to apply it concretely.

The summoning of this energy belongs to religion, or more correctly, adds a dimension to religion that was missing in its focus on the interiority and the transcendent (although, we might add, one that he himself would not miss in his later writings):

> Traditionally, a religious standpoint means that the past can be revived at any time. But what is needed at present is a standpoint of religion that will embrace modern ideas of progress—a pragmatic idealism that will yet resist becoming an idealistic religion.

Religion, like ethics, remains abstract if not linked to historical knowledge—not the facts of history but the philosophy of history that is the ground of those facts. Since the effect of this practical ethic extends beyond Japan, simple attention to local tradition will not do. This is the task of leadership that Japan needs to awaken to, then: to transmit its moral energy to its Asian neighbors so that they in turn can recover similar strength from their own background. It is particularly necessary for China, whose own spiritual resources have been depleted, to yield to the moral energy of Japan as a matter of historical vocation:

> The most basic issue is the "China-consciousness" of the Chinese as having always been the center of East Asia and of Japan as having been educated through the grace of Chinese culture.... The main thing is somehow to make them realize that Japan is now the leader in the construction of the Greater East Asia of today, and *must* be the leader as a matter of historical necessity. ... Only then does it become possible to think of showing moral energy in East Asia at large.

This call for the submission of China to the will of Japan is accompanied, at least in Nishitani's interventions, by a clear sense of resentment toward the world's "contempt" for Japan as always playing second-fiddle to the great civilization of China. Chinese culture had once made Japan strong, but now it is the science and technology of Europe that backs up Japan. This train of thought leads him to make what I see as the most embarrassing statements he makes in the discussion, if not in his entire public life. I cite the passages at length, the first two from the second discussion, the third from the last:

> I am reminded of something that happened on the ship to Europe. A Filipino from Shanghai told me that he was envious of Japan, and that the Filipinos must take in more of Japanese culture if they want their country to become like Japan. I remember thinking to myself at the time that things are not so simple. Japan's spirit has been refined through a long historical process. Before the arrival of European culture, Japan was possessed of an extremely high spiritual culture of its own, and an extremely vital dynamic was at work. Since that is lacking in the Philippines, even if they take in the same European culture the effect will be extremely different.

> Japan's population is too small for the construction of the Great East Asian Sphere.... Is it not possible to turn those among the races of the area with superior qualities into a kind of half-Japanese? The Chinese race or the people of Thailand, having their own history and culture, have a sense of brotherhood that inhibits such a transformation. Or again, there are the Filipinos who have no culture of their own but have had to indulge in America's culture; these are perhaps the most difficult to handle. In contrast, races that have no historical culture of their own but are possessed of superior qualities, such as the Malays.... Well, I am thinking that it is not impossible to take such a race, or the Filipino Moros (here I am speaking secondhand, but they

> are said to be good also), races of high quality, and from their early years educate them and turn them into half-Japanese.... This would be one measure to counter the small numbers of Japanese, and at the same time would call forth from them their racial self-awareness as well as their moral energy. I have been thinking of this as one possible plan.
>
> In the case of Korea..., the general idea of a "Korean race" has been too rigid and inflexible to be of use any more.... Now that Korea has been subjected to military inscription and what has been called "the Korean race" has entered into Japan in a completely subjective form, that is, where they have become subjectively Japanese, the small idea of "race" that has so far been considered something fixed now seems to have fused into a larger notion. In some sense the Yamato race and the Korean race can be said to have become one.

There is no point straining to justify these comments, let alone to see them as part of Nishitani's political philosophy. They are unreflected bias pure and simple, no less banal than if they had rolled off the tongue of one of the ultranationalists whose ideas the discussions were supposed to be repudiating. It is not their depth, and certainly not their empirical base, that gives them weight but the context in which they were spoken, making it all the harder to suspend judgment in the light of the circumstances.

The final discussion, held eight months after the second, was more daring than the previous two in that it took up the question of the meaning of war. In them Nishitani distinguishes himself for his support of the war effort both in philosophical principle and in fact. As is almost universally the case with those caught up in war, the claim is made that theirs was "a different war from all previous wars." Militarily speaking it represents a shift from "total war," which is focused on military equipment and personnel alone, to an "all-out war" that mobilizes the entire economy, social structure, and spirituality of a people in a comprehensive state ideology.

Nishitani argued that the very life or death of Japan as a nation is tied up with the coprosperity sphere, and that the war over the coprosperity sphere is a war over the end of modernity in Asia or the continuation of western colonial influence. He tidily bundles up Japan's mission in Asia, its identity as a world-historical people, the end of modernity, and the engagement of the entire nation as a single unit in all-out war:

> Not only is it a matter of the life or death of our own country, but of the life or death of the coprosperity sphere, that is, of a new world order. Our nation's life and death hangs in the balance with it.... In the present war the consciousness of the people has unfolded into what could be called the consciousness of a world-historical people, the subjective awareness of a people that it is theirs to decide the order of the world as a whole.... Externally, the

> goal is the reform of world order... Internally, what is called for is a reform deep in the consciousness of each member of the country.

What we have here is not a conclusion from the discussions but a reiteration of their starting point, the assumption that they share with the war government, not a matter for debate. The discussion's focus is rather to locate this kind of war in a philosophy of history.

Nishitani's own interventions in this regard are considerable. Basically there are five points, which I will summarize using his own words as far as possible, supposing that the citations already supplied should have made clear enough the manner in which he was expressing himself.

First, the national or racial consciousness that is made manifest in war between races slides into a support of imperialism or colonialism if it does not include consciousness of the identity of the new world being shaped through war, a world that takes in also the enemy nations. This does not mean simply accepting the self-understanding of other nations as it has been, but guiding them to a new self-consciousness. To do so requires a high level of awareness of one's own subjectivity, in both its ethical and spiritual dimensions. This awareness is the "primary essence" of a people that must serve the political and economic forces of the country as its own spiritual foundation and guide the new world in the making, and to do this it must appeal to reason. Without it, there is no way to overcome the effects on Japan's Asian neighbors of the "ceaseless propagandizing" of England and the United States, let alone to win their consent to the reality of what is happening.

Second, political leadership has to provide a clearer overall structure with more exhaustive regulations—a comprehensive "net in which all the holes have been filled in—so that the freedom and autonomy of individual citizens are the kind that negate the sort of mere individualism we find in the west, particularly in the Anglo-American hypocrisy of promising Asian countries independence "under the cloak of democracy so that they can keep on exploiting them." To do so, it must act as a single unit and avoid all internal schism. Only with such a unified structuring of the nation, "a kind of Hegelian objective spirit" or a "body working as an organic unit," can the truly "creative power" of all-out war come into play.

Third, war gives the opportunity for a "purifying of the spirit" if its negative aspects can be inverted to create a new standpoint in life that transcends times of war and times of peace. He suggests something along the lines of a revitalization of the samurai ethic of the unity of "arms and letters" to "uproot Anglo-Saxon ideas of democracy and human prosperity" without at the same time falling into mere self-centered totalitarianism.

Fourth, in what may be the single new addition to his own political philosophy, Nishitani suggests that the democratic nation embodies the Hegelian subjective spirit while the totalitarian state is the equivalent of the objective spirit. Japan fits in neither, but is rather an "objective spirit as the expression of an absolute spirit." This absolute spirit, he claims, was there from ancient times in Japan and is now expressing itself as the call for a new world order arising from history itself. This is what makes Japan's position "rise above that of other nations."

Finally, he adds a remark along the lines of a "just war" near the end of the discussions. Taking Nietzsche's remark that it is not a good cause that make a war holy, but a good war that makes a cause holy, he twists its obvious sarcasm around to a literal meaning. It is usually thought that the Greater East Asian Coprosperity Sphere makes the present war holy, but he suggests that the quality of the spirit in which a war is waged, "the goodness that shines forth from those who shoulder its cause actively and embody it in their own persons" is what makes that cause truly good. The volume ends on this note, with Nishitani's claim that "the war in the seas of Hawai'i has reawakened this spirit. We may call it all-out war, but it is also an all-out effort to enliven that spirit in every area of the nation."

54 OVERCOMING MODERNITY. In 1942 a leading intellectual journal in Japan, *Literary World,* organized a symposium to discuss the impasse in Japan's reception of western civilization, under caution that the participants were to avoid political statements. Published the following year under the title *Overcoming Modernity* with a first printing of 6,000 copies, the work was dismissed in the postwar years as no more than another expression of the fascist ideology that had led Japan to its distressful state. But as the problems it took up were clearly of relevance broader than that exploited by the ideologues of the day, there was a revival of interest which led to its reprint and reexamination, including the extent to which it reflected the views of the Kyoto school at large.

Nishitani, who, at the time was already involved in the *Chūōkōron* discussions, was one of the ten of the thirteen participants to deliver an opening paper. For some reason it was not included in his *Collected Writings,* nor is any mention made of it in the list of his writings appended to the final volume. The Confucian scholar Minamoto Ryōen, who had edited a dictionary of philosophy on which Nishitani collaborated during his time of exile from Kyoto University as well as others of his works, and who had transcribed the talks that were eventually to become *Religion and Nothingness,* concludes his examination of the symposium sympathetically but firmly:

> There is no denying the fact that Nishitani was a nationalist and that he supported the war. Still, we cannot leave the fact that he was a universalist out of the picture... At the same time as he made a case for a "national ethics" in his presentation to the symposium, Nishitani recognized the pitfall of a national egoism and argued also for a "world ethic."

I do not intend here to detail what Nishitani's critics have had to say. The extensive treatment of Tanabe's critics provided in the previous chapter will have to suffice as a general picture of how Nishitani's political philosophy was received. More important is to see, as we have already begun to see, the difference that his explicitly religious standpoint made to the views that earn him the judgment that Minamoto and others have passed.

As he states in his inaugural lecture, Nishitani understood modernity as the result of a historical development that began with a break with the middle ages, passed through the Protestant Reformation and the Renaissance, and ended in the emergence of modern science. The relationship between the individual self, God, and the world that had once given a spiritual base to culture had shattered, and in their wake religion, science, and culture have fallen into a state of permanent conflict.

These are all ideas that we had already met in *Elemental Subjectivity* and *View of the World,* and indeed one has to assume that the fact that they were known was a major factor in inviting him to participate in the conference. Here he takes them up in much the same context to contrast two views of the world. On the one hand, there is liberalism, which he sees as a unified position based on individual rights as setting the limits to the imposition of a world order; and on the other, a confrontation of the individual and the world—and hence also of the unity they found in liberalism—found in socialism, communism, and extreme forms of nationalism. In place of these, he recommended a new view of the world and of the human person. For him, the questions were wider than the problem Japan was facing from its own historical position; these were "problems we share with all of humanity." The new view he suggests gives a special role to Japan based on a rejection of the liberalist view.

Taking up from where he had left off in *View of the World,* Nishitani speaks of the need to construct a new ethic grounded in a religious standpoint of absolute nothingness, and from there to stimulate a "moral energy" among citizens to support a view of nation-*in*-world and world-*in*-nation within which the task of Japan becomes manifest:

> It is a moral energy of the nation in which individuals in their respective occupations wipe out the private and offer it up to the public.... At present, our country's national life is being poured into world history, as if pumping blood into a vein. And at the same time, the fountainhead of our national life, the ideals that infuse its history, can become leading ideals within the reality of world history.... If individuals can find their footing in a subjective nothingness..., from the bottom of the historical world they can awaken to the opening up of an original religious, or what we may call transhistorical, world.

Aside from the overtones that talk of "moral energy" had during a time of war, in comparison with the *Chūōkōron* discussions, much of the rhetoric here is tame.

Neither in his paper nor in his comments does Nishitani give any indication of having done further historical research into the themes he is treating—leading a prominent Marxist critic to accuse him of being "completely wrapped up in abstract sermons purporting to give a philosophical grasp of what is supposed to be overcome." If he has a unique contribution to the symposium, it is that he saw the relationship between the individual and the state as justified only by its contribution to the wider world.

He concludes his paper with a statement that makes his point by what can only seem to us today a rather clumsy combination of a classical Buddhist statement of moral altruism with a subtle rewording of one of the slogans of the ultranationalists of the day:

> Japan today shows a standpoint deeply rooted in the self-existence of the nation that we can only call a self-negation of "benefiting oneself by benefiting others," through which the founding ideal of "bringing all the world under one roof" can become an ideal for history and for the world. In this way Japan can take a self-affirmative standpoint that can claim for itself the authority of a leading nation.

A careful reading of his written and spoken remarks shows that he does not suggest that traditional Japanese social values, let alone the shape they took in the current political order based on the emperor system, *as they are* can make a contribution. Rather, they need to be relocated in a world setting where they will be tested by fire. This is an experiment that must be done energetically because, he seems to imply, what is of world value within Japanese culture will otherwise be swept along in one or the other current definition of how a nation should shape itself. His own insistence was that this moral energy needs to be based on an understanding of what he saw as the basic religious impulse of the human: to transcend its humanness in the direction of an absolute.

The fact that Nishitani's brand of nationalism was criticized by the imperialist ideologues angered him. Not that he thought they shared much in common, but that their way of arguing seemed to him closer to propaganda than to reasonable discussion. He writes in a commemorative piece on Tosaka Jun after his death in prison, that he was tempted in 1944 to enter into discussions with the rightists to defend himself, but that Tosaka dissuaded him:

> The last time I met him was just before he was put into prison.... It was after I had also been attacked by rightists from behind the shield of the Army. Even then, journalists of the very magazines that were attacking me would come and invite me to take part in discussions they were sponsoring. Their meanness was transparent and I refused to go along with them, but somehow they had gotten under my skin and I even thought about going with them on my own and speaking my mind. When I told him this, he stopped me in my tracks, telling me to give up such nonsense and to have nothing to do with that pack of mad dogs.

After the war, he complained that Japanese intellectuals had amputated the debate on overcoming modernity from history in the attempt to hide the wounds from memory—*Kritiker ohne Not* he calls them, borrowing a phrase from Nietzsche. Rather, he says "we must confront the past and make it our own past." He did this in a number of essays between 1946 and 1949, during the first years of his removal from his teaching post, and then stopped. One can only assume that his turn away from the political arena reflects not so much a loss of interest as a recognition that his own contribution would best be made by letting go of his animus for his own anguish and towards the regime that had brought it all about, and turning his thought in a direction more in line with his own strengths.

55 THE RELIGIOUS DIMENSION OF THE POLITICAL.

Nishitani made a few attempts to recast his earlier political philosophy, to salvage what he could of its ideas, but then let it go. In a 1946 essay on "Popular Culture and Humanism," for instance, he retains the idea of the dialectic of subject and substrate, but the substrate is now identified as a "principle of life" that checks the subject's attempts to define itself on the one hand, while on the other it brings "a freedom embodying infinite possibility" when brought to awareness in the subject. Or again, for a while the "moral energy" he had seen as requisite for all-out war reemerges as an innate "spiritual energy" that has permitted the Japanese to accept cultural influence from everywhere without prejudice and without being colonized. Even this use will disappear completely in the end.

When I say he let his political ideas go, I do not mean that he finally thought it best to return to where he had left off in 1940, bracketing the whole misadventure of the war years as something best forgotten and retreating to the safer realms of the philosophical clouds. Had this been so, we would expect him to shy away from any further comment on Japan's role in the world, perhaps with an occasional *lapsus linguae* breaking through the shield. What we find is quite different. The narrow horizons of Japan's role in history are widened and deliberately trimmed of political ambitions. Its task is no longer aligned with the socio-economic improvement of Asia but with the rescue of the heart of religion from the slow erosion that inattention and the fossilization of tradition were working on it. Japan's problem in this regard gradually comes to disclose itself as a worldwide problem in which Japan's response is not peculiar to Japan nor is its contribution advanced from a position of superiority, but as one perspective on a common concern. It was as if the philosophical ideal he had inherited from Nishida in the abstract had been appropriated *through* the experience of its abuse, not *in spite* of it.

A 1958 symposium published under the title *The Postwar Intellectual History of Japan* gives us a hint of this struggle for appropriation. In its course he talks of not having dissuaded his students from accepting military conscription, and then feeling that a little piece of himself was dying each time news of the death of one of them reached him. He goes on:

> My position was, well, one of cooperation in the war. Of course I didn't feel approval for the war from the start, but I considered it a kind of karma to cooperate. Once the war was going, though, there was something meaningless about those deaths.... And yet—I don't quite know how to put this—there was a strong sense of a kind of "karma" to it all: If it was meaningless for the losers, than it was also meaningless for the victors. It was a feeling, if you will, of "this world." At the same time, beyond the world of karma, or perhaps behind it, the presence of those who had died cast a shadow over my own existence.

This way of thinking about the war, as a religious fact for all involved, independently of who was right or who was wrong, runs throughout his comments in the symposium, and although other participants express their agreement from time to time it is Nishitani who brings the religious dimension to the discussion. He speaks of the deep insight behind the ancient custom of offering Buddhist rites for the souls of all who have fallen, friend or foe. Just as the fundamental evil of the human condition does not discriminate between persons, he argues, so, too, our confrontation with it should not.

In this same vein he notes how the expropriation of the categories of good and evil by the victors after the war is no less blind than that which existed on both sides during it. In particular, the "universal values" appealed to in the name of "God" and "civilization" at the Tokyo war trials were as "ungodly and uncivilized" an imposition in peace as they were in war. This imposition is aggravated by the fact that the Christian west assumes that its own way of apportioning "guilt" is a universal religious pattern, which is given the lie by the Buddhist preference for the "sorrows of impermanence."

The appeal to the religious dimension is only one of the wedges Nishitani uses in the discussions to free the idea of Japan—and more immediately those among the discussants preoccupied with what is "distinctive" about Japan—from its localism and open it on to a "world perspective." In one passage he complains about the Japanese discomfort at seeing their traditional arts and religions taken over and practiced in the west:

> That the traditional culture of Japan, despite its distinctiveness—or rather because of it—should be able to have a worldwide quality to it has not yet dawned on the awareness of the Japanese but is being pointed out from abroad. We are being opened up by those outside of Japan.... The global perspective always seems to slip away when it comes to the self-criticism of the Japanese.... Having lost our subjectivity, the idea that true distinctiveness can be truly universal and global doesn't occur to us, and we think of "the world" as pointing to an abstract, nondistinct universality.

It is in this context that his remarks on preserving the consciousness of being a "country," and even a country with an emperor, despite the abandonment of particular political models of "nation" and the "emperor system," need to be understood. It is also the context in which he qualifies his criticisms of a democracy imposed from without as unacceptable "in principle" to argue that it needs to be cultivated in Japan hand in hand with the religious, ethical, and cultural conditions of a Japan that does not share the history from which the principles of democracy arose.

In later writings, too, his references to Japan, its ancient spirit and role in the world, completely lose their racial and nationalistic edge. To dismiss Nishitani summarily for the statements made during the war, with no consideration of how he got through that position, is a far greater prejudice than Nishitani's own prejudices had been. I will cite two examples of his views on the other side of this conversion of viewpoint, and then let the matter drop for the rest of my treatment of his thought.

In 1971 Nishitani wrote a short piece reminiscing on his studies in Europe and how it made him realize for the first time the connection that exists between oneself and one's homeland. He is referring here not to any political or ethnic entity, but to the fact that one's bodily existence is conditioned by the natural environment, including the food one has been raised on, and this in turn provides a physical link with one's ancestors, through whose blood the environment has passed on its special traits. Though carefully worded to avoid any suggestion of a link with the *Blut und Boden* ideology to which he had consented before, it tries to reappropriate what remains true in the myth that had been expropriated with such disastrous effects. Eating his first bowl of rice after a steady diet of Western food, he was overwhelmed by an "absolute taste" that went beyond the mere quality of the food:

> This experience made me think of the meaning of the notion of "homeland," which is fundamentally that of the inseparable relation between the soil and the human being, in particular the human being as a body.... The vital link that since time immemorial has bound together the rice, the soil, and those countless people who are my ancestors forms the background of my life and is actually contained in it.

One notices the absence of any reference to this experience as distinctively Japanese, which it surely would have had if it had occurred to him to mention it in the wartime discussions.

A second example, dating from a 1967 essay, concerns the way he preserves the idea of a special role for Japan in the world. Only the most wooden-headed of critics would class his words in the same genre as his earlier nationalistic statements:

> We Japanese have fallen heir to two completely different cultures.... This is a great privilege that westerners do not share in, ...but at the same time it puts a heavy responsibility on our shoulders: to lay the foundations of thought for a world in the making, for a new world united beyond differences of east and west.

The passage from his political philosophy to the mature thought that will leave his mark on the history of philosophy was negotiated through the struggles with nihilistic thought that took over with redoubled force during the years after the war.

56 OVERCOMING NIHILISM. The problem of nihilism had already appeared in Nishitani's earlier writings, but did not become the focal point of attention until the years after the war. Allusions to nihilism continued to appear regularly in his writings for a few years after *Religion and Nothingness,* but then faded away from his late works. In the midst of his renewed interest in the subject, he recalls the importance that nihilism had for his philosophical vocation:

> I am convinced that the problem of nihilism lies at the root of the mutual aversion of religion and science. And it was this that gave my philosophical engagement its starting point, from which it grew larger and larger until it came to envelop nearly everything.... The fundamental problem of my life... has always been, to put it simply, the overcoming of nihilism *through* nihilism.

The struggle with nihilism that led Nishitani to philosophy also led him back to his philosophical vocation after the forced exile from his post at Kyoto University. In both cases, it was Nietzsche and his idea of "overcoming nihilism by means of nihilism" that accompanied him. If Nishida and Tanabe found their original inspiration in the writings of Kant and Hegel, Nishitani found his initially in *Thus Spoke Zarathustra.* Neither the philosophical tutoring he received in the circles of Nishida and Tanabe nor the influence of Suzuki Daisetsu that turned him to Zen undid his early affections for Nietzsche. Quite the contrary, they matured into a profound understanding that more or less coincides with the rediscovery of Nietzsche in the West.

The high point of his confrontation with nihilism was a series of lectures he delivered on the subject in 1949, published later in that year, along with a short book on *Russian Nihilism.* As the title we chose for the English translation of those two books as one volume, *The Self-Overcoming of Nihilism,* indicates, Nishitani was not simply concerned with laying out the contours of western ideas of nihilism, but with trying to find a way to overcome it, or more correctly to letting it overcome itself—a problem in which his philosophical concerns and his personal concerns drew together as never before.

What is so surprising about *Nihilism* is that, despite his clearly stated agenda of seeking a way through nihilistic thinking, he is able to present a fair and readable account of the authors whom he takes up at the same time as he gropes beneath the surface of the text for the heart of the matter. His chapter on Max Stirner's *The Ego and its Own,* a work virtually forgotten in western intellectual history, for instance, is outstanding.

The conclusion at which he arrives, by a process of argument far too intricate to reproduce here, is that Europe and Japan show different but related ways of resolving the crisis of nihilism. In Europe one sees the emergence of a creative, affirmative nihilism that faced human finitude foursquare—a kind of double negative that amounted to an affirmative. On the one hand, there is a transcending of the phenomenal world in the recognition that it is basically void of meaning to sustain itself. On the other, the eternal world of essences that rises up to fill that void is also negated as an inauthentic alienation from the pain and burden of having nowhere to stand. The transcendence of the world is thus returned to the world enriched by having been robbed of its promise of a route of escape. Finitude becomes final, and the world has to be embraced as it is, as eternal recurrence (Nietzsche), as the property of the individual (Stirner), or as the transcendental ground in nothing (Heidegger).

Japan, in contrast, did not come to nihilism by way of a shaking of the foundations of its native religious tradition, as Europe had in relation to Christianity. Instead, it inherited the technological and social structures of the modern world that had emerged as part of that process of spiritual upheaval. Granted that it cannot simply inherit at one swipe the wider reach of spiritual resources within which all of this happened, its only recourse is to appeal to resources of its own. But the necessary spiritual wellsprings have all but dried up in the consciousness of its people:

> The West still has the faith, ethics, ideas, and so forth that have been handed down from Christianity and Greek philosophy.... No matter how much this basis is now being shaken, it is still very much alive, and one battles against it only at the cost of fierce determination. For us in Japan, things are different. In the past, Buddhism and Confucian thought constituted such a basis, but they have already lost their power, leaving a total void and vacuum in our spiritual ground.... The worst thing is that this emptiness is in no way an emptiness that has been won through struggle, nor a nihility that has been "lived through." Before we knew what was happening, the spiritual core had wasted away completely.

The very source of spiritual strength that a few years earlier he, like others of his generation, had believed would fill up what was wanting in China and Korea and other countries of Asia, the deep bonds of the Japanese soul with the spirit of the ancients just within reach, are now recognized to have been no more than a fiction of a mass self-deception he, too, had been made to believe in.

Still worse, he says, is that people do not even realize that all of this has happened. The self-identity of the Japanese has split down the middle and its "moral energy" (he uses the term, but without its earlier enthusiasm) has drained away almost imperceptibly. The problem, he now sees, is one of recovering a will towards the future grounded in the past, or what he calls with Nietzsche, learning to "prophesy towards tradition."

The study of European nihilism is important in three senses, he concludes. First, it can help us realize that the problem exists in Japan as well, even if in a different form. Second, it can show us that overcoming requires that we recall the importance of spiritual depth. And third, it can show us that tradition must be recovered not by orienting ourselves towards the past but in terms of the direction in which we are headed. He ends on the proposal that this be done by way of the Buddhist standpoints of emptiness and nothingness.

One might suppose that he would immediately turn all his efforts to take up his own suggestion, given the freshness of the question to the age and the intensity of his own personal involvement. This was not the way Nishitani did his best work. One may assume that his experience with political philosophizing had made him cautious of rushing head-on to tackle apparently clear questions as if they were no more than obstacles blocking the way in the road ahead. More importantly, one may also assume that he realized that any genuinely philosophical problem needs to emerge from within oneself more than once and in more than one form before one is ready to respond to it. The source of the spiraling logic we see in his late work, it seems to me, lies precisely in a respect for the problem at hand that supersedes the immediate desire to apply one's education as widely as possible.

His own approach to the proposal was to return to reflect on the philosophies of his teachers, Nishida and Tanabe, and at the same time to rethink some of his own earlier ideas about evil, God, mysticism, myth, and religion—but always keeping that proposal in sight. Thus, however wide-ranging the essays he wrote in the following several years, he had the sense that he was walking in circles, ever smaller circles that would bring him one day back to the problem of nihilism in a Japanese context. And bring him back it did, in what was to prove to be the crowning achievement of his published writing, *Religion and Nothingness.*

57 FROM NIHILISM TO EMPTINESS. *Religion and Nothingness* is Nishitani's masterpiece. It is also a giant step in the advance of Japanese philosophy and religious thinking onto the stage of world intellectual history. In order to introduce others of his writings, it will be necessary to

shorten our account of this book and fracture the structure of the whole into a number of themes, but not without a word about how it came to take shape.

Nishitani says in the preface that the book began in response to a request for an essay on "What is Religion?" In fact, the opening essay was not written but revised from the transcript of a lecture he delivered on the subject. His answer to the question was not, as the title might suggest, an attempt to offer yet another definition of an already overdetermined term. Needless to say, by now he was thoroughly disillusioned with the idea of aligning religion to the construction of a practical ethic for a world-historical Japan. In reverting back to his earlier concern with religion, he took a position that drew on, but also was different from, that of both his teachers. Tanabe had felt that Nishida turned philosophy into religion, while for him philosophy had its own standpoint and domain independent of religion. Only by pursuing philosophy to its limits does it self-negate and open into religion. Nishitani sides with Tanabe in seeing philosophy as a kind of irrepressible "absolute insolence." Its essence is free thought that will, if that freedom is stubbornly maintained, eventually break through religion. For Nishida, it was enough for philosophy to explain the world opened up in religion. Philosophy is thus absorbed into religion and forfeits its own standpoint. Nishitani began where Nishida had ended, as he says, in the idea that "religion means to become aware of a unique relationship to the absolute in one's self."

In this return to the primacy of self-awareness, the question of what religion is became an invitation to examine what has happened to the religious way of being and thinking in our day, what could happen to us if we lose it, and what can be done to restore it to its original purpose. To this end, he felt that a new philosophy of religion was needed, different from the classical systems of the nineteenth century that had been based on something immanent in the human individual such as reason or intuition or feeling.

In the course of laying all of this out, Nishitani quickly found that so many ideas had come up that he had to add another essay, and then another, and so on until he had folded into the work a philosophical position that, as he says, while lacking the unity of a systematic plan, nevertheless aims at a unity of comprehensiveness. Looking back over the work as a whole, he locates his approach in the history of western philosophical thought in contrast to classical systems in this way:

> In my view, it has since become impossible to institute such a standpoint, given the nature of the questions that have meantime given rise to the

> thought of the later Schelling, Schopenhauer, Kierkegaard, or even Feuerbach and Marx, and above all, because of the appearance of positions like the nihilism of Nietzsche. Consequently, our considerations here take their stand at the point where traditional philosophies of religion have broken down or been broken through. In that sense, they may be said to go along with contemporary existential philosophies....

At the same time, he dislocates his approach to religion from western philosophy by employing general Buddhist terms and ideas, as well as more distinctive ideas associated with particular sects such as Kegon, Tendai, Pure Land, and, of course, Zen:

> Removed from the frame of their traditional conceptual determinations, they have been used rather freely and on occasion... introduced to suggest correlations with concepts of contemporary philosophy.... This way of using terminology may seem somewhat careless and, at times, ambiguous. As far as possible, it is best to avoid this sort of trouble but it is not always possible when one is trying, as I am here, to take a stand at one and the same time within and without the confines of tradition.

The initial project of finding a way to overcome the nihilism in Japanese consciousness is the core of the opening essay and of the work as a whole. At the same time, he honors his commitment to make use of specifically eastern and Buddhist ideas that would deepen what he had found in western responses to nihilism as well. Accordingly, we do not find him preoccupied with distinguishing Japan's situation but rather with a deliberate attempt to overcome that viewpoint. Not that he has taken to talking about an abstract, generic idea of the human—his approach remains fixed on the individual—but that he has reached a point in individual consciousness that a shifting of cultural and historical conditions cannot reach, however much they may stimulate us to reach that point.

In the same way that Descartes took up the challenge of scientific method to traditional religious belief by engaging himself in the discipline of a radical doubt, Nishitani takes up the challenge of nihilism to religion by a disciplined doubt of his own. Rather than end up in the certitude of the "I am," however, he has to begin by questioning that certitude in a still more radical doubt—the Great Doubt, as he calls it, employing a term from Zen—in which one lets go of even the thinking ego in order to *become* the doubt.

Like Descartes, and indeed like the mystics whom he continues to draw on here, Nishitani's engagement with doubt is a kind of spiritual ascent through descent into radical finitude. The stages of the process are, crudely put, three. It begins, first, when the ordinary encounter with personal limits turns into a conscious question about the whole of one's own life: the simple, most trivial event in which one's own desires or ambitions are frustrated by the lack of one's own ability or by a conflict with the desire and ambitions of others. It is as if a crack had appeared in one's view of the world and with it a sense that it is only the mask of a deep darkness that lies on the other side.

Typically, we seal this crack up as quickly as possible, chalking it up to "just one of those things" of life. It is only when one deliberately decides not to seal it up but to allow it to grow that a second stage becomes possible. It is, he says, as if the frustrated ego were seen to be like the shell of a bean that had begun to crack, and as if the darkness inside were trying to break out and swallow up the light. If one lives with the doubt and allows it to take its course, this frustration is transformed into a great abyss of nihility at one's feet. The original questions—Why did this happen to me? What can I do about it?—are transformed into the questions: Who am I? Why do I exist? Nishitani calls this conversion the "realization of nihility."

Nihility is understood here as the nullification of the self by the nullification of the ground it has to stand on. It is not that the self is annihilated out of existence, but that all certitude is completely absorbed in doubt, and that this doubt becomes more real than the self or the world it belongs to. It is a Great Doubt:

> This Doubt cannot be understood as a state of consciousness but only as a real doubt making itself present to the self out of the ground of the self and of all things.... It presents itself as *reality,* ...with an inevitability quite beyond the control of the consciousness and arbitrary willfulness of the self. In its presence the self *becomes* Doubt itself. The self *realizes* the doubt about *reality.*

Nishitani is playing here on the double-entendre of the English word *realization* to express the fact that the subjective awareness of nihility is at the same time an actualization of something nonsubjective.

A doubt that simply makes me aware of my personal finitude, or even of the finitude of the human condition as such, does not go far enough. Or again, to turn one's back on the doubt through an act of faith in salvation from beyond is not to overcome the nihility but to disassociate oneself from it. *Becoming the doubt* must go a step further.

The unfolding of the Great Doubt reaches a third stage when that nihility is itself nullified—again, not annihilated but transcended through its negation—in the awareness that the world of being that rests on the nihility of the self and all things is only a relative manifestation of nothingness as it is encountered *in* reality. Beneath that world, all around it, there is an encompassing absolute nothingness that *is* reality. Nihility is emptied out, as it were, into an absolute emptiness, or what Buddhism calls *śūnyatā*. This absolute is not a further aggravation of the original frustration and the abyss of nihility it contained within it, but rather a complete negation of that aggravation. It is an affirmation, *in* those negations, of the fact that all frustration and nihility belong to a greater reality whose nature it is to empty all things of that desire and ambition that makes what is only relative appear to be absolute rather than what it really is: a manifestation of an absolute self-emptying.

This affirmation of an absolute nothingness beyond the world of being and the self awakens consciousness to the original face of the self and world, a consciousness enriched by the fact that it no longer confuses what is only relative for the absolute. The self, such as it is, discloses itself as no-self. The world of becoming, such as it is, manifests itself as a world emptied of being. He calls this, again with a Buddhist term, an awakening to the "true suchness" of things and the self.

As should be clear from what has been said above, for Nishitani doubt is always a matter of mental energy, not a simple *blanking* of the mind but a disciplined *emptying* of mind. Only in this way, he insists, can it pass beyond the bounds of a private mental exercise to metaphysical insight into reality as such. As he says, "ontology needs to pass through nihility and shift to an entirely new field, different from what it has known hitherto." Moreover, as with all spiritual process, there is no way to leap to the final stage without having passed through earlier ones. For one thing, it is precisely because of the passage that the final stage takes on what meaning it has. For another, it is not a question of ascending to a higher, truer self on one's own but of a letting go of self acting on its own. At the same time, to be sure, Nishitani's final stage of no-self may seem, at least to the everyday ego, a rather disagreeable place to land up; and in any case that it is a higher and more real state is not self-evident from the start. By the same token, not every insight that Nishitani records along the way—including the reformulation of a great many western philosophical and theological ideas—is necessarily justified by his own passage, or even by the fact that it has a long tradition in the east standing behind it. There is no proof or disproof of what he is arguing, any more than was the case with Descartes's experiment with doubt, without the experience of having followed the path oneself.

So much is sacrificed here in the telling, not only of the careful way Buddhist and western philosophical ideas are interwoven but also of the existential feel of Nishitani's prose, that I am tempted to run page after page of quotation from the book into the text at this point. But even that, I fear, would not breathe the soul into the bare bones of this summary that Nishitani has inspired. I return, instead, to a number of remaining motifs, most of which appear in one or the other form in *Religion and Nothingness,* to present an overview of Nishitani's mature philosophy.

58 EMPTINESS AS A STANDPOINT.

Nishitani includes himself in the company of Nishida and Tanabe, whose respective logics, he says, "share a distinctive and common basis that sets them apart from traditional western philosophy: absolute nothingness." As we noted, however, without abandoning this lineage he gradually came to prefer the term "emptiness." As we will see, this also represents the first step in what was to be an ever more courageous attempt to integrate Zen ideas and images into philosophical discourse.

He also came to speak of his own position as a "standpoint" rather than a logic. There seem to be two reasons for this. First, he turned away from Nishida's logic of locus in favor of something closer to what Nietzsche had called "perspectivism" because it seemed better to express the existential reality of what goes on in coming to awareness: the ground one stands on changes and the horizon of what one can see broadens. Second, the image of a standpoint better expresses the Buddhist ideal of a "middle way" between the outright acceptance of the world as objectively real and the outright rejection of it as subjective and illusory, namely a standpoint from which one can see both ideas as two sides of the same reality. These motives are reflected in his use of language. Thus he often speaks of a standpoint as both a "foothold" from which to see more clearly, and also as the actual "point" from which reality can show itself more clearly. It is on the standpoint of emptiness that, as we stated above, things and the self show themselves for what they are:

> True emptiness is nothing less than what reaches awareness in all of us as our own absolute *self-nature.* In addition, this emptiness is the point at which each and every entity that is said to exist becomes manifest as what it is in itself, in the form of its true suchness.

The standpoint of emptiness, then, is not so much a philosophical "position" as it is the achievement of an original self-awareness (our self-nature), compared to which all other consciousness is caught in the fictional darkness of ignorance, or what the Buddhists call *avidyā*. It is a point from which to philosophize, not a doctrine. In this sense it may be called a "standpoint of standpoints"—the practical dimension of Nishida's ontological judgment of absolute nothingness as the "universal of universals." At the same time, it is the point of contact with the real as it is in itself (in its suchness), and therefore not only a matter of a conscious state. This conjunction of the real and our realization of the real means that the standpoint of emptiness unites what is dichotomized in ordinary consciousness.

To illustrate this conjunction of the illumination of mind and the illumination of reality in emptiness, Nishitani draws on the Tendai Buddhist dialectic of *fact* and *theory*. The opposition between the phenomenal world, in which facts appear, and the noumenal world, in which one becomes aware of them, is overcome not by tilting the balance towards one or the other—whether by harmonizing it or absorbing it outright—but by shifting the opposition to a higher level of insight in which phenomenon and noumenon flow one into the other without impediment. Emptiness is thus neither fact nor theory, but a level of awareness at which the two interpenetrate each other. It is not an erasure of this dialectic of fact and theory as a mere fiction of the world of form, but its relocation on the field of emptiness, of the formless. Thus he takes over the description of enlightenment in Zen as a field on which it can be said that "form is emptiness, emptiness is form."

While the conclusion of the argument is clear, its logical progress is not always clear, and the circularity can be annoying when one wants explicit rational connections. The appeal to a standpoint of higher insight in which the world of fact and our thinking about it in theory are said to show themselves just as they are, so that the opposition between them is overcome, echoes Nishida's central concern with the subject-object dichotomy. Like Nishida, Nishitani never questioned that such a level of consciousness existed, and that while it appears "higher" to those tangled up in rational thought, it is in fact the most immediate and down-to-earth form of experience. He did not, however, detain himself as long as Nishida had in examining the place of this dichotomy in the history of western philosophy. Nishitani's description of the problem and its overcoming are much more quickly displaced into the Buddhist tradition, not as a matter of principle but because it seemed to him—without having to repeat Nishida's demonstrations—that western philosophies of being lack the requisite categories.

As if recognizing that something had been lacking in his idea of the standpoint of emptiness as a process of overcoming the dichotomy between fact and theory, object and subject, reality and realization, Nishitani tries to get to the bottom of the question in a late essay on "Wisdom and Reason." In it he argues that the assumption of an original separation of knowing and being is itself mistaken. Theory, logos, needs being as the object of a thinking subject, and the thinking subject needs becoming, the rational process, to achieve its end. But the Buddhist idea of awakened wisdom *(prajñā)* does not belong to being, and emptiness *(śūnyatā)* does not belong to becoming. Emptiness is the standpoint of a wisdom in which the opposition is not so much overcome as seen through as illusory.

Nishitani traces the dichotomy of knowing and being in western philosophy to its culmination in Hegel's idea of *noesis noeseos,* the knowledge in which knowledge is self-conscious of knowing, as the completion of the process of becoming in absolute being. This end point is already present, he says, in Hegel's initial assumption that in order to understand that "only the absolute is true, only truth is absolute," one must follow a developmental process of the conscious subject thinking about objective reality. Nishitani accepted the initial intuition, as stated in the preface to the *Phenomenology of Mind,* but rejected the claim that it requires a subject-object process to be explained. *Prajñā* wisdom, the "knowing of not-knowing," has no such requirement. The truth of emptiness of the self and all things is immediately present all at once. Being is originally in nothingness and nothingness in being.

59 EMPTINESS AS THE HOMEGROUND OF BEING.

As with Nishida, for Nishitani the structure of self-awareness was a paradigm of how all of reality is constructed, "the nonobjectifiable mode of being of things as they are in themselves." Being aware is not like an activity that one schedules for a certain period, and then sets aside in order to do other things. It is the original activity that defines what it means to be human. When birds fly and fish swim, when fire burns and water washes, they do not do so as a pastime, but *by being what they are.* So, too, the mind is, by its nature, aware.

Nishitani has recourse to the Buddhist notion of *samādhi,* usually associated only with a state of complete concentration, to make the connection, playing on the polyvalence of the single character the Chinese used to express it. *Samādhi* is not merely a state of settled mind, he argues, but also a state of being settled that applies to the true form of all things. We may distinguish three elements here.

First, *samādhi* it is an elemental activity that defines a thing and settles it in its own homeground. This is intended to replace the idea of a fixed substance or self that defines itself by the activities it is caught up in, by its "being-at-doing" as he calls it. To be settled in *samādhi* is to be substantially unsettled; its homeground is in its homelessness in the world of being and becoming.

Second, *samādhi* does not simply confine individual things to their nature but defines them relationally with all things. Its being centered is not only a concentration of its whole nature in everything it does, but represents a central point for everything about it, just as it is part of the concentration of those things. Since it is acting freely and naturally, it is not preoccupied with protecting itself against the activities of others. Self-centeredness is at the same time other-centeredness. At the homeground of the self and all things, every action takes place naturally, without the interference of a reaction. Nishitani closes *Religion and Nothingness* with an image of this aspect of concentration in emptiness from the life of St. Francis of Assisi. About to have an infected eye cauterized, St. Francis addresses the hot iron as "Brother fire," making over it the sign of the cross:

> For St. Francis the purpose of making the sign of the cross was to solicit the love of his beloved brother, fire. This love occurred at the point that he emptied himself and consorted with the fire, and where the fire emptied itself (ceased to be fire) and consorted with him.... And, in fact, the fire did not cause him any pain. As the doctor applied the cautery, drawing it from the earlobe all the way up to the eyebrow, St. Francis laughed softly, as a child feeling the caress of its mother's hand.

Third, this state of acting naturally, in according with the self-nature of oneself and all things, allows a thing to be fully present in all of its forms without being locked into any one of them. Lacking substance, every manifestation shows instead the formlessness of true suchness, that is "that form is emptiness and emptiness is form." This means that whatever is done in *samādhi* is done spontaneously, and not tailored to the form of one's personal wishes or even of one's ideals. There is no form to conform to because there is no self to be formed. It is like free play, a "self-joyous sporting in *samādhi*" as Dōgen calls it, in which forms come and go because there is no model to impede them. Behavior on this homeground of emptiness does not observe custom or rule, nor is it the practice of principles. It is the spontaneous observance of a self no longer attached to itself so that it can "realize" its surroundings."

The common ground of mind and reality in *samādhi*-being is what makes "knowing by becoming" possible. Nishitani takes up this idea of Nishida by citing a haiku verse by the poet Bashō:

From the pine tree
  learn of the pine tree,
And from the bamboo
  of the bamboo.

From the ordinary standpoint of substantial being, this can only make sense as a metaphor for "observing closely" or "studying objectively." But Bashō's intent, says Nishitani, is different:

> He invites us to betake ourselves to the dimension where things become manifest in their suchness, to attune ourselves to the selfness of the pine tree and the selfness of the bamboo, ...making an effort to stand essentially in the same mode of being as the thing one wishes to learn about. It is on the field of emptiness that this becomes possible.

Thus we see the way in which the standpoint of emptiness entails an ontology and yet is not itself any philosophical position. As a way of seeing, the standpoint of emptiness allow one to see through both native fictions of the mind and the optical illusions that the world throws up to us. In a particularly moving passage in *Religion and Nothingness* Nishitani speaks of seeing the world as if in a "double exposure," allowing it to show both its surface and its depth at the same time. He imagines walking down Tokyo's fashion center, the Ginza, and seeing it as a field of grass:

> One can see the Ginza, just as it is, in all its magnificence, as a field of pampas grass. One can look at it as if it were a double exposure—which is, after all, its real portrait. For in truth, reality itself is two-layered. A hundred years hence, not one of the people now walking the Ginza will be alive, neither the young nor the old, the men nor the women.... We can look at the living as they walk full of health down the Ginza and see, in a double exposure, a picture of the dead.

While Nishida and Tanabe had both spoken of life and death as correlatives that entail each other, Nishitani's standpoint of emptiness relates them to our way of viewing this world just as it is, in its "true suchness," as a synchronicity of life and death:

> I mean that while life remains life to the very end, and death remains death, they both become manifest in any given thing, and therefore that the aspect of life and the aspect of death in a given thing can be superimposed in such a way that both become simultaneously visible. In this sense, such a mode of being might be termed life-*in*-death, death-*in*-life.

In Buddhist terms, he explains this idea of seeing through the endless cycle of impermanence or *saṃsāra*—the coming-to-be and passing away of all things—to their liberation in *nirvāṇa.* This "transcendence into emptiness" while living in the midst of the world, a kind of *saṃsāra*-in-*nirvāṇa,* is a higher transcendence than the rejection of this world for another. Here again, while it is only the mind that can "realize" this in awareness, it is something that is already "realized" in the fundamental structure of reality itself. Hence, the freeing of the self from ego-centeredness is not something simply internal to the mind, but takes place in the encounter with the world as it is. As Nishitani remarks rather cryptically, "The fact that this staff is a staff is a fact in such a way as to involve at the same time the deliverance of the self."

Seeing things from the standpoint of emptiness can also help us to see through the objectifying tendencies of mind to its true activity of awareness. In this regard, for example, he argues that myth can be understood as a surface fiction that invites deeper insight. Nishitani also offers it as a kind of tool to cut through the demythifying debate, which he sees as a consequence of the faith-reason dualism built into Christian self-understanding, and as a result of which theology and philosophy run parallel in the same direction without being able to work together. After a careful review of Bultmann's basic idea and the criticisms against it, he takes up the doctrine of the virgin birth (which he mistakenly identifies with the doctrine of the immaculate conception) as an instance of that dualism. The idea of being "stained" in the natural, physiological sphere and yet unstained in the spiritual sphere rests on a split between body and soul that he finds understandable but incapable of addressing the question of the "original purity" of the human, which is what he believes the doctrine is meant to express. He rephrases the question this way:

> What if we posit in the fundamental nature of human existence an unlimited and simple immaculateness that transcends both what is stained and what is unstained (in body and in spirit), and if we further assume that men and women can only be comprehended in their true concrete wholeness when they are seen as beings that bear such a fundamental nature in itself?

His answer to the question is that from such a standpoint, original purity can be seen both in being stained and in being unstained, whether physically or spiritually, and that this purity is what gives persons a unity so fundamental that it cannot be stained. To talk of such things, we need a language different from the language of scientific or objective facts, and this is what the mythical language of the doctrine provides. The doctrine of virgin birth thus points to the awareness that we are all born of a virgin in a very important, if neglected, sense. Neither scientific method nor belief in the intervention of the gods can touch this primary, *religious* fact. Only a renewed sense of what myth is can give us the language we need. It is a language, he says, that replaces vertical transcendence, which demands that we step beyond this world, with a horizontal one, which "does not entail an either-or decision vis-à-vis science... or any conflict with nature," and yet remains "wholly other from the world of nature." This nature-*in*-non-nature is what Buddhism calls "emptiness."

While Nishida had seen the locus of absolute nothingness as a self-identity of the opposites of being and nothingness, Nishitani seems to take the formula "being-*in*-nothingness" and place himself squarely at the point of the "-*in*-." At the same time, echoes of Nishida's acting intuition reverberate beneath the surface of his text as he struggles to delineate a conversion to the world in its "true suchness," a world that is neither subjective nor substantial but a "middle way" that affirms itself in negating them both.

60

EGO AND SELF. From what has just been said, it should be obvious that for Nishitani the idea of the true self cannot be a permanent, unchanging principle of identity somehow encased within the person, an individuated soul, a cluster of human potentials waiting to be realized, or even an ideal of expanded consciousness. It has to be, rather, a mode of being in which everything done is done "naturally," and in that sense has to serve as a paradigm of the mode of being of the nonhuman world as well. It must also be a mode of selfhood that does not complement the ordinary ego but displaces it.

The distinction between the ego and the true self is crucial for Nishitani, but is posed in terms different from those familiar to us from twentieth-century psychology. He understands ego to include the Aristotelian idea of substantial individuation and the *res cogitans* of Descartes. By self he means a self-identity based on the negation of both of these. In a splendid but demanding 1962 essay on "Western Thought and Buddhism," he tries to show how the idea of the non-ego can help to solve a problem inherent in western philosophy and above all in its mystical tradition, namely the addiction to the category of selfhood in defining the human and the absolute.

(We should note here a subtext to this essay that Nishitani was certainly aware of but which may not be immediately apparent if it is read on its own: the terms he uses to contrast substrate and subject are the very terms he had used in his early political philosophy. Here not only are they purified of all political overtones, but the logical connection between them is also completely revised.)

He begins with Plotinus, for whom the soul (the egoistic, self-centered subject) must go beyond thinking, perception, and being in order to lose itself in the One. The final barrier to cross to get there is materiality, the formless non-entity that underlies all entities. Thus we see an opposition set up between two apparently nonsubstantial original principles: matter and the One. But in fact, since each of these is self-enclosed and has its identity in itself independent of the other, they are both still substantial: that is, they stand on an underlying substrate (a *hypostasis* or *sub-jectum*) that gives them their self-identity. What is supposed to lie beyond the sensible and intelligible world as nonsubstantial ends up being substantialized there by virtue of its opposition to something else.

This pattern of not being able to think of an ultimate without substantializing it he sees running throughout the western philosophical tradition. Although modern idealism and materialism, for example, define their basic principles differently from Plotinus, one can recognize in both the same basic attachment to an intelligible and real substratum. As he says elsewhere, "If idealism's 'in the mind' loads the rock into the front of the mind, materialism's 'outside the mind' sticks the mind onto the back of the rock." Underlying the antagonism of apparently differing standpoints is a common rooting. Rather than seek to deal with the antagonism by siding with one or the other, Nishitani wants to uproot the question from its traditional form and pose it in terms of the fundamental, nonsubstantial, nonsubjective—or without substrate—nature of reality.

The connection between material or spiritual "substance" and "subjectivity" here looks to be merely a play on the double meaning of the Latin word *subjectum*. For Nishitani it is more than that. It is a simultaneous projection of the substantiality of the material world into the core of the human, and of the subjectivity of consciousness into the core of reality, so that consciousness has a kind of "substance" and things have a kind of "ego." This has two consequences. First, the hypostatic ground that passes itself off as a true non-ground offering human beings a firm foundation, in fact only hinders them from getting to the bottom of what they are. Second, the idea of a God as the perfection of reality transcending all opposition is made into an absolute subject that stands in opposition to other subjects and renders them finite and relative. The ground of the world of being, including human being, is the *nihilum* out of which they were created. In them this *nihilum* becomes something real, standing opposite the self-identical, self-grounded God.

It was Nietzsche, says Nishitani, who uncovered this opposition between God and nothingness as something more fundamental than that between idealism and materialism, but without questioning the attachment to substantiality:

> Nothingness is deepened to the point that it can assault the very throne of God. The nihility that has untied itself from any and all support wrestles with God for authority and succeeds in offering itself as the absolute groundless ground. The split between these two fundamental principles... came about because the concept of God and the concept of nothingness still arm themselves with the character of a subjectum or substratum and, as a result, cannot but appear as permanently opposed one to the other.

The only remedy, for Nishitani, is to find an original principle that does not stand in opposition to anything else and does not block the way to recover our most elemental self beyond subjectivity, free of any substratum. This principle cannot be the cosmos in the sense of the totality of everything that is, but must be a kind of an absolutely open "field" in which everything material and spiritual has its place and its ultimate truth. Neither itself spiritual nor material, it is a nonsubjective field on which the human being can discover essential selfhood. Put the other way around, attaining to the self is itself a manifestation of the nonsubjective, ungrounded ground of reality. Self and reality are one in the realization of true selfhood.

The idea of self as non-ego therefore cuts away the idea of subjectivity in the human and in reality itself to disclose a true absolute:

> The absolute is not thought of as any kind of subject or any kind of substance. To think it so is a complete misunderstanding. We cannot speak of the absolute in the sense of "something" or "someone" that "appears." The absolute is a non-subjectum—or what Buddhism calls "nothingness" or "emptiness."

There are two ways of viewing the self, and they need to be interlocked. First, there is the self-centered in which the mind is seen as the unity or possessor of a variety of faculties. Since the self grasps the world through these faculties, it naturally comes to see itself as the center of the world. Nishitani calls this "the self-centered mode of being." It is a mode of being of self-consciousness, the knowing of an ego that at the same time as it knows things, knows itself to be different from them. But the exact opposite is possible, a cosmocentric view in which mind is seen from the standpoint of the world. In this case the faculties of mind are seen as applying to all things that live. Mind becomes a universal and the human mind only one instance of it. This has found its way through myths into various religions and philosophies east and west, though in the west the advance of Christianity has brought the egocentric view to the fore. There the personal as a privileged state of existence becomes central in the relation with God and among humans.

In psychological novels and in scientific psychology, the attempt to know the self suffers from a basic split, since one is always thinking of oneself in terms of a universal idea of the human. Everything that is true is true because it can be universalized, or conversely, one rediscovers the universal form in one's own particularity. This is the core of Nishitani's critique of self-attachment at the heart of Sartre's humanism, which sees in ego-consciousness "an image of humanity" from which one can act categorically. The Zen way of seeing the self makes no such split. It is a union of the seer and the seen.

Sartre begins from consciousness as the source of meaning because it is the one thing that protects the individual from becoming an object among other objects in the world, which is the greatest disvalue that can be done to the human. Nishitani says that the problem is that to become a subject vis-à-vis objects is no less demeaning of the true self and in fact ends up putting the self on the same substantialized ground as the objects it apparently lords it over and therefore closes itself off to its true nature. Sartre grounds ego-conscious on nothingness, and therefore sees through the unreality of the world, but this is only a "relative nothingness." By the same token Nishitani rejects Heidegger's solution since, although he goes further than Sartre in decentering the ego and has a certain cosmocentrism, still he sees nothingness as a thing "outside" of being and existence.

In Buddhism, on the other hand, the self-centered and cosmocentric have both been preserved, which leads to a different view of the human and of the absolute. Buddhism preserves the awareness of the individual ego that puts consciousness at the center, but also recognizes the egoity of all living things capable of sensation and perception. Both are self-determinations of the same universal mind, and this is what defines them at the core. This universal mind can even be considered a kind of unconscious, provided one takes it in an ontological sense, and not simply an epistemological one as western psychology is prone to do. It is a "oneness of minds and things" that Buddhism calls emptiness or *śūnyatā*. It is here, in the awareness of nondiscriminating knowledge, that things manifest their true form, which is lacking a self-centered nature or substance.

Awakening to one's true nature is therefore a kind of death to the self, what Zen refers to as the Great Death. It is not death in the ordinary sense of leaving the world of the living, but a liberation from the endless stream of birth-and-death, or *saṃsāra*. It is an existential liberation, in the midst of life, from constant change and the anxiety it brings with it. It is thus a rebirth at the same time, or as we stated above, a *saṃsāra*-in-*nirvāṇa*. This liberation is not a physical freeing from death or a being reborn in another world. It is a freeing of oneself from the prejudices one has towards the self and the world, and also a freeing of oneself from all dependence on liberation from another world or transcendent power. It is at once "a freedom from all things and a freedom to all things." In this context Nishitani cites Eckhart's position here of "taking leave of God." In contrast, a position like Tillich's, which finds ultimate concern to come to rest in participation in a "ground of being," still thinks in terms of an other, and from the Zen point of view is not yet a final step.

For Nishitani, the ultimate concern is not to find an absolute other on which to rely, but to see that "the examination of God or Buddha must become an examination of self":

> The quest of God or Buddha arises as an inevitability inherent in the essence of what it is to be human.... It cannot be cared for simply be redirecting it into a social "love of humanity," or by analyzing it as an issue of class theory seen from a materialistic view of history, or by reducing it to a psychoanalytic problem of the sexual libido.... As long as the investigation into the matter of self is not resolved, all being, all things within humanity and the world itself, will, as seen from the self, be something "other".... This other-centered point of view will always function as a hammer pulverizing the various forms of return to the self that present themselves as answers in the course of one's questioning.

It is not that Nishitani means to reject God or Buddha as mere fictions, and in fact he alludes to Vaihinger's idea of the "as if" only to reject it as inappropriate. If what they point to is a fiction, then "it is a fiction that has more reality than what is usually called real,... a reality in the background." The self is not a Kantian "thing in itself" that cannot be known except through such indirect pointers. It can be known, but only as formless, not as thing, not as consciousness.

Nishitani's descriptions of the liberation of the self, or the encountering of true selfhood, are more mystical in tone than philosophical. Philosophical language is used more as a *via negativa* to show what this liberation does *not* mean. In this sense, Nishitani does not give philosophy an epistemology or ontology of the self so much as a permanent critique of all such ways of thinking. This does not mean that it stops with Zen at reminding us of the ineffability of experience or of the limits of rational thought, the "Great illness" of not doubting words. His discussion of the self and its liberation also points to the goal of his own quest: "philosophical awareness of one's own self." Like the pure or direct experience that Nishida held before him in his thinking, Nishitani's experience of the self is the lodestone of the truth of philosophy.

61 **SELF, OTHER, AND ETHICS.** As with Nishida, the I-you relationship in Nishitani is given a place of special importance but does not form part of the paradigm of all of reality. In a word, interpersonal encounter is made the handmaiden of self-awareness, and within it the "other" is viewed as a dimension of no-self. On this basis he tries to generate a kind of moral imperative. Although all the ingredients for this step are already present, the connection will take some explaining.

The principal model of the self-other relationship in Nishitani is that of the Zen dialogue between master and disciple, tales of which abound in the most outrageous symbolic acts. In his praise for these "direct body attacks" one can of course see Nishitani's own love of a good intellectual discussion. He was always convinced that parlor etiquette is the antithesis not only of true rational dialogue but also of dialogue in which reason is cast aside as an impediment to awareness. It is this latter that is central to the Zen dialogue, whose focus is not clarity of ideas but the recovery of self through the encounter with the other.

Nishitani saw in these exchanges not only the spirit of Zen but a paradigm of all authentic encounter between one person and another: namely, an encounter that realizes—actualizes and becomes aware of—the reality of the self as it is. As long as one or both parties do remain on the ground of the ordinary ego, only words and ideas can be exchanged. Sharing in experience, speaking "mind to mind" or "heart to heart," requires rather a standpoint of non-ego.

As he sees it, Zen begins precisely at the point where Buber's I-you stops because it challenges a contradiction built into it, and indeed to all notions of interpersonal relationships based on a substantial ego. Namely, although individual subjectivity is made an absolute so that no one can take the place of another, as long as this absoluteness is located in the substantial ego, the relation between individuals either entails the absorption of the two into a universal *tertium quid*, whether in the form of a substantial nature or in the form of a transcendent mediating principle. In either case, part of that absoluteness is taken away. Remove the substantial ego, as is the case with Zen and the standpoint of emptiness, and the contradiction disappears with it.

In the encounter of one with another on a ground of nothingness, the self-identity of each is absolute; and yet each is absolutely relative in the sense that relationship requires both a self and an other. Therefore, the negation of one's own individual freedom in affirming that of the other is at the same time a reaffirmation of one's own individual freedom. In the "therefore" one can hardly fail to see Nishida's earlier construction of the I-you relation:

> The absolute discrimination between the two sets up an absolute two. But precisely because it is *absolute* the absolute discrimination is at the same time an absolute self-identity: the absolute two are absolutely one. Within the absolute two, one and the same absolute openness dominates. Absolute discrimination is here the same as absolute equality. This means that there is a true and direct communication between two human individuals, but without anything being communicated.... Each in knowing himself essentially knows the other... This can take place only on a non-subjective ground.

As nonsensical as this sounds, Nishitani insists that "the absurd notion that absolute enmity is at the same time absolute harmony" is in fact the Zen foundation for the I-you encounter.

He makes it clear that the harmony he speaks of here is not just a logical entailment of self requiring other the way son requires mother. Nor is it the same as the simple nondifferentiation that comes from absorbing all individuals into a single One, so that self and other simply disappear and with them all individual personhood. Rather each is absolutely nondifferentiated from the other as part of its own identity, and in this sense all relationship between them as relative absolutes is transcended. When two individuals meet at this homeground of the self, they face the "unbounded horror" of a self-identity that negates their ordinary identity as a free and absolute ego relating to other egos. Yet it is precisely here that love in a religious sense is possible:

> I stress "in a religious sense" because it is a case of emptiness or no-self that has absolutely cut off self and other from each other and from their relationship as self and other. Thus absolute opposition is at the same time absolute harmony.... *Self and other are not one, and not two.* To be not one and not two means that they are related, with each retaining its absoluteness, and while still being relative are never for a moment separated.

This is what it means to speak of love as a non-ego in which the other is "present" as other and not simply as "a projection of one's own ego."

Throughout Nishitani's later work, he seems to have understood ethics as more or less circumscribed by the search for what humans *should be* in order to act in accord with their true nature. He was more concerned with locating the source of ethical behavior in the self-awareness of non-ego, and therefore distinguishing it from rational or lawful behavior, than he was with establishing the practical dimension to religion he had once found so important. Despite the occasional reference to "selfless activity" in the ordinary sense of "not acting selfishly," the bulk of his references to religious love seems to have maintained a rather typical Zen distance from identifying or applying actual ethical norms. In what follows I have picked up remarks from a number of his writings and organized them more or less *ad libitum*. At best they will show a mixture of openings and closures to ethical questions, with no concrete indication of what he found morally unacceptable, or why.

The moral vacuum of the present age did not, of course, escape his attention. He saw the "fundamental relativism" of values as an unreflected consequence of modern nihilism. It was neither embraced in full consciousness as an alternative to the once dominant absolute values of tradition, nor experienced in a somber despair over the loss of something essential to existence. The fact that values have been subsumed under the category of "fashion" seems rather to have been accepted as part of modern life. This is why the very word *ethics*, he says, has become for modern men and women "like an empty, dried up bean-shell."

This does not mean that the solution lies in restoring the ethical values of tradition. That ground has been taken, and for all the distress it brings, opens the possibility for a spiritual advance, just as nihilism itself does. In the same way that no one can eat or sleep for another, no tradition or institution can ground the ethical objectively for individuals. If the *logos* of science tries to look at the world as it is only from the viewpoint of the world and to minimize the human ingredient, the counterposition of *ethos* that is content with trying to look at the human from the standpoint of the human simply replaces one imbalance with another. Even an ethic that purports to be concerned with taking care of the world falls into this same one-sidedness if it does not issue from an enlightened awareness of world and self just as they are, in the no-self of their true suchness. In other words, it is only by deliberately breaking through the ethical to the religious sphere—he draws on Kierkegaard in this connection—that one can return to true ethical behavior.

By "breaking through," he does not mean simply overstepping or sidestepping the ethical sphere, but facing the aporia built into all ethical systems, both those rationally devised and those haphazardly lived out. This is why morality cannot be based on divine law and commands, on self-interest, or even on some Kantian idea of the categorical imperative, which retains the form of a transcendent command even though it seems to come from within the self. Only a sense of responsibility that issues naturally from a deep awareness of the utter contingency of life on the one hand and the openness of the future on the other is the proper foundation for human action. But today ethics seems paralyzed by the inability to restore this transcendent ground on the one hand and its captivation by nihilism's relativization of all values. If there is to be a way out, it cannot be a matter of rejecting ethics but of appropriating the outer problem as one's own and "wrestling with the devil" within:

> Fundamentally ethics today is enveloped in a deep enigma. The simple rejection of ethics we see today is, of course, no answer; it is no more than decadence and a sign that the enigma has been trivialized. The split this causes in life reaches all the way to the religious dimension.... If there is any heartfelt desire left to seek the Buddha and the patriarchs outside of the self, the Buddha and the patriarchs must also become the "devil."

Consequently, the ethical spirit of social movements must also be internalized if they are not to be self-defeating. Nishitani's complaint against Marxism was that, having divested itself of the ruling Christian values as supportive of the status quo, it obliged those who practiced it to forfeit the inner tranquility and love of humanity that those traditional values also represented. It thus lent itself easily to be taken over by objective, "scientific" accounts of what is ultimately of value for society and the individuals who make it up.

In this connection, I recall his reply to a question I put him in 1980 at what was probably the last conference of the extended membership of the Kyoto school. Just back from war-torn Nicaragua, where I had met with friends in the Sandinista government and former students, and from a broader research tour of Latin America, where I had had occasion to see the seamy side of multinational investments in oppressive social structures, I asked him for his thoughts about the equivalent of a "liberation theology" for Zen and the philosophy of absolute nothingness. The immediate occasion for the question was a remark he had made in his own lecture the day before:

> Buddhism and Christianity need a "place" to come together to talk, ...and that place is the world of historical reality where the two religions meet head-on.... Even the confrontation of the traditional doctrines of the two religions must take place in the actual situation of the world today. It must not be an in-house discussion.... It is necessary to dialogue on the problems of present

society, ...problems for which both carry responsibility, if only in virtue of the fact that they had not been able to prevent them.

He made it clear in his reply to the question that no ideology of "liberation" was to be trusted, that they were all "pseudoreligions" because the call for the one true liberation, changing one's heart and mind, was smothered in the clamor of collective reforms. It was substantially the same position he had argued in a 1957 essay:

> Interpretations of religion not only in Marxism but in all modern social ideologies... only interpret the human being from the standpoint of the "I." This is because they only know self-awareness in the form of an awareness of an "I" and not in that of a "non-I".... This is also the reason why social reform is considered apart from the reform of the human person.

The transcript of that interchange does not reflect the temper of his remarks, indeed his annoyance at the way the question was put. Still, it is not difficult to read between the lines of Nishitani's allusions to Marxism, Nazism, Imperialism, and so forth a disillusionment with the ideologies that had swept through Japan when he was a young professor. As he knew only too well, the scars of complicity still mar the reputation of the Kyoto philosophers at home and abroad. But, at least as long as I knew him, this was clearly a matter to be kept between the lines. It was not, and perhaps had never been, part of the main text.

Be that as it may, this distrust of institutions or the preoccupation with reforming institutions has also its theoretical basis. Beginning with Socrates, Nishitani notes, the problem of knowing the self was "linked to that of ethical relationship with other people in the *polis.*" The connection is made by the self's ceasing to be simply a problem to itself. The way of investigating the self as the great doubt of Zen, in contrast,

> refuses any ready solution established from such a standpoint. For the self questioning its very existence, anything come from outside the self itself is not acknowledged as having authority.... In this sense, the self is through and through self-centered. The answer that solves the problem of the self can only arise from within the self itself.

This answer from within does not take the form of principles, universal or concrete, but rather that of a "demand for liberation from self" that is locked away from awareness by self-attachment. Once the Great Negation of denying the self has been performed, the Great Compassion of living selflessly for others follows naturally, as a matter of course.

The mark of the self liberated from self-attachment is an undifferentiated love for all things, like God's making the sun to shine and the rain to fall on the good and the bad without discriminating. This liberation from judgment of good and evil points to an emptying out of self. It is not like the detached, disinterested view of scientific objectivity, which abstracts from the human and also from the concrete reality of the things it studies in order to find the laws that govern reality. It is a religious indifference that functions not from principle but from the immediate encounter with the concrete reality of this evil person and that good one. It was only in this sense that he was prepared to recognize the importance of working passionately for what one believes in as an essential dimension of religion. In his terms, along with what Zen calls Great Faith and Great Doubt, we cannot not forget the ingredient of Great Anger. By this he does not mean mere fury or animosity, but a passionate overflowing of no-self.

This ambiguity towards the ethical dimension of religion affects Nishitani's critique of science and technology as well as his revised view of history, to which questions we may turn next.

62 SCIENCE AND NATURE. In condensing Nishitani's views on science, we have to understand that his context was defined by the overcoming of nihilism, whose advent and consequences he saw at the heart of the modern world; and by the fact that Christianity was both the womb of science and its chief antagonist. His views were framed, accordingly, in terms of a face-off between religion and science in which the latter had swallowed up the former. While he will agree *in principle* that some kind of a convergence of the two is necessary, *in practice* he was more given to the critique of science and its visible effects than to making positive steps towards an alternative understanding of science, and not at all given to examining trends in the philosophy of science that took that next step and has struggled with concrete ethical questions.

Nishitani's critique of science has three aspects, which come and go freely in his writings on the subject and all of which need to be kept in mind at all times. First is the idea that science itself is a critique of all former modes of thought, challenging their survival and at the same time forcing them to deeper reflection on their own biases:

> We must have the courage to admit that the spiritual basis of our existence, that is, the ground from which all the teleological systems in religion and philosophy up to now have emerged and on which they rested has been completely destroyed, once and for all. Science has descended upon the world of

> teleology like an angel with sword, or rather a new demon.... The problem here is one of philosophical conscience inquiring existentially and essentially into what science is, ...submitting to science as to a fire with which to purge and temper traditional religions and philosophies.

It is not only the remarkable achievements science has brought that give it this critical power, but the fact that its claims against prescientific thinking are so often well-founded, as well as the fact that it has constellated the basic questions of life in a new form from which no philosophy or religion can claim exemption.

Second, just as nihilism needs to be overcome from within nihilism itself, and ethics from within the enigma of ethics itself, so the scientific mode of thought that lies at the core of nihilism must be made to face and break through its own limitations. If the scientific standpoint were lived to the full, Nishitani suggests, as a total and exclusive way of being in the world, it would soon enough run up against the fundamental questions of human existence before which its powers would collapse. At this point, it must not turn back but cast itself into the dark night of its own irrelevance in order to resurrect in another, more self-conscious, form.

Third, science needs to be submitted to the critique of a religion and philosophy grounded on a standpoint that transcends both science and its own respective traditions. Such a standpoint is to be found, at the crossroads of the natural world and the no-self, in what Nishitani calls—returning to an idea he had introduced in his early work on elemental subjectivity— "naturalness." It is here that he sees the philosophy and religion of the east making a distinctive contribution.

This three-dimensional critique of science is seen by Nishitani as a chapter in the history of self-awareness. Though it is ultimately only the individual who can advance to self-awareness, the process must begin from within the setting of a scientific and "mechanized" world, by making that world, such as it is, a problem of the inner life. "The essence of science," he says, "is something to be brought into question in the same realm where the essence of the human becomes a question to human beings themselves." Technology is, of course, a fact of modern life, but it is *also* a state of mind, and for the philosopher this is the primary concern. What has happened is that the mindset of technology has led to a rationalization of external society, in its work and in its human relationships, in such a way as to erase the human from the picture—or rather, to think of it in mechanistic paradigms—with the result that it has brought about the exact reverse in the inner life: a derationalization in which people no longer think about what is happening to them. In effect, the certitudes of science have become the new dogma of an unreflected faith. Questioning the foundations of these certitudes begins from a recognition of how we came to believe in them in the first place.

The opposition of scientific rationality to the irrationalities of religion fractured the mythical view of the world—a single world in which God, self, and world interpenetrated and even interchanged each other's identities. Western philosophy, Nishitani claims, has not been able to stop the two from "stabbing each other in the heart" but all along has kept up the illusion of being able to live in two worldviews at the same time. Prior to the Enlightenment and the emergence of modern science, the idea of God as the author of ultimate truth served to join secular and religious knowledge. When science dispensed with God, the unity collapsed. The effort to reconcile religious dogmas with scientific explanations is an attempt to restore this unity at the level of rational understanding. The more basic problem, for Nishitani, is the split between opposing ways of *Existenz* or being human in the world represented by religion and science. What has happened is that instead of allowing this problem to flower into full frustration, a new form of humanism has arisen, bring calm to the situation by focusing on the meaning of human life and leaving the world of nature to science. It is this separation of the human from nature that Nishitani finds deluded, both because it is not as peaceful a coexistence as it seems and because it glosses over the opportunity to face a more basic question brought to the surface by the clash of worldviews.

In the shift of the source of authority from tradition to expertise and scientific method, then, the image of the human underwent a radical change along with the idea of nature. The self detached itself from unity with God and world to assert its independence. A different way of "seeing and being" in the world arose, what Nishitani calls, recalling again his early work on elemental subjectivity, the rise of "the awareness of subjectivity." The turn to modernity meant a drive to get to the core of the human, casting off the outer shell of religious authority as an "unnecessary accessory."

Meantime, in the mechanized world of science, nature had been redefined as energy. Only by abstracting from the traditional and symbolic value of things in nature could technology advance to the most efficient manipulation of the nature world. Water, for instance, which had meant different things at the same time and in the same culture to the tea master, the poet, and the religious person, is redefined in scientific culture as a "source of energy" to the exclusion of all other meanings. As the idea of nature was thus adjusted to the ends of the new worldview, it was necessarily dehumanized. Along with religious and cultural meanings, all subjective significance was drained off in order that it could be understood and controlled. This ongoing process of "mechanization," as Nishitani liked to call it, did not simply run parallel with the "humanization" of the interior life; it competed with it until it had taken over. Subjectivity, in effect, retreated from nature.

The alienation of the subject from nature is not simply the result of scientific method having gotten the upper hand. It has become an accepted way of life, so that even the wonders of the natural world drive us back deeper into our own frustrated selves. The following passage from a late lecture, though somewhat broken in the transcript, makes the point clearly:

> Humans are born from the world of nature, which means that nature is part of their very existence. They are like each tree or each blade of grass, like the birds and the beasts: no matter how much one looks at them, there is no explaining why they are or what they mean. But humans, unlike the rest of nature, came to form themselves into societies.... The urban life in which we pass our days is a world that has room only for things that can be understood. We have gotten used to this world. Its shallowness became second nature to us, and as a result our minds grew shallow and narrow, giving rise to discontent and dissatisfaction. Since no return to nature could provide an answer, we turned around and grew discontent with nature itself.

The consequence is that the subjective awareness that was gained with the emergence of the scientific worldview began to be eroded. Not only the world of nature, but also the human itself became an object of increasing mechanization, both directly through science and technology, and indirectly through the effect of the scientific standpoint on the rationalization of social institutions. Mirroring the words of Buber, though not citing him, Nishitani argues that our age is turning everyone, and everything, into an "it," with the result that the "I" is also turned into an "it":

> If all "yous" completely cease to resist the "I" to the extent that they even cease to be "yous" any more, the standpoint of the "I" also evaporates at the same time. "I" becomes the dominant power in a world of power.... As everything becomes an "it" to be freely manipulated and controlled, the humans who do the manipulating have their quality as subjects taken away. Subjective awareness suffers a gradual degeneration under the sway of the technological.

At the same time, the weakening of the self and the objectification of nature cloaks a subtle anthropocentricism in science. Despite its mechanistic view of the human, the scientific mode of thought has allied itself with economics and philosophy in settling on the human, individual and social, as the measure of all things. Where one set of human traits had once been projected on to the world of the gods, another set is now projected on to the world of nature. The natural world is carved up into individual items that become kinds of "abstract subjects" that "function" in a law-regulated community of other subjects. In this sense the Christian myth of the cosmos centered on the human as the crown of creation and ruled over by a personal God continues to nourish science from the roots, despite the surface antagonisms.

The east did not produce out of itself either the scientific culture of the west or the idea of subjective awareness that is the foundation of western democracy. The former Nishitani sees as having its origins in Greek culture, the latter in the personal relationship with God in Christianity. The science and subjectivity we see in the world today run counter to their origins, even though the "fatal affinity" remains like a stiff muscle that refuses to relax. In such circumstances a return to the origins—such as we see in the Renaissance or Reformation—will not suffice, since the origins themselves have become problematic. Nishitani reckons that eastern culture may be of some help in regaining the pristine meaning of Greek and Christian culture by seeing something in it that western eyes have missed, namely the non-subjective, non-objective, primary "naturalness" of nature.

In the east we see the pristine "naturalness" that objectifying, functional thinking has come to trivialize as romantic and irrational. The naturalness of nature as a whole and of everything in it is that of something that is "as it is and of itself." Not by outside force of law or will, or by any inner necessity of an underlying substance, but just simply by its "suchness." There is no "self" in either the personal or impersonal sense—just a "self-nature." In place of the duplicity of essence and existence that both science and subjectivity rely on, nature is a unicity of nature. As a consequence of the duplicity, each thing has its own "framework of being" so that it cannot be any other, as reflected in the logical law of noncontradiction. In the unicity of "natural being" there is no such framework, and this means that what are "essentially" two can be seen as "naturally not two." This, in a word, is what Nishitani proposes as the standpoint from which to carry out the three-dimensional critique of science.

63 TIME AND HISTORY.

For many, if not most, of Nishitani's western readers, the chapters on time and history in *Religion and Nothingness* are the most dissatisfying because of their irrelevance to lived history. What has to be remembered here, however, is that a large part of the reason for his apparent abstraction of history from the concrete actuality it normally has, is that his only serious attempts to do otherwise were in his political philosophy and particularly in the *Chūōkōron* discussions. The abstraction is, I believe, as clear a sign as we have that Nishitani wishes deliberately to distance himself from that earlier thinking. In fact, already in 1949 he had altered his use of the term "philosophy of history" to remove its political implications and make it refer instead to the pure search for a metaphysical ground to human existence. The result is a far more valuable contribution to Kyoto-school philosophy than his earlier orientations would have ever produced.

In the *Chūōkōron* discussions he had talked of the absence of history in the east in the sense that the transhistorical and the historical have traditionally been one, in contrast to western historicism, which separates the two. He recommended then, in a passing remark, that "overcoming historicism seems to work better if it proceeds by way of historicism." This was to be the starting point for a revised idea of history.

For Nishitani, the normal ways of looking at history, as an endless cycle of repetitions or as a linear advance into an indeterminate future, are neither of them adequate because each represents only one aspect of time. Nor does any attempt to combine them into the sense of a spiral progression that continually recapitulates as it moves ahead get to the true nature of history. All of these view the making of history from the standpoint of being. He proposes a view from the standpoint of a dynamic nothingness in which time and becoming are seen as the self-emptying of reality. This will take some explaining, though the basic insight is a simple one.

He begins from Arnold Toynbee's contrast of history east and west. Christian theology has carried the idea of linear time through the history of western philosophy by accepting its fundamental form of an infinite past advancing into an infinite future and at the same time trying to complement that idea of time with an idea of eternity that transcends the temporal, historical world. What it sees as eternity, however, is allowed to break into the immanence of history only on condition that it submit to the absoluteness of unidirectional time. Time was originally the creation of God, but its essence is such that God rules over it only by becoming a player in its story, that is, as a *dramatis persona*. This idea of time thus reduces the idea of eternity to a mere infinity stretching in both directions. This creates a kind of "optical illusion" in which one strains to explain history by looking back to the mind of God before the beginning of the story and ahead beyond its end. But the actual meaning of history unfolds within the drama itself and is therefore centered on the action of the individuals who make it up, including God.

Eastern ideas of time, including the Buddhist way of thinking, instead tend to be circular or cyclical. The order of things is entirely impersonal, and its meaning undetermined by any overarching story. This gives it its own internal contradiction. On the one hand, since meaning becomes a function of the human intellect and will, history is open. On the other, since meaning cannot alter the nature of history's universal indetermination, the individual self is absorbed into the universal and deprived of any novel contribution. Unlike Christian history, this view is centered on nature rather than on the self.

Nishitani accepts the view of western history as accurate, but claims that Toynbee has read a western bias into the eastern view. It is in correcting that bias that Nishitani offers his own view. He sees the present moment not as a point in a progression, be it circular or linear, but as an opening to the "homeground" of time itself, in which not only past and future, but all the meaning of history has its elemental, and infinitely renewable, source. The passage cited above (§55) of connection with the past through a bowl of rice is one example of this. In that same context he speaks of the appropriation of the wisdom of the great figures of the past as a way of transcending history from within history.

In overcoming the apparently stifling impact of a circular view of time, he claims, Christianity has in fact served science with the tools for an anthropocentric objectivity that locates the meaning of things in the story of their genesis and their effects. Already from the time of the European Enlightenment it was clear that this worldview would one day undermine Christianity, and the rise of secular nihilism has borne this out. (At the same time, he acknowledges that this view of history has given a foothold from which to wrestle with the problems of the present, which Buddhism has not yet found.) Not even Nietzsche's attempt to bend time back on itself in eternal recurrence can overcome this problem because it, too, leaves the human as the sole center of time and telos of history.

If the nihilism built into the modern view of history is to be overcome, it can only be by a return to the origin of history itself. The point of return is the present moment, or the "eternal now" as he calls it, borrowing the phrase of Kierkegaard that Nishida and Tanabe had also made use of. In the here and now, "directly underfoot of the present," past and present are both transcended and made simultaneous—without destroying the temporal sequence just as it is. The pattern is familiar: the same nothingness disclosed in the world of being without annihilating that world is here discovered in the essence of time. Only eternity can ground the infinity of time, just as only nothingness can ground the world of being. It is not that there is another world outside time called eternity, but that the world of time and being *is* the self-emptying of absolute emptiness. Emptiness is history, history is emptiness.

64 GOD. As we have seen with so many of the other ideas Nishitani takes up—nihilism, self, interpersonal relationship, ethics, science, history—Nishitani neither simply rejects traditional ideas he wants to rethink nor does he simply modify them in the light of his own standpoint. Rather, he tries to think ideas through to the point where they collapse before what they are trying to express, and at the point of collapse disclose what had been neglected. What he calls "breakthrough" always implies a rebirth, not only of the self but also of that which has been broken through. From there he begins his reconstruction, relativizing what had gone before in the light of this disclosure. The similarities to Nishida's idea of "transdescending" negation to affirmation and Tanabe's "absolute critique" are evident. What comes through more strongly in Nishitani than in his predecessors is the existential dimension of this way of approaching a question.

Whether or not this method always works, and one has the sense that the assumption of its applicability is more tacit than examined at times, it is Nishitani's way of recognizing the authority of tradition without being bound to that authority. The same holds true of his treatment of God, which too many of his commentators have seen as a simple rejection of the Christian God in favor of a God fashioned in the image and likeness of absolute nothingness. It is probably more accurate to say that his inquiry into the idea of God sharpened his idea of absolute nothingness, and indeed provided an ontological grounding for his existential method of dealing with traditional ideas: not only rational reflection, but all of reality is by nature self-emptying.

It is clear that Nishitani rejects the traditional western idea of divine transcendence, but he does not reject the idea of God or the possibility of transcendence altogether. Rather, he insists that it is necessary for Christianity itself. And in working out his argument for a reform of the Christian notion of God, Nishitani is not simply wagging a Buddhist finger in the direction of Christian doctrine and asking it to wake up to rational criticism and modern philosophy. Rather, he is wrestling with the problem of God with one foot in Christianity and one foot in Buddhism precisely because it is a problem that opens up into a fundamental human problem for religion, independently of Buddhism or Christianity. This is true of his writings on God in general, where what was only implicit in Nishida and Tanabe is brought into clear relief: a philosophy of absolute nothingness needs the idea of God as a central ingredient.

The principal reasons for his rejection of divine transcendence we have already seen. The emergence of the scientific worldview brought with it a freedom of thought from all external authority, which begins with a declaration of independence from God. Christianity has countered the blow to divine authority by insisting on God's absolute otherness and transcendence from the world, and at the same time that this transcendent authority is omnipresent in the world and in all human activity, including that of reason. The perennial problem of working out an ontological relationship between God and creatures thus becomes still more acute when it is made to challenge the autonomy of scientific reason, and still more when the principles that had once ruled unquestioned in daily life, thought, ethics, and society, fall one by one to the advance of skepticism, secularization, and atheism.

Unless one believes that the self-awakening of the Enlightenment, science, and modernity has all been one gigantic mistake whose time will soon be spent so that faith can return to its former pride of place, then something must be done about the fact that the traditional standpoint of Christianity stands at loggerheads with this "awakened subjectivity of modern man." Nishitani is unequivocal on the point:

> Christianity cannot, and must not, look on modern atheism merely as something to be eliminated. It must instead accept atheism as a mediation to a new development of Christianity itself.

This new development begins with a reassessment of transcendence as that which "deprives us of a locus to stand in self-existence, a locus where we can live and breathe."

Throughout western intellectual history, the omnipresence of the transcendent God in history has risen up like a great iron wall that one cannot get around. It rises up before us and presses on us the constant reminder that creatures cannot be God. "Insofar as God is the one and only absolute *being*, all other things consist fundamentally of *nothingness*." No appeal to the analogy of being can compensate for the fact that we have been created not from the same stuff as God but *ex nihilo*, so that our nothingness is more immanent in us than our being. Nor is the basic imparity between God and creatures really overcome by personalizing God and opening the way for an interpersonal relationship. Such personalizing can never be complete because God lacks the fundamental nihility that is the mark of human personhood. A simple atheism that negates the creator does not eliminate the nothingness, since the experience of nihility is thrown up to us quite independently of whether we accept the religious doctrines or not. Better to seek a way *through* the nothingness with which God's presence confronts us.

Though not a historical argument, Nishitani claims that the reason for personalizing God—or for continuing to keep him a person—is to paint over the nihility at the core of human existence with an image of harmony between the world and human existence in it, so that "the meaning and *telos* of human existence formed the criteria for the meaning and *telos* of the world." The world is pushed to the periphery and the special qualities of human existence are put at the center, with the result that God's place at the center is secured only by taking on the personhood of the human. Today the world is back in the picture, and the vertical axis of a personal relationship between God and humanity is cut across by a horizontal axis that makes the world spin in a different direction. We can no longer think of our place in the world as fundamentally personal; we must think of it as material and biological.

If the idea of God is to survive, it can only be by finding a more fundamental impersonality beyond the personality of God. Here again, the point is not to reject the God of tradition but to reestablish it. And the grounds for that do not lie in any privileged access to knowledge of the nature of divinity but in a recognition of the self-attachment at the core of our image of God. The mark of liberation from self, as we saw earlier, is an undifferentiated love for all things, like God's making the sun to shine and the rain to fall on the good and the bad without discrimination. It is that image of God, of a lover who is "impersonal" in the noblest sense of the term, that he urges on Christianity: a person "that appears out of what cannot itself be called personal and does not entail any confinement of self-being." At the same time, just as the awakening to true selfhood beyond self-attachment is a paradigm for how reality as such works, so the image of God must conform to that paradigm. In a word, Nishitani's treatment of God as an impersonal person is part of a wider reappropriation of the idea of God. The basis of this rethinking—to massively simplify an idea he turned around and around in his head for most of his life—is what the mystics called "the God beyond God" and what he called "an absolute nothingness reaching a point beyond even God."

The reexamination begins with the idea of the creation of the world *ex nihilo*. This *nihilum* that is elemental in the human, and that at first encounter seems to be no more than a meaningless nihility, is not a total negation of all meaning but only a negation of meaning that has been centered on the self as the telos of life. Put the other way around, its meaning lies in the affirmation of a self not attached to, and not centered in, itself. The nothingness beyond God of which the world is made is also the nothingness out of which God works. It is more absolute than God, not in the sense that God becomes its creature but in the sense that the elemental nature of a thing is more absolute than any particular manifestation of it. From his early years Nishitani was caught up in Eckhart's idea of the "godhead" as pointing to just this idea of an elemental divinity from which all activity of God proceeds and to which all our ideas and images of God must return for rejuvenation.

It is also and at the same time the point to which the self returns in quest of its own true nature:

> The nihility of *creatio ex nihilo* may be spoken of as a simple relative nothingness... Truly free existence can only be posited on and rooted in absolute nothingness. This, it seems to me, is the kind of nothingness Eckhart has in mind when he says, "The ground of God is the ground of my soul; the ground of my soul is the ground of God."
>
> ...
>
> He calls this the "desert" of the godhead. Here the soul is completely deprived of its egoity. This is the final ground of the soul, its *bottomless ground.* Although it marks the point at which the soul can for the first time return to be itself, it is at the same time the point at which God is in himself. It is the ground of God.

Thus the nature of God—which is at the same time the elemental nature of the world of being and of human existence in it—is absolute nothingness, and the nature of absolute nothingness is the absence of all substance or self. Hence that nature is most manifest where self is emptied out.

The principal image of this in Christianity Nishitani finds in the self-emptying of God in Jesus, what Paul's hymn in the epistle to the Philippians (2: 6–11) calls *kenōsis.* Nishitani distinguishes the *kenōsis* of God from the *ekkenōsis* of Christ. By the former he sees it as the nature of God to be self-negating, empty of self; by the latter he understands a deliberate and free choice to act in accord with that nature. Thus we say that God *is love* and in Christ God *loves.* If the latter is an act of self-emptying, the former is a further emptying of emptiness beyond will. In this way God, the godhead, and

Christ are taken out of the frame of reference of a personal, anthropocentric view of world and relocated in the spontaneous, natural state of *samādhi* in which things and persons are what they are and do what they do from a standpoint empty of self.

Nishitani was fond of citing to theologians who would come to visit him Paul's statement that "It is no longer I who live but Christ who lives in me" (Gal. 2: 20) and turning it into a *kōan* to ask, "Who is talking here?" The question, and the answer, rest on a Buddhist reading of God as no-self. What he seems to have wanted in reply was a recovery of the mystical search for God by letting go of God.

65 THE EMBODIMENT OF AWARENESS.

Beginning with *Religion and Nothingness* Nishitani takes ever longer Buddhist strides in his treatment of philosophical themes. It was only after completing the last chapter of that book that he was to publish his first essay on Zen, "Zen and Science." But once he had taken that step he gained in confidence to deal directly with the texts of the Zen tradition, culminating in two volumes of commentary on Dōgen's *Shōbōgenzō* running to over 830 pages. This is not to say that he was simply applying Zen ideas to the philosophical questions. Beginning with the central idea of emptiness, these were borrowed concepts that he rethought and transformed in a philosophical context. In this sense, his interest is less in clarifying Zen for rational discourse than, as Horio Tsutomu, one of his leading disciples, has said, "in breaking through those ideas to pressure them to a new position."

In general, Nishitani cites the western mystics in their talk *about* experience or its ineffability. When he wants to talk of the ineffable experience itself, he prefers to cite examples from Zen and the Chinese classics. He states his reason succinctly:

> If silence is golden, then Zen may be called an alchemy that transforms all things into gold by purifying them in the fire of the negation of all words and letters, names and concepts, logical methods and theoretical systems. Zen is, so to speak, an anti-ontological alchemy.

This may be said of the way he uses Zen in his own thinking. Zen examples fall into his texts fresh off the tree. After chewing the dried fruits of his philosophical arguments, they taste all the sweeter, at least until he interrupts the savoring to let us know that they are really the same thing in different form. What is more, Zen seems to preserve its traditional authority because of its detachment from established authority. Like the gold that was the standard of the alchemical *opus,* Zen remains a standard because of its elusiveness and its commitment to break through all reasoning about and imagination of the "one great matter" of the true self.

At the same time, as we have seen, this activity of breaking through was not an end in itself. The purpose of Zen imagery and discipline was always a coming to awareness. It is like the eagle driving a small bird high into the sky by flying circles around it, and when the air has become too rarefied for its prey to breathe and flap its wings, clutches it at the moment it is about to fall. Its dependence on its prey, we might say, is its way of keeping itself from trying to soar over itself. So, too, the body and the images it feeds to consciousness are a way of keeping the pursuit of the true self tied to the everyday.

In a late series of lectures, completed when Nishitani was seventy-five years old, this theme figures strongly. He explains that if there is no substance to things and the self but all is change and becoming, then even the words and ideas we use to capture things are empty of substance. In fact, he suggests, it is words and concepts as much as anything that created the idea of substance in the first place and hold it in place.

This naturally leads us to ask what can carry the weight of the manifested world in reason if not words and ideas. In a late essay completed several years after these lectures, he suggests that at the standpoint of emptiness the world is reconstituted in its immediacy as "image" that is grasped not by feeling or thinking but in a "sensing" that includes both. As we have seen, just as the overcoming of nihilism does not entail the erasure of nihility but only the erasure of the anxiety connected with it—an affirmation of the nihility in the negation of the anxiety—so, too, the world does not simply cease to exist in awakening to nothingness but is reaffirmed just as it is, while our idea of it passes away. The world, he now suggests, "becomes image" on a field of emptiness. This "imaging" is not the work of the ordinary imagination in which the subject reproduces the world mentally. It is the work of emptiness making itself manifest in awareness while transcending the subject-object world.

Nishitani likens the imaging of the world to the "empty sky" (a metaphor that is also adopted in Buddhist texts), in the sense that it is both visible and yet opens up into an invisible, infinite expanse. This unity of an infinitely open reality and the manifold of appearances it takes in the world of being points to a kind of inner landscape of awareness. It is here that we speak of knowing things by becoming them. At the same time, we might add, it broadens the notion of viewing the world in double-exposure, which previously had the negative connotation of seeing through to the transience of the things of life, to give it a positive sense as well.

Using an image to talk about images, Nishitani says that in imaging, the thing and our knowing it are one, much as the chirping of a cicada—or even talk about the chirping of a cicada—calls up the image of the cicada, which is neither the cicada itself nor our knowing, but the "immediately given" point at which these two intersect. Seen in this light, ordinary knowing that sees the knower as standing in one spot and the known fact in another is overcome. In imaging, the external, stubborn facticity of a thing, its "being," is, as it were, "relocated" to a common ground at which it becomes "transparent," showing its true form while maintaining its "place" in the world of being as a fact:

> It is as if an inner landscape hidden in "being" were opened up. This is the basis for seeing facts themselves "from within." Basically, this relocation constitutes a shift from a real "fact" to its image. Or rather, it means that from within the "fact" an image that is one with it shows its individual form *as image*.

For Nishitani this imaging is not merely the work of consciousness, or work done on consciousness, but is an awareness in emptiness. Returning to the expanse of sky—which, incidentally, is written with the same Chinese character as that for emptiness—he asks us to think of someone lying on the ground and looking up. The sky above, though too expansive to be converted into a concrete image itself, seems to offer a field on which emptiness, the body that holds the images of the reality that the sky embraces, and the earth to which the body belongs, intersect. In other words, the sensing of an image represents an awakening to the fact that emptiness is the elemental source of all things, embracing them and permeating them through and through. He is thus able to use imaging as a way to reconfirm the transition from fact and idea interpenetrating each other to the interpenetrating of all things beyond all reasoning. It is, he says, like a recovery of original "chaos" behind the unified "cosmos."

The body that "holds" images of the world in their true, empty form is not body in the ordinary sense of the physical body, but more like a corporeal life that includes but is not limited to the skinbound individual. It is not susceptible to scientific investigation but neither is it a merely spiritual metaphor. It is the sense in which the full appropriation of insight—Nishitani introduces a term that means "bodily recognition"—belongs to the entirety of the living self because that living self belongs to the world around it. The body is that which breaks through the skin of the private individual to relate to the environment around it. In this way attention to the body does not oblige him to reintroduce the subject-object dichotomy that awareness on the standpoint of emptiness is intended to overcome. In fact, it is not in terms of the body-mind duality at all that he treats the body, but rather in terms of the relation between body and earth.

To express the unity of bodily self and environment, he borrows a term Kierkegaard uses in *Sickness unto Death* to speak of the unity of the self with its ground, namely that in the body self and environment are "transparent" to one another

> in the sense that no borderlines or partitions are present. This is what makes it alive. For the self to be alive means that life flows or breathes in the wider nature.... The fact of one's being alive means at bottom that there is a point where the center of the world and the center of the self are one,... a transparent point through which light can pass freely.... It has no walls, and where a wall appears it is the doing of the ego.

The idea of the body and the function of the image were never formally organized by Nishitani, nor did he go beyond these intimations to an interpretation of imagery that would have required some kind of symbolic theory. Numerous passing references in his late lectures to psychology—most of them, let it be said, to reject various models of the psyche—at least suggest that he recognized the question of the interpretation of images as deserving serious attention. What is more surprising is the lack of connection to art and literature, where his ideas would have taken off in a number of different directions. One has to suppose that, as an old man who had found a position that basically sufficed for his inquiry into ultimate questions, he faced the twilight of his life with the almost ascetical refusal to distract himself in novelty.

66 THE CRITIQUE OF RELIGION. We may conclude our account of Nishitani's philosophy by noting his general orientation to organized religion, in particular Buddhism and Christianity. Although he never addressed the subject of institutional religion at any length, comments that surface here and there in his works and late talks make it clear that he understood the task of the philosopher as one of recovering for those religions the soul that they seem to have lost in preoccupying themselves with doctrinal, ritual, or structural reform. "There is no 'present age' in religion," he liked to say, "and no religion in the present age." The relationship

between science, religion, and nihilism that had formed the heart of all his work up to *Religion and Nothingness* yields in his later work to a concern with turning religion back to the basic human drive from which it first emerges:

> Religious observances and doctrines developed through historical tradition to give support to religious bodies. But they have to be brought back again to their source, that is to their roots in the religious needs of people.... Religion is, after all, a way of living... and this is what religious institutions have to face ever and again.

The response to this situation will be different for Christianity than for Buddhism.

Apart from the doctrinal developments Nishitani saw necessary if Christianity is to face the contemporary world, he roundly rejected what he saw as an abiding intolerance toward other religions. As reprehensible as this is from the standpoint of simple reason, when the exclusion of the truth of other faiths passes itself off as a "certitude of faith" it offends the very heart of religion. "The domain of faith becomes like the court of a despotic monarch: open upwards to the Absolute one, but closed off downwards in the direction of the common man."

The reconciliation of faith with free thinking in Christian tradition is crucial precisely because the doctrines in question are too important to be cloistered in a self-centered dogmatism. For example, protecting the idea of a universal God from anthropomorphism or intolerance is a concern that goes beyond the boundaries of Christian theology, because sectarian fixation on such ideas easily falls into using particular ideas of God to support private notions of what constitutes the human or even simple national interests, in both cases human-centered perspectives passing themselves off as God-centered ones. Although he sees the Christian problem as a type of problem that traditional religion in general faces, one cannot help feeling that beneath his complaints of Christianity's failure to reexamine itself he felt a deep personal disappointment. This is borne out by the clear affection he shows for so many of the great Christian ideas and images that were so important to him in his own life.

As for Japanese Christianity, he saw it as a kind of "hothouse" religion, "having no contact and even isolating itself from the actual life of Japan" in order to keep its western form intact. He is not concerned with the extent to which western colonialism may be behind this, but only with the lack of a Japanese response to Christianity. In particular, he notes the lack of attention to Japanese ideas and sentiments toward the world of nature. At the same time, he sees the failure of "inculturation" in the Christian community as belonging to a more general malaise of the gradual alienation of the Japanese from their own cultural heritage.

Buddhism, meantime, though out in the open air of Japan, had got stuck in outdated institutional forms of funerary rites and temple transference, so that its temples are no longer a place of religious practice primarily. Its response to the arrival of nihilism was one of "simply passivity." So serious a problem was this, he predicted, that "if a reform of Buddhist institutions is not brought about, Buddhism will soon fade away." Lest one think that he is introducing a different brand of exclusivism in his claim that Christianity needs to become Japanese, he makes a contrary claim equally strong against Buddhism for its failure to open up to the rest of the world. This is complicated by the fact that Japanese Buddhism, he says, lacks the ability of European Christianity to see how its own distinctiveness is enhanced, rather than menaced, by its opening up into a more universal perspective. "Only when Buddhism becomes a world Buddhism," he predicts, "will it be brought back to life in the hearts of the Japanese people of today and in the future."

Buddhism also comes in for criticism over its doctrinal rigidity and sectarianism, at the very time that it "exerts practically no influence on life in society." He calls for a "Buddhist theology" to rethink the idea of the Buddha as well as the meaning of the death of the Buddha. Compared with the lively debate in Christian theological circles, "Buddhism, in its present tepid and inactive state, almost seems to be like a kind of geological relic from the past." This criticism of Buddhism for a lack of self-reflection extends to the absence of a clear ethic to respond to changes in the world of economics and politics, of a clear sense of historical consciousness, and a direct confrontation of tradition with problems of science and technology.

Thus he sees reform needed for both—like the great reform of Kamakura Buddhism or the changes that occurred in Christianity as it spread to the Hellenic and Roman worlds. Both need to face Japan as it is today and take on a new form. Nishitani considered himself a Buddhist, but not in a traditional, sectarian form nor in the general Japanese cultural form of plural affiliations. His affections for Zen and his practice of Rinzai Zen stopped short at "belonging." In a 1968 discussion of Tanabe's thought, he commented on his teacher's remark about being a *gewordener Buddhist* and a *werdender Christ* saying that as a philosopher he had taken a different position:

> I have the impression that I understand Tanabe's problem very well. I myself am in a similar situation. I do not feel satisfied with any religion as it stands,

> and I feel the limitations of philosophy also. So, after much hesitation, I made up my mind and have become a *werdender Buddhist*. One of the main motives for that decision was—strange as it may sound—that I could not enter into the faith of Christianity and was nevertheless not able to reject Christianity.

To understand these words, one has to recall that during Zen meditation one has to transcend religion in all forms, including that of one's own personal beliefs. This position seems to have found its way into Nishitani's philosophical reflections, and from there back again to his approach to Zen in its institutional form.

Even though the religious question itself, the question of the self, is not tied to any particular religion, Nishitani did recognize advantages that Buddhism and Zen had over Christianity in phrasing this question and in making it central. At the same time, he saw that the question is always imbedded in the history of the religion that poses it, so that for Christianity to try to simply take over Buddhist ontology—or vice-versa, for Buddhism to take over Christian ontology—is to miss the point. Only by recovering the primary question can both of these historical traditions, with their respective ontologies, be renewed.

That said, the renewal is one in which Christianity and Buddhism can collaborate to the benefit of both, provided they accept seriously that what is ultimately at stake is not the relativization of other traditions to their own absolute faith, nor even their own self-preservation, but religion itself.

Given Nishitani's lifelong interest in religion and the wide use to which he put his philosophy, it is possible to string together his remarks and make him sound like a soap-box preacher. But to read his works is to see a first-rate philosophical mind at work, who took very seriously his discipline and carried it out with high conscience. Despite his call for openness and its multifaceted richness, there is a kind of self-enclosed, all-or-nothing quality to Nishitani's thinking. One can cite his words as applying to this or that problem, but his standpoint was too much his own to be taken over by others as their own. Indeed, only rarely can the whole of one of his arguments be taken over. What one can take from his standpoint, though it is far more difficult to do so, is the reverence *within philosophy itself* for what is written on the calligraphy penned by D. T. Suzuki and hanging over the portal to Nishitani's house: "Ordinary mind."

Prospectus

67 PLACING THE KYOTO SCHOOL.

As I write, the study of Kyoto-school philosophy both inside Japan and abroad is alive and well. As major currents of thought around the world go, it is a small stream, but one that continues to course swiftly and deep across the wasteland that has long separated philosophy east and west. The number of younger scholars attracted to its ideas, the new translations in preparation, the confrontations with contemporary questions as well as with traditional religious thought—all of this suggests a vitality in its fundamental inspirations.

Like any "school" of thought, its survival depends on two elements. On the one hand, the main corpus of its writings needs careful and critical attention, both in its own right and in conversation with other modes of thought. On the other, its ideas need to be carried further and into new directions. In some measure these two elements are inseparable, but in the case of the Kyoto school the signs of the former are much easier to detect than those of the latter. Perhaps it is still too early, a mere ten years after the death of its last principal figure, to expect any more. All the same, one has to wonder whether a new generation of thinkers will find something new to paint with the three primary colors of Nishida, Tanabe, and Nishitani on their palette, and just what that might be; or whether it will all pass quietly into history as another movement whose time simply came and went.

I do not ask the question in order to predict an answer. But I do think the foregoing pages warrant some conclusions about the place of these thinkers in the history of philosophical ideas. One needs to place them not only to honor their achievement but also in order to know what is the primary context for teaching their thinking, for criticizing it, and simply for knowing what to expect of it and what not.

Set in the context of western philosophy, the Kyoto philosophers need to be seen as a derivative school of thought. None of them represents the kind of revolutionary originality we associate with the thinkers who were most influential on them: Kant, Hegel, Nietzsche, James, and Heidegger. At the same time, neither do they stand out as specialists in the thought of any of these thinkers. Their contribution to western thought as such was to have built on what they received, critically and creatively, but without an upheaval of the same proportions that we see, for example, in the phenomenological and existentialist movements.

That said, their importance to the history of western philosophy surpasses that of the neo-Kantians, a major current in Europe at the time Nishida began his philosophy but also fundamentally a derivative movement. While the sheer volume of material by and about Rickert, Cohen, Windelband, Natorp, and Cassirer far exceeds what is available on the Kyoto school, and while their influence on later Continental and American philosophy has been greater, it is my judgment that Nishida, Tanabe, and Nishitani will be seen to have made the more lasting impact on twentieth-century philosophy.

When we widen the horizon to look at the steady influx of eastern thought into western intellectual history in the past hundred years, the stature of the Kyoto school needs to be adjusted. There is nothing—be it the thought of an individual or a school of thought, be it in oriental studies or in philosophy strictly speaking—to compare with the appropriation of eastern ideas into western philosophy that we find in Nishida, Tanabe, and Nishitani. As tall as they stand in this regard, their contribution to Buddhist studies, or indeed to oriental philosophy in the traditional sense, is rather diminished in the western context. I say this as a point of fact, since very little attention has been given to the Kyoto school by scholars devoted to the classical thought and texts of the east. One may argue that the neglect is not entirely fair and that the Kyoto philosophers could bring some measure of synthesis to the study of eastern ideas in the west, which has tended to concentrate itself in highly specialized scholarship at one extreme and popular hodgepodge at the other. At least so far, this synthesis has not been.

But the western context is only half of the picture, if even that. As I stated at the outset, and as the intervening pages have strained to show, Nishida, Tanabe, and Nishitani do not really belong to the history of philosophy as we know it and under the assumptions that have dominated it up until now. Unless one is prepared to dismiss out of hand the idea of opening up western philosophy to the standpoint of world philosophy, there is literally no place to locate the Kyoto school properly. They have positioned themselves in a place as unfamiliar to the eastern mind as it is to the western. The question of locating them in effect questions the way we have located philosophies east and west. In this context, theirs is not a derivative contribution but something original and revolutionary.

If we assume, at least for the sake of argument, that philosophy needs a world forum in which Europe and the Americas do not enjoy privilege of place; that the time has come for the west to accept as part of its philosophical inheritance ideas that have flourished in non-western cultures but foundered in the west; that the age of isolating traditional eastern thought from the full weight of western criticism is drawing to an end; and that these were precisely the working assumptions of the Kyoto-school thinkers; then one has to conclude that they belong to that tradition of philosophy in-the-making more properly than any leading movement in western or eastern philosophy of our day. Of course, having reviewed their achievement, one may also conclude that they have demonstrated that it is too early to think in terms of a world philosophy except as a general ideal to be aimed at in the future. Either way, we cannot locate the Kyoto school without at least asking that question.

68 STUDYING THE KYOTO SCHOOL. Trying to condense a shelf of heavy volumes into a single essay, as I am only too well aware, risks misunderstanding. Attempting it three times in the same book makes it inevitable. Careful arguments are made to look like wild conjecture, the flavor and nuance that build up an author's style are pared away to the most basic ideas in the rawest form. What is worse still, in the time that it takes to read enough of the material to construct a summary, one's attention fades in and out, and the memory of what was read at one sitting often dims before its place in the wider picture has had time to register.

It is too late to be apologizing for this, but I mention it because it gives me the chance to flip to the other side of the coin that may not be as obvious from these pages: there is also in the writings of Nishida, Tanabe, and Nishitani a fair share of commonplace and ordinary ideas elevated to philosophy by context and language more than by any depth of insight or precision of argument. I have drawn attention to this only in connection with certain of their views on culture and politics, but this is by no means all of it. The fact is, the philosophical genre has not always suited them for clarity of thinking. There is no substitute for reading the original texts, but one does have to be prepared to cut through pages of verbose, and to all appearances pointless, thicket before coming to a clearing where one can stand up and get the lay of the land again. As often as I have reread difficult passages to my own profit and surprise, I have not infrequently come away regretting the lack of a competent editor. The truth of the matter probably lies somewhere closer to their genius than to my impatience, but having drawn attention to their distinctive philosophical styles, it is not something I can pass over without comment.

That said, there are a number of aspects of Kyoto-school philosophy that I have let pass but which seem to me to merit further study. Leaving aside a host of specific questions, I would single out three general areas where adequate research seems to me lacking.

First of all, we do not have enough knowledge about the relationship among the three central figures considered here, both in terms of the historical development of their ideas and in terms of comparative thought. Of the many connections I suggested in the course of this book, most of them lack documentation or proper analysis. There is no question of the importance of Nishida and Nishitani, but there are many, and they are a majority in both Japan and the west, who would prefer to take a detour around Tanabe. And those who have concentrated on Tanabe have given short shrift to the interplay of his ideas with those of Nishitani. Everything I have read tells me this is an unfounded and unfortunate choice.

The influence Tanabe's criticisms had on sharpening Nishida's thinking is too obvious (distastefully as those criticisms may have been served up) to pass over. Conversely, reading Tanabe in the light of Nishida helps to dispel the image that great blocks of his thinking or expression were idiosyncratic to him. Tanabe was able to deal with the same ideas in a different way and give similar expressions a different twist of meaning. Knowing his thought helps protect Nishida from the image of a solitary genius. At the same time, Nishitani's own essays on Tanabe are different from his essays on Nishida. The former concentrate on the relationship between his two teachers, with a generous tilt in the direction of Nishida. The latter are an explicit attempt to appropriate ideas and wrestle with the texts directly. None of them speaks of the connection of his own ideas to Tanabe's.

In particular, without Tanabe in the picture, the dimension of social praxis in the thinking of Nishida and Nishitani remains bound to the flirtations with a Japanism that we find morally unacceptable today. In Tanabe we at least see a clear call for engagement with the historical world built formally into the philosophy itself, on the same level as the dominant ideas of Kyoto-school thought. Most attempts simply to integrate one or the other form of moral philosophy from the western tradition to supplement the lack in Nishida and Nishitani do so on the assumption that this dimension is somehow alien to their eastern way of thinking. A closer study of Tanabe's ideas, including how their underlying idealis were offended in the practical applicaiton, could be of great help.

Second, I would welcome some study of the major ideas of the Kyoto philosophers as metaphors of the ambiguities that marked Japan's entry into the modern world. Again, I was able to do no more than hint in this direction, as many others before me have done. These half-ideas need to be gathered up and examined in the light of the history of ideas and the social changes taking place at the time these thinkers were writing. Without it, we end up sliding into one of the two available positions, neither of which seems to me justifiable: to see them as simply mirroring their age uncritically from the grandstands of academia, or to see them as having tried to rise above their age to concentrate on transcendental philosophical questions. There is a vast web of connections between their thinking and the historical changes of the day, much of it unconscious to them but clearer to us in hindsight, which begs to be used as a hermeneutic to reread their work.

Finally, the role of "experience" in the philosophies of the Kyoto school and its relationship to the eclipse of "authority" in modernity has yet to be studied. I would resist the simple idea that the primacy of experience is more marked in eastern thought and religion—*pace* Zen—than it has been in the west. The emergence of the psychology of religion, the arrival of eastern spiritualities, and the spiritual vacuum that has carried over from industrial to postindustrial society, are all part of a wider phenomenon of the shift of authority from the keepers of tradition to a new priesthood of experts whose paradigm is the scientist. Japan has not been exempt from this same shift, and it is hardly a coincidence that its philosophical call of "back to experience" was originally stimulated by the work of James and Bergson.

The question is whether experience itself is able to provide the foundation of a worldview or of a philosophy as Nishida thought and as Tanabe and Nishitani basically concurred. It should be clear, at least in their case, that the withdrawal from historical reality into the problems of interiority, the "bourgeois" mentality that Tosaka criticized, was not enough to return them to the historical world. Even if we reject as entirely too simple the judgment that, in time of crisis, they wrapped their philosophy in the flag, one has to admit at least that it demonstrated in concrete form the limits of a philosophy oriented to the contemplative. This is not a matter to be examined from within the framework of the Kyoto school itself nor from the framework of a contemporary political agenda, but is a type of a larger question to which the school, it seems to me, needs to be exposed critically.

69 QUESTIONS FOR WORLD PHILOSOPHY.

No doubt much in the foregoing chapters will have struck many readers, particularly those conversant with contemporary western philosophy, as interesting hypothesis but far removed from the currents of intellectual history today. In the years in which the Kyoto school's philosophies were taking shape, the philosophical mood was changing in the west. Even continental philosophies concerned with the same sort of questions have taken a different direction. The Kyoto school surfaces on the other side of Whitehead, Wittgenstein, Foucault, Derrida, Habermas, and Gadamer to look like something of an anachronism. What is more, a great many ideas in the philosophical tradition out of which Nishida, Tanabe, and Nishitani worked have been rejected by advances in science.

Nevertheless, in addition to historical research on the Kyoto school as such, there are certain questions that emerge from their writings that cannot be answered from their native context but seem to require an opening of the very philosophical forum that seems to have marginalized them. Perhaps only to the degree that such questions are recognized as genuine contributions from the east that need to be taken up also in the west, can we say that Kyoto-school thought has found its place in world philosophy. If they end up being dismissed as "orientalizations" of questions no one is interested in asking, they have literally nothing to say to the west. If this is indeed what is at stake, I hesitate to take on myself the burden of identifying just what those questions might be. But having posed the dilemma, I leave myself no choice except to at least make an attempt. Once again, I limit myself to three questions.

To begin with, there is the question of introducing the idea of the no-self as a subject of moral choice. Any cross section of the religious and intellectual history of the east in which the idea of no-self has figured prominently will show that it has always been a polyvalent notion. As a guiding principle of meditation or ascetic practice aimed at deliverance from the ordinary self, the idea of no-self can function without directly entailing any consequences for everyday morality. Conversely, as an ideal of basic human goodness in daily life, the idea of no-self can be understood as a reminder of the moral obligation to act selflessly in personal and social relationships without implying the radical denial of self central to meditation and ascesis. And when no-self is located in the realm of metaphysical or epistemological ideas, it takes on other meanings which have no necessary connection either to the practice of self-liberation or the morality of selflessness, both of which can function fully without coming to any decision regarding the nature of subjectivity or the ultimate structure of reality. If we look at the way the idea actually works in these different settings, this polyvalence may be seen as an enhancement of our understanding of no-self and need not simply be dismissed as a confusion of terminology or a logical failure to reconcile internal contradictions.

Clearly this was not the way the Kyoto-school philosophers were prepared to handle the idea of the no-self. Rather, they sought the same sort of singular and univocal meaning that western philosophy has always required of an idea of the subject. The subject of experience and artistic intuition could not be described differently from the subject of reflection and knowledge. This, they assumed, led to a higher mode of understanding than a more phenomenological or operational approach. Put the other way around, to the extent that such consistency was lacking, the idea was not a properly philosophical one.

The fact is, however, that the moral aspect of no-self was denied a proper place in their thought, thus compromising this goal of a univocal and comprehensive meaning. As we have seen, they simply absorbed the moral dimension into their general understanding of the subject, reducing the practice of virtue, along with the notion of practical will, to a question of experience and knowledge. As we have also seen, none of them clearly states the univocal definition of no-self (or its correlatives, true self and non-ego) that they were assuming as necessary. The result is an obscuring of the moral layer of meaning which has historically been at the heart of the idea of the no-self. My suggestion is that this is not simply a matter of a lacuna in their own thinking that needs filling up, but is a question central to the encounter of philosophies east and west, without which there will be no satisfactory answer.

Second, there is the question of the relation of self-awareness to the critique of the anthropocentric view of reality. The challenging of the subject-object model as an imposition that covers up more of the nature of reality than it enlightens is, of course, crucial to the thought of all three philosophers. In a sense, the whole of their thinking may be considered an experiment with removing that assumption, and this is carried out uniformly with regard to each of the traditional thinkers with whom they wrestle. The logic of locus, the logic of the specific, and the standpoint of emptiness all stand or fall on this critique of tailoring the real to suit the purposes of subject-centered consciousness. In the process, attention is drawn to cognate ideas in classical philosophy—albeit generally in more mystical and esoteric thinkers or in the world of art and literature—that they try to move from the periphery to the center.

At the same time, again and again it has been noted in these pages how the idea of a self-awareness without a subject was made to function as a paradigm for the structure of reality itself. Because this connection is not directly questioned, let alone justified, much of the anthropomorphism that is thrown out the front door returns creeping in through the back. The progress of the individual towards awareness is measured in terms of its liberation from self-centeredness and its resignation to the reality of things just as they are. Moreover, the selfless "subject" of this progress is said itself to transcend the skinbound individual person and to show the working of reality. In other words, the real is most fully real when it reaches consciousness, a consciousness in its purest form but a consciousness nonetheless. Since there is no question of a self-awareness in the inanimate world, or even in the world of nonhuman sentient beings, the human is set more firmly at the center of reality than it is in the subject-object model.

The problem raises an important and unresolved question that it seems to me the philosophy of the Kyoto school is better able to phrase than their western counterparts, namely, the limits of the overcoming of anthropocentricism in consciousness. If no-self is a cipher for the ideal of the most radically detached, liberated, and awakened state that the human individual can attain, the value of this state needs to be clarified relative to other states of existence. Otherwise there is no way of assessing what is worth sacrificing to attain it and what greater values there are to which it may have to be sacrificed. Even if one grants, as the Kyoto school seems to require that we do, that philosophy is, after all, about the awakening of the human individual, this only pushes the question a step further back, forcing us to ask what value the pursuit of philosophy has relative to the rest of reality. Even before one gets to the moral implication of the relative importance of human survival and well-being in the larger picture of reality, the epistemological question of whether and to what extent the anthropocentric assumption is a necessary condition for the possibility of knowing reality has to be articulated more clearly than it has been so far.

A third question they have left us has to do with a radically depersonalized and relativized notion of God. Looking back over the way Nishida, Tanabe, and Nishitani deal with God, we see two different ideas running throughout their works, both of which use the same word without qualification. On the one hand there is the Christian idea of God, who belongs irrevocably to being and whose absoluteness, therefore, has to be seen as relative to the true absolute of nothingness. On the other, there is their own reformed idea of God as an image of nothingness locked away from recognition by doctrinal assumptions but transparent to the philosopher who does not share these assumptions or the commitment to reality as being.

These two ideas cross paths occasionally, most notably in references to a kenotic theology of "self-emptying," which suggests a Christian idea of God as a no-self that approaches absolute nothingness. This crossing falls less hard on western ears today than it did when they began writing about it. The contemporary philosophy of religion, as well as more and more theologians sympathetic to the philosophical critique of the past century, have broken with the idea that the search for truth in scriptural tradition requires a literal interpretation of the foundational ideas, including the idea of God. The approach to religious truth as symbols pointing to basic and intangible impulses in our common human nature, to particular experiences that fall outside of normal patterns of relationships with the world or other persons in it, or to some form of moral or intellectual task that needs to be worked on and appropriated by the individual in order to become "true," has loosened the previously unassailable connection between God and being.

This means that the ambiguity in the Kyoto philosophers due to their parallel ideas of God—their own and classical Christian ideas—has in fact become a mainline question for the west as well, and that the possibility of transferring the weight of "God exists" to "God is nothingness" is no longer as farfetched as it once seemed. And precisely because it means this, it also means that the notion of God, whether understood metaphysically or symbolically, can serve as a focal point to bring criticisms from the philosophy of being to bear more directly on the question of the adequacy of a pure philosophy of nothingness.

70 THE ENCOUNTER BETWEEN BUDDHISM AND CHRISTIANITY. The three questions I have singled out above—the no-self as moral subject, the limits of the anthropocentric, and the detachment of God from being—can hardly be said to have found their way into western philosophy. But they are among the many ideas from the Kyoto-school tradition that have stimulated discussion between Buddhist and Christian scholars, particularly in Japan. Since this has been one of the principal forms in which their thought has gained attention outside of Japan during the past twenty years, it is worth pausing a moment to consider the factors that combined to bring this about.

Nishida and Tanabe did not themselves take part in or encourage formal discussions with Buddhists or Christians regarding their religious ideas. For one thing, the practice of such "dialogue" was almost unheard of at the time. For another, they would probably have felt uncomfortable representing either tradition or brokering an encounter from neutral, philosophical ground. I do not think it fair to say that what they offer is a religion beyond religion, any more than interreligious dialogue takes that as its aim. At the same time, the idea that parties professing different faiths might step away from the traditional doctrinal formulations of their profession in order to discuss them from an alternative religious or philosophical perspective would hardly have struck them as irreligious. One has to think they would have welcomed it. Still, their commitment to philosophy was such that they could not conceive of religious doctrine other than as philosophical ideas.

Things were different with Nishitani, who was more openly committed to Buddhism and who lived to see the birth of its dialogue with Christianity in Japan. Not only did he welcome invitations to participate as a Buddhist, he saw it as a concrete response to the spirit of exclusiveness and authoritarianism that had long infected Buddhism and Christianity alike. Though I think the ideas of the Kyoto school would have found their way quickly into the dialogue in Japan in any case, the fact that Nishitani lent his support was an important element in the fact that within a few short years it reached a high level and attracted serious attention in academic circles.

The complaint that Christianity's turn to intellectual dialogue with Buddhism is simply the old, expansionist proselytism with the lining turned out is off the mark. Even the slimmest of acquaintance with the facts will show that at least as many Christians have drifted away from the church as have been drawn into it as a result of these encounters, and that in either case the numbers are insignificant. On the other hand, insofar as the criticism is aimed at the spread of patterns of self-understanding, attitudes toward doctrine, and ethical agenda that are promoted as transcending any specific religion but in fact are more strongly rooted in Christian tradition than in any other, caution is completely warranted. This is not the case with the Kyoto school, however, and this has to be considered another of the reasons for the attractiveness of its ideas as a stimulus to dialogue.

Since the seventeenth century, when Leibniz and others took an interest in the reports sent back to Europe by Jesuit missionaries in China of Confucian thought, these traditions have remained by and large esoteric to the western intellectual world. At first the property of a cultural and intellectual elite, with the emergence of religious studies a new academic elite arose to claim them in the west. All of this changed in the twentieth century, which has seen eastern traditions enter the popular history of ideas. Though not yet part of the philosophical and theological mainstream, through their introduction into general education in the humanities, and through the fact that the western world became missionary territory for eastern religions, we can hardly speak of them as esoteric any longer. There is every indication that the west is on the verge of a major upheaval of its traditional spirituality, if not already well into it, and the wisdom of the east is a major influence. The spectrum of responses from the intellectual establishment continues to range from the superficial to the serious, but seems to have had little impact on the pace of events.

What is interesting is that this incursion of eastern thinking into the popular imagination was taking place in Europe and the Americas at the same time as Japan was discovering western philosophy, as if in a mirror-image of the arrival of eastern thought to the west. In fact, by the time the Christian lands of the west had at last begun to open to dialogue with the east, the Kyoto philosophers had already produced a body of literature based on the interpenetration of the two worlds. And they did it in a way very different from anything that religious studies in the west had done.

Aside from the fact that the introduction of the Kyoto school to the west coincided with a readiness within the Christian world for such a challenge, the fact that it was posed in a religious but nontheological discourse, devoid of any confrontation between faith and reason and yet phrased in a more or less familiar philosophical idiom, meant that their challenge could speak directly to the religious individual, Buddhist and Christian. In this sense, it is precisely its difference from ordinary interreligious dialogue that has made the Kyoto school the stimulus to dialogue that it has been.

Lest too much be read into this, threatening the right to call these thinkers philosophers, some qualification is in order regarding the peculiar, and at times questionable, approach of the Kyoto-school thinkers to philosophy and religion east and west.

71 PHILOSOPHY AND RELIGION, EAST AND WEST.

In the opening pages, mention was made of the absence in the Kyoto school of a distinction between philosophy and religion like that found in the west. Later we came to see how Tanabe at first resisted the position and then came to embrace it more enthusiastically than either Nishida or Nishitani. Whatever their own views in the matter, the reader accustomed to western philosophy can hardly fail to ask at some point whether these thinkers have not in fact forsaken philosophy for religion. I would suggest that the question cannot be answered as such, but only deflected, because it hides a fundamental confusion of categories.

In the same way that Gershom Scholem insists there is no such thing as "mysticism" beyond tradition but only a Jewish mysticism, a Christian mysticism, an Islamic mysticism, and so forth, so, too, there is really nothing like a "philosophy" or a "religion" floating free of the language, imagery, and cultural meanings that each uses to express itself. Hence, when we speak of the Kyoto philosophers as having erased the borderlines between the two, this must not be understood as something carried out not within a western context but within a different frame of discourse.

For this reason, the way in which thinkers like Hegel and Jaspers, for example, can be said to have absorbed religion into philosophy, cannot directly be compared to the strategy of the Kyoto school. The philosophizing of religions means one thing in a Judaeo-Christian context and quite another in a Buddhist one, and both of them are again different from the "scientific" study of religion. For Nishida, Tanabe, and Nishitani, the primary frame of reference for the coincidence of philosophy and religion is always Buddhist, and more specifically a Buddhism focused on the pursuit of self-awareness. Theirs is not an attempt to harmonize propositional disagreements from a neutral, higher ground, nor to use one set of "truths" to criticize another. It is always and ever a view of philosophy and religion from a Japanese Buddhist perspective. The object of their attention—reality and the place of human consciousness within it—is not bound to any specific culture or intellectual history, but their attention is.

The distinction is as important as it is difficult to preserve in the execution. Whether they were applying western philosophical ideas to a distinctively Japanese way of thinking or to something more universal in human nature, their aim was to see what that perspective would enlighten and what it would obscure. This was their way of freeing themselves from bondage to the traditional Japanese way of looking at things in order to enhance it and broaden it. From start to finish, their aim was, as I insisted early on, an introduction of *Japanese* philosophy into world philosophy while at the same time using western philosophy for a second look at Japanese thought trapped in fascination with its own uniqueness.

This is the same framework within which they attempt to criticize, appropriate, and adapt Christian tradition. Of course, there are many areas—and some of them we have pointed out along the way—in which a wider knowledge of Christian history than what the Kyoto philosphers found through philosophy and the mystics, could temper some of their generalizations. By the same token, their commitment to the western philosophical tradition sometimes yields rather peculiar interpretations of their own native Buddhist religion and ideas, which has hardly won the unqualified support or even interest of most Buddhologists. But at no time, as I said, did they delude themselves that they had discovered a philosophy beyond the history of philosophy or a religion beyond the history of religion. The problem of how to approach the rather unique amalgam of philosophy and religion we find in the Kyoto school is, therefore, very much of a piece with their aim of negotiating a route between east and west. Unfortunately, the results are far easier to criticize than the process is to emulate.

The west of which they write is a highly selective one, centered on intellectual history, and within intellectual history on philosophy, and within philosophy on the Continental philosophy from Descartes to Heidegger. The art and literature that has been important in that history also figured in their writing, though to a greatly diminished extent. But the living culture of the west within which that history took shape is absent. And more than absent, it is assumed—usually without adequate reason—to be radically different from the living culture of Japan.

In a sense, then, the "east" that the Kyoto philosophers set up against the "west" they had constructed for themselves was also something of an invention. At best, it is one constellation of a heritage too long and too plural to be represented fairly by Japan. And even within the Japanese context, there is a distinctly modern bias to what counts as oriental and what not. It was its quality of being non-western that accounts for much of the power of their talk of the east, and this holds as true for western readers as for the Japanese. Much, but not all.

As the Kyoto philosophers were well aware, the efforts they exerted on the borderlands of philosophy and religion to bridge the gap between east and west were no match for what science and technology were accomplishing almost automatically and with far less conscious effort. One of the chief motives for their critique of science was to show that fixation on results often entailed a kind of self-deception. The spread of scientific method had not been transcultural, transreligious, and transphilosophical, but every bit as colonial in structure as modernity itself had been. The gaps it filled were filled not with understanding but with tacit assumptions.

Still, much of what they have to say about science may sound dated to our ears today; many of their complaints have become almost clichés as the catechesis of the scientific view of the world has all but taken over our imagination. Even at the time they were writing, their thoughts lacked the persuasive power of similar analysis done in the west. The sort of "oriental" view of nature that the western reader has come to expect of Japanese philosophy and religions is by and large absent. One of the reasons for this is that when Japan imported the scientific method from the west, it did so without very much of the critical environment that had grown up around science. Literature, science fiction, and varieties of scientific ethics belong as much to the story of the "scientific mentality" as do the laboratories and technological innovations. To base a critique of science on the erosion of the inner life or religious consciousness—as, for instance, Nishitani does throughout his writings—may leave us dissatisfied. But then again, for those educated in the western culture that produced the idea of science as a global gift to the human race, there was little awareness of the kinds of cultural sacrifice this demanded in the countries of the east.

Even with these limitations, the Kyoto-school philosophers give the west a way into the east like none other. Theirs is not an eastern thought diluted for foreign consumption, nor is it a simple transference that assumes a background in the history of oriental ideas. It makes an unsolicited contribution to world philosophy that both respects the traditions of philosophy and expands them. In this respect, the development of the school from Nishida to Tanabe to Nishitani is a rising crescendo. Never has the west produced an intellectual movement whose contribution to the east can compare with what these three thinkers offer the west. If we are poised at the brink of a new age of world philosophy, one in which the confluence of east and west will take up the task of redefining one another without either reducing the other to one of the available common denominators, the thought of Nishida, Tanabe, and Nishida may help push the weak in spirit to take the next step. If so, they shall more than have earned a place of honor in the history of twentieth-century philosophy.

Notes

In general, the notes follow the order of the text, only occasionally reorganized for the sake of readability. Chinese glyphs for proper names that have been omitted can be found in the general index. References to works in Japanese that appear in the bibliography are referred to here by their English translation.

Orientation

1 THE KYOTO SCHOOL. The original article of Tosaka cited here appeared in 『経済往来』 for September 1932, and was later included, along with the essay on Tanabe, as back-to-back chapters in a book entitled *Talks on Contemporary Philosophy* (TOSAKA 1970, 3: 171–84).

Tosaka (1900–1945) had studied the philosophy of mathematics under Tanabe. At first he was attracted to the neo-Kantians, but later followed the lead of Nishida and Tanabe in abandoning this interest. Instead of following Nishida into metaphysics, however, he turned to Marxism and, beginning with a book on *The Logic of Ideology* in 1930, wrote widely in this vein. With the outbreak of the Sino-Japanese War in 1937 he joined a socialist movement and within the year was silenced, then later removed from his post, and imprisoned. After release he continued to speak out and was put in prison again in 1944, where he died the following year. He was teaching in Hōsei University at the time the article cited here was written, in a post vacated by Miki Kiyoshi, who had been his first inspiration to Marxist thought but was later dismissed for his political activities. Miki had also criticized the "school" from his own Marxist perspective, but never to the point of distancing himself from Nishida. The only allusion I could find in his works to the "school" around Nishida was made in 1939 (MIKI 1986, 19: 728). ➤ Tosaka had also studied at Kyoto with Nishitani, with whom he remained on good terms to the end, despite their political differences, as evidenced in an *in memoriam* Nishitani penned after his death (NKC 39: 129–33, cited in the text of §54; see also the short piece *Fragments of a Memory* by Aihara Shinsaku in the leaflet appended to volume 12 of Tanabe's *Complete Works*).

Phenomenology was little known in Japan at the time, and although Nishida was one of the first to speak of it, he never identified with the movement (see NITTA, TATEMATSU, SHIMOMISSE 1979, 8).

Neither the 1954 edition of the standard *Dictionary of Philosophy* 『哲学事典』 (Tokyo: Heibonsha) nor its 1971 revision include mention of the Kyoto school. It is not until the 1998 edition of the *Dictionary of Philosophy and Ideas* 『哲学·思想事典』 (Tokyo: Iwanami) that an entry on the subject appears. In addition to the three central figures, the names of Kōsaka Masaaki, Kōyama Iwao, Shimomura Toratarō, and Suzuki Shigetaka are listed as members; and Miki Kiyoshi and Tosaka Jun are mentioned as belonging to the school in the "wider sense of the term." Watsuji Tetsurō and Kuki Shūzō, both of whom had taught philosophy and ethics at Kyoto for a time during the period of Nishida and Tanabe, are properly listed as peripheral.

Takeuchi Yoshinori, a disciple of Tanabe who succeeded Nishitani in the chair at Kyoto and who is often associated with the school, suggested that the clearest way to define the school is to "triangulate" it around Nishida, Tanabe, and Nishitani (1981, 198). Regarding Takeuchi's career and connection with the thinkers of the Kyoto school, see Heisig 1983. ➤ A fuller listing of the "galaxy" of scholars and students around Tanabe and Nishida, based on the memoirs of one of the minor participants, can be found in Yusa 1998a, 341. See also the somewhat looser description of the school and its membership in Ōhashi 1990, 11–19. ➤ I find no documentation to support the account of the formation and consolidation of the Kyoto school given by Vianello in his otherwise instructive essay (1996, 28–32). His misnaming of the group as *Kyōtoha* (the Kyoto faction) repeats an error by Piovesana (1963, 85; repeated in the 1994 revision, but corrected in the Japanese translation of the work published in 1965), and his assignation of membership seems to have the same source. Particularly odd is his own idea that the group found its identity in the polemics after the war and, with the catalyst of Tanabe's *Philosophy as Metanoetics,* was able to publish Nishida's *Collected Works.* It seems to me, though, that the postwar polemics scattered the group, and that Tanabe's act of philosophical repentance had no impact at all on the publication of Nishida's works. Finally, his distinction of three generations of Kyoto school philosophers is entirely his own invention.

In many cases the inclusion of Hisamatsu Shin'ichi in the Kyoto school seems to be the doing of his disciple, Abe Masao (e.g., 1997, 787), who has passed the idea on to a number of others outside of Japan (Ng 1995, Prieto 1989), who then take the next step and include Abe himself as the "leading representative" of the Kyoto school today—a title that Abe himself would be the first to distance himself from in Japanese circles, but that he has clearly used to identify himself in the west, as in his *Buddhism and Interfaith Dialogue* (Honolulu: University of Hawai'i Press, 1995), 122. Abe had studied under Tanabe in Kyoto, but his chief influence was Hisamatsu. Tanabe's ideas are all but absent from his work, except as they were shared by Nishida and Nishitani, on whose work he has written several commentaries and original interpretations. For a readable summary of the work of Abe centered on his encounter with western theology, one can hardly do better than the little book by Angelo Rodante (1995), which contains a good bibliography of his works.

Shibayama uses the term "Kyoto school" to cover everything from Nishida to Watsuji, whom he goes out on a limb to call "a most preeminent member of the Kyoto school" (1994, 7). As a result, his general statements about the school in the postwar years are difficult to support. Happily, this misnaming is only a minor blemish on his general thesis: to focus an appreciation of these thinkers only on their wartime positions and in particular on the pan-Asian dimension of their thought, is to miss out on the broader context of questions that had been discussed since the early years of the Taishō era, and to avoid the question of the importance these thinkers still have for us. ➤ It should be noted that Ueda Shizuteru, the most immediate successor to the school, speaks consistently of "Nishida philosophy," assiduously avoiding the term "Kyoto school." ➤ The 1982 publication of a collection of essays entitled *The Buddha Eye,* in a series that I myself edited, bore the misleading subtitle *An Anthology of the Kyoto School.* The inclusion of pieces by D. T. Suzuki, Abe, and Hisamatsu no doubt did its share to contribute to the confusion of the membership. ➤ A more recent study of Japanese philosophy since 1868 by HAMADA introduces still another classification by speaking of a "Nishida school" with Miki and Tosaka on a "left wing" of the school, Mutai Risaku, Shimomura, and Yanagida Kenjūrō in the "center," and Yamanouchi Tokuryū, Kōsaka, and Kōyama at the "right wing" along with Tanabe and Nishitani. This right wing she calls the Kyoto school in the strict sense of the term (1994, 56). No one else seems to follow her, though a different alignment of rightists and leftists can be found in YAMADA Munemutsu 1975, 44. ➤ NG has come up with a scheme he devised with the help of Abe (on whose writings he relies heavily in his presentations of the more central figures of the school), according to which Hisamatsu belongs with Nishitani to a "second generation" after Nishida and Tanabe, and Takeuchi, Abe, and Ueda to the third and current generation (1995, 1; 1998, iv–v).

In 1977 Nishitani wrote in the introduction to a commemorative volume of essays in honor of Zen master Yamada Mumon:

> The name "Kyoto school" is a name journalists used in connection with discussions that friends of mine and I held immediately before and during the war, but in the present volume indicates purely a school of thought. This is also the way Americans and others use the term at present. (NKC 11: 207)

In Japan, the negative connotations of the term "Kyoto school" have been revived by the "critical Buddhism" of Hakamaya Noriaki, who argues that it has lent support to popular Buddhist heresies, such as the idea of the "Buddha nature," that have tended to uphold social injustices in the status quo (see HUBBARD and SWANSON 1997). ➤ As a general indication of how little the political question was discussed in the 1970s and 1980s among those engaged with the thought of the Kyoto school in Japan, Jan VAN BRAGT, one of the key figures in the story of the introduction of the school to the West through his essays and translations, gives a good account of how these issues were revived and how important they are (1995, 233–42). ➤ For a wider overview of the fate of the study of Nishida's thought after the war, and the conversion of former critics to a more balanced view, see YUSA 1995A.

The nearest thing to an official continuation of the Kyoto school in Japan are groups that have been organized among the disciples of Nishida and Tanabe. The first of what could be called the "Nishida Kitarō Commemorative Lectures" was delivered in 1945, the year of Nishida's death, by D. T. Suzuki. The next year a number of Nishida's students and interested scholars formed a group to preserve their teacher's memory and perform a memorial service for him each year. The group called itself the "Sunshin-kai" (after Nishida's lay Buddhist name) and took over the responsibility of hosting the annual commemorative lectures, which continue to this day. ➤ The Kyūshin-kai (Society for the Pursuit of the Truth) was founded in 1977 by Tanabe's disciples and students of his thought. After sponsoring a series of symposia and seminars, it was given new focus in 1994, at which time it inaugurated the publication of an annual journal of the same name as the Society, 『求真』. ➤ In 1995, on the occasion of the fiftieth anniversary of Nishida's death, commemorative lectures on Nishida and Tanabe were delivered in Kyoto. The two lectures were delivered by UEDA Shizuteru (essentially 1995A, ch. 1) and myself (HEISIG 1995B).

A good indication of the effect of Kyoto-school thought on Christian theology in Japan can be seen in a 1997 symposium on the subject "What does Christianity Have to Learn from Buddhism?" (NANZAN INSTITUTE, 1999). See also HANAOKA (1988) and the creative attempts to rethink the role of the Holy Spirit in the light of Nishida's thought by ONODERA (1992). The pioneer figure in this regard, still largely unknown in the west, was Takizawa Katsumi, whom Nishida considered one of the most astute readers of his thought. ➤ In general, the influence of Nishida and Nishitani is most marked. Perhaps the most constructive use of Tanabe's thought by a theologian is the work of MUTŌ Kazuo (see especially 1986, 2: 143–65, 3: 93–166).

Although there have been many Buddhist scholars, particularly from the Rinzai Zen tradition, who have welcomed the philosophies of Nishida and Nishitani as a contribution to their own self-understanding, Tanabe seems to have been entirely passed over in this regard. Even in the case of Pure Land Buddhism, where one might expect a better reception, Tanabe has been all but entirely ignored, while Nishida's philosophy, long dismissed for having disagreed with traditional interpretations of Shinran, has made some inroads. The most notable example of this latter is a long section devoted to it in a massive collection of essays by TAKEDA (1991, 239–305).

2 **JAPANESE PHILOSOPHY AS WORLD PHILOSOPHY.** The translations of Tanabe and Nishitani that revived interest in Nishida in the west are *Philosophy as Metanoetics* and *Religion and Nothingness*. ➤ I have argued the underlying problem of parochialism of "world philosophy" masquerading as a universalism in the context of the Kyoto school by making use

of Tanabe's logic of the specific (HEISIG 1995B). ➤ To my knowledge, no one has tried to place the Kyoto philosophers in the history of philosophy as a whole or to assess their achievement in this context. Western studies have rather focused on locating them within the general Japanese history of ideas (see references in notes to §6 below). Japanese studies have tended to be still more narrowly focused. While one has to take into account the circumstances in which they wrote and the audience they had in mind, to get stuck here or even to see this as primary, as not a few Japanese seem to do in order to get over the problem of their wartime writings (for instance, YUSA 1992, 153–4), is to miss the greater question of their worldwide contribution.

3 **THE BACKGROUND OF WESTERN PHILOSOPHY IN JAPAN.** The best overview of the origins of the study of western philosophy in Japan is still that done by PIOVESANA (1963). While it does not go into much depth in terms of the actual ideas, it is a valuable resource for the principal persons and their works. A shorter but useful synopsis can be found in SHIMOMURA 1966. ➤ KASULIS (1995), as always bringing clarity to bear on questions others have smothered with technical apparatus, presents a shorter introduction to the intellectual context in which philosophy landed in Japan, with a focus on Nishida's attempt to reject the isolation of scientific thinking from philosophy and religion.

Nishi Amane (1829–1897) was sent to Holland from 1863 to 1865 by the Tokugawa government, and on returning tried to give an encyclopedic account of western academia (which he called "philosophy"). He organized the work along the lines of Auguste Comte's idea of the three stages in the development of knowledge, in the course of which he provided Japanese with a number of its key translations of technical philosophical terms. The citation from his *Encyclopedia* is taken from Thomas Havens, *Nishi Amane and Modern Japanese Thought* (Princeton: Princeton University Press, 1970), 108.

In saying that the Japanese did not come to philosophy through demythification, we should note that at the height of the "thought control" during the war, right-wing elements in the government did in fact take the founding myths of Japan to be "historical fact" and even indicted Tsuda Sōkichi, a scholar of classical Japanese history, for writing a book that treated the legends scientifically, as well as his publisher, Iwanami Shigeo. For details, see Abe Yoshinshige, 『岩波茂雄伝』 *[A biography of Iwanami Shigeo]* (Tokyo: Iwanami, 1957), 224–32.

Resistance to western philosophy and religion that was prevalent among the Japanese intelligentsia of the time found its way to Europe and the United States in books published by Japanese living abroad. Looking at this material today, one realizes how ridiculous these ideas must have looked in their foreign clothes to western readers anxious to know something about Japan. I cite two examples of this overlooked body of literature. A little book purporting to challenge western philosophy with the wisdom of the East was published in 1931 by Sakurazawa Nyoichi, *Principe unique de la philosophie et de la science d'Estrême-Orient* (Paris: Librairie Philosophique J. Vrin). In it the author bemoans the state of his country as having forfeited its own spirit for a half-digested "salade russe américanisée." His own version of "oriental thought" is even more badly digested. I cite his words because they are the very antithesis of what Nishida and the others of the Kyoto school were aiming at:

> In short, the Japanese spirit is a realism that surpasses at bottom all subtle discussion, all partial teaching, all philosophy, all science, assimilating them in a practical life and doing so in an aesthetic manner. It does not allow for specialization. It asks that one be from the start an ordinary and natural individual, and from there that one possess a clear and precise instinct-intuition, the awareness of "emptiness" (119).

An example of resistance to the world hegemony of Christianity and its cultural influence can be found in the popular (though written in a clumsy and at times nonsensical English) *Discovery of Japanese Idealism* by Satomi Kishio (London: Kegan Paul, Trench, Trubner, and Co., 1924). This, too, is the antithesis of the Kyoto school in that its method lacks the discipline of logic and the understanding of the West needed to reach its conclusions. ➤ In the postwar period, the Kyoto school was lumped together with this sort of approach and accused of having fused Japanese and western traditions uncritically. A classic example of this kind of thinking is a book by MIYAKAWA Tōru, which argues for a reconstruction of ethnic tradition based on a rejection of its past, and in this light dismisses Nishida and Tanabe, in considerable detail, as academic ideologues of the past (1956, 101–4).

4 **WORKING ASSUMPTIONS OF THE KYOTO PHILOSOPHERS.** There are any number of short résumés of the general philosophical position of the Kyoto school as a whole. See BRÜLL 1989, 155–79; HEISIG 1990A, 1998, 1999A, 1999b; MARALDO, 1997, 1998A; ŌHASHI 1990, 11–45.

Religious studies was introduced to Japan as part of philosophy, and therefore as part of western thought. When Nishida was an undergraduate, Inoue Tetsujirō taught a course on "Comparative Religion and Eastern Philosophy," indicating the shift that was taking place. By the turn of the century, religious studies had more or less established itself. ➤ The overlap of philosophy and religion, though uncommon among teachers of western philosophy, was not unique to these thinkers but was also present in some Buddhist thinkers in Kyoto at the time, such as Saitō Yuishin. On this see HANAZAWA 1999, 44–5.

The echoes of Tanabe's idea of metanoetics are unmistakable in TAKEUCHI Yoshinori's comment (1959, 292–3), but the general point is valid for all the Kyoto philosophers.

5 THE MATTER OF LANGUAGE. To give an idea of how much had to be done to create a philosophical idiom for Japanese, and how late it was done, UEDA Shizuteru notes that it was Nishitani who introduced the translation of the term "subjectivity" (主体性), in his translation of Kierkegaard—a translation that seems obvious to us today but that had not been settled up to that time (1992A, 4).

MARALDO's sustained criticism of sloppy and literal translations of Nishida as almost unintelligible in English (1989) is certainly true, and the worst of these are not translations made by Japanese and corrected by native speakers. Unfortunately, nearly all the major criticisms he raises can be applied to a recent, and important, anthology that seems to have taken no account of his censorship (DILWORTH and VIGLIELMO 1998).

If I am permitted to recount a personal experience of the clash of ideas involved in translating Japanese philosophy: in the summer of 1987 Abe Masao spent two months in our home where we were to work together on a revised translation of Nishida's *An Inquiry into the Good*. Time and again we locked horns, faced with the choice between a literal but artificial English rendering and a more interpretative rendering based on the western philosophical texts that Nishida had open before him—Professor Abe convinced that I lacked the feel for the genius of Nishida's style, I convinced that Abe was ignoring Nishida's sources. In the end, we decided it best to abandon the collaboration and part friends, which we remain to this day.

The same thing happens again and again with Japanese translators of western philosophy, who, lacking a feel for the soul of the text they are reading, render it into an artificial Japanese on the basis of textbook expectations about how the grammar of the language they are dealing with works. A steady diet of these kinds of translations, in turn, feeds the conviction that the more natural style of works composed in their own language is based on a different way of thinking. A good instance of this can be found in NAKAMURA Yūjirō's first book on Nishida's thought. In it he argues that Nishida's logic of locus is bound to structures natural to Japanese but not present in European languages (1983, 96–102). But the "structures" he is comparing are actually the formal grammatical rules of European languages on the one hand and the full, living, and nuanced language he is familiar with. If it is not saying too much, I have the impression in reading remarks of Japanese philosophers on linguistic differences that they imagine themselves potters free to slap and shape the wet clay of their own language to fit their intuitions, while when faced with western texts they turn their own language into preshaped bricks to be laid in neat rows. When I say, therefore, that nothing important of the ideas of the Kyoto philosophers need be lost in translation, I do so on the grounds that this fantasy of linguistic incompatibility is largely an affront to the facts of the matter.

6 THE STUDY OF THE KYOTO SCHOOL IN THE WEST. In a newspaper poll taken after the end of the war, readers were asked which books they would like to see republished. The first author on the list was Nishida, indicating that the revisionist criticisms did not, at least initially, have popular support. See John F. Fairbank, Edwin O. Reischauer, Albert M. Craig, *East Asia: The Modern Transformation* (Boston: Houghton Mifflin, 1965), vol. 2, 544. ➤ The works whose English translation was funded by the Ministry of Education included: Nishida's *A Study of the Good* (1960), Watsuji's *A Climate* (1961), and Suzuki's *Japanese Spirituality* (1972). These works were later reissued in the United States by Greenwood Press in the 1980s in facsimile editions, at inflated prices that have kept them out of reach of the ordinary reader. Tanabe's *Philosophy as Metanoetics* was also originally part of this translation project, but foundered in manuscript form due to an unacceptable translation until it was completely reworked and published in 1986.

SCHINZINGER was living in Japan at the time he wrote his first essay on Nishida (1940), and consulted with Nishida personally over the German translation of his essays (see YUSA 1998A, 428). That first essay on Nishida, as well as his introductions to the collected translations, *Die intelligible Welt* (1958), really only strings together Nishida's technical jargon and does very little to illuminate his thought. One wonders how it could have made sense to those who read it at the time. LÜTH's work on Japanese philosophy, although weak by today's standards, gives a good idea of what was known of Japanese thought at the time in Europe (1944). See also the posthumously published attempt to synthesize Nishida and place him in the context of Japanese philosophy (1983). ➤ KASULIS (1982) was among the first working outside Japan and not directly involved in the translation of Kyoto-school philosophical texts to recognize the importance of the school for the appropriation of Japanese Buddhist thought in western philosophy. ➤ In 1982 (English translation, 1997) Fritz BURI published a lengthy résumé of several thinkers associated with the Kyoto school, a work marred by misinterpretations, many of them the result of his own theological agenda. It is not that he had only the translated texts to work from, but that he seems to have summarized what was available to him in a rush to get to the theological questions that interested him most. I say this with some disappointment, since I was among those who encouraged him during his visit to Japan in the late 1970s to use the Kyoto philosophers as a bridge to Buddhism in his own Christology. ➤ Regarding the reception of Nishida's thought in the United States in general, see YUSA 1995B.

When it comes to locating the Kyoto school in the intellectual history of Japan, western historians have taken a rather more generous perspective than their Japanese counterparts by including the history of ideas predating the arrival of western philosophy proper. Thus BRÜLL, who tries to show Japan's philosophical face without imposing a western definition of philosophy from the outset, devotes well over half of her account to an overview of Buddhist ideas as they were accepted in Japan before the Meiji era (1989). ➤ In a careful and detailed study of philosophy in Japan from the sixth to twelfth centuries, PAUL combines a culturally transcendental definition of philosophy as including every sort of "critical reflection, based on logic and experience, of fundamental human questions" with a studied resistance to what he sees as the inveterate chauvinism and revisionism of the idea of a "Japanese philosophy" that Brüll advances (1993, 4, 15–16). His working assumptions that the principles of logic (identity, contradiction, and the excluded middle) are a universal and innate human function, and that Japanese history shows its thinkers "for a long time placing the same questions as the European philosophers," fulfils its predictions in remarkable detail. As I have made clear already, I will here assume both that the idea of philosophy is always in part culturally determined, and that the "logic" of which the Kyoto philosophers spoke was not merely a collection of rules of rational discourse but a way of thinking aimed at enhancing and transforming the awareness of the thinker. ➤ For a general understanding of the Kyoto school, by far the best work available is a recent study by GONZÁLEZ (2000) that came to my attention when I was in the midst of my own work. The bulk of the book, after a brief but adequate introduction of Buddhist, Confucian, and Neo-Confucian thought in Japan, is devoted to twentieth-century philosophical currents. In it, the ideas of Nishida, Tanabe, and Nishitani figure prominently and are presented with an eye to the texts themselves. ➤ HAMADA's (1994) work more or less covers the same ground as PIOVESANA had (1963), filling in some of the lacunae as far as dates and titles of works go, but with often confusing résumés of the ideas of the philosophers she treats.

The dozen or so doctoral dissertations written in United States universities on the Kyoto school began to appear in 1972 (WARGO). In Germany, the groundbreaking works were the postdoctoral theses of WALDENFELS on Nishitani (1976) and LAUBE on Tanabe (1984). In 1990, a dissertation was prepared at the University of Leiden on Tanabe's work by a young Japanese (OZAKI), a solid piece of work marred by substandard English. ➤ The privately published volume of the Monumenta Nipponica series referred to is Nishida's *Fundamental Problems of Philosophy* (1970). Shortly therafter, in 1973, the East-West Center of Hawaii published an English translation of Nishida's *Art and Morality* (1973).

In Spanish the efforts of Agustín Jacinto at the University of Michoacán in Mexico deserve special attention. Not only has he done translations of extended sections of the works of the major and several secondary figures of the Kyoto school, he has also done long commentaries on specific areas in Nishida's thought and provided general historical background to the philosophical scene in Japan as a whole. His work, though published locally and difficult to come by, has made mine much the easier.

The 1980 symposium with living representatives of the Kyoto-school tradition was subsequently published under the title *Absolute Nothingness and God* (NANZAN INSTITUTE 1981). ➤ The proceedings of the Kyoto Zen Symposia were published in a dedicated annual journal, *Zen Buddhism Today*, between 1983 and 1998.

➤ In 1982 an academic association known as the Society for East-West Religious Exchange was begun and a series of annual meetings held. Beginning with Nishitani's addresses to the assembly in 1985, the thought of the Kyoto-school philosophers has been a major driving force in the meetings, which have continued up to the present. The results are published annually in the pages of *Mahāyāna Zen* 『大乗禅』, which includes special issues on Nishida (1992) and Nishitani (1996, 1997).

7 ARRANGEMENT OF THE MATERIAL. In dealing with the criticisms of the political views of the Kyoto school, I have limited myself mainly to early criticisms from the Japanese side and a few recent studies. I am not unaware that there are any number of intellectual historians, on both sides, who have taken a few politically oriented texts of the philosophers treated in this book and relocated them in the general history of Japanese ultranationalism. As I am convinced, from what I have read, that this is the wrong context from which to understand either their thought as a whole or their political ideas, and as I have taken part already in a serious attempt to construct a more adequate context (see Heisig and Maraldo 1995), there seemed no point to making a lengthy detour through those arguments. For an overview of this question, see Parkes 1997. Also indispensable is a recently published collection of reprints of critical essays, along with responses from Nishida scholars, that was appended to a new edition of selections from Nishida writings (Fujita Masakatsu, 1998a).

The Prospectus with which this book closes is not annotated. Nevertheless, I wish to acknowledge the influence of Jan Van Bragt, who has been putting hard questions to the Kyoto-school philosophers in his writings and public lectures for as long as I have known him, and many of whose thoughts have become my own over the more than twenty years of our collaboration.

Nishida Kitarō (1870–1945)

8 NISHIDA'S LIFE AND CAREER. An exhaustive listing of Nishida's movements through the course of his life has been prepared by Yusa (1998a) as an appendix to her careful account of Nishida's life based on his diaries and letters, as well as on considerable secondary literature. A revision of this work is being prepared for an English edition. In the meantime, the only source in a European language of detailed information on Nishida's early life has been Viglielmo 1971 and the still very readable and useful essay on the diaries by Knauth 1965. I have also drawn on Uesugi 1988. Concerning his university teaching and practice of Zen years, see also Ueda Shizuteru 1991, part 3; 1995a, ch. 3. ➤ Also not to be overlooked is a collection of reflections and recollections by

his contemporaries (SHIMOMURA 1977). ➤ A schematic outline of the diaries has been prepared by JACINTO (1984, 159–93).

Though Nishida never did complete his history of ethics, the bare bones of Green's divisions of ethical theories reappear in his first book, *An Inquiry into the Good.* ➤ Already from the time of his high-school years, when he joined with a group of friends to form a society called the "Self-Respect Society" to share literary writings, Nishida was fond of writing.

Nishida had known of Zen from his high-school teacher, Hōjō Tokiyuki, who set up a circle of interested students around Master Setsumon, abbot of the Kokutai-ji temple in Toyama. The circle included Suzuki (Daisetsu) Teitarō, who eventually also dropped out of that high school as Nishida had. He entered university in what is present-day Waseda, until Nishida talked him into shifting to the same program in philosophy at the Imperial University of Tokyo where he was enrolled as a special student. Along the line Suzuki disappeared down the road to Zen practice. For details see UESUGI 1982. ➤ For a light and readable history of the relationship between Suzuki and Nishida, see MORI Kiyoshi 1991. More personal information, based on firsthand memories, is included in OKAMURA and UEDA (1999, 298–383). ➤ There are different interpretations of the meaning of the name Sunshin, combining two characters for *mind* and *inch*, but it seems to be no more than an ironic play of Zen master Setsumon, who recognized in Nishida a great mind. Nishida seems to have taken to the name from the start (see YUSA 1998A, 125). ➤ Setsumon first gave Nishida the character *mu,* or "nothing," as a *kōan* to meditate on, but five years later changed it to "the sound of one hand" when it was clear Nishida was stuck. For all his intuitional gifts, Nishida could not keep up with young colleagues in Zen who passed from one *kōan* to the other with less strain. When he eventually resolved the *kōan* "nothing" to the satisfaction of his master, Nishida himself was unsatisfied. D. T. Suzuki is reported later to have remarked, "That's what can happen to rational, logical brains like Nishida" (cited in TAKEUCHI Yoshitomo 1970, 161; the original reference was unfortunately cut by the editors of SHIMOMURA's recollections, 1990, 62). ➤ For a Zen master's assessment of Nishida, see the brief essay by HISAMATSU, who considered him a "thoroughly Zen-like individual" (1985, 45).

UEDA Shizuteru's comment that "in the person of Nishida Kitarō, for the first time in world history Zen and European philosophy truly encountered each other" (1998B, 42) requires qualification. During the decade that he carried on the practice of *zazen* while devouring western philosophy voraciously, this encounter seems to have been more a matter of finding a psychological balance for his future life than part of any adventure of ideas. And after he gave up Zen meditation, the encounter focused on the intellectual side of Zen. Strictly speaking, the two are so much distinct—non-thinking as opposed to disciplined thinking—that one or the other must take preference in the encounter. If there is any middle-ground for encounter, it can only lie in an idea of "experience," which can be spoken of in philosophical categories that in the end collapse in awe in the face of the unknowable, unspeakable. In Nishida's case the attempt to "explain all things on the basis of pure experience as the sole reality"—the explicitly stated goal of *An Inquiry into the Good* (Nishida 1990c, xxx)—was clearly an attempt to create a Zen philosophy. As that idea receded into the background, so did its goal. ➤ The first in-depth study attempting to relate the place of Zen in Nishida was made by Takeuchi Yoshitomo in 1970.

Other citations: NKZ, 17: 117; 18: 35.

9 nishida's philosophical style. The reference to taking in the husk of foreign cultures without imbibing their spirit alludes to a well-known Japanese phrase, 和魂洋才—Japanese spirit, foreign (Western) learning (NKZ 12: 162). ➤ The passage on Nishida in the classroom appears in Nishitani 1991a, 11–12. ➤ A short piece composed on the occasion of his retirement from teaching (Nishida 1995b) was used by Ueda Shizuteru as a starting point for a book on the "biographical life" of Nishida as contrasted with his "personal life" (1995a). I have drawn on this work frequently in the course of these pages. ➤ See also the reminiscences of Nishida in the classroom by Kan Enkichi in the publisher's leaflet to NKZ 5.

As an example of how the creative unfolding of Nishida's thought can be obscured by the attempt to impose a systematic consistency, see the four-volume work by Sueki (1988), which unabashedly flattens out the entire historical and personal context of his thought in order to apply the tools of linguistic analysis to the writings and produce a philosophy of self-awareness. I read the work seriously in my early years of reading Nishida, only to conclude that while the results are impressive they are fundamentally flawed by the presuppositions of a logical positivism that only rarely suits Nishida's work.

One exception to the failure of translators to pay attention to Nishida's obfuscation of his sources is the work of O'Leary (1987), who tracked down numerous unacknowledged quotes in *Intuition and Reflection in Self-Consciousness* by comparing Nishida's text with his personal library. As to how far this practice was followed in his other works, one can only have suspicions.

For a discussion of the philosophical differences between Nishida and Kobayashi, showing how each was trying to deal with the same problem of analyzing the ego and the sick consciousness of modern Japan, see Nakamura 1987, chap. 5. ➤ Nakaoka seems to reflect a general opinion among Nishida's admirers that, while his writing lacked "the elegance of Watsuji or the high-spirited prose of Kuki," it indicated the careful way in which he thought, "as if chipping away at a great rock a little bit at a time" (1999, 19–21). Miki adds to this the fact that the reason he kept reading Nishida despite the difficulty of his prose is that "suddenly an enlightened phrase would surface from the inner recesses of the soul in the midst of all the sophistry and throw light on the whole of the text" (1986, 17: 299–300). The rest of this essay talks about Nishida's open-minded attitude towards his students and their ideas. The passage cited in the text about his way of writing also appears here (306–7). ➤ Even among Nishida's admirers, some have strong words for his writing. YUASA, for instance, calls his writing "a recondite soliloquy, lacking clear and theoretical organization and method" (1987B, 49). For differing opinions on Nishida's style, see FUJITA Kenji's brief contrast with the style of Natsume Sōseki (1993, 15–22), as well as those of NAKAGAWA (1994) and ŌMINE (1995). UEDA Shizuteru's reflections on Nishida's style are a mixture of attention to its genius and an attribution of originality vis-à-vis the style of "western philosophy" that seems to pass lightly over the vast variety of ways philosophy has been written through the centuries, including by Heidegger, whom he in fact mentions (1998B, 233–43; English translation, 1995C). His metaphor of the miner was also cited earlier by TAKEUCHI Yoshitomo (1978, 10), who also neglected to add Nishida's conclusion to the metaphor. SHIMOMURA calls his writings "monologues" and "meditation journals," which give them the sense of a musical theme repeated again and again (1988, 197). ➤ The only full-length attempt to take up the question of Nishida's style critically was made by KOBAYASHI Toshiaki (1997). I have borrowed from it some of the citations given here from Nishida's work.

Nishida's counter to criticisms, though not extensive, can be found in letters in NKZ 19: 122–3, and in a short piece for a publisher's monthly, "The First Time I Wrote in Colloquial Style" (13: 153–4). It might also be possible to read between the lines of his philosophical idea of "expression" (especially in the form it took in his late writings) a certain defense of his style.

MARALDO alerts us to four methods of argumentation in Nishida's writings. The first is his way of laying foundations only to subvert them; second, undermining anthropocentric assumptions about the nature of knowledge and reality; third, relating ideas of logic and metaphysics to the process of self-awareness; and fourth, turning traditional hierarchies or explanatory schemes on their head (1998A). Though I am not sure this covers the whole of his philosophical style, nor that these four are all on the same methodological level, Maraldo's point is well taken.

Regarding the "handicap" that Japanese faces in terms of the close affinity of western languages to philosophical argumentation, see NAKAMURA 1987, 159–60. ➤ The first translations of Nishida's work to appear were done when he was alive, and the translator, Robert Schinzinger, visited Nishida on several occasions in 1938. On one of his visits, Nishida responded to a question about a passage, "I really don't know myself what I've written there" (cited in YUSA 1998A, 428). In addition to Schinzinger, the year before Nishida had received Eduard Spranger, a disciple of Dilthey, and Karl Löwith (see KNAUTH 1965, 356). On the relationship between Löwith and Nishida, see STEVENS (2000, 21–5).

Umehara Takeshi, who is known in Japan today as a popularizer of Japanese thought and Japanist theories, is one of those who insist that Nishida could have used simpler language (cited in KOBAYASHI Toshiaki 1997, 11). ➤ Nishida's insistence on getting the "knack" of a philosophy is cited by NISHITANI (1991A, 65). NISHIDA uses the same term elsewhere in speaking of consummate artists as well

(1990C, 32). ➤ During the war years in particular, Nishida recognized the importance of having a circle of disciples whom he could direct to clear thinking beyond the biases of the time (NKZ 18: 465). ➤ Nishida's occasional pieces are mainly gathered together in volume 13 of his *Complete Works.*

Other citations: KOBAYASHI Hideo 1968, 7: 84; NKZ 14: 267–8, 19: 36.

10 AN ADVENTURE OF IDEAS. The lengthiest presentation of Nishida's thought in a western language is MAFLI's 1996 study, a ponderous but rigorously outlined synopsis based on several of the important works available in English and German. The most exhaustive study in English, dissertations aside, is perhaps CARTER's, written in lighter and more accessible prose (1997).

Nishida did not concern himself with developments in logical positivism nor indeed with even the differences between symbolic and formal logic. His concern was not with the *method* of the principles of discourse but with the use of principles themselves. Hence even when he is discussing the Aristotelian syllogism, he has in mind its function as a way of talking about the world of experience. PAUL misses this point entirely in accusing Nishida and his followers of ignoring the fundamental rules of formal logic, based on his own assumption that the idea of a distinctively "oriental logic" is nonsensical (1993, 136–7). In an earlier pamphlet, he had dismissed outright the idea that Nishida's philosophy was representative of Japan or even very good philosophy (1986, 41–2). Nishida's aim was precisely to challenge the assumptions behind such judgments.

If my suspicions are correct, though I have no way to confirm them, Nishida had a solid scholar's knowledge of philosophical German, was unsure in French (he read Bergson in German and Japanese translation) and somewhat better in English. Latin and Greek were lost on him except for the handful of phrases he met in philosophical texts. He spoke none of these languages, and we may assume that whatever feel he had for western literary language was secondhand. This is in part the reason why he all but abandoned his early interest in great stylists like Bergson and James to lose himself in the neo-Kantians.

NODA recalls that Nishida often referred in his lectures to his aim of seeking rational foundations for the "certain characteristic truth" of Zen (1984, 101–2). ➤ The quotation from NISHITANI (1991A, 25) telescopes Nishida's ideas about Zen. In fact, at several points in his diaries we find him eager to flee the world, not confront it. For example: "My mind must leave the world to Providence and give itself over to practice. I only diminish myself when I expect anything from such a stupid, fleeting world" (NKZ 17: 16). It is only later that he sees this as a lack in Zen. ➤ The fact of Nishida's having kept his practice of Zen secret from his students is attributed to Kataoka Hitoshi (see HORIO 1992, 95).

Examples of Japanese commentators who swallow Nishida's generalizations about the west and the east wholesale are too many to mention. Worse, although Nishida himself preferred the original sources, it is ironic to find so many Japanese thinkers attracted to his ideas who rely on him for their understanding of western philosophy rather than study the texts themselves. The inevitable confusion in what they write reflects badly on Nishida, and is one of the reasons the zeal of his disciples has not succeeded in drawing new readership to the master. ABE Masao is perhaps the most illustrious example of this tendency. See his introduction to the revised translation of *An Inquiry into the Good* (1990) and his explanation of Nishida's "corrections" of Hegel and Aristotle (1995). MARALDO has carefully demonstrated the "veiled cultural nationalism" at work in the background of Abe's way of thinking (1995, 241–6).

DILWORTH, summing up decades of pioneering work in the study and translation of Nishida, has made a solid presentation of the development of Nishida's thought in terms of his overall aim of uniting east and west (1987).

Other citations: NISHIDA 1958D, 355–6; MIKI 1986, 20: 728–9; UEDA Shizuteru 1995B, 35.

11 THE QUEST OF THE ABSOLUTE. Regarding the preoccupation among Meiji intellectuals with clarifying the idea of the self, see NAKAMURA 1987, 161–3. ➤ As might be expected from the intensity of Nishida's commitment to Zen in the midst of a teaching career, his diaries and letters are full of references to the self and its pursuit as more important than the vanity of worldly preoccupations. At the time he was trying to position himself in a kind of "radical individualism" that did not fall into the trap of what he saw as the egocentric tendency of European thinking, whose history he tried to trace in a short piece called "The Doctrine of Self-Consciousness" (NKZ 13: 90–5). This was a position to which he clung vigorously, insisting to the end that totalitarianism in any form has to be rejected precisely because of its negation of the individual. In this connection, see the brief interview with Yamamoto Ryōkichi in the publisher's leaflet to NKZ 15.

STEVENS (1998, 2) has gone out on a tender limb in claiming that not only the later philosophy of Nishida "but also the various aspects of the philosophy of the Kyoto school as a whole" are "seminally contained" in *An Inquiry into the Good.* Fortunately his essay focuses on his own reappreciation of the work and does not try to justify the claim. This view, let it be said, is not uncommon even among many students of western philosophy in Japan who treat it as the culmination of his thinking. As an example of how badly skewed the results can be, see OGAWA's comparison of Nishida with Husserl (1979). ➤ Twenty-five years after *An Inquiry into the Good* was published, Nishida recognized the fact that he had made consciousness the center of the work, giving it a kind of psychological flavor that he had not intended (NISHIDA 1990C, xxxi). ➤ NISHITANI's remarks (1991A, xxvi, 96, 101) appear in the course of a long and extremely readable commentary on the work which, however, I conclude are best read as reflections in hindsight than as a merely objective account.

Regarding the title and publication of *An Inquiry into the Good,* see YUSA 1998A, 242–3.

Other citations: NKZ 17: 74, 18: 44.

12 THE ABSOLUTE AS PURE EXPERIENCE. Miki is reported to have said during his high-school years that *An Inquiry into the Good* was his "favorite reading." The remark appears in the recollections of Kōyama Iwao (cited in HANAZAWA 1999, 24).

The first translation into English of *An Inquiry into the Good* in 1960 (reprinted in NISHIDA 1988) badly needed redoing, and has improved greatly in the new translation, though still with a fair share of Japanese literalisms marring the English (1990C). The most recent Spanish translation based on this latter shows everywhere the marks of a direct translation from the English (1995A), while the earlier Spanish translation, made directly from the Japanese, is in general reliable, but also, unfortunately, out of print (1963).

NISHIDA's discussion of "Various Worlds" at the conclusion of his next project, *Intuition and Reflection in Self-Consciousness,* is his way of speaking of a single unity refracted in a variety of viewpoints or ways of classifying the items of reality (1987A, 154–9). His attraction to Leibniz's theory of monads is of a sort with this, in that the theory relies on the assumption of an *unus mundus* ruled over by a single, unifying principle.

The passage that I have rendered as experience having an individual rather than the other way around (NISHIDA 1990C, XXX; NKZ 1: 4; the German translator, for some reason, simply left the whole prefatory section of the book out) plays on the double meaning of the Japanese word *aru:* to exist and to have. Literally, the rephrasing contrasts the clause "there being an individual, an experience is had" with "there being an experience, an individual is had." The rendering "experience exists because there is an individual" not only adds the element of causality, but misses Nishida's inversion of the conditioning and the conditioned. The rest of the mistranslation involves confusion of where the relative clauses begin and end. I have reworked it in order to communicate something of the twist of meaning communicated to the Japanese reader. ➤ The obliquely stated criticism of FUJITA Masakatsu against the "purity" of pure experience on the grounds that all human experience is colored by language (1998B, 58–60) seems to be dealing with experience that has lost the pristine purity to which Nishida wants to return. ➤ FEENBERG finds four distinct meanings of the notion of "experience" in *An Inquiry into the Good* (1999, 29–31).

The citations from William James are taken from his *Essays in Radical Empiricism* (Cambridge: Harvard University Press, 1976), 45, 57, 59. Fur further enlightening comparisons, one can turn to the unpublished doctoral dissertation by ABE Nobuhiko (1993, 53–75), which argues convincingly that Nishida took pure experience the full distance as a philosophical idea, while James, despite his intentions to do so, never quite did. Where I disagree is with his idea that pure experience survived as a general concept (Abe coins it "immanent transcendence") in Nishida's later philosophy. ➤ Dilworth challenges Nishida's understanding of the idea of consciousness in James, particularly in terms of the "flow" of experience (1969). ➤ Ueda Shizuteru's is perhaps the most thoroughgoing attempt to see the notion of pure experience as a kind of intuitive flash that continued to glow at the foundation of all of Nishida's later thought (1991). ➤ Nakamura (1987, 163) repeats the idea that James's pure experience was tied to his pragmatism while Nishida's was looking for "transcendental foundations." This view, which can only be based on a rather severe ignorance of James's work, is rejected by Nishida himself, who recognized in James an "ideal" combination of judgment towards inner events and outer events (NKZ 13: 206–7). ➤ In fact, the only text of James's he seems to have studied thoroughly is the *Varieties of Religious Experience* which he first mentions in 1902 (NKZ 18: 59). Even so, he seems to have missed the important concluding chapter to that work. At the pace Nishida was reading, it is likely that the command of metaphor and literary sentiment required to understand James would have made it impossible to give the texts the necessary attention they deserved. That said, it is not surprising that Nishida took his idea of pure experience in a different direction, avoiding some of James's oversights while making errors of his own that James could have spared him from. ➤ Nishida himself only writes briefly, in 1910, of his disagreement with James (NKZ 13: 97–8). ➤ My question about the depth of Nishida's early understanding of Hegel is extended by Funayama to Nishida's later work as well, which he criticizes as too bound to an "ego philosophy" to open up to the "world philosophy" of Hegel (1984, 10–42). For a reorganization of *An Inquiry into the Good* around the idea of pure experience, see Sueki (1988, 1: 19–33). His attempt to "systematize" the work runs longer than the original text. ➤ Shimomura sees no less than twelve different functions for the idea of pure or direct experience in *An Inquiry into the Good,* which he condenses into the five stages on which I have based my summary here (1947, 172ff). This work has been shortened for inclusion in the volume of his *Collected Works* that deals with Nishida and Tanabe, and this scheme was lost in the excision (1990, 80–1).

The term I have translated "demand" or "drive" is 要求. For a listing of its uses in *An Inquiry into the Good,* see Takeuchi Seiichi et al. 1996, 366–70. I would also note a passage in a 1916 essay in which Nishida distinguishes between private desire and ambitions and a deeper impulse, of which he goes so far as to say, "this internal necessity is God" (NKZ 13: 113). ➤ Nishitani argues that by shifting the foundation of western metaphysics to pure experience, "we find something fundamentally different from any metaphysics known to the history of western philosophy; so much so that it is not really proper to continue speaking of the book's standpoint as metaphysical." He claims that the only other philosophy to offer the same kind of appeal to experience as a middle ground between traditional metaphysics and positivistic science is in Bergson (1991A, 79, 108–9). On the influence of Bergson on Nishida's thinking, see the biographical data in Yusa (1998A,

237–8). I find SUZUKI Sadami's attempt to read vitalism into Nishida's thought, and further to associate this with his attitude towards world history, farfetched (2000). ➤ The two passages on the will are mistranslated in the English (NISHIDA 1990C, 25, 123). In the case of the latter, the will is made *the* unifying activity of consciousness, which would contradict everything Nishida had been saying about thinking and willing being united in pure experience or immediate intuition.

When Nishida talks about religion, it is nearly always Buddhism and Christianity he has in mind, and then their doctrinal and mystical traditions rather than any institutional affiliation or ritual practice. A short piece he wrote in 1901 on "Religion Today" criticizes the bearers of religious tradition for turning it into a professional occupation and scholars for trying to invent a replacement of their own—both missing out on the heart of the matter, which is concern with life and awakening the individual to the religious dimension of the human. In uncompromising terms he calls on Christianity to take its own truth to heart (NKZ 13: 81–4). While the style is atypical for its moralizing attacks on the religious establishment, it shows a position from which Nishida never backed down.

Other citations: KAWASHIMA 1997, 59; NISHIDA 1990C, 59, 79–81, 171.

13 THE ABSOLUTE AS WILL. My remarks on this book draw freely on O'LEARY's introduction to the English translation (1987), which itself is a fruit of the long months we worked together to prepare the translation. ➤ The young professor to whose criticisms Nishida responded (NKZ 1: 299–316) was Takahashi Satomi, who would later come close to reconciling Nishida's idea of absolute nothingness with the notion of finitude from neo-Kantianism and Heidegger, based on a dialectics of love that prefigures Tanabe's late thought. A good résumé of Takahashi's thought, showing his relation to Nishida, can be found in KOSAKA (1997, 157–91). ➤ Nishida is said to have been the first Japanese to cite Husserl in a philosophical publication. That was in 1911, when he saw Husserl as in the same camp as Rickert (NITTA, TATEMATSU, SHIMOMISSE 1979, 8). Nishida exchanged letters with Husserl in 1923 and with Rickert in 1924 (YUSA 1998C, 63). When news reached him of Husserl's passing in 1938, Nishida wrote that "the twentieth century has lost its first grand old man" (NKZ 19: 32).

On Nishida's general idea of voluntarism at this time, and its roots in his earlier thinking, see DILWORTH 1970. ➤ The idea of absolute will as extending beyond conscious subjective ends to cover all of reality as a fundamental principle is Schopenhauer's. Nishida does not cite him in the work, but he was moved by his ideas during his undergraduate years, and he had read his life and dipped into his writings during the years preceding the publication of *An Inquiry into the Good.* A 1902 letter alludes to his preference for grounding the absolute in will with Schopenhauer rather than in intellect with Hegel (NKZ 18: 61). Much of his interest in artistic expression also bears the mark of Schopenhauer's thinking, though again it is not cited.

NISHIDA suggests that the Gnostic cosmology may be worth pursuing for its ideas of the God of non-existence and the abyss of creation, though he does not do so himself (1987A, 156, 167). As far as I know, no work has been done on comparing gnostic ideas to the philosophies of nothingness of the Kyoto philosophers. ➤ I can do no better than repeat O'LEARY's judgment of the concluding chapters of *Intuition*: "These chapters mark a turning-point: behind them lies Nishida's long apprenticeship as an imitator of western voices; before lie the grander themes of his later philosophy. No student of the Kyoto philosophy of absolute nothingness can afford to ignore these pages" (1987, XVII).

Other citations: NISHIDA 1987A, XXIII–XXIV, 125, 133–4, 166–7; NKZ 1: 209; O'LEARY 1987, X.

14 SELF-AWARENESS. The term "self-awareness" is a rather ordinary Japanese term, and appears as such in *An Inquiry into the Good,* where it replaces "self-consciousness" no more than 5% of the time without any particular technical meaning. By the time of *Intuition and Reflection in Self-Awareness,* as we have seen in the previous section, it has taken on a meaning of its own, different from self-consciousness. Accordingly, in the text and notes I have adjusted the title under which we published the English translation of that work. ➤ It is worth mentioning that the confusion in English between the European Enlightenment and Buddhist enlightenment is avoided in Japanese by the use of a special technical term reserved for the former.

UEDA Shizuteru sees three dimensions of awareness, corresponding to three of the meanings pure experience carried for Nishida in *An Inquiry into the Good:* (1) simple *awakening* is like the fact of pure experience, a unity of words and things (言 and 事, both of which are joined at the roots in the Japanese language by having the same pronunciation but differing Chinese characters: *koto*); (2) *self-awakening* points to the fact that pure experience is a dynamic self-unfolding in which all awareness of others is at the same time a self-awareness; and (3) *understanding of the self and world* reflects the fact that pure experience is the principle by which everything can be explained (1991, 249–57). In this way he tries to see the core of the idea of pure experience surviving in Nishida's later work.

In general, I agree with UEDA's view that self-awareness is a central idea of Nishida's philosophy (1981). The fact that some, like KŌSAKA, have been able to see Nishida's concern with self-awareness as no more than the stage in his development associated with *Intuition and Reflection*, indicates how little attention Nishida gave to refining his definition of the term (1961, 71–117). What is clear is that he intended it as a refinement of the traditional idea of self-consciousness, for which reason he spoke for a period of "self-aware self-consciousness" (NKZ 4: 286). ➤ Elsewhere I have argued that the idea of the true self owes as much, if not more, to western thought as to eastern (see notes to §60 below). NISHITANI's reading of Nishida's idea of the self (1991A, 112–44) is a very skillfully executed stringing together of passages from *An Inquiry into the Good* to show that they represent a consistent idea. Although Nishitani had the advantage of studying directly with Nishida and therefore is a more reliable guide than I in regard to what ideas Nishida had and did not have, my suspicions are that his own concentration on the notion of the self were more at play in his reading of Nishida than Nishitani gives them credit for. ➤ Unlike some of his disciples, notably Nishitani, who drew more on Buddhism, Nishida uses terms like non-I (無我) and self that is not a self (自己ならぬ自己) sparsely. In their place he prefers the positive expression of true I (真の私, e.g., 3: 146) or true self (真の自己).

Part of the problem is language, since use of the term "self" is often less technical than it is a matter of grammar. Thus when NISHIDA writes that "one without an ego, that is to say one in whom the self has been destroyed, is the greatest," the word "self" (自己) functions like a pronoun referring to "I" (我) and not a noun as translators tend to do in order to make the sentence read more naturally (1990C, 77; 1995A, 123; 1997A, 91). Lacking definite and indefinite articles, Japanese enjoys an ambiguity of expression here that English does not. See also notes to §44 below.

NAKAMURA Yūjirō finds a cognate to Nishida's distinction between ego and true self in the psychology of C. G. Jung, where "ego" is said to refer to mere self-consciousness and "self" to self-awareness (1984, 66–71). While there is a certain overlap in the intention behind the distinction, the comparison of terminology is mistaken, and breaks down as he carries it further into its psychological ramifications. If one is looking for points of contact, it would seem more accurate, and more useful, to trace the idea in the west directly to Nietzsche, beginning with the third of his *Untimely Meditations.* ➤ YUSA thinks that the true self is a kind of matrix, or locus, for the ordinary ego, and in this sense can be seen as a "pure consciousness" (1998B, 27–8). Though her choice of words is not particularly good, this is indeed one of the meanings one can find in Nishida, particularly in his final essay.

The use of "self" to mean "self-identity" is clear, for instance, in an occasional piece he wrote in 1936 (NKZ 13: 124–5). When he speaks in a 1901 diary entry of the need to "let go of petty ambitions to philosophy and fame and make peace in the self" or "conquer the self" (NKZ 17: 50–1), for example, the contexts make it clear that he means no more than what we would call finding peace with oneself and overcoming one's baser desires.

15 ACTIVE INTUITION, KNOWING BY BECOMING. Nishida's two major essays on active intuition, over one hundred pages each, were completed in 1935 and 1936, and one shorter piece was published in the following year (NKZ 8: 107–218, 273–393, 541–71). A reconstruction of the 1936 essay, "Logic and Life," is offered in YUASA, who inserts in his account a comparison with Watsuji and a contrast of Heidegger with Nishida (1987B, 50–2, 65–72). ➤ The combining of the active and passive dimensions of intuition recalls Fichte's idea of facts as never merely given but always in some sense made—what he

called *Tathandlung*. While Nishida was sympathetic with Fichte's idea, he balked at the turning of the I into a substantive. Active intuition may be considered his best formal answer to Fichte. ➤ See also CESTARI's lucid description of active intuition (1998). ➤ TAKEUCHI Yoshitomo's late study of active intuition (1992: 9–93) contends that this remained pivotal in Nishida's thinking to the end.

JACINTO suggests, in an overview of Nishida's idea of body, that we distinguish three forms: the biological, the historical, and the productive, each of which mediates a different aspect of the self's relation to reality (1989, 22–32). Despite his efforts to show how the idea was Nishida's way of making his epistemology concrete, I find myself in sympathy with KETA when she suggests that Nishida's abstract notion of "body" did not succeed in introducing "bodily thinking" into his philosophy. Given his long practice of *zazen*, she faults him for the omission, or rather the collapsing of the Zen idea into a philosophical one (1985, 171–2). I would add that Nishida could also have come to a far more concrete understanding of bodily thinking by reading further in William James.

The distinctive expression NISHIDA uses for "becoming" a thing, 成り切る, had appeared already in *An Inquiry into the Good* (1990C, 61, 77). In commenting on the first passage, the one cited in the text, NISHITANI interprets the concomitant idea of "working at one with" something as the equivalent of an appropriation of that thing into awareness (1991A, 116–17). Besides knowing, Nishida also speaks of thinking about, acting on, and seeing a thing by becoming it. ➤ It is curious that although the idea of *becoming* is important in Nishida's later thought, the editors of the quasi-biblical concordance of *An Inquiry into the Good* neglected to single it out (TAKEUCHI Seiichi et al. 1996).

Other citations: NKZ 8: 163–5; NISHIDA 1958D, 362.

16 ART AND MORALITY AS SELF-EXPRESSION. In two 1919 essays Nishida links the individuality of the artistic production to pure experience, and sees active intuition as something that combines the highly objective with the highly subjective, singling out van Gogh and the cubism of Picasso as examples (see NKZ 3: 116, 13: 123). These seem to be the first indication of his interest in relating artistic activity to his own philosophy. ➤ A short essay NISHIDA wrote in 1900 (1987C) is his first suggestion that the sense of beauty, as well as of morality, is to be found in the no-self. ➤ The distinction between eastern and western art in relation to the idea of nothingness is also expressed in his essay on Goethe (NISHIDA 1958B, 145–58). ➤ Nishida's calligraphy was of high quality, but he refused to allow an exhibition while he was still alive (see the comments by Ueda Juzō and Shimatani Shunzō in the publisher's leaflets to NKZ 7 and 9).

In a brief essay on Nishida's aesthetical theory, YOSHIOKA attempts to distinguish Nishida from the west's concern with "certain knowledge" in virtue of a starting point in the "pathos" of existence (1996, 137). It is true Nishida uses a term uniting feeling and intention 情意 in a distinctive way already from *An*

Inquiry into the Good. The English and French translators separate them as "feeling and volition," one of the latter adding a note to the effect that he doesn't understand the term (1997A, 16). JACINTO opts, incorrectly, for simply "emoción." And on first encountering the term, the German not only misses the sense of the word *(Gemütsbewegung)* but also the grammar of the passage (1989, 31). In any case, it has nothing to do with the pathos of existence. The term "pathos" only appears twice that I know of (NKZ 7: 113, 147), where it is cited as synonymous with the Hegelian idea of *Leidenschaft.* Alternatively, one could consider "pathos" present in Nishida's location of the starting point for philosophy not in "wonder" but in "the sadness of life" (6: 116), which ŌMINE sees as an underlying current running throughout Nishida's thought (1990, 101). I have to say, deferring to those who knew Nishida personally, that on the basis of the texts I find the argument stretching things. If anything, I find the element of pathos distinctively absent in Nishida, whether in the Japanese aesthetic sense or a more general philosophical sense, and one of the areas in which Nishitani made a significant contribution.

A clear statement of the identification of the "ought" with the "real" in the heightened awareness of the subject appears in his earliest attempt at an ethical position (NISHIDA 1990C, 126).

Other citations: NISHIDA 1958B, 145–6, 159; 1958C, 175–6, 181; 1973A, 104; NKZ 6: 14–15; 12: 150–1.

17 **ABSOLUTE NOTHINGNESS.** Nishida calls his shift to nothingness part of a turn to "religion" (NKZ 4: 3), though curiously the essays to which this applies, those gathered in a book he entitled *From Working to Seeing,* are devoid of references to traditional religion and to God. The religion he seems to have in mind is the religiosity he had discovered in artistic creation.

Passages in *An Inquiry into the Good* referring to nothingness as an ontological principle, either in western or eastern thought, can be found in NISHIDA 1990C, 46, 55, 167–8. ➤ Near the end of *Intuition and Reflection in Self-Awareness* we find clearer indications of an idea of nothingness on a par with that of being, such as the following:

> Like our will, which is nothingness while it is being, and being while it is nothingness, this world transcends even the categories of being and nothingness..., for here being is born out of nothingness. (NISHIDA 1987A, 166)

Nonetheless, these are no more than hints, and what is more, hints drawn mainly from western philosophy. ➤ In the same work, we find a passing reference to nothingness as μὴ ὄν in distinction to οὐκ ὄν not develop the idea of absolute nothingness until some years later, neither does he speak of a "relative nothingness," as the translator has interpolated (50).

The idea of ontology was so foreign to Japanese thought and its Chinese ancestry that Nishi Amane, one of the first modern thinkers to struggle with translating western philosophical concepts into Japanese, could not decide exactly how to render the term itself. Sometimes he calls it 虚体学, or the study of nonentities, at other times, the study of principles of order 理体学, and at still others 本体学, or the study of original forms. See『西周全集』(Tokyo: Munetaka Shobō, 1960), 1: 36, 146, 161.

The attempt by Hisamatsu Shin'ichi to lay out the various definitions of nothingness east and west is naïve to much of the history of western philosophy, and insofar as it co-opts Nishida's thinking for Zen and indeed for "oriental nothingness" as a whole, to much of the history of eastern thought as well. See his "The Characteristics of Oriental Nothingness," *Philosophical Studies of Japan* 2, 1960: 65–97. Hisamatsu had studied under Nishida, was strongly influenced by him, and is still revered by his followers and students as a philosopher who belongs alongside Nishitani and Tanabe as one of the pillars of the Kyoto school. See the comments by SWANSON in this regard (1996, 100).

MARALDO notes, in defending Nishida against Tanabe's criticism of intuitionism, that "Nishida never writes of the pure or immediate experience of nothingness" (1990, 251) but uses language that suggests nothingness as either a condition for the possibility of experience" or even as that which experiences. He is correct that Nishida never writes of the pure experience *of* anything, since by definition pure experience does not distinguish an object. But we should add that Nishida did not begin using his concept of nothingness until after he had stopped using that of pure experience, and that the former replaced some of the functions of the latter. Nishida does not talk of a consciousness of absolute nothingness like the consciousness of objects in the world that allows for a *knowing by becoming*. But he does in fact relate experience to nothingness in the only way one would expect him to: as a "self-awareness." This I take it be *precisely* what he means by seeing nothingness as the locus of all experience (rather than the actual experiencer). For example, Nishida explicitly writes that "in religious consciousness the body-mind is dropped off and we are united with the consciousness of absolute nothingness" (NKZ 5: 177). On the other hand, Nishida *does* state clearly that God or Buddha, as absolutes, cannot be experienced directly but only through the mediation of experiences that constellate the sentiment of no-self (see notes to §22 below).

Other citations: NISHIDA 1970B, 17, 49, 77, 237; 1973A, 41; NKZ 4: 221, 245, 254; 7: 445; 8: 324–5.

18 IDENTITY AND OPPOSITION. NISHIDA's first treatment of the idea of the *coincidentia oppositorum* was a short lecture delivered in 1919 (1997B). ➤ He gave a concentrated series of lectures on the *coincidentia oppositorum* in 1919 at Ōtani University. The lengthy essay referred to was published in 1939 as "The Self-Identity of Absolute Contradictories" (NISHIDA 1958C).

PAUL rejects out of hand Nishida's idea of identity in contradiction and of absolute nothingness as a distorted reading of the idea of "nonsubstantiality" or of Nāgārjuna's logic (1993, 136–7). See notes to §2.

DILWORTH relates the interest in a logic of contradictions to Nishida's general interest in bringing east and west into encounter, noting, however, that he did not develop the consequences of the former for the latter (1987, 129–31). ➤ The etymology of the Chinese glyph for *soku* or *sunawachi*, 即, is said to derive from the sense of "taking one's seat for a meal," from which it took the general sense of "arriving at," "being attached," or "following on."

TREMBLAY is wrong to argue that the absence of the term *absolute* in the phrase "self-identity of contradictories" is without meaning (2000A, 108). For example, he uses that phrase to refer to the identity of subject and environment in Greek culture (NKZ 12: 354) and to speak of the relation of the temporal to the spatial world (12: 294). In religious contexts, such as St. Paul's idea of Christ living in the self (12: 369), he invariably includes the qualifier "absolute." UEDA Shizuteru concludes that this makes his elimination of the term "absolute" in referring to the imperial household significant in that it denies the emperor the religious meaning he was given at the time (1998A, 482–5).

The distinction between *what* things are and *that* they are things of experience is carried in Japanese by the vernacular Japanese terms *mono* and *koto* respectively. This latter term serves a variety of grammatical functions that enhances the distinction from the former, which refers simply to something or someone. Although commentators on Nishida are fond of drawing attention to the resistance of *koto* to translation by any single word in European languages, it seems perfectly clear in paraphrase. See, for example, Kimura Bin, "Self and Nature: An Interpretation of Schizophrenia," *Zen Buddhism Today* 6 (1988), 20–1; and FUJITA Masakatsu 1998B, 61–3.

D. T. Suzuki, who was aware of the same differences between ways of thinking east and west, took the opposite stance from Nishida, seeing logic as no more than a tool for communication with those who think in terms of logic. Thus in a 1951 letter regarding Nishida's continued reminder of the fact that Zen does not have a logic, he writes, "If we are going to convince the westerners, somehow or other we are going to need a logic." Akizuki Ryōmin, 『鈴木大拙の言葉と思想』 *[Thoughts and sayings of D. T. Suzuki]* (Tokyo: Kōdansha, 1967), 187.

Other citations: NKZ 8: 616; NISHIDA 1958D, 355–7, 359; 1970B, 16.

19 THE HISTORICAL WORLD. Details on the relations between Nishida and the Navy can be found in HANAZAWA 1999, 150–67. There is no need here to reproduce his careful documentation of each of the details given here in résumé. ➤ To get an idea of the intellectual confusion after the war, see SHIBAYAMA 1994, 110ff. ➤ The argument for the nation as the primary "moral body" can be found in NKZ 12: 376. ➤ For the relationship between morality and absolute nothingness, see especially NISHIDA 1973A, 133–9.

NISHIDA 1958D, 351–3, 358; 1973A, 165-6; 1970B, 237, 254.

20 THE LOGIC OF LOCUS. Others have variously translated the logic of *locus* as a logic of *place* or of *topos*. The verbal and adjectival cognates for "place" in English are too clumsy to use to translate Nishida's imagery of location and being located. The Greek term *topos*, which Yusa and Jacinto are fond of, apparently for its philosophical ring, bring additional problems. Nishida does suggest the term, to be sure, when he says that "the word *basho* was taken from the idea of the place of the Ideas of the Platonists" (NKZ 11: 73), and NISHITANI—whether on the basis of something Nishida said or not, we cannot tell—associates it with *χώρα* of Plato's *Timaeus* (1982A, 21). Neither of these connections is pursued in Nishida's own writings. Nor does there seem to be any connection with Aristotle's use of the term, let alone the more technical uses the term has taken in modern logic. NAKAMURA has given a popular account of the range of meanings that the ordinary terms *place*, *topos*, and *locus* have taken in western science and philosophy, and contrasted them with the way Nishida took the equivalent term in Japanese, the everyday word *basho* 場所, and gave it still another meaning (1988). ➤ DILWORTH has rendered *basho* as "horizon" in his translation of *Art and Morality*, and in his translation of Nishida's last essay alternates mainly between "place" and "matrix" (1973A, 1987B). On his account of the logic of locus as a "matrix ontology," see 1987, 14–20. An earlier essay of his that tries to show how the logic of locus (he called it "topos" then) became a final resting point for Nishida is one of the clearest introductory pieces to Nishida's mature thought I know of in a western language (DILWORTH, 1979).

In a later essay on the philosophical foundations of mathematics, Nishida uses the logic of locus generously, but makes no mention of the idea of "field" (rendered as 場 or 体 in Japanese, depending on the meaning) in either its classical or modern senses there (1995G). The closest allusion to the scientific use is a passing reference to the "locus of material force" (NISHIDA 1973A, 48). ➤ For a general overview of the role of mathematics in his thinking, see SHIMOMURA 1985B.

YUASA (1987B, 42, 67) reckons that Nishida, like Watsuji, followed a general oriental preference for spatial thinking, unlike the western preference for the temporal. A similar position is taken by ARISAKA, who also takes Watsuji's idea over into her reading of Nishida's logic of locus (1996B). This is not an uncommon view among Japanese philosophers, but NISHIDA himself is not so clear about it. In fact, he claims that the Greeks were spatially oriented and the Japanese, in contrast, temporally oriented, so that "whereas the Greeks subsumed time within space, the Japanese subsumed space within time" (1970B, 248–9). I would argue that the idea of locus abstracts from *both* space and time.

UEDA Shizuteru, on whose helpful essay I have drawn liberally for my summary, argues that Japanese language more easily lends itself to the idea of something "becoming conscious" as an event independent of the subject because of its preference for intransitive statements in contrast to European languages ("The sound of the bell is heard" rather than "I hear the bell") (1995B, 31). Though he later qualifies his remarks to avoid the impression that the Japanese language is better suited to Nishida's thinking, his remarks point to two common mistakes made by a great many of Nishida's commentators. First, not all European languages adopt the grammatical demand for stating the subject of the transitive verb as English and German do; and second, the presence or absence of the grammatical subject does not necessarily accent, either in Japanese or in western languages, the presence or absence of a sense of the subject, despite the literal meaning. See also the notes to §21 below.

NISHITANI says that with the logic of place the last vestiges of psychologism were gone from Nishida (1991A, 91–2). ➤ O'LEARY's remark that Nishida's locus is "an oriental equivalent of the Platonic or neo-Kantian *mundus intelligibilis*" (1987, ix) is only true if one extends the notion of intelligibility to include the fusion of subject and object, and the notion of world to include nothingness. NISHIDA discusses this in two 1929 essays (1958A and NKZ 5: 5–57). ➤ KŌSAKA, from whom I have drawn the model of the three circles (1961, 119–20), also refers to these levels as location in being, location in relative nothing, and location in absolute nothingness (1935, 37–8).

Other citations: NKZ 4: 5–6; NISHIDA 1973A, 37.

21 SUBJECT, PREDICATE, AND UNIVERSAL. The résumé on subject and predicate appears in the concluding chapter of Nishida's 1926 essay on "Locus" (NKZ 4: 272–89). ➤ A recent study of Nishida's idea of the universal based on volume 5 of his *Collected Works* (TREMBLAY 2000A) gives a much more detailed account of this idea and its relation to the logic of locus. It could profitably be completed by the efforts of KOSAKA to schematically relate the various kinds of universals of which Nishida speaks (of action, intelligibility, expression, self-awareness, and judgment) to one another and to his logic of locus (1991, see especially 283–7). Both of these authors make me all the more conscious of how simplistic my own résumé is and how many questions it leaves unanswered.

ABE Nobuhiko (1993) argues that languages centered on a subject-predicate structure (the model of which is English syntax) are not suited to translating Nishida's central ideas. The argument challenges an important assumption in western philosophical circles: that the "deep structure" of all languages is fundamentally identical and that this structure can be called to the surface with the help of logical thinking in order to produce a universally valid mode of thought. At the same time, he weakens his case by introducing an oblique assumption of his own: that the grammars of western languages function in the same way in deliberately logical, scientific discourse as they do in habitual modes of thinking and communication. On that basis he is able to contrast Japanese with English and arrive at certain incompatibilities relative to philosophical discourse. I prefer to think of language as less monolithic, and to recognize the way in which the "subject-predicate" modes of European languages accommodate themselves naturally to modes of thought of a quite different nature, namely to communicating exactly what the Japanese "topical" grammar is designed to express by its elimination of the subject-predicate demand. I also think that this everyday experience of language plays a much greater part in philosophical thought and expression than is ordinarily given credit. No one knew this better than William James, whom Abe contrasts well with Nishida. In any case, these are not claims Nishida himself made.

The term Nishida uses for *working*, 働くもの, carries the sense of the *worker* as well. In introducing the term, he defines it as "the ongoing transformation of the self in time" (NKZ 4: 176–7), thus setting up the contrast with seeing, which will rely on non-temporal, spatial metaphors.

Other citations: NKZ 4: 254, 279; 6: 279; NISHIDA 1970B, 45, 79–80, 172–3.

22 SELF AND OTHER. TREMBLAY has put the subject of self-awareness in context by distinguishing it from other kinds of "self" in Nishida (2000B). What is interesting about her helpful summary is that she overlooks the self of self-and-other. I say this, even though I am questioning here whether the presence of the other adds anything to the notion of self covered by her categories.

Elsewhere I have argued a comparison of Nishida's ideas with Buber's *I and Thou*, focusing on the question of what happens to the moral imperative of the self towards the other in each. I also take issue there with UEDA Shizuteru's comparison (1991, 352–8), which tilts the scales of the comparison in Nishida's favor, for having confused the notion of *Verhältnis* and *Beziehung* in Buber, and for having failed to ask the ethical question. I conclude that his allusions to Buber are intended primarily to accent an originality in Nishida's ideas that cannot be accounted for in classical western philosophy (HEISIG 2000). ➤ For a more favorable assessment of Nishida's book, see KOPF 1999. ➤ I have left out of my account the element of the third person (the "he" or "she"), which HIROKAWA sees as the whole orientation of the I-you relationship in Nishida (1999). ➤ A lengthy comparison of Nishida and Buber by TSUNODA (1994, 123–54) covers much the same ground as Ueda, whom he does not cite, but also fails to take into account the moral imperative of Buber absent in Nishida. ➤ Nishida cites Gogarten's *Ich glaube an den dreieinigen Gott* near the end of his own book (NKZ 6: 417), a work in which Buber's influence is evident. This may even have been a major stimulus for his own interest in the I-you relationship. In any case, the first allusion to Buber's work appears in Nishida's diaries in 1934, two years after the publication of his own book. UEDA (1991, 350-1) reconfirms my suspicion that Nishida could not have known any more than the title of Buber's work when he composed his own.

The introduction of the idea of the "eternal now," of course, suggests a comparison with Kierkegaard. Kierkegaard's idea of the self constituting itself by encountering the power of an absolute other in self-reflection is not basically different from Nishida's, where the I-you relationship is a stage in the "self's relating itself to itself." But this was the very "sublime mistake" whose rejection set Buber on the path of the I-Thou; for Nishida, it is a logical entailment of seeing reality as absolute nothingness. I do not know that Nishida ever cited, or even knew, Kierkegaard's famous passage about the self grounding itself in the absolute.

To get an idea of how the I-you idea survives in later works, minus the connection with love and simply as a logical device, one can refer to the essays written immediately after and collected as the first volume of his *Fundamental Problems of Philosophy* (for example, see Nishida 1970b, 18–19, 24–27, 69–71, 139–41). One may also cite the concluding section of a 1934 essay that paraphrases the structure of the I-you, which also stresses the logical structure alone (NKZ 7: 266ff). ➤ The only extensive treatment of the relation of Nishida's idea of self and other I am aware of is a collection of essays by Noguchi (1982), in which the author attempts to show the continuity between the two essays of Nishida's treated here and Nishida's earliest work, and to reply to criticisms. The question of morality is not raised.

The influence of T. H. Green on Nishida's maiden work, *An Inquiry into the Good*, is well known. But while Nishida took over Green's idea of reality as something spiritual that transcends both reason and the world, from the start he never personalized reality the way Green had. This was a question Nishitani would wrestle with directly, but Nishida did not. On the contrary, the loss of self in mystical union he sees as undercutting the personalist view rather than supporting it, as is common in western mystical theology. Given Nishida's views of the fundamentally impersonal nature of reality and his radical relativization of the personal aspect of the I-you encounter, there is no way to put him in the "personalist" camp, as was done early on through a secondhand knowledge of Nishita's work before anything had been translated (Piper 1936). ➤ At the same time, the claim that Nishida's is "obviously a *Japanese* philosophy" based on the idea of a distinctively "Japanese ego" (Miyakawa Tōru in publisher's leaflet, NKZ 12) is not only not self-evident, it seems to me completely mistaken.

The first clear mention of the idea of love as the combining of the opposites of self and other in such a way as to confirm the self appears in a short 1919 essay, where he states that "to love the other is to love the self" (Nishida 1997b, 11). In that same place he indicates that God (and Buddha) cannot be known directly but only indirectly through the emotion that accompanies the union of the opposites, which, together with his rejection of a personal God, helps explain the absence of an Eternal Thou in his thought.

Other citations: Ueda Shizuteru 1998b, 243; NKZ 6: 265, 343-4, 348, 385-6, 408, 424; 7: 266].

23 LOVE AND RESPONSIBILITY. Nakamura Yūjirō sees the tendency to ignore the ethical dimension of love in Nishida already from the time of *A Study of Good* where the highest moral category was that of 誠, "authenticity" or "sincerity," which is too subjective to ground moral

outrage against the status quo.「《誠》という道徳的価値について」[On the moral value of 'sincerity'] in『内なるものとしての宗教』*[Religion as inner]* (Tokyo: Iwanami, 1997), 20. HASE (1998B) parries the criticism by challenging Nakamura's understanding of Nishida's later work on the I-you relationship without, however, coming to grips with the fundamental abstractness of an ethic whose *terminus ad quem* remains a heightened sense of self-awareness.

The references to the love of God and the citation of Augustine should not be taken in their ordinary Christian sense. Already from a 1916 essay on "Within and Without the Mind" Nishida characterized the question of "whether the gods and buddhas are to be found within the mind or without it" as important to believers but unacceptable to his philosophical logic, in which reality is the same, whether it appears at one moment as mind and another as some thing outside the mind (NKZ 113:109). Hence the allusion to the love of God, far from supporting the idea of an independent thou, only reconfirms the self as an absolute center of reality.

Other citations: NKZ 6: 260, 273, 348, 390, 391, 420–1.

24 JAPANESE CULTURE, WORLD CULTURE. The essay comparing cultures east and west is partially translated in 1970b, 237–54. ➤ Although based on a rather limited set of translations, Yoo's doctoral thesis (1976) brings together a readable summary of Nishida's general ideas on Japanese culture, and does so with a sensitivity to the questions generally lacking in western appreciations.

Until quite recently, the leading representatives of the Kyoto-school philosophy in Japan had made no serious attempt to parry the criticisms that had been raised against Nishida's political statements during the war. A conference to discuss the question was organized in 1994, at which time UEDA Shizuteru prepared a lengthy judgment on Nishida's political philosophy (1995D) in which he argues his position of the "tug-of-war over meanings." Although I edited out a good deal of the text while working on the translation, Ueda himself later published a still longer version of the original in Japanese (1998A). YUSA's paper, prepared for the same symposium, slants the events entirely in Nishida's favor, casting aside all criticism with citations from his works and private papers (1995C; see also her earlier account of 1989, where many of the same points are made). ➤ LAVELLE (1994B) flatly rejects as "inexact" the claim that Nishida took formulas from official doctrines and gave them different meanings, claiming instead that he used them to probe the deeper meanings of those doctrines. There is no evidence given for this and plenty of evidence to the contrary. At the very least, his opinions should be read in tandem with the no less critical but withal fairer presentation of STEVENS (2000). ➤ FURUTA makes a case that Nishida's conscious opposition to fascism and ultranationalism had no effect for the reason that it added the "ideal dialectic" to the very thing he was opposing (1956, 452), concluding that therefore embracing Nishida's aims requires overcoming the content of his philosophy (465).

By 1942 Nishida was completely fed up with the Ministry of Education's "insanities" and encouraged his disciples to have nothing to do with them (Kōyama 1949, 85). ➤ Miki is surely correct when he says that Nishida's departure from mere imitation of western philosophy "was not the result of any Japanism or Orientalism but lay at the fountainhead of his own political philosophy":

> From here on, philosophy will have to be *world philosophy*, and what I have in mind in saying this is that it is here that Nishida's philosophy can make its distinctive mark. The point is important. The "logic of nothingness" that seems to leave you prostrate in awe, is in fact a world logic.

The context makes it plain that Miki means both that Nishida's philosophy is *for* the world, and that it is a philosophy *about* the world (Miki 1986, 10: 412, 419–20).

Other citations: Nishida 1970b, 237, 249; nkz 12: 385–94; 13: 116; 18: 544–5, 621; 19: 28–9, 110.

25 **THE TURN TO POLITICAL PHILOSOPHY.** The slogan 富国強兵, *enrich the country, strengthen the military,* goes hand in hand with another, 尊皇攘夷, *honor the emperor, expel the barbarians,* to express the desire of the Japanese leadership to extricate Japan from the treaties that had been imposed on it at the time it reopened its doors to the rest of the world.

In making his educated guess as to what Nishida's idea of the state would be, Miki adds a farsighted criticism of his own to the effect that he finds Nishida too "idealist" and thinks that he weakens his dialectic by removing the ingredient of praxis from the time of the historical world. He recognizes here the point of Tanabe's logic of the specific (see §§33–34) but thinks that in the end both Nishida and Tanabe seem to see only discontinuity in the relations among particular societies (1986, 10: 419–26).

The passages from his diary can be found in nkz 17: 129–30. Ueda Shizuteru cites the second passage from the diaries, critical of the war celebrations, conveniently neglecting the former (1995b, 41). ➤ Many helpful details about Nishida's reactions to the events of the 1930s have been gathered together and carefully documented, though with a clear bias towards Nishida's innocence and a tendency to value passing bits of comments made in personal correspondence the same as extended statements made in published texts, by Yusa (1995c, 1998a, 445–91). ➤ The most famous attack on Nishida from the right was written by Minoda Muneki in the pages of a rightist magazine called『原理日本』*[Principium Nipponica]* 14 (1938), 3–22. Nishida dismissed it as fascist claptrap (nkz 19: 33). ➤ Arima suggests that Nishida's aim was an "emancipation of the self from society" for an inner harmony, which in turn required harmony and the absence of conflict in the political sphere. He places Nishida among those who retreated to academia "as a way of nursing the emotional wounds they had experienced in being removed from the limelight of historical events" (1969, 11–13). I have a difficult time reconciling these opinions with the more complex facts of the matter.

A short piece by KRACHT (1984), concluding that Nishida had replaced Hegel's theodicy with his own "satanodicy," may be cited as an example of the sort of extreme and uninformed bias Nishida's political ideas have prompted. ➤ One finds this kind of bias prevalent in present-day Japan among conservative Christian intellectuals opposed to the imperial system. To cite one recent example, a dialogue between Shinpo Yūji and Tomioka Kōichirō, 『日本の正統』 *[The true tradition of Japan]* (Tokyo, Chōbunsha, 1995) refers to Nishida's philosophy as a "Battleship Yamato" in that it defined its task primarily in terms of an attack on the west (28–9), and adding later that the reason there are so many interpretations of Nishida is that he did not even understand himself (136). ➤ A fair overview of postwar reactions to Nishida can be found in UEYAMA, who argues that attempts to dismiss Nishida as fascist are too one-sided and often based on an incorrect association of him with his disciples, notably Tanabe and the *Chūōkōron* discussions (see the text and notes to §52 below). His own conclusion is that Nishida's political philosophy was abstract and bourgeois, basically extracted from ideas in his early writings (1971, 75–138), more or less supporting my conclusion that his political philosophy was not very remarkable.

Ueda suggests that in referring to the imperial household Nishida deliberately spoke of a self-identity of contradictories, omitting the qualifier *absolute* in order to distance himself from those who preached the divinization of the emperor (see NKZ 12: 334–5). The reference can be found in the notes to §18 above. ➤ YAMADA Munemutsu, a critic of the Kyoto school's involvement in the politics of the day, defends Nishida's philosophy as not having shared in the support of the imperial system (1978, 221–304).

Other citations: NKZ 12: 375–83; 14: 405–6.

26 RUDIMENTS OF A POLITICAL PHILOSOPHY. Nishida's remark on the occasion of his brother's death appears in NKZ 13: 170. ➤ Although the page references of the translation of extracts from *The Question of Japanese Culture* indicates that the last section has been included, in fact it is omitted in its entirety (NISHIDA 1958D). ➤ Quotations from the 『国体の 本義』, *Principles of the National Polity,* can be found in *Kokutai no Hongi: Cardinal Principles of the National Entity of Japan*, translated by J. O. Gauntlett (Cambridge: Harvard University Press, 1949), 134, 126. ➤ The symbolism of the Shinto myths and their relation to the emperor system is already referred to in *The Question of Japanese Culture* (NKZ 12: 335–8), where he parallels it to the Christian west and the Holy Roman Empire.

JACINTO has gone to great lengths to pull out from Nishida's works ideas related to one or other aspect of political philosophy and weave them into a composite whole (1994). I have found his efforts helpful for composing my résumé here, particularly because of his constant reference back to the original texts. At the same time, I think he is being entirely too generous in presenting these ideas as a significant contribution to Nishida's thought, let alone to the political philosophy of Japan at the time, or political philosophy that transcends Nishida's day. ➤ In his 1988 doctoral thesis Huh takes a still more favorable view of Nishida's political thought, placing it on a par with his theory of self-awareness. For a time, Nishida may have agreed with him; I cannot.

Regarding Nishida's attachment to the imperial family, Yusa is surely correct in seeing this as the normal attitude of the day, opposed by very few (though hardly "only the Communist party," as she suggests), and undeserving of criticism from the postwar viewpoint (1989, 292–3). The same could be said of Tanabe and Nishitani as well. ➤ A most helpful, though of course partial, survey of the views of Nishida's political involvements has been prepared by Arisaka. Her own casual and unimaginative conclusion, that Nishida could have chosen to remain silent had he fundamentally disagreed with the government's expansionist policies (1996a, 95), is no indication of the care with which she has done the rest of her work. If I understand her correctly, I agree with the conclusion she presents in her doctoral thesis, that Nishida's use of his thought for political purposes is merely "contingent"—but not for her reasons (1996b, 237–8). ➤ Regarding the strange composition of the 1943 essay on "The Principle of the New World Order," see Yusa 1989, 288–90; 1998a, 469–70.

Kume has given us a useful critique of Nishida's fundamental failure to introduce the social dimension in his philosophy, as Tanabe had pointed out, along with a critique of Tanabe for having failed to follow through on the consequences of his "logic of the specific" (1999). ➤ Agustín Jacinto informs me that my assessment of Nishida's failure to produce a political philosophy was the viewpoint Shimomura Toratarō presented in late lectures on Nishida's thought, but I have not been able to locate a clear statement to this effect in his writings on Nishida.

Other citations: nkz 10: 333; 12: 271, 337, 403, 405–6, 409–10, 417; 19: 418.

27 **religion, god, and inverse correlation.** Regarding the composition and publication of Nishida's final essay, see the reminiscences of Ōshima Yasumasa in the publisher's leaflet for nkz 4. ➤ Recognizing the difficulty of reading the essay on its own, Dilworth has attempted an interpretative translation, transplanting terms from continental philosophy freely and paraphrasing arguments to give connections that he, as a seasoned reader of Nishida, reckons to be consistent with the wider framework of his thought (Nishida 1987b; a partial earlier draft was published in Nishida 1970c). I would, however, refer the reader rather to Yusa's more literal rendering (Nishida 1986) on the assumption that the previous pages of my explanation have not been in vain.

By combining *soku* 即 (see notes to §18 above), with the negative particle *hi* 非, we have the formula of *soku-hi* 即非, or affirming by negating. The classic source for this is the *Diamond Sūtra* saying that "All things are because all things just as they are, are not." Nishida cites the passage without identifying it (nkz 11: 399). The reference was provided by D. T. Suzuki, who had been prompted to seek out a philosophical logic for Zen by reading Nishida. In citing Suzuki indirectly, Nishida is acknowledging the importance of Suzuki's change of heart in this matter (see notes to §§18 and 45). Regarding the differences of the two in the interpretation of this notion, see TAKEMURA 1997. ➤ From a Zen standpoint the reactions are mixed. HIGASHI (1985) has questioned Nishida's way of applying Suzuki's idea of *soku-hi* to his idea of no-self and its effect on his reading of Dōgen (as well as his rejection of Tanabe's reading of Dōgen). HASHI, in contrast, takes the opposite view of Nishida's reading of Dōgen, and finds that it opens Zen's horizons (1997). AKIZUKI Ryōmin, while acknowledging the discrepancies, shows how Nishida's idea of inverse correlation addresses the difference a philosophical approach requires (1996, part 1).

The idea of inverse correlation was introduced too late to be further developed, but those closest to Nishida considered it a major development. Perhaps it is best understood in contrast with that of *soku* as another way of speaking of the "self-identity of absolute contradictories." To take the paradigmatic example of the God-human relation, instead of speaking in terms of the direct correlation of a "divinity-*in*-humanity" (or Buddha and sentient beings, absolute and relative, finite and infinite), Nishida reverses the role of the "in" to mean that the more God is fully divine (self-emptying) and therefore the greater the distance from humanity, the more we who relate to God become fully human (self-aware); and the more fully human we are and the greater our distance from God, the more our idea of God is truly divine. If God is a negation of humanity, that very negation reaffirms humanity; and vice-versa. In this sense, it is a principle of "paradox" that goes beyond a mere dialectic of mutual negation to include the negation of the negation. ➤ On the importance of the idea of inverse correlation for Nishida, see, for example, the comments by Yamanouchi Tokuryū in the publisher's leaflet for NKZ 1. For a much fuller and more nuanced treatment, see KOSAKA (1994, 278–343), and the shorter treatment in NUMATA 1984, 213–27. A brief summary of the relationship of the idea to Nishida's earlier logic of relationships can be found in SASAKI (1977, 93–102). ➤ It may be noted that, in a rare reference to Nishida in his late writings, Tanabe accepted the idea of inverse correlation as having bettered the idea of the self-identity of absolute contradictories as a description of the relationship between being and nothingness (THZ 11: 492). ➤ DILWORTH prefers to render "inverse correlation" as "inverse polarity" and stresses the relation between God and the self as one of mutually mirroring images, each inverting the other (1987, 31–2). Although the idea of opposite poles on a field of force, imported from Whitehead, does not strike me as appropriate, the idea of the mirror-image is surely one Nishida would have known from the mystics (for instance, in Angelus Silesius, for whom the eye with which I see God is the eye with which God sees me).

The sense of religion as something the self *requires* (NKZ 1: 169) or *demands* (NISHIDA 1990C, 149) recalls the notion of "drive" in *An Inquiry into the Good* (see notes to §12 above). ➤ Nishida wrote an introduction to the second edition of *Philosophy as Repentance* (『懺悔としての哲学』) of Nozaki, which appeared after

Tanabe's similarly titled *Philosophy as Metanoetics* (『懺悔道としての哲学』). For further details about Nozaki and his relationship with Nishida, see Kamimura Takeo, 『哲学徒と詩人—西田幾多郎をめぐる短い生の四つの肖像』 *[Philosophy students and poets: Portraits of four brief lives surrounding Nishida Kitarō]* (Osaka: Henshūshobō Noah, 1985), 197–246. ➤ Nishida's lecture notes from his first course on religion have been included in his *Complete Works* (NKZ 15: 221–381). On the basis of these notes, YUSA has tried to present a more or less composite picture of Nishida's view of religion, but the contexts and time period separating the ideas cited are really too motley, and his generalizations of Christianity and Buddhism often too much adjusted to the purposes of the classroom, to justify the simple weave of word-associations she uses to fit everything on the same loom (1998B). ➤ Details of the way in which Nishida taught religion are provided by Hisamatsu Shin'ichi in the concluding commentary of NKZ 15.

A consequence of NISHIDA's lack of concern with religious practice and its relationship to received tradition is that he lands himself easily in a position that contradicts what scholars have seen to be the most distinctive qualities of Japanese religiosity, namely, its focus on ritual as the keystone of tradition. Rather than contrast this with the western preoccupation with doctrine, he sees concern with ritual form as characteristic of what Christianity took from the Greeks (1970B, 279–80). This, however, was part of his general cultural theory that by the time of his final essay had been laid quietly to rest. ➤ Although NISHIDA himself refers to his idea of God as an "absolute," not as "Absolute Being" as Yusa's translation has it throughout (1986), the context makes it clear that God belongs to the world of being.

Only at the end of his essay does Nishida make one last attempt, in a most confusing if brief final section, to salvage the outlines of his cultural and political philosophy under the rubric of the historicity of religion. What he intends to argue is that religion must be independent of the state and culture, and yet belong to both of them at the roots. In his earlier political writings he had claimed that it was not the salvation of the individual but surrender to the absolute that was the main goal of religion, which can then be shown to be present, analogically, in surrender to the state as the incarnation of the absolute ethnic society in the historical world. Hence he had concluded that "the state, as moral substance, does not contradict religion." His appended remarks in the final essay add the necessary qualifications to liberate those ideas from the ideological context, but probably would have been best omitted, given the weakness of the original theory and the focus of this essay. ➤ The ellipses in the passage disassociating religion from personal salvation and peace of mind (NISHIDA 1958C, 236) add the comment that national ethics can be seen as the fruit of religion and therefore as not contradicting it.

Other citations: NISHIDA 1958C, 238; 1973A, 118–19, 236; 1986, 25; NKZ 11: 399; 13: 72, 76–7; 19: 417.

Tanabe Hajime (1885–1962)

28 TANABE'S LIFE AND CAREER. Tanabe's self-deprecating remarks about his abilities in mathematics (THZ 5: 95) are given the lie by his series of books and essays on mathematics, as well as his work on the natural sciences. See TAKEUCHI Yoshinori 1986, xxxii. ➤ Tanabe first met Nishida in 1913 at a supper after a lecture Nishida delivered to the Tokyo Philosophical Society (NKZ 17: 313).

I use the term "Freiburg school" in accord with the use of the time. It is now more commonly known as the Southern German school. ➤ TAKAHASHI, who had himself studied with Husserl three years after Tanabe, reports that Husserl was not impressed with Nishida's "intuitionism" as Tanabe presented it (1973B, 221). Tanabe's dissatisfaction with Husserl was due at least in part to his heavy psychologism (TANABE 1986, 70). ➤ Tanabe shared an office with Gadamer when he was studying with Husserl (YUSA 1998C, 63). ➤ Colleagues of his at the time remember that Tanabe spoke of his task as "bringing logical rigor to Nishida's thought" (see the recollection of Akizuki Yasuo in the publisher's leaflet for THZ 2).

If I have omitted mention of the conflict between Tanabe and Nishida in the chapter on Nishida, it is because, having reviewed what I could find on the subject and discussed it with those who have recollections closer to the history of their relationship, I conclude it was by and large Tanabe's problem. Where I disagree is with the conclusion that there was no major philosophical disagreement among them. For example, even so astute a reader of Nishida and Tanabe as TAKIZAWA wrote as late as 1947 that "Tanabe's thought does not take so much as a single step beyond Nishida's early thought" (1972, 10: 153), an opinion that further investigation of the texts seems to have changed (see notes to §46 below). ➤ Nishida's remark on Tanabe's heartlessness appears in a letter in which he vents his own feelings in no uncertain terms: "That fellow—if you don't look closely, you're not even sure if he's alive or not" (NKZ 18: 629). ➤ The last work Tanabe published while Nishida was alive, *Philosophy as Metanoetics*, nowhere mentions the name of his teacher, though in a number of contexts it is clearly Nishida he has in mind in his criticisms. Nishida's final essay, published in the same year, treats Tanabe in the same way.

The saying on the gravestone is a quotation from a tribute Tanabe wrote for Heidegger on his seventieth birthday under the title "Ontology of Life or Dialectics of Death?" (THZ 13: 529). The phrase was intended, in its original context, to temper his praise for Heidegger with an assertion of his own prior commitment to philosophy. It was inspired by a proverb Tanabe had found in Carlyle: *Amicus Plato, magis amica veritas* (*Sartor Resartus*, chap. 2). The saying itself goes back to Plato (*Phaedo*, 91), and was rendered later in Latin by Ammonius in his *Life of Aristotle*. The idea to use it on Tanabe's headstone was suggested by Tsujimura Kōichi, who had done the German translation of the piece on Heidegger with the help of Hartmut Buchner (Tanabe, 1959a), and approved by the family and Nishitani Keiji. The Chinese characters for *search* 希求 are particularly appropriate here in that the first of them, an abbreviation for "Greece," was used in one of the first names Nishi Amane devised to translate the term "philosophy," 希哲学. Regarding the motives for Tanabe's self-enforced isolation, see the reminiscences of Kōyama 1964: 160. On life in the mountain villa, see Kawashima 1997, 63–4. ➤ In addition to the sources mentioned above, further information about Tanabe's life and temperament can be found in: Abe Yoshishige, 1951; Ōshima 1951; Takahashi 1962; Nakano 1975, 425–58; and the personal recollections in Takeuchi, Mutō, and Tsujimura, 1991, part 2. I would also mention the recollections of Nunokawa Kakuzaemon of the Iwanami Press, which show the brusque, even offensive, manner he had of treating people (publisher's leaflet to thz 2). After Tanabe's death, at his request, a portion of his personal library went to Kyoto University and the majority, some 8,000 volumes, to Gunma University along with the land and buildings of his mountain villa, which Ishizawa Kaname rehabilitated for use. The library also contains 206 notebooks, which should provide clues to the development of Tanabe's thought. For further details, see Ishizawa 1996, 33), and Kawashima 1998b, 323–5.

Other citation: Aihara, 1951, 270.

29 tanabe's philosophical style. Tanabe's inveterate search for systematic unity and logical consistency is confirmed in a commentary on his late work by Nishitani Keiji (thz 13: 646–7). ➤ The closest Tanabe came to "journalistic" writing are the essays gathered in volume 8 of his *Collected Works*, which contains his comments on politics national and international, but always written with the same logical rigor and, as Ōshima Yasumasa calls it, "Platonistic" style (see commentary to thz 8: 485). Additional short pieces and a small sampling of the classical-style poems that were regularly written at the end of his notebooks—as many as 1,000 in all—are included in the second half of volume 14. ➤ One of his university classmates recalls how Tanabe was introverted and totally given to his academic work. He would compare his teachers' interpretations with the original texts, "until eventually one had to wonder whether he had come to the school to learn or to criticize his teachers' lectures" (Fujiwara Yuishin, publisher's supplement to vol. 3 of thz). ➤ The recollection of Tanabe as "the trawler" comes from a remark by Kuyama Yasushi in 1961 (see Nishitani 1981b, 143). Kuyama also suggests that Nishida was like Dostoevsky, who was able to gain a deep sense of life from everything he read and saw, whereas Tanabe was more like Tolstoy for his concern to reshape reality and criticize religion.

Regarding his presence in the classroom and attitude towards his students, see Takeuchi Yoshinori 1990, 2–4; Hanazawa 1999, 42; and the recollection of Saitō Yoshikazu in the publisher's leaflet for vol. 1 of nkc. Kimura Motomori is reported to have said of Tanabe as a mentor that he was like a lion that tossed its cubs into the valley and would only raise those that could climb up out of it (from Kuyama's recollections in the publisher's leaflet to THZ 10).

Takeuchi suggests in those same reminiscences that if Tanabe had given in to the impulse to resign, "to this day it is my belief that he would have ended up committing suicide" (5).

Tanabe's writings on literature include only essays on Valéry and Mallarmé, in both of whom he sought correlates to his own philosophical ideas rather than an appreciation of their role or value as literature. We also know that Tanabe read and was moved by Rilke's *Book of Hours* (from a letter, cited in TAKEUCHI Yoshinori 1986, XXXVII). ➤ Tanabe's *Complete Works* were published between 1963 and 1964, and reprinted during 1972 and 1973. ➤ A scattered, and now largely dated, list of works on Tanabe was appended to the publisher's leaflet for THZ 15.

30 **PURE EXPERIENCE, OBJECTIVE KNOWLEDGE, MORALITY.** For an overview of Tanabe's early work, see KAWASHIMA 1998A. ➤ Tanabe took the expression *thetic judgment* from Alois Riehl, under whom he would later study. Riehl's use of the term more or less coincides with the way Husserl used the word, namely, to distinguish the pure judgment about an object from any perceptual interference on the part of the perceiving subject. The essay, which opens the first volume of his *Complete Works*, runs to a mere eight pages but shows the breadth of Tanabe's reading in European philosophy.

MARALDO's conclusion, like that of Nishitani, that Tanabe did not differ as much from Nishida as he thought, seems by and large correct. But he slights Tanabe's originality, and this shows up in the short remarks he makes about Tanabe's dialectics in a splendid overview of contemporary Japanese philosophy (1997, 817–18).

Other citations: THZ 1: 92; 2: 4, 152–3; 3: 69.

31 **PURE RELATIONSHIP, ABSOLUTE MEDIATION.** Concerning Tanabe's reading on the boat back to Japan, see Kōyama Iwao's "Commentary," THZ 3: 525. ➤ In his 1948 comments on the essay on Kant's teleology, Tanabe acknowledges that it was a topic he had no reason to select except that he was under obligation to do so. That he should credit "fate" with its importance rather than Nishida, who made the request of him, indicates a certain distance from his teacher already at that time (THZ 3: 8).

In *An Inquiry into the Good* NISHIDA had already insisted that "reality comes into being through interrelationship" (1990C, 59) and in an essay published just prior to that book claimed that his idea of pure experience allowed for "internal" (that is, self-unfolding) connection among experiences whereas James's had been merely external (NKZ 13: 97). Tanabe knew this essay, of course, but it is gratuitous to say that he "took" these ideas from Nishida, just as it is to downplay the differences between Tanabe and Nishida on the grounds that the same things can be found in both of them. To compare a *bon mot* from Nishida—in which his works abound—with the developed arguments of Tanabe is to see Nishida as a kind of scripture in which all doctrine is prefigured.

The concept of "dialectics" initially owed more to Cohen than to Hegel, though its usefulness may have been instrumental in turning Tanabe closer to Hegel in later following years (Kawashima 1999, 54). ➤ Tanabe acknowledges the helpful suggestions he got for his idea of absolute dialectics through discussion with Miki and Tosaka, whom he refers to as his friends (THZ 3: 78). ➤ It was not only from Hegel that Tanabe took over the idea of a logic that supersedes the law of noncontradiction. He had already struggled with this question in a 1925 book on *Studies in the Philosophy of Mathematics,* where he attempts to show the generation of numbers through a series of contradictions (THZ 2: 419–24), and to suggest cryptically that this supports Nishida's idea of thought as a "system of self-expression" that takes place through changes in the self (427). Kawashima says that Tanabe relates these mathematical discussions to Fichte's idea of the ego as an act-fact (1998a, 50), but I have not been able to locate any such reference in Tanabe's text.

Nishitani sees the impact of the shadow of Nishida at work elsewhere, noting, "Curiously, it almost seems as if the principle of negation that thoroughly opposes and rejects the tendency of the self-awareness of absolute nothingness to embrace all things gives us a mirror-image of Tanabe himself desperately struggling to escape the embrace of Nishida's philosophy" (1991a, 167). ➤ The debate between Fredericks, who published an essay for *The Eastern Buddhist* dealing with the difference in the idea of absolute nothingness between Nishida and Tanabe (1989), and Ives, who tried to parry the charges against Nishida (1989), is weakened from the start by the absence in both accounts of attention to Nishitani's considerable reflections on his two teachers. Unfortunately, Maraldo does no better when he later adds his remarks to the debate (1990, 249–55).

The most notable exception to the neglect of Tanabe in the west is the book-length study of Laube (1984) of Tanabe's idea of absolute mediation. Laube bases his study principally on a popular series of introductory lectures on philosophy, to which he overlays his own schematic of the interplay between the immanent and the transcendent in history. From Tanabe's later works he concludes that Tanabe, as indeed all of the Kyoto school philosophers, basically aimed for a synthesis between traditions of Buddhist and Christian inspiration (1994, 423). Laube has done more than anyone to stimulate interest in Tanabe in the German-speaking world (Brüll 1989, 169–81, and Koch 1990, 34–46, rely on it almost exclusively), and to relate it to theological concerns. My chief disagreements with him are two. First, there is the question of emphasis. The idea that he finds central in Tanabe I see as having gradually moved to the periphery as a working assumption, and as too abstract to explain the core of Tanabe's achievement. Secondly, no attempt is made to explain Tanabe's fall into nationalism and the consequences for his philosophy.

The use of the *soku* copulative appears throughout Tanabe's work in much the same sense as it had with Nishida. Tanabe does not draw any particular attention to it, but beginning with *Philosophy as Metanoetics* it appears with much greater regularity than before.

32 A REINTERPRETATION OF ABSOLUTE NOTHINGNESS. It should not be forgotten that from early on Nishida was also swept up in the imaginative power of the Hegelian system and its aftermath. His own response focused mainly on the relationship between transformation of consciousness and the self-transformation of the world. The similarities with Tanabe's response are far more striking than the differences, though the particular circumstances in which their two philosophical systems took shape tended to obscure the fact during the years of Tanabe's mature work. On this point, see Nishitani's important essay, "The Philosophies of Nishida and Tanabe" in 1991A, 210–11.

It is Nishitani who compares Tanabe's absolute nothingness with Nishida's in terms of the distinction between the differential and the integral, a distinction that actually comes from Tanabe's *Metanoetics.* Basing himself on a distinction he had introduced in his 1931 book *Hegelian Philosophy and Dialectics,* Tanabe distinguishes the former as the standpoint of faith-act and the latter as immediate intuition. Nishitani is correct that he has Nishida in mind for the latter.

IENAGA has brought many of Tanabe's early comments on the state together nicely in his *Studies in the History of Tanabe's Thought*, 35–46. Even though Tanabe was later to be accused of identifying the providential advance of history with the Japanese nation, as late as 1936 even so astute a critic as TAKAHASHI Satomi could criticize him for having slid a Kantian subjectivism back into his view of history (1973A: 221–67).

The passage on nothingness as central to philosophy (THZ 9: 273) appears in a context that reads almost like a paraphrase of the pattern relative nothingness–nihility–absolute nothingness (279-85), which is central to Nishitani's *Religion and Nothingness*, a work whose composition would begin only seven years later. ➤ The expression *absolute nothingness* originates with Nishida and the Kyoto school, but the Chinese term they use for *absolute*, 絶対, had already found its way into standard philosophical translation. Literally it means "cutting off of any opposite" in contrast to *relative*, 相対, which means "facing an opposite." Earlier Chinese philosophy has used the term 絶待 and 相待 to stress the cutting off of mutuality or dependency. For precedents to the idea of an absolute, nondependent nothingness in Chinese thought, see LAI 1990, 258–60.

On Tanabe's idea of the need for bridging the gap between the ideal and the actual, see ŌHASHI 1991. ➤ Tanabe left his studies in Germany with the idea of combining a philosophy of life with a philosophy of the human sciences.

Other citations: TANABE 1986, 98; THZ 6: 156.

33 THE ORIGINS OF THE LOGIC OF THE SPECIFIC. On Tanabe's reading of Bergson, see HASE 1994, 2. ➤ Regarding Tanabe's own account of the origins of logic of the specific, see "Clarifying the Logic of the Specific" and "Response to Criticisms of the Logic of the Specific," both in vol. 6 of THZ. These two essays speak more of the formal logic of the idea, in response to his critics. Regarding criticisms of the political consequences, during the formative years of the idea he omits mention of his critics or their criticisms. ➤ Although Tanabe does not later draw particular attention to the fact, during the early years of his idea he penned an essay on "The Relationship of Religion and Culture" (1934) in which he took up the "dialectical theology" of Barth and Brunner, suggesting that his dialectic could overcome the polar opposition their idea of the absolute alterity of God set up between religion and culture, and between faith and reason (THZ 5: 61–80).

In 1946 Tanabe wrote that his idea of a logic of the specific was "originally suggested by Hegel's objective spirit" (TANABE 1969, 274; see also TAKEUCHI Yoshinori 1990, 7–10). Standing between the subjective spirit of individual consciousness and the absolute spirit of history, the customs, traditions, and laws of a society are the objective spirit that specify and limit the absolute spirit on the one hand and bind and control the subjective spirit on the other. Only to the extent that this determination is an embodiment of the absolute nothingness that is the true ground of the absoluteness of history can it be said to enhance, rather than frustrate, the freedom of the individual.

Despite a small number of references to this connection with Hegel in his earlier essays, it seems to me that the introduction of the notion of the specific to explain objective spirit was rather an attempt to break his idea of absolute mediation away from the imposing shadow of Hegel's scheme. I must admit I have trouble understanding this claim as far as the purely logical structure of the scheme goes. Tanabe's first outline of the logic of the specific opens with a brief critique of Hegel's lack of concreteness in the *Science of Logic*, and makes a brief allusion to the *Phenomenology of Mind*. But in reading through the third part of the *Logic*, where the idea of the concrete universal is discussed and where Hegel makes his case for the cooperative interplay of universal, species, and individual, I have to say I find nothing terribly suggestive of Tanabe's reading. Tanabe's idea is that the three parts of the *Logic* correspond to logics of the specific, the individual, and the universal, respectively. I know of no one else who reads Hegel this way, and in fact Tanabe himself may have realized this later, as his main point here—that the logic of general predication found in part 1 (Being) "leaves no room for doubt that it corresponds to a logic of the specific"—is not repeated in later writings (THZ 6: 71–4). On the other hand, the influence of the *Philosophy of Right* on Tanabe's development of the idea of the nation is both explicit and to the point in his early essays.

Not too much should be made of the term *race* here, which did not have all the connotations it has today. The Japanese term Tanabe used, *minzoku,* could as well mean *ethnos* or simply *Volk*. On this, see DOAK 1995. ➤ HIMI is right that a careful reading shows that Tanabe used the phrase *Blut und Boden* as an example of a closed totemic society (1990A, 97–8); I do not find reference to the term, however, in the 1934 essay, but only in a later essay dating from 1940 (THZ 8: 146). After the war, when it was clear where Tanabe's new logic had eventually led him, the phrase *Blut und Boden* was cited as proof of his rightist tendencies, without regard for its original context. See YAMADA Munemutsu 1975, 47. ➤ On Tanabe's critique of this idea and of Heidegger, see THZ 8: 8.

Other citations: THZ 1: 444; 3: 76–7; 6: 466.

34 THE SPECIFIC AND THE SOCIOCULTURAL WORLD. The direction in which Tanabe took his conviction that mediation is real and not just an abstracted reflection of the real, is as different from Nishida's logic of place as it is from what Hegel does with the same conviction in the *Science of Logic*. Tanabe's rejection of Nishida's "self-identity of absolute contradictories" as slipping into a contemplation of a static, quasi-Plotinean One that neglected the role of negative mediation (TANABE 1986, 45, 89; THZ 4: 307, 315) has to be read today, I think, less as a fair appraisal of his senior colleague than as his way of underlining the utter reality he wished to grant to mediation (NISHITANI 1991A, 173–5). Nishida never challenged Tanabe on this directly in print, but KOSAKA has argued that the idea of "inverse correlation" was Nishida's attempt to answer Tanabe's criticism (1994, 281).

Tanabe's departure from Hegel is more studied. Hegel saw logical mediation as a misty reflection of reality, a self-estrangement of Thought from itself, a temporary detour away from phenomenal being in search of the essential substrate of things, which would eventually wind its way back to the self-consciousness of Spirit. In this way he argued that logic needs to be freed of its traditional attachment to abstract notions of the universal and the specific as mere names for common features shared by concrete individuals in order to show Thought functioning in the unfolding of history as a concrete universal and a concrete specificity.

In addition to comments in the opening pages of the 1932 essay responding to his critics (THZ 6: 3ff), he suggests in a 1938 essay on "Logic from Kant to Hegel" that Hegel's critique of Kant needs to be complemented by a reverse critique in which Kant's concrete "Platonic" practical reason could challenge the abstract and "Plotinean" aspects of Hegel's Absolute Spirit (see especially THZ 5: 400–4). There he fills out an idea that he alludes to in a 1931 essay on "Dialectics and Hegel's Philosophy" (THZ 3: 134). In addition, his longer essays on Hegel at that time often refer to taking the ethical and historical dimension of Hegel more seriously than Hegel himself had. ➤ The rethinking of the classical syllogism was not something Tanabe thought he had accomplished with a single stroke. He tracked his idea through the history of the syllogism from Socrates through Aquinas and Scotus (THZ 7: 213ff).

Other citations: THZ 6: 145; 7: 261–2.

35 THE SPECIFIC AND THE NATION. PIOVESANA's account of Tanabe's thought (1963, 145–58), though providing valuable historical information, is somewhat confused on the whole. In particular, it rather badly misses the place of the nation in Tanabe's logic of the specific. ➤ LAUBE glosses over the role of the state as a relative absolute in concluding that for Tanabe "religion by its nature represents genus, while the state represents species" (1984, 280). For a more careful but condensed account of the place of the nation in Tanabe's logical scheme, see HIMI 1990A, 104–17, and 1990B. ➤ On Tanabe's critique of Bergson, see THZ 6: 147; on theocracy, 6: 149–53.

36 AN AMBIVALENT NATIONALISM. HIMI argues that there was an unquestioned bias at work in Tanabe's mind that made him read the species not as a philosophical category in the strict sense but as "no more than a euphemism for Japanese ethnic unity" (1990B, 311). I think he may be simplifying Tanabe's motivations, but his conclusion is certainly correct as far as the results go.

Tanabe had trouble drawing a straight line from Taishō democracy to Taishō philosophy, which for him was a humanism and a "cultivationism" and did not represent a true basis for the ideals of Taishō democracy. The political Taishō democracy and cultural Taishō humanism and cultivationism ran parallel but rarely communicated with each other. Apart from a slight overlap in the "concept of culture," the waves of Taishō democracy hardly reached Tanabe at all. IENAGA (1988, 5–6) argues that he accepted the positive significance of *culturism* only in the sense of a metaphysical culturism that broke through the crude antipolitical and antisocial culturism he saw as distinctive of Taishō thinkers. He draws on the analysis of Funayama Shin'ichi, 『大正哲学史研究』 *[Studies in the history of Taishō philosophy]* and compares it with an essay of Tanabe's on "The Concept of Culture" (THZ 1: 423–47).

The book on the case of Takigawa, 『先輩の見た京大事件』 *[The Kyoto University affair as seen by senior colleagues]*, appeared in July of 1933, just three months after the affair broke out. Just how important Tanabe's role was is difficult to say. His name is not mentioned in the account of Takigawa and those immediately involved, which was published in October as 『京大事件』 *[The Kyoto University affair]* (Tokyo: Iwanami, 1933) under the editorship of Takigawa Yukitoki and six others involved in the events.One has only to glance through the account of the events to realize how ridiculously complicated the Ministry of Education made things, and to understand perhaps something of how ideological differences at the time could flame passions on the slimmest of pretexts. The only intellectual content has to do with the supposed danger of Takigawa's views that crimes against society do not emerge merely from some evil in the individual but can also be the result of society itself. Particularly interesting is how the government substituted the term *nation* for *society* in representing Takigawa's views (101); and also how the counterargument that runs through the book, once all the political maneuvering is set aside, is that the reason for making criticisms against the state was really to strengthen the sense of the "people's" identity (16). This seems to have been the mood of the time: a choice between ultranationalism and nationalism.

The quote on Heidegger appears in THZ 8: 8. When this volume of his collected works appeared, the editors thought it had never been published (8: 463). In fact, it appeared in the『朝日新聞』*Asahi News* of 4–6 October 1933 (see YUSA 1998c, 70). Two months later, MIKI singled it out as one of the leading events in the world of thought for that year (1986, 20: 106).

The letter to Jaspers is mentioned in IENAGA 1988, 64–6. His attempt to aid Jaspers—or more precisely his wife, who was Jewish—was related by Ōshima Yasumasa to TAKEUCHI Yoshinori, who was later told in person by Jaspers of his gratitude for the assistance Tanabe had lent him (1990, 11). Robert Schinzinger recounts his role as intermediary between the German ambassador and Tanabe, and Mutō Mitsuaki also recalls meeting with Jaspers after the war, who confirmed how helpful the interventions had been (see publisher's leaflet for THZ 6 and 7). ➤ Tanabe would draw on Jaspers's philosophy of religion in his late thought (e.g., THZ 9: 457ff).

Regarding Nishida's position in all of this, IENAGA quotes from the biography of Iwanami Shigeo here (1988, 50). He cites the postwar reflections of Nakajima Kenzō to support Tanabe's voiced opinion (51, 53). Tanabe's fear for his life is reported by Ueda Yasuharu in an explanatory postscript (THZ 5: 110). In *Metanoetics* Tanabe makes a similar remark about being ready to die for his views (189), which IENAGA surmises to have been exaggerated by Tanabe (1988, 65).

In defense of Tanabe, KAWASHIMA (1997, 61–2) sees the conflict of philosophies between Nishida and Tanabe as not simply the personal conflict they were aware of, but as also affected by the times in a way neither of them was fully conscious of. Nishida's attempts to secure the identity of the self within the context he was living, he says, were misread by some who shared his context and experience as a way to stand up to the rest of the world, and this misreading gave wings to his thought in places he never intended to fly. Tanabe was caught up in that draft, so that his critique and alternative logic of the specific ended up driving the delusions of those who wanted to bully the rest of the world into giving the Japanese nation a leading role it had never before known. It was precisely because their philosophies touched the feelings of emptiness in the Japanese soul that they were liable to abuse. True as this may be, and as much as one admires Kawashima's appreciation of Tanabe's genius and scholarly discipline, this kind of thinking begs the important question of the extent to which Tanabe agreed with this use of this thought. Kawashima himself admits that this is a question Tanabe's successors have yet to sort out satisfactorily (66).

The rightist attacks on Tanabe can be found in MINODA 1933 and MATSUDA 1933. Tanabe's response appears in THZ 8: 11–31. ➤ Tanabe's distinction between the *within* and the *without* is an attempt to locate himself in counterposition to the "humanitarianism" of Kōyama Iwao and the "individualism" of Nishida. ➤ The idea that service to the emperor was Japan's way to enter the community of nations as an open society is present in a book Tanabe wrote on *Historical Reality* (THZ 8: 166). ➤ I find it important that he avoided mentioning the *corpus mysticum* theology of State Shinto that saw the emperor as the *arahitogami* or God-appearing-in-human-form, who was the living soul of the Japanese nation.

The appeal to the cadets was printed in the *Kyoto University Newspaper* under the title "Farewell Words to Students on the Way to War: Awaken to the True Meaning of Conscription!" (THZ 14: 414–16). As far as I have been able to ascertain, it was not delivered orally, despite the rhetorical tone. ➤ The statement by Nishida on Tanabe's "fascism" was made to Aihara Shinsaku, who reports it in a brief "Recollections" affixed to vol. 12 of Tanabe's *Complete Works.* It is difficult to know how much of this was based on his distance from Tanabe, without knowing what Nishida thought of Nishitani's political views. ➤ Mention should also be made of Tosaka, who already in 1934 singles out Tanabe as a "fascist" (1970, 3: 170–84). ➤ Nishida's views on the relations of specific societies to the state are cited from NKZ 8: 288–9, 451; 9: 113, 144, 146.

Other citations: THZ 7: 30–2, 41, 79, 362; 8: 207–8; 6: 163, 232–3.

37 **CRITIQUES OF TANABE'S NATIONALISM.** At the time Nanbara's original book was published, Japan had already signed a treaty with the Nazis. As IENAGA points out, a close reading shows that, despite his criticism of Tanabe, Nanbara in fact judiciously avoided an explicit attack on the Nazis (1988, 143). ➤ Nishitani's remark can be found in『哲学年鑑』*[Philosophical yearbook]* 2 (1943): 93–4. The review was not included in his collected works. ➤ Nanbara's complaint that Tanabe's logic had slackened the tension between the ideal and the real was hardly original. In the same year that his book appeared, Akizawa Shūji raised similar doubts about the implicit "totalitarianism" of Tanabe's dialectical method (cited in IENAGA 1988, 196). ➤ Nanbara was attracted to Christianity in general, but in particular to the No-Church movement whose founder, Uchimura Kanzō, was still more outspoken against the government during the war years. After the war, Nanbara served a term as president of Tokyo University. ➤ An appendix was added to *State and Religio* for its inclusion in Nanbara's collected works and an apparently expurgated phrase restored. See IENAGA 1988, 142–3. ➤ The essay in which Tanabe acknowledges Nanbara's criticisms (THZ 7: 366–7) was actually composed during the war but only published in 1946.

Among those who attributed Tanabe's nationalism to his affections for Hegel is FURUTA Hikaru (1959, 278), who levels a general accusation against the thinkers of the Kyoto school, but later is more favorable to Nishida (1983, 145). ➤ YAMAMOTO Seisaku suggests that in fact the critique spurred Tanabe on to develop his idea of "metanoetics" and to reconsider the possibility that latent authoritarianism in the nation needs to be submitted to a higher, divine judgment of history (1987, 122). Yamamoto fails to mention, however, that after the war Nanbara sent Tanabe a collection of his own poems lamenting the war. This, together with Tanabe's response praising Nanbara for his efforts on behalf of freedom of thought, indicates that there was no lasting ill will between them over the public criticism.

Regarding Yamada Munemutsu's view that Tanabe's philosophy had shielded itself systematically from social questions, see IENAGA 1988, 185.

Other citations: IENAGA 1988, 143; NANBARA 1972, 264–5, 268–9, 274; YAMADA Munemutsu 1975, 46, 61, 87–8.

38 CRITIQUES OF TANABE'S POLITICAL NAÏVETÉ. Umehara's comments occur in the course of a criticism of remarks supporting the war made by the four principals of the *Chūōkōron* discussions: Kōyama Iwao, Kōsaka Masaaki, Suzuki Shigetaka, and Nishitani Keiji (see §52). ➤ KŌYAMA recalls the weakness philosophy teachers like himself felt in trying to face their students in class after the attack on Manchuria (1943, prologue).

The imperial philosophy (皇道哲学) to which Umehara alludes is associated with figures like Kihira Tadayoshi and Kanokogi Kazunobu. It should be noted that UMEHARA's conclusion that "Nishitani was a believer in the myth of the emperor's divinity" (1959, 34) is not only wrong, it squares clumsily with the claim of Umehara that he himself, while taken in by the ideology, was too sophisticated to swallow the idea of the emperor's centrality. Ironically, Umehara himself would go on to become known, at home and abroad, as one of the most outspoken ideologues of postwar Japanism.

Katō's quotation makes a literary reference to Shikitei Sanba, an early nineteenth-century satirist who wrote of conversations that took place in the public baths.

Other citations: KATŌ 1959, 346; THZ 8: 50, 64–5, 166, 178.

39 RESPONSE TO THE CRITICISMS. On Tanabe's hurt, see IENAGA 1988, 71. ➤ HIMI (1990A) argues that after *Philosophy as Metanoetics* the logic of the specific is no more than a smoldering ember that Tanabe never again managed to fan into flame. TAKEUCHI Yoshinori disagrees, claiming that his later work on the logic survived but underwent a major change (1986, xliii). If Takeuchi is correct, this change would have to lie in the return to religion as a complement to ethics, an idea already present in Tanabe's first reading of Bergson. ➤ For redefining the specific with looser ties to the nation, see THZ 7: 257–60. ➤ The suggestion of identifying the specific community with the church is HIMI's (1990A, 168).

The notion of the communion of saints, though a Christian one, seems to have been taken from Jaspers. On Tanabe's serious study of Jaspers's thought, see TAKEUCHI Yoshinori 1990, 6–7. ➤ At the prodding of Takahashi Satomi, Tanabe realized early on that there was a problem with exempting the specificity of society and nation from the rule of absolute mediation. But as the term he used for *immediate* did not on the surface indicate *unmediated*, it was not until he dislodged the nation from its central position in the logic of the specific that he reached a satisfactory solution to the criticism.

In his *Metanoetics* Tanabe repeats his claim that western democracy needs the "special characteristics of particular racial and social groups" in order to work in Japan and that "the imperial ideal at work in the political system of our nation is also democratic... at least in principle." Somehow, he continued to feel, only an amalgam of socialism and democracy would do for the modern world, and he claimed that this could come about only if all nations, democratic and social, engaged in metanoesis (TANABE 1986, LXI–LXII, 94). Obviously LAVELLE's claim (1994A, 450–53) that Tanabe had turned to western democracy in the *Metanoetics* is mistaken, as is his wholesale conclusion that Tanabe was an ultranationalist who saw Japan alone as capable of providing a model government for the new world order. His further assertion that Tanabe's politics were cut of the same cloth as Nishida's with the one exception that he saw the emperor, rather than the nation, as the unifying element for Japan, is also based on ignorance of the texts. The patchwork of phrases he slaps together is easily refuted by reading the very texts he himself cites, and all the more so by knowing more of their context.

Other citations: THZ 6: 452; 7: 253; 8: 370–1; 14: 439; THZ 7: 258; TANABE 1969, 278.

40 REPENTANCE. The phrase "without a single thing," a Buddhist term for detachment, is used again by Tanabe to refer to Japan's position towards democracy after the war (THZ 8: 319–21). In this context he refers to the Japanese people and the imperial household as forming "a single body above and below" (322). ➤ The letter to Nishida (NKZ 19: 3–4) was written in rather stilted prose, which I have simplified in the translation. ➤ Information about Tanabe's plan for the emperor has been taken from HANAZAWA's thorough study of the matter (1999, 171–4). See also Ōshima Yasumasa's remarks, THZ 8: 482.

Other citations: TAKEUCHI Yoshinori 1986, XXXVI, XL, LVIII; NKZ 19: 669.

41 PHILOSOPHIZING THE REPENTANCE. Regarding thinkers who doctored their writings after the war, Akashi Yōji has gathered together an expressive essay on the subject, "The Greater East Asian War and *Bunkajin*, 1941–1945," *War and Society* 11/1 (1993): 129–77. None of the Kyoto philosophers engaged in this (Watsuji did doctor his *Ancient Japanese Culture*), apparently all of the same mind as Nishida that "thought is something that belongs to its age and should not be adjusted afterwards" (cited in KŌSAKA 1978, 208). ➤ TSUJIMURA notes that what happens in *Metanoetics* is not that the logic of the specific disappears but that it is given different expression. "The three ele-

ments of absolute dialectic—individual, species, genus—each show up in a new form in the ideas of 'death-resurrection,' 'nothingness-in-love,' and the 'fellowship of mutual forgiveness'" (1965B, 47). See also YAMAMOTO 1987, 123.

Takeuchi's book, *The Philosophy of the Kyōgyōshinshō* was published in 1943. ➤ Three years before Tanabe's work came out, a book entitled *Philosophy as Repentance,* almost identical in name to his own, was published. Actually it was a revision of an earlier book, first published in 1920 as the posthumous notes of a brilliant young student of Nishida named Nozaki Hiroyoshi, who had died suddenly in 1917. In content there is almost nothing of overlap with Tanabe, but the appearance of the work at a time when Tanabe must have begun writing leaves open the possibility of an influence on his own choice of title. See notes to §27 above.

In an essay published while Tanabe was alive, Nishitani took up the argument of *Philosophy as Metanoetics*, points to some of its precedents in Tanabe's earlier thought, pulls out its implicit criticism of Nishida, and highlights what he sees as Tanabe's misreadings of his teacher's thought. The result is perhaps the most informed and careful critique of Tanabe's book to come out of the Kyoto circle. Unfortunately, Tanabe did not respond to it in print.

The reference to "saints and sages" is based on a Pure Land term, 自力聖道門, which refers to the wise and holy persons as those who seek salvation through the path of self-power.

Other citations: TANABE 1986, L; NISHITANI 1991A, 174–5.

42 **THE LOGIC OF ABSOLUTE CRITIQUE.** For a different way to organize the progression of Tanabe's metanoetics from philosophy to religion, see WATTLES (1990). Though I question the imposition of stages, he seems to me to have caught all of the essential ingredients in good form. ➤ For a solid and readable analysis of the main philosophical arguments of the *Metanoetics,* see FREDERICKS 1990A, based on his 1988 dissertation at the University of Chicago.

MARALDO (1990) shows well how Tanabe's attempt to combine absolute critique with a religious posturing has no real parallels in the various trends of the critique of rational faith in contemporary western philosophy. He also argues that Tanabe's position is a purely mental one that overlooks the critical role of body and emotions as part of what Descartes had called "everything opposed to reason" (1990, 252).

Tanabe came to Nietzsche relatively late. For years Tanabe had considered *Zarathustra* a kind of "book of seven seals, whose treasures I was only able to unlock with the metanoetics" (TANABE 1986, 102). It is my suspicion—though I cannot support it, because Tanabe gives no indication—that it was Nishitani who stimulated Tanabe's interest in Nietzsche. ➤ A positive assessment of Tanabe's reading of Nietzsche in the *Metanoetics* and a comparison of the idea of negation in the two (supported by material of Nietzsche that has come to light well after

Tanabe did his work) has been made by KOCH (1990). Although his outline of Tanabe's thought centers on the idea of absolute mediation (a function of the author's dependence on LAUBE's work, 1981 and 1984) his comparison with Nietzsche rests on comments in the *Metanoetics* where that idea does not figure. The author would have been much better advised to have read Nishitani, where the notion of *amor fati* is not only central, but more explicitly related to the Buddhist thinking he reads into Tanabe.

Passages on his aim of leading the Japanese people to repentance come from two personal letters of 1944 and 1945 cited by TAKEUCHI Yoshinori 1986, XXXVII–VIII.

Other citations: TANABE 1986, 26, 44–5, 113, 118, 195.

43 RELIGIOUS ACT, RELIGIOUS WITNESS. For the relation of absolute nothingness to Pure Land doctrine, one may be referred to the essay by HASE (1990), which I have drawn on here. One should, however, note that although Hase speaks of Tanabe's views in general, he in fact restricts himself to Tanabe's late work. ➤ FUNAYAMA reckons that if Tanabe had broken from Nishida earlier, his thought might have developed in a more profitable, and less religious, direction than the metanoetics and later philosophy of death (1984, 208–9). He is not alone in his dislike for Tanabe's later thought, but blaming it on his attachment to Nishida seems rather far-fetched.

The terms *gyō* and *shō* are present in the title of the *Kyōgyōshinshō*. The term *kyō* refers to the teaching of the *Larger Sūtra (Sukhāvatīvyūha-sūtra); gyō* to the practice of the *nenbutsu* or invocation of the name of Amida Buddha; *shin* as sincere mind and authentic faith; and *shō* to the dual movement of transforming love, "going to the Pure Land" *(ōsō-ekō)* and "returning from the Pure Land to this world" *(gensō-ekō)*. Tanabe speaks of his metanoesis as a unit of "act-faith-witness." While this omits the element of teaching, it is clear that metanoesis includes in its idea of witness that of reforming his own philosophical position in the light of the teaching.

On the contrast between Zen and Eckhart on the one hand and Pure Land on the other, see TANABE 1986, 185–92. ➤ Tanabe's remarks on western mysticism really only encompass Plotinus, the Neoplatonists, and Eckhart, which he refers to as "ordinary mysticism." Its chief common trait of contemplative union, as far as he was concerned, was that it takes place in the common medium of Being which either keeps the self-identity of the individual and the absolute intact or has the two of them absorbed into that common medium. The same applies to Zen mysticism, whose common medium of the Buddha-nature relates the individual to the Buddha like water and ice: both share the same nature (TANABE 1986, 169). Only an absolute nothingness that functions as an Other-power mediating the way between the relative individual and the absolute (be it God or Buddha) can effect a radical transformation of both. And only such a model, he argues, does justice to the Christian symbolism of death and resurrection.

Regarding Shin Buddhist views on Tanabe's reading of the *Kyōgyōshinshō*, it must be said that it is generally neglected in doctrinal studies. NAKAYAMA (1979), for example, takes Tanabe to task for missing the radical otherness of Other-power, for failing to distinguish the faith achieved in the Pure Land from that of one coming to faith in the world, and for misrepresenting Shinran's notion of repentance. Unfortunately, the author seems to be far more out of his depth in the world of philosophical discourse than Tanabe was in Shin Buddhist studies. A more studied and important criticism can be found in UEDA Yoshifumi (1990), who accuses Tanabe of reading Shinran through the lens of an idea of repentance (*zange* 懺悔) that does not square with Shinran's own idea (*zangi* 慚愧), in which the self that Tanabe sees as resurrecting from its death as a new self is simply abandoned altogether in Shinran. Similar criticisms are raised by UNNO, who adds to them a criticism of Tanabe's reading of the going-to and coming-from the Pure Land (1990, 126–32).

Tanabe's most controversial reading of Pure Land doctrine has to do with his reading of the symbol of the bodhisattva Dharmākara. In carrying out disciplines and accumulating merits over five *kalpa*, Dharmākara represents the way in which the practice of repentance of relative beings belongs to the internal transformation of the Buddha himself. His self-discipline becomes a transcendent ground for our own repentance. For Tanabe, in contrast, he is a symbol of the transformation of the self—that all self-determination entails an other-determination—and the Tathāgata becomes a symbol of absolute mediation. Tanabe tries to show how Shinran's idea of the three stages of transformation corresponding to the three original vows of the Buddha (argued in the final chapter of the *Kyōgyōshinshō*) supports the idea of an absolute mediation in absolute nothingness.

In speaking of Tanabe's rethinking of philosophy from a religious point of view, TAKEUCHI Yoshinori refers to his thought as a "philosophy of religion," the term he uses literally means philosophy-religion (1986, XL–XLI). ➤ Concerning Tanabe's views on demythification, see MUTŌ Kazuo 1986, 3: 155–66.

Other citations: TANABE, 1986, LI, 42, 149, 211, 238; THZ 9: 328; 11: 238.

44 SELF AND SELF-AWARENESS. The term "self that is not a self" is Nishitani's. As far as I know, it does not appear in Tanabe, though it sounds very much like something Tanabe might have used in the classroom. NISHITANI's choice of the term as a common ground for Nishida and Tanabe (1991A, 175) is not without a certain irony if one recalls that Tanabe had used the pattern in a positive sense to speak of his own "metanoetics" as "a philosophy that is not a philosophy," while at the same time he used it negatively to dismiss Nishida's logic of place as the attempt to pass off "a logic that is not a logic" (226).

At the time, Tanabe freely uses the term "active self-awareness," working the idea out through metaphors of the new physics in which the subjective and objective coalesce in the theory of scientific observation at the atomic level (THZ 12:

3–58). Throughout, his distance from Nishida is clear and blunt. The active intuition he sees at the foundations of the logic of locus is accused of being formalistic and transcending content, "a reduction of the temporal element of intuition to the spatial," "a conventional dogmatic metaphysics," "a secularized theology," "an abstraction of religious faith to a one-sided intuitional immanence," and so forth (12: 224–5).

Laube finds *self-awareness* "one of Tanabe's most difficult terms" because of its double meaning of ordinary self-consciousness and religious awakening. Rather than allow the ambiguity, he has decided for the reader which meaning is intended (when often they *both* are) by translating the former as *Selbst-bewusstsein* and the latter as *SELBST-Bewusstsein*. At the same time, he badly overstates the importance of self-awareness in Tanabe in claiming that, like Hegel, he regarded "absolute knowledge" as the ultimate goal of philosophy (1990, 317). The point is not unrelated to his strenuous efforts to provide a rational scheme for Tanabe's thought and to his general judgment that Tanabe remained a kind of "unchurched religious vagabond" who roamed from one religion to another without making a home in any of them (1984, 27–8, 222). Rather, self-awareness *was* Tanabe's religious home, and it is not fair to reprimand him for lack of religious affiliation.

For the shift from the "finality of self-awareness" to the self-awareness of praxis, see thz 3: 78-81. Hanaoka (1990) glosses over the details of the controversy, both historical and philosophical, in an attempt to overcome the difference between Nishida and Tanabe by arguing that each is concerned with a different dimension, Nishida the vertical and Tanabe the horizontal, both of which we need as we try to make our way in real life, where the two dimensions intersect. ➤ As for Nishida's turning the self into a God and philosophy into religion, and to treat the true self as ahistorical, see thz 4: 305–28.

Other citations: Tanabe 1986, l; thz 3: 4, 64; 6: 185; 7: 41 (emphasis added); 8: 260; 11: 186–7; 14: 439; Nishida 1986, 25–6.

45 a synthesis of religions. Shida Shōzō traces Tanabe's route to Dōgen through Watsuji and seems to reflect the general opinion of scholars in the field that his commentaries are more a platform for his own philosophy than they are a fair appraisal of Dōgen's own ideas (publisher's leaflet to thz 9).

Regarding the distinction between philosophy and religion cited in the text (thz 11: 429–30), see Hase 1994, 5–6, and §67 above. ➤ In a 1961 round-table discussion, Nishitani takes the view that Tanabe never really made the leap to integrate religion into philosophy, but on this count I think him mistaken and would very much side with Mutō Kazuo's views in the discussion (1981b, 136–44). ➤ The best attempt I know to sort out the question of Tanabe's views of the relation between philosophy and religion is a beautifully structured essay by Takeuchi Yoshinori. Rather than focus on the disagreement with Nishida, he lays out three patterns for the philosophy of religion: a clear separation of the religious experience from philosophical reflection, the pursuit of a kind of thinking which sees philosophical thinking as at the same time belonging to religious experience, and the search for a unity in the tension of these two positions. These three patterns are then shown to represent transitions in Tanabe's own philosophy (1999, 5: 47–65). ➤ Nishitani notes that whereas D. T. Suzuki had reacted strongly against the philosophizing of Zen, he later changed his views, under the influence of Nishida's idea of the "self-identity of absolute contradictories," at which point he began to seek in Buddhism what he called the "logic of *soku-hi*" (see §28 and its notes above). As far as I know, Tanabe never makes any reference to Suzuki's idea of *soku*. Nishitani's own conclusion, at this point, is that the relationship between Zen and philosophy remains an open question, one that he himself wrestled with late into his life (NISHITANI 1986D, 153–4). Coincidentally, in an essay published the same year this discussion was held, Nishitani cites Suzuki indirectly by repeating his reference to the *soku-hi* pattern from the *Diamond Sūtra* (1982B, 55).

In his late years, Tanabe was more convinced than ever that Buddhism needed to recover its sense of social responsibility. In a 1955 letter, reflecting a rather widespread view in the postwar period, he refers to the "duty of Zen to leave the meditation halls and go out to the street corners and to work its liberation among the people" (to Tsuji Sōmei, cited in the publisher's leaflet to THZ 13). ➤ Tanabe's early attraction to Christianity for its social teaching is apparent throughout the treatment of ethics in his *Introduction to Philosophy* (THZ 11).

For a general look at his use of scripture, and his neglect of the Old Testament, see YAMASHITA 1990. ➤ Tanabe saw the turn away from Paul and back to Jesus as the challenge of a "second reformation" facing Protestantism in particular. See Mutō Kazuo's commentary on this point in THZ 10: 328–32. ➤ Tanabe summarizes the purpose of *Existenz, Love, and Praxis* succinctly in the preface to *The Dialectics of Christianity* (THZ 10: 14). The preface to *Existenz, Love, and Praxis*, incidentally, contains probably Tanabe's clearest published statement on his own religious background, his interest in Christianity, and his search for a religion of self-awareness. Combined with his reflections on being a "Christian in the making" (THZ 10: 258–61)—an idea repeated later by Nishitani (§66)—they give as clear an image of his own relationship to organized religion. ➤ For a concise but thoughtful résumé of the differences in approach to Christianity of Tanabe and Nishida, see Mutō Kazuo's comments in the publisher's leaflet to NKZ 17. ➤ Regarding Tanabe's late political thought, see MUTŌ 1951. ➤ On Tanabe's late views on natural science, see TAKEUCHI Yoshinori 1981, 216. Regarding the metanoetics aspect, see UEDA Yasuharu 1985.

Besides omitting Shinto from his synthesis of religions, Tanabe also passes over the Taoist and Confucianist traditions. LAUBE observes that Tanabe's personal library suggests that he had read in the area, as well as in Islam and Judaism, even though he only makes passing remarks to them in his writings (1984, 219–20).

Citation: THZ 10: 300–1.

46 A DIALECTICS OF DEATH. HOSOYA refers to Tanabe's final essays as a "dizzying transformation, a leap amounting to a conversion of fundamental principles" that is nonetheless prefigured in his earlier work (1988, 7). I rely on his painstaking work on the texts for my abbreviated account of his struggles with symbolism here. ➤ UEDA Shizuteru, in addition to locating Tanabe's philosophy of death in his late thought, shows how it relies on a reversal of his inaugural critique of Nishida (1997, 125–68). It is, I believe, his best appreciation of Tanabe's differences from Nishida.

Tsujimura Kōichi observes how the series of lectures that became *Introduction to Philosophy* gave Tanabe the opportunity to sum up his earlier thought clearly and to take the first step towards his "philosophy of death" (commentary to THZ 11: 634). In this sense, the transition to his final philosophical position was more studied and natural than his earlier turning points to the logic of the specific and the metanoetics had been.

Tanabe's critique of Heidegger is the lengthy essay entitled "An Ontology of Life or a Dialectics of Death?" (THZ 13: 525–76). ➤ On the criticism of Heidegger cited here, see TANABE 1986, 149. On Tanabe and Heidegger, see TSUJIMURA 1991. Unfortunately, Tanabe's relation to Heidegger is given short shrift in the volume dedicated to the influence of Heidegger on eastern thought (YUASA 1987A, 158), even though he seems to have been the first person to introduce Heidegger's thought to Japan (see the commentary by Kōsaka Masaaki to THZ 4: 432). ➤ For comments by Nishitani Keiji on Tanabe's disagreements with Heidegger, see NKC 9: 304, 315–24. ➤ The longest treatment of Heidegger's thought appears in Tanabe's final but incomplete work, *Philosophy, Poetry, and Religion,* the bulk of which centers on a critical appreciation of Heidegger (THZ 13). ➤ I find the remark made by Nagao Michitaka that Heidegger is closer to Nishida than Tanabe was unsupportable (publisher's leaflet to NKZ 8).

In the light of Whitehead's thought UEDA Yasuharu (1985) criticizes Tanabe's lifelong pursuit of a philosophy of science, concluding that in the end Tanabe had failed to come to terms with the limits of physics. ➤ On Tanabe's idea of "practising death," see THZ 9: 190ff. ➤ The passage criticizing Christianity's lack of a true dialectics of death appears in an unpublished fragment, THZ 13: 637–8. ➤ Regarding Tanabe's use of Leibniz, he had already hinted at a move in this direction in a 1944 letter (TAKEUCHI Yoshinori 1986, XXXVII). Although the Kegon idea of the harmonious interpenetration of principles and things, and among things *(jijimuge, rijimuge)*, had already appeared in the *Metanoetics* (TANABE 1986, 221), there was no reference to Leibniz. One should also note here the remarkable affinities with Nishida, whose interest in Leibniz was much more sustained, beginning in 1918 and continuing until his final essay. Even though Tanabe does not mention Nishida by name, the use of the Kegon idea is one more sign of a restoration of sympathy for his teacher. Similar interpretations of the Kegon idea of mutual interpenetration, incidentally, figure prominently in Nishitani's *Religion and Nothingness.*

In addition to the two essays on Valéry and Mallarmé, which together run to over 260 pages in Tanabe's *Complete Works*, the final work mentioned above, *Philosophy, Poetry, and Religion*, deals extensively with Rilke and Hölderlin. The judgment that Tanabe "neglected" literature is based less on the quantity of his writing than on the fact that he read literature as philosophy. ➤ Tanabe's chief source for his knowledge of the symbolists seems to have been a 1924 book by Suzuki Shintarō that bore a title curiously like his own, *A Memorandum on the French Symbolists*. For details on the connections, see Hosoya 1998, 15–26.

Other citations: THZ 11: 32; 13: 29, 100, 171, 173–4, 185, 204, 221, 266, 290, 529, 554, 576; NKC 9: 283; Takizawa 1972, 1: 460.

Nishitani Keiji (1900–1990)

47 NISHITANI'S LIFE AND CAREER. There is no biography of Nishitani available, and the only reliable data appears at the end of the final volume of his *Collected Works* (NKC 26: 345–64), with certain supplementary material in the second volume of a memorial collection (1993, 2: 310–13) and in a memorial edition of *The Eastern Buddhist* (1992, 155–8). Nishitani himself provides additional information in two autobiographical essays (1985D, 1986A), and in a series of enlightening discussions held late in life with Yagi Seiichi (1989D) and Sasaki Tōru (1990D). The publisher's leaflets for each of the volumes of the *Collected Works* are also full of personal reminiscences. ➤ The inaccuracies in Jacinto's sketch of Nishitani's life (1995, 209–11) were taken over by Dilworth and Viglielmo 1998, 373–4. The cause of these mistakes, and perhaps those in the German translator's introduction to *Was ist Religion?* (Nishitani 1986A), seems to have been Van Bragt's account (1982, xxxiv). ➤ There is also no reliable comprehensive work on Nishitani's thought available that I know of, either in Japanese or in a western language. Ishida (1993) gives an overview, but it is more interpretative and less representative of Nishitani's own thinking. Sasaki attempted an overview of his thought while Nishitani was still alive (1986), but the work was not well received.

The original German text of Nishitani's presentation in Freiburg seems to have been lost. The Japanese version opens the first volume of his *Collected Works*. ➤ Nishitani's undergraduate thesis was published in the second volume of his *Collected Works* and his doctoral dissertation in the first volume. The story of Tanabe's difficulty with it is mentioned in Shimomura 1992, 126 (see also the publisher's leaflet to NKC 13). Nishitani himself notes that on rereading it in his late years he was surprised to find so many Zen terms in it (1985C, 4).

On Nishitani's practice of Zen, see Horio (1992). In a later essay he corrects the dating of the earlier piece in the light of information from D. T. Suzuki's correspondence (1997A, 22–4). For Nishitani's own comments, see 1987B and 1989D, 60–69. He himself says that the reason he went to Gyōdō was that he had asked

Suzuki to recommend him to the greatest living Zen master (1985C, 3). In a late interview, Nishitani admitted, after considerable prodding, that he had passed all the *kōan*, though not in the normal order in which monks do so, to attain what is called 大事了畢, the "completion of the great deed" (1987B, 8). ➤ When it is said that Nishitani "practised" Zen, it was of course a layman's practice, different from the intense routine of the monk. At first he received instruction six times a year during the concentrated *sesshin*, which then slowed to once a week and later once a month on his Master's retirement. ➤ He refers to Hisamatsu Shin'ichi out of deference to disciples who interviewed him on this and other occasions, but he does not refer to Hisamatsu in his autobiographical or other writings.

NISHITANI mentions going to Kamakura to meet Sōseki (1986E, 26), whose novels were influential in his youth and whose ideas have often been compared to Nishida's (see notes to section 10). He would later write an essay on Sōseki's *Bright Darkness*, which he considered the novelist's finest work (NKC 15: 25–46). ➤ THOMPSON goes overboard in calling Nishitani one of the "heirs" of Heidegger who has taken on the important task of appropriating Heidegger's ideas into eastern thought (1986, 237). It is true that NISHITANI near the end of his life wrote that he found the encounter with Heidegger "meaningful and groundbreaking" (1989A, 269), but the influence went both ways. Indeed, one could with more justice claim the opposite, that Heidegger had taken a leading role in introducing Asian metaphysics to Europe. ➤ His essays on Nishida and his talks on nihilism have both been translated into English (NISHITANI 1991A, 1990C). ➤ Regarding his tranquility in Zen practice after having been purged from his post, see the recollections of KAJITANI (1992, 98). ➤ After Nishitani's restoration to his teaching chair in 1952, Tanabe wrote a letter in which he spoke of his great relief. The letter from Tanabe to Kano Jisuke is dated 14 April 1953. Kōsaka Masaaki was reinstated in 1955; only Kōyama Iwao, a junior professor who had served as the go-between between the Kyoto school and the Navy, was not (HANAZAWA 1999, 248, 365). ➤ The remark of Nishitani's wife and the comment by Tanabe are reported by TAKEUCHI Yoshinori, a student of Nishitani's and Tanabe's and a close friend of the family (1992, 129).

Published interviews with NISHITANI are really indispensable for understanding the liveliness and breadth of his thinking, though it is difficult to cite them because of their nature. The *Chūōkōron* (1943) and *Overcoming Modernity* (1979) roundtable discussions, however, because of their careful preparation and review by the authors, will be cited as freely as the published works.

In 1941 Nishitani mentions having been attacked by the right because of his association with the "Kyoto school" (NKC 21: 132). ➤ The comment on being slapped on the cheeks is cited by HORIO (1995, 291) and also from a 1984 letter of Nishitani's (YUSA 1992, 152). It is a rather well-known phrase of Nishitani's, and the fact that he cited it so late in life is an indication that he considered himself falsely accused. While one pities him the slap on the left cheek, it is harder to say he did not deserve at least a tap on the right, as we shall see in what follows. ➤

The statement that the Second Order of the Sacred Treasure was awarded to members of the armed forces as well as academics (Dilworth and Viglielmo, 1998, 374) is to confuse practices during the war with those after the reform of the awards in 1947. Of the 78 laureates of 1970, 46 are from academia, 26 from government, and 10 from the private sector. See『朝日新聞』*[Asahi news]*, 29 April 1970, 4.

Nishitani's posthumous lay Buddhist name is 西来院空谷溪聲士. ➤ The catalogue of Nishitani's personal library is to be published in October 2001.

Other citations: Nishitani 1986a, 28; 1989d, 27.

48 NISHITANI'S PHILOSOPHICAL STYLE. In the exchange with Kobayashi over philosophical style (Nishitani 1979, 248–51), the scholastic philosopher Yoshimitsu Yoshihiko also comes under Kobayashi's sharp knife, but his response is little more than a lame resignation to the fate of trying to introduce abstract thinking into Japanese, with an implied criticism of those who sacrifice that task for simple clarity of expression. The gist of Nishitani's response, incidentally, is also repeated years later in another context (1961b, 307–8). ➤ The remark on Nishitani's preference for communicating his ideas through spoken conversation rather than through being read in print was made by one of his oldest colleagues, Shimomura Toratarō (1992, 128). ➤ Kasulis's suggestion that Nishitani should "avoid coining terms that are more puzzling than illuminating" (1982, 143) is a judgment made, it seems to me, without sufficient attention to the attempt to introduce Buddhist ideas into world philosophy without restricting himself to traditional Buddhist terminology.

The completion of the English translation of *Religion and Nothingness* was known by several publishers in the United States who expressed interest in publishing it. The translator, Jan Van Bragt, and I narrowed it down to two, one heavily theological, the other a secular university press. Nishitani at once opted for the latter on the grounds that he did not want to be known as a theologian. This desire to disassociate himself from theology is confirmed in an essay by Van Bragt (1989, 9). Part of the decision, though I have no way of confirming this now, may have been that the only extensive treatment of his thought in the west (Waldenfels 1976) was overtly theological in nature, and Nishitani wanted reaction from the philosophical world. It may be noted here that roughly two-thirds of his writings deal with religious themes. Where Nishida and Tanabe had ended is really where Nishitani began, and remained. ➤ The last time I went to see Nishitani was in 1988, when he was 88 years old, to clarify ambiguities in passages in translation. He set aside all our questions. He was detached from his writings at this time and preferred to talk about the flower blooming on the table rather than justify or correct anything he had written before. During the same visit, a phone call came requesting another talk, and I was surprised at the alacrity with which he asked his daughter to handle the details (Heisig 1992b).

His aside about debates with Tanabe can be found in NKC 21: 130. ➤ The comments concerning his posthumous papers were conveyed to me by Horio Tsutomu, who was entrusted with the task of sorting them out. ➤ It should be noted that many more of Nishitani's writings than the eleven volumes that appear as lectures in his *Collected Works* in fact had their origins in transcripts of talks he had given. ➤ The three references to passages on his style can be found in NKC 17: 60–3, 18: 24–5; NISHITANI 1982A, 283–4.

Other citations: UEDA Shizuteru 1992A, 3; MUTŌ Kazuo 1992, 99.

49 A STARTING POINT IN NIHILISM. The reference to Jaspers, which appears in the first chapter of his *La filosofía* (México: Fondo de la Cultura Económica, 1949) is mine, but NISHITANI himself states clearly that his philosophy did not begin in wonder and doubt but in nihilism (1986A, 26). ➤ On Nishitani's early psychological condition, see also HORIO 1997A, 21–2. His early optimism towards Japanese spirituality is reflected in the concluding section of *A Philosophy of Elemental Subjectivity*, where his wording is very close to the conclusions Nishida advanced in his essays on Japanese culture (NKC 1: 147–50). ➤ The idea of the "bottom dropping out of" ego or being (脱底) is generally translated as "bottomlessness," as if it were simply the same as *Grundlösigkeit* (for which Nishitani himself uses a different term, NKC 10: 108), which misses the existential nuance that Nishitani intends. ➤ On his change of attitude towards Japanese religiosity after the war, see VAN BRAGT 1971, 273–4.

It is worth noting that at the time Nishitani saw the struggles with nihilism as his own personal philosophical starting point, not as a general rule. The nature of philosophy itself, already from its roots in the west, he characterizes simply as a union of the two dimensions of specialized "scholarship" and "subjective self-awakening" (NKC 15: 237).

KETA sees Nishitani's struggles with nihilism as taking the appropriation of "the west" a step further than Nishida and Tanabe had done, making what he saw as its central spiritual problem his own, blurring the sharp line of separation between east and west (1991, 33–4). ➤ The passage from NISHITANI's memoirs appears in 1985D, 25.

Other citations: NISHITANI 1986A, 27; 1961B, 341; 1964B, 4, 8.

50 ELEMENTAL SUBJECTIVITY. In summarizing Nishitani's early thought, I have made generous use of the essays of MORI Tetsurō, who carefully documents his synopses in Nishitani's writings (1994, 1997). ➤ As remarked in the notes to §5, it was Nishitani who gave philosophy the Japanese term for "subjectivity" (主体性) Kierkegaard. ➤ The term I have translated as *elemental* (a term that we also decided on in revising the translation of *Religion and Nothingness*), 根源, literally means "fountainhead" or "root source." It carries the sense of the primal spring of life from which subjectivity flows. Nishitani first used it in his undergraduate thesis, which dealt with "elemental evil." The early Greek philosophers' search for the basic elements of real-

ity, as well as the *Elementalphilosophie* of K. L. Reinhold, that attempts to locate in subjectivity the common source of sensation and understanding in Kant, seem to suggest this as a workable translation.

Unlike many of his later essays, which are divided into untitled sections (as were the essays of Nishida and Tanabe), these early works provide clear subtitles which seem to help focus the progression of the argument and also make it easier for the reader to find the way back to passages in the text. Accordingly, passages dealing with each of the main ideas treated here in connection with elemental subjectivity can be found by consulting the contents of the first two volumes of Nishitani's *Collected Works.*

As Mori Tetsurō rightly points out (1997, 12), the passage on "love as life itself" (NKC 1: 87) suggests the influence of Schelling's idea of love as *Ungrund,* although, I would add, this does not figure in his thesis on Schelling. ➤ It is interesting to note that while Nishitani speaks of two faces of God, he does not relate these to the Old Testament and New Testament, as was often done from early Christian times and throughout the esoteric tradition of Europe.

Other citations: NKC 1: 77–8, 86–9; 3: 153–4.

51 A PHILOSOPHY FOR NATIONALISM. The motivations for his political philosophy are stated in an afterword appended to a 1946 reprint of *View of the World, View of the Nation,* where he speaks of "overcoming ideas of ultranationalism from within" (NKC 4: 384). This way of viewing the project seems to me a reading-in of the approach he was taking to nihilism at the time and not to be present in the original work. ➤ The remark on his own assessment of the originality of the work is cited from a personal letter (Yusa 1992, 152).

The piece on Hitler's *Mein Kampf* can be found in NKC 1: 144–7. Incidentally, a copy of the book is to be found in Nishida's library of western books, though the uncut pages indicate that he never read it (Lavelle 1994b, 163). ➤ The political theorists Nishitani uses are Rudolf Kjéllen, Friedrich Meinecke, and Otto Kroellreuter, as well as Hegel and Ranke, familiarity with whose thought was *de rigeur* in Japan at the time.

English translations of parts of this book (Nishitani 1998a–c) appear in an anthology that limits the selection of essays on Nishitani to these pieces as representing the foundations of all his philosophy. The translations tend to be sloppy (there are numerous interpolations and even a paragraph skipped in 1998c, 399) and should be read with care. The claim of the editors that all of Nishitani's postwar writings simply "amplify his prewar themes, but with a certain loss of the 'Japanese spirit' that animated his wartime writings" (Dilworth and Viglielmo 1998, 380) is ridiculous in the extreme. I should take this occasion to note, as I did not in my review of the work (*The Journal of Asian Studies* 58/4, 1999: 1135–6), that Jacinto's selections and comments show a much more balanced approach to

Nishitani's thought (1995, 309–14), but were effectively ignored, even though his name appears among the editors of the work.

It is interesting to note that Nishitani offers a reading of the Pure Land idea of "returning from the Pure Land" that suggests something quite similar to what Tanabe performed in his *Philosophy of Metanoetics* (NISHITANI 1998C, 400). Tanabe surely read this work, but makes no mention of it.

Other citations: NKC 4: 262, 276, 279, 286, 304–5, 348, 357, 374, 382; NISHITANI 1998A, 382, 384; 1998B 389; 1998C, 392–3, 400.

52 HISTORICAL NECESSITY. The report on Nishida's meeting with the Navy, the response of the Kyoto school, and the composition of the "brain trust" is reported and documented in some detail in HANAZAWA, who draws heavily on the recollections of Kōyama, the pivotal figure in the preparation of the *Chūōkōron* discussions (1999, 136–41). ➤ A solid overview of the discussions, their history and the aftermath of criticisms, has been prepared by HORIO, who—more out of a deep sense of loyalty to Nishitani, one feels, than a balanced assessment of what his teacher actually said—concludes that the discussions were not an unqualified failure, despite attempts by critics overcome by emotional prejudice to bury them in history, since compared with those who simply swallowed the propaganda without question or remained on the sidelines, at least these young scholars *tried* to do something (1995, 295, 315). A great many of the citations and ideas that I have singled out do not figure in his résumé of the discussions. Horio draws on an earlier draft of Hanazawa's researches for certain historical details. In fact, it was Horio who first introduced me to the important work that Hanazawa had done, with the request that I act as an intermediary to present them to the publisher. ➤ The comment accusing the discussants of having led the country to war can be found in Matsui Yoshikado, 「世界史 的哲学」 [A philosophy of world history], Takeuchi Yoshitomo, ed., 『昭和思想史』 *[Intellectual history of the Shōwa period]* (Kyoto: Minerva Shobō, 1958), 420.

STEVENS argues that Nishitani was politically naïve and actually inconsistent with the ethical position implied in his own thinking (1997). Part of the blame, he says, lay in a "déformation professionnelle" that combined the long western tradition of trying to deduce political opinions from metaphysical principles, and part of it in the Zen tradition of seeking the absolute not in a transcendent realm but within this relative world. In making his case, he includes an important ingredient often overlooked in moralizing over the Kyoto school: the self-reminder that it is what they supported that must be battled against at all costs and on all fronts, not the totality of their thought or the character of the individuals in question. As he himself notes, he has been limited to translated sources, which in this case has ruled out any assessment of just what Nishitani's general philosophical views were at the time he turned to political thought. (In fact, his philosophical reflections on Zen, nihilism, and self-awareness had not yet been thought out.) Instead, Stevens assumes that Nishitani had accepted Nishida's views in large part as his own—not an altogether misguided assumption, but one that needs more refining in order to reach the conclusions that Stevens does. Moreover, the inconsistency he sees is based explicitly on ideas Nishitani had worked out much later (52–3).

In 1994 I prepared a translation of about one-third of the discussions, including all the interventions by Nishitani. I did not carry it any further towards publication, on the advice of the head of a team that was about to complete the same work. Alas, their work never reached press. ➤ The speech of the military officer, a certain Kimura, took place in 1945 and was reported in the newspapers (Ōshima 1965, 131).

Other citations: Takeuchi Yoshimi 1979, 322; Nishitani 1943, 2, 5, 11, 19, 33, 73, 85–6, 148.

53 MORAL ENERGY AND ALL-OUT WAR. The term *moralische Energie* was taken from the German historian Leopold von Ranke, but retained very little of its original, empirical sense in Nishitani's use of it to promote a world ethic as a response to historical necessity. ➤ Nishitani cites the essay he contributed to the *Overcoming Modernity* symposium in a reference to moral energy in the closing stages of the discussions (1943, 393). ➤ Aside from the reference to racialism and nationalism as a counterpoint to western democracy (Nishitani 1943, 186), the only other allusion to "nationalism" in the discussions is to allude to it as something distinct in Japan from the merely ethical (310). None of the other participants used the term.

It may be noted that in the *Chūōkōron* discussions Nishitani twice refers to ideas from Tendai and Zen, though it can hardly be said that he brings them to bear on anything political. In responding to one of the participants who mentions the Buddhist idea of "no-self," he starts to say something, and then cuts himself short (Nishitani 1943, 420). This is only one indication of the much greater resources that Nishitani had at his disposal that would serve him once he had put all of this behind him.

The idea of "all-out war" was not Nishitani's, but simply his recapitulation of an idea expounded by other participants at the opening of the session. Horio, or at least his translator, gets the German terms *totale Krieg* (total war, 全体戦) and *Generalmobilisierungskrieg* (all-out war, 総力戦) backwards in his essay (1995, 311).

Other citations: Nishitani 1943, 160, 168, 262–3, 282, 309–10, 317, 326, 328, 337–8, 351, 360–2, 396, 422, 443–4.

54 OVERCOMING MODERNITY. The essay by Minamoto from which the opening citation is taken (1994, 229) gives a good overview of the intellectual background of the right at the time of the symposium, the revival of interest in it after the war, and the positions of the principal

participants. ➤ The criticism of Nishitani's lack of solid historical research was made by HIROMATSU (1980, 246) in his extended review of the discussions.

The member of the group most sympathetic to the military and the emperor-centered patriotism was Hayashi Fusao, a convert from communism. Nishitani has two exchanges of words with him during the discussions. In the first Hayashi complains that although many thinkers in Japan continue to sympathize with the recapitulation to western civilization that began in the Meiji period, the war being waged in the Pacific has for the time being nailed the lid shut. Nishitani cuts him off at just this point to agree, and carries on the lament about the preference for western dance and music to the neglect of Japan's own culture. He also notes that a national unity of Japan centered on the imperial household requires getting past the individualism and liberalism of the west. In the second, which is at the end of the final session, Hayashi laments the fact that he was given a "modern education" full of western ideas, and that a closer link between the objectivity of scientific education and resignation to the demands of ordinary life is necessary not only for the young men who make up the Army and Navy but for all true patriots and military people. Nishitani only questions whether what is straightforward for the military is so easily carried over into those who devote themselves to the study of science (NISHITANI 1979, 239–43, 268–9).

The form of the slogan that the rightists used was "all the world under one roof" (八紘一宇), adapted from the eighth-century classic, *Nihon shoki* (Chronicles of Japan). Nishitani alters it closer to the original to give 八紘為宇. This was the same form, incidentally, in which the term had been introduced into the *Chūōkōron* discussions some four months earlier, where the source was misidentified. NISHITANI himself, however, in a final reference to the phrase, cites it in the form of the current slogan (1943, 225, 396). The first time Nishitani uses the term, however, is in the final two chapters of *View of the World, View of the Nation*. In his afterword to the postwar reprint, he insists that he did not intend the term in the sense used by the ideologues of the "imperial way," but only to point to the idea of a "selfless" nation (NKZ 4: 384). This only makes one wonder why he did not say so at the time, as the term was sure to be misunderstood without qualification. ➤ I recently stumbled upon a complete "philosophical" tract on the subject by Arima Junsei, 『日本思想と世界思想』 *[Japanese thought and world thought]* (Tokyo: Keiseisha, 1940), which shows the standard meaning the term had at the time.

Other citations: NISHITANI 1979, 35–7; NKC 4: 409, 455, 461; 21: 132–3.

55 THE RELIGIOUS DIMENSION OF THE POLITICAL. References to the inner "spiritual energy" of the Japanese can be found in NISHITANI 1961B, 314–16. ➤ The passage on incorporating the ancestors through a bowl of rice (NKC 20: 192) recalls Nietzsche's use of the body as the medium for inheriting the archaic levels of the past (see PARKES 1993, 67). ➤ The importance of the idea of ethnicity (blood) and a common natural environment

(land) for self-identity is one NISHITANI never let go of. See, for example, 1961B, 48–9. ➤ His revised remarks on democracy appear in NISHITANI 1981B, 156.

The citation on Japan's role in overcoming east and west appears in a preface to a symposium edited under his name (NISHITANI 1967, 2–4). It does not appear in his *Collected Works.*

Other citations: NISHITANI 1961B, 72, 93, 104–5, 319–20.

56 OVERCOMING NIHILISM. I have found HORIO's overview of Nishitani's project of "overcoming nihilism through nihilism" useful in preparing my remarks (1997B). Although the problem of nihilism is mentioned as central throughout the years of composing *Religion and Nothingness* (see, for example, NISHITANI 1960D, 17), VAN BRAGT is the first to point out, as far as I know, that after the publication of that book, the term "nihilism" appears very rarely in Nishitani's writings (1992, 30). ➤ The conversation in which Nishitani talked about the role of Nietzsche in his youth is referred to in PARKES's superb and meticulously documented introduction to the translation of *The Self-Overcoming of Nihilism* (1990, xx). The absence of Nishitani in a volume he edited on *Nietzsche in Asian Thought* (Honolulu: University of Hawaii Press, 1991) is indeed as glaring an omission as he feared it would be (13). Complementing the general background of the study of nihilism in Japan that Parkes provides, KETA broadens the field to show its connections with Buddhist thought (1999). See also STEVENS (1996) for an overview of the place of nihilism in Kyoto-school thought in general. ➤ By NISHITANI's own account, Watsuji Tetsurō's 1913 and 1918 books on Nietzsche were the stimulus that first led him to *Zarathustra* (1991A, 6). ➤ MORI Tetsurō sees the combination of Nishida's death and Japan's defeat in the war as marking a turning point in Nishitani's thought (1997, 2). ➤ In an interesting dialogue with Abe Masao in 1976, Nishitani recalls his bout with Nietzsche's nihilism and how it led him to views of evil different from those of Nishida and Tanabe (reprinted in NISHITANI 2000).

As ALTIZER correctly notes, even though Nishitani does not identify Nietzsche as a Christian thinker, Nishitani's running dialogue with Nietzsche represents the deepest encounter in his thought between Buddhism and Christianity (1989, 78). ➤ SHANER claims that it was Zen that enabled Nishitani to give Nietzsche's nihilism a positive twist, and that without it "it is likely that he would have joined the camp of early Nietzsche interpreters who dwelt almost exclusively upon the superficial themes of pessimism and negativity" (1987, 117). The claim can only be justified, of course, by seeing how other Zen Buddhist intellectuals accepted Nietzsche, and there he would find himself on thin ice. In fact, I know of no Buddhist thinker in Japan contemporary with Nishitani, Zen or otherwise, who read Nietzsche the way he did—neither as thoughtfully nor as affirmatively.

As PARKES points out, even though Heidegger was lecturing on Nietzsche at the time Nishitani was studying with him, their appraisals of Nietzsche are too different to suggest much influence (1990, XXII). Heidegger's two-volume study, incidentally, was not published until 1961. ➤ NISHITANI rather magnanimously accepts the criticisms of the German philosopher, Karl Löwith, that the Japanese lack self-criticism (1990, 176). ➤ A concise and clear statement of NISHITANI's approach to the inheritance of western problems without its spirituality can be found in the transcript of a talk he gave on a national radio station (1960D).

Other citations: NISHITANI 1986A, 24, 27; 1990C, 175, 177.

57 FROM NIHILISM TO EMPTINESS. It is hard to understand how JACINTO can claim that Nishitani's approach to nihilism through Buddhist emptiness "essentially refined Nishida's ideas" (1995, 314; repeated by DILWORTH and VIGLIELMO 1998, 376). ➤ Although Nishitani had turned his view of nihilism around to a human problem that Buddhist ideas could serve, some years later UMEHARA Takeshi reprinted the concluding essay to *The Self-Overcoming of Nihilism* with an editorial comment twisting Nishitani's efforts to the aim of "overcoming nihilism for the Japanese themselves" 『ニヒリズム』 *[Nihilism]* (Tokyo: Chikuma Shobō, 1968), 99. Umehara's general introduction to the work, stuck in the pursuit of the uniqueness of Japanese nihilism, makes it clear why he chose Nishitani's earlier piece and ignored the eventual solution he offered.

VAN BRAGT's introduction to *Religion and Nothingness* (1982) gives us a splendid galaxy of Nishitani's ideas centered around that book like planets around the sun. In fact, it is one of those summaries that is *so* good that, apart from lifting out its citations, almost no one of the many people who use it cites it directly any more. This helps explain why some of the errors in his dating (see notes to §47) keep getting repeated in western publications. ➤ ABE Masao, in whose life work *Religion and Nothingness* holds pride of place, has written a thoughtful appreciation of the work that brings together many of the themes I have discussed in this section. In particular I would note his analysis of the main traits of Nishitani's idea of emptiness (1989, 27–35). The volume in which this appears in English translation (UNNO 1989A) contains numerous valuable reflections from theological and philosophical points of view, only a few of which I have cited here. ➤ Since so many commentators make a point of noting that the original Japanese title of *Religion and Nothingness* was *What is Religion?*, I suppose I should make clear that it was in fact I who renamed it. There were two reasons. Giving it the name of the title essay did not cover the whole of the book; and the literal rendering made it sound like a catechetical tract, of which there were several in print at the time with just that name. It took some time for the translator to persuade Nishitani himself of the change (see VAN BRAGT, 1989, 7). I think it fair to say, in hindsight, that the title has served the book, and the diffusion of the concept of nothingness, positively.

Regarding the distinction between Tanabe and Nishida on the role of philosophy, see HASE 1994, 4–6. HANAOKA argues that Tanabe's whole criticism is rendered invalid by his own later metanoetics, whose view of the relationship returned to a position that Nishida had already found in his inaugural idea of pure experience (1995, 5). It is clear that Tanabe reversed his position regarding religion's relation to philosophy, but I find it difficult to read anything approaching the metanoetics in *An Inquiry into the Good.*

Although he does not, as far as I know, ever take up the question of whether or to what extent the Other-power salvation of Pure Land Buddhism involves a retreat from doubt to a salvation from beyond, NISHITANI is openly critical of the adoption of the *nenbutsu* (invocation of the name of Amida Buddha) as a *kōan*, on the grounds that it weakened the doubt and mental energy of the *kōan* (1975B, 92–3).

Other citations: NISHITANI 1960D, 12; 1982A, XLIX, 18, 112; NKC 18: 193.

58 EMPTINESS AS A STANDPOINT. Nietzsche speaks of perspectivism as an approach "by virtue of which every force center—and not only man—construes the whole rest of the world from its own viewpoint." See *The Will to Power,* trans. by W. Kaufmann and R. J. Hollingdale (New York, 1968), §636. NISHITANI mentions it as Nietzsche's way of affirming the world while at the same time recognizing it as illusion (1990C, 145). ➤ One should not overlook the possibility that the idea of speaking of a "standpoint" rather than a "logic" as Nishida and Tanabe had done was also influenced by D. T. Suzuki's 1916 book『禅の立場から』*[From the standpoint of Zen]* which Nishitani had read as a young man. In 1967, Suzuki and Nishitani began editing a series of volumes called *Lectures on Zen,* the opening volume of which was Nishitani's *The Standpoint of Zen.* An English translation of the opening essay of the same name can be found at NISHITANI 1984A. ➤ Nishitani seems to bend over backwards to avoid using the ordinary word *basho* that Nishida had chosen for what we have called his logic of locus (see VAN BRAGT 1982, XXX–XXXI). We should note, however, that at two points he does use the phrase "the locus of nothingness" (1982A, 21, 38), both of which suggest an indirect allusion to Nishida. See note to §20 above.

The long critique of Hegel's basic position was written when Nishitani was seventy-nine years old, and although rather far removed from the texts of Hegel, it is a serious meditation on Hegel's starting point (NKC 13: 31–95). On several counts his criticisms echo and complement those of Tanabe in *Philosophy of Metanoetics,* especially his insistence on an absolute negation, though he makes no mention of any connection. A short essay by KADOWAKI on this piece is helpful in placing it in the context of Nishitani's own thinking (1997).

NISHITANI first suggested that Bultmann's demythifying was not going far enough (1959, 56–7), but after more thorough reading he altered his views (1961). Once he had met Bultmann some ten years later, he seemed to confirm his view that they were both on the same track (MUTŌ 1992, 100). ➤ The idea of disassociating myth from a separate realm of time and returning it to the present is also at work in his reading of Shinran's explanation of salvation (NISHITANI 1978, 14–15). ➤ In addition to Nishitani's confusing the idea of virgin birth with immaculate conception, he also confused other elements of Christianity (Van Bragt 1992, 38–9). I would add to the list his confusion of Catholic "veneration" of Mary with "worship" of her (NKC 21: 206–8). ➤ According to Nishitani, unlike Christianity, which is in need of demythologizing, "Zen is a radically demythologized religion" (1982B, 53).

The graph on the standpoint of emptiness and additions to its explanation in *Religion and Nothingness* (Nishitani, 1982A, 142) have an error: "a^n, b^n, c^n" should read "n^1, n^2, n^3, ..." I thank Bowers for pointing this out (1995, 185).

The Chinese glyph 定 by itself simply means "settled." Buddhism has used it to indicate a mind concentrated or at peace. Thus, when prefixed with the character for Zen, it came to signify "Zen meditation." ➤ I have drawn upon Maraldo's essay for this brief summary of Nishitani's understanding of *samādhi*-being. Readers will find helpful his garnering of related texts scattered throughout the pages of *Religion and Nothingness* (1992, 14–20).

Citations: Nishitani 1991B, 15, 21; 1982A, 106, 179.

59 EMPTINESS AS THE HOMEGROUND OF BEING. Concerning the several Buddhist terms that show up here and later, the reader to whom they are unfamiliar is advised to consult the brief glossary we prepared for the English translation of *Religion and Nothingness.* ➤ Although the Kyoto school's idea of absolute nothingness is something of a Zen-flavored add-on to traditional Buddhism, one that classical scholars are not always fond of, Nishitani's restatement of the idea as a standpoint of emptiness is fully in line with classical teaching on the middle way, as Swanson points out in an important essay based on the threefold truth of Chih-i (1996; see also the essay by Matsumaru 1997B). Actually, Nishitani himself describes his idea of religious philosophy as just such a middle way between religion and philosophy in their traditional, western senses. It does this by criticizing them from within and mediating them from without (NKC 6: 61–2, 69). ➤ Takeda notes, however, criticisms that can be raised from a Shin Buddhist perspective (1996).

Other citations: Nishitani 1991B, 51, 93, 128; 1982A, 158, 284.

60 EGO AND SELF. Although Nishitani, like Tanabe and Nishida before him, avoided all psychological descriptions of the true self, the tendency to reification that psychology inherited from the nineteenth-century transformation of the pronominal "I" into a substantive "the I" is not entirely absent. As noted earlier (see notes to §14), the Japanese language, which can get along without definite articles, camouflages this tendency fairly well, though there are telltale signs of it in the way Nishitani attributes an idea of "the ego" to the Cartesian "cogito." He sometimes speaks as if Descartes had an idea of "the ego" that he means to reject; at others, as if it is Kant's reading of Descartes (1981A, 33–4). This very same idea can be found previously in Nishida

NKZ 3: 159). Strictly speaking, it is neither. Descartes has no such term, and the closest Kant comes to giving him one is his allusion to "das ich Denke." The substantive "I" enters European languages with Fichte. The point, that Descartes and Kant had an idea of subjectivity corresponding to what we now call "the ego," however, stands. It is most likely the post-psychological texts of Sartre and Heidegger, with whose critiques of Descartes he takes issue, that are responsible for the anachronism. I consider this whole question not only unresolved in Kyoto-school philosophy but not even properly asked yet. See HEISIG 1991, 1997. ➤ As an indication of Nishitani's resistance to overtures from psychologists, see his discussion with the Jungians David Miller and Kawai Hayao, where Nishitani plays the skeptic in a playful but decisive manner (NISHITANI 1988).

The way Japanese handles the technical Buddhist term *anātman* suggests "non-ego" as the best English equivalent. Otherwise, Nishitani tends to use the term "ego" to refer to the Cartesian subject and "self" as a generic term for the subject, which can be qualified as self-centered, no-self, or true self. It is a mistake simply to overlay modern distinctions of self and ego (such as that found in Jungian and other psychologies) on Nishitani.

The essay on "Western Thought and Buddhism," first printed in German under its subtitle "Die religiös-philosophische Existenz im Buddhismus" and taken over in that form in an English translation unreliable in the details (1990E), shows Nishitani's way of thinking at its finest, introducing the question from a contradiction in western thought and offering a Buddhist alternative. ➤ Concerning the confluence of the notion of ego and substance in Western philosophy, see also NISHITANI 1969, 91. ➤ The clearest résumé of NISHITANI's critique of Sartre appears in 1982A, 30–5.

There is some question as to whether Nishitani was fair in his critique of Heidegger's *Nichts* as a relative nothingness still bound to human subjectivity. DALLMAYR suggests that from 1929 on Heidegger had taken a position that separates nothingness from *Dasein,* something he had not done earlier in *Being and Time* (1992, 45–6; see also THOMPSON 1986, 247–8). Some of the works Dallmayr cites in his support, however, were published well after Nishitani's remarks. In addition, the influence of certain of Nishida's ideas on Heidegger through Tanabe, who had been with him several years before he adjusted his position, cannot be discounted. That of Kuki Shūzō, also a student of Nishida's who had been with Heidegger, is also clear. The thought of Nishida seems particularly in evidence in Heidegger's later idea of the overcoming of the dichotomy of subject and object, expressed clearly in his 1959 work, *A Dialogue on Language* (a fact completely overlooked by ENNS, 1988). Dallmayr's is a question on which a clear judgment, based on all the facts, has yet to come forth.

Other citations: NISHITANI 1990E, 4, 9; 1984A, 5, 13, 16, 25–6; 1996, 9, 14–15, 19–21; NKC 17: 93, 101.

61 SELF, OTHER, AND ETHICS. On Zen dialogue, see Nishitani 1975B, 86–7. ➤ He does not in fact take up Buber's position regarding dialogue in any detail, but only mentions it as having been surpassed by the Zen position (Nishitani 1982B, 51). Yamamoto Seisaku reports that in 1976 Nishitani remarked, on reading an account of Buber's thought, that he found it remarkably close to his own on a number of points (see publisher's leaflet to NKC 17). ➤ For his comments on Marxism, see Nishitani 1985D, 26. ➤ The exchange with Nishitani over liberation theology can be found in Nanzan Institute 1981, 274–5. The passage from his talk appears in NKC 18: 128–30.

The Zen term for Great Anger, 憤志, suggests a deliberate indignance. Nishitani himself plays on the ordinary Japanese word for anger, おこり, to suggest the image of something "rising up" from within the depths of the individual (1986B, 121–2). ➤ On logos and ethos, see Nishitani 1959, 59. The longest résumés of his position on ethics can be found in NKC 6: 303–26. See also the remarks scattered in 1969 and 1986B. ➤ The most perceptive critique of Nishitani's reading of Kantian ethics I know is by Little (1989). To my knowledge, no one has ever taken his points up further.

Other citations: Nishitani 1982A, 32; 1982B, 56; 1984A, 11; 1996, 26–8; 1990E, 16–17; NKC 6: 303, 325–6; 17: 11–12, 86–7, 112.

62 SCIENCE AND NATURE. A good résumé of Nishitani's ideas on science, though based on limited resources, has been prepared by Robinson (1989). ➤ Hase tries to show how Nishitani's early struggles with nihilism survived in his later work in the form of his critique of science (1999). ➤ Concerning developments on the convergence of science and religion in philosophical circles and their relation to Nishitani's thought, see Heine (1990). Although he relies on only a couple of representative sources and passes over the bulk of Nishitani's writings about science, his conclusion, that Nishitani does not translate his ethical ideals into a contemporary ethical code, seems correct. But the claim that Nishitani overlooks "the liberating consequences of science and technology" (188) is true only insofar as the former claim is true. Nishitani often has high praise for scientific and technological accomplishments. He repeats his conclusion in a later piece, while insisting nonetheless that the ethical dimension in Nishitani's critique of science is more important than the metaphysical (1991).

It may be noted in passing that in a 1975 lecture Nishitani refers to Whitehead's philosophy as one of the most illustrious of the day (NKC 24: 326), but with no hint of its central critique of substantial thinking or its attempt to relate religion and science. One has to suppose that he had not read any of the work and was simply reporting from secondary sources.

NKC 6: 334–45 treats the movement from the absence of the human in science to the presence of the human in the example of medical science and its service to humanity. Only then does he make the radical step of saying that this anthropocentricism needs to be overcome. ➤ For a lengthy comment on the relation between mechanization of the human, the transformation of the meaning of work, and the deterioration of human relations, see NISHITANI 1961B, 350–4. ➤ For extended treatments of the relation between science, religion, and myth, see NISHITANI 1959 and 1991B.

Other citations: NISHITANI, 1982C, 118–19; 1959, 53; NKC 18: 24–5.

63 TIME AND HISTORY. I myself had to persuade the publishers to let the chapters on time and history in *Religion and Nothingness* (1982A, 168–285) stand, and then again to resist their compromise that we shorten and combine them. ➤ The new understanding of the philosophy of history is mentioned in NISHITANI 1993, 3–5. ➤ HEINE takes up the question of Nishitani's view of time and history in an attempt to parry criticisms that Zen's reconstruction of the historical past in the service of individual enlightenment engages a kind of systematic scotosis that blinds it to the demands of historical accuracy and shields itself against criticism of its own past deeds (1994). Although making rather limited use of Nishitani's ideas, it does draw attention to the tacit assumptions that Nishitani took over from Zen. ➤ For a fuller résumé of Nishitani on history, and important criticisms of his allusions to western intellectual history, see KASULIS 1989.

Although NISHITANI mentions Eliade's work only briefly in connection with his thoughts on myth and makes no reference to it in his own treatment of time and history, he was certainly familiar with the contrast of linear time and circular time from *Le mythe de l'éternel retour,* originally published in 1949. Eliade himself was in Tokyo and Kyoto in 1958, but I have not been able to confirm if the two met on that occasion. In any case, there is no mention of it in Eliade's memoirs. ➤ Nishitani cites Kierkegaard's idea of the moment as an "atom of eternity" in time but also speaks of it as a "monad of eternity" to stress the self-enclosure of all of time (1982A, 189, 266).

Other citations: NISHITANI 1943, 45; 1969, 70, 83–4, 87–8; 1982A, 266.

64 GOD. The idea of overcoming God by God is also applicable in Buddhism to the Buddha. In a 1980 symposium, Nishitani calls on the Zen idea of "killing the patriarchs and Buddhas" to interpret the notion of "ascent to the Buddha" along these lines (NKC 18: 121–50). This essay is followed by a transcript of a discussion with other members present at the symposium, only one of two discussions to appear in his *Collected Works.* ➤ On Nishitani's reading of *creatio ex nihilo* and an assessment of its possibilities for Christian theology, see KRISTIANSEN (1987, and the shorter account in 1989). ➤ In an otherwise remarkably clear exposition of the central thesis of *Religion and Nothingness,* George JAMES is off the mark in finding in Nishitani an "unqualified rejection of western theism" (1991, 296). On the contrary, as ALTIZER has recog-

nized, it gives us "both a pure conception and a pure image of God... perhaps only possible within the horizon of Buddhist thinking" (1989, 70). ➤ BURI's argument that "the idea of God plays no central role in the thought of Keiji Nishitani" is wildly mistaken. As his explanation makes clear, what he means to say is that it does not play the same kind of central role that it does in Christianity, which is self-evident (1972, 49).

Nishitani makes a clear connection between the nothingness of the godhead and the ground of the soul in his earlier volume on *God and Absolute Nothingness* (NKC 7: 70–1), the bulk of which is devoted to Eckhart. ➤ Regarding his idea of breakthrough as a rebirth, see NKC 7: 32–3. ➤ In addition to Eckhart's explicit distinction of God from godhead, Nishitani finds this pattern implicit in other mystics as well. For example, in a sensitive but rarely cited essay on the thirteenth-century Beguine Mechthild von Magdeburg, he cites her idea that "separation from God is more desirable than God himself" (NKC 3: 119–47). He later expands this in a 1948 essay (NKC 7: 137–40).

On the effects of personalizing God for the scientific worldview, see NISHITANI 1982C, 132–3. ➤ Nishitani, like Nishida and Tanabe, does not distinguish Jesus from Christ, but generally prefers the latter. I have adjusted the vocabulary where necessary throughout the book. ➤ A brief connection is made between *kenōsis* and *ekkenōsis* in Christianity and the dual aspect of the Buddha as Tathāgata: Thus-Gone and Thus-Come. The point of contact is the idea of compassion as a "self-emptying" (1982A, 288). ➤ Nishitani is often credited with having originated the *kōan* of Paul's statement, supported by a comment of VAN BRAGT to that effect (1971, 281), but the idea seems to have been Nishida's NKZ 19: 93–4).

Other citations: NISHITANI 1982A, 36–8, 49, 62, 66, 68–9.

65 **THE EMBODIMENT OF AWARENESS.** For further detail on Nishitani's turn to Zen themes in his published works, see HORIO (1997A, 19–24), to whom I also owe the comment on breaking through Zen with philosophy. Nishitani himself explicitly acknowledged a few years after he completed *Religion and Nothingness* that "I have gradually come to think things through in Buddhist categories" (NKC 20: 185).

UNNO's characterization of *Religion and Nothingness* as "a modern hermeneutic of Zen Buddhism" seems right to me (1989B, 315). While it seems to me going too far to claim with VAN BRAGT that "Nishitani's whole opus is an attempt to build a *theologia fundamentalis* of Zen" (1971, 279), it does fulfill the proper theological role of liberating religion from the stagnation and routine of unquestioned traditional practice, a role that NISHITANI himself valued highly (1968A, 111). ➤ PASLICK's attempt to rescue Nishitani from criticisms of being anti-intellectual and obscurantist by comparing his imagery to that of Boehme (1997) has slightly skewed Nishitani's ideas in the direction of a philosophy of will. It is unfortunate that Nishitani's own essay on Boehme in his *History of Mystical Thought* has not yet been translated, since it focuses on somewhat different aspects of Boehme's thinking than Paslick does, namely, the "naturalness" at the base of light and darkness, the emergence of the self, and the problem of evil (NKC 1: 125–52).

The combination of feeling and willing in sensing is already present in Nishida's early expression of direct experience (see notes to §16 above). ➤ The term Nishitani uses for imaging, 構想, is different from the ordinary term for the psychological function of the imagination. The essay in which he deals with the relation of this imaging to the standpoint of emptiness was published in 1982 under the title "Emptiness and *Soku*" (NISHITANI 1999B). It is taken up in an essay by HASE as "the crystallization of Nishitani's lifelong thinking on the problem of imaging" (1997, 70). I am grateful to this essay for pointing to several texts of Nishitani's I had not paid attention to before. The only other treatment of "imaging" in Nishitani that has come to my attention is a piece by HIGASHI, which approaches the question in terms of aesthetic feeling (1992). ➤ The image of Zen as an alchemy of the heart also appears in NISHITANI 1961B, 349.

The Chinese glyph for "sky", 空, is the same as that used to translate the Sanskrit term *śūnyatā* (NISHITANI 1999B, 179). ➤ His term for "incarnate understanding" is 体認. He uses it frequently in *Religion and Nothingness*, where it has been translated as "appropriation" (see NISHITANI 1982A, 293).

The lectures referred to in which his most extended comments on the body appear, were delivered between 1964 and 1975 and gathered together in volume 24 of Nishitani's *Works*. ➤ Nishitani does not at any point see his theory of "imaging" as a critique of Zen, though as Bernard Faure has gone to great lengths to show in *The Rhetoric of Immediacy* (Princeton: Princeton University Press, 1991), the repudiation of imagery is closely tied to the traditional taboo on social practice in the Zen tradition.

Other citations: NKC 13: 127, 141, 145; 24: 392–3; NISHITANI 1981A, 35.

66 **THE CRITIQUE OF RELIGION.** On the general parameters of Nishitani's idea of the "religious quest," see HORIO 1993. ➤ I have found VAN BRAGT's essay on Nishitani's late thought helpful in locating some of Nishitani's comments on organized religion, which he liberally paraphrases (1992). ➤ Nishitani's ideas of differences between Catholicism and Protestantism, though not very profound and badly discolored by the distinctive shape each has taken in Japan, can be found in NISHITANI 1961B, 144–5. It is later in this same discussion that he refers to the openness to the universal that Buddhism has to learn from Christianity (327). ➤ It comes as little surprise to learn that the evangelical Christian finds Nishitani "much closer in assumptions, agenda, and conclusions to nonevangelical Christian theologies—such as radical, process, and mystical theologies—than to historic, evangelical faith," which leads him to conclude that this leaves only an either/or choice: either self or non-self, either a personal God or an absolute Nothingness" (BOWERS 1995, 140, 144; see also the chart of differences on page 148). That this is precisely the view that

Nishitani was inviting Christianity to overcome seems to have been lost in the reading.

The call for rethinking the meaning of the Buddha's death appears in NKC 17: 285–7. For references to other lacks in Buddhist religious thought, see NKC 17: 141–2, 148–50, 155–68; 18: 171–4. ➤ One has to take THELLE with a grain of salt when he writes about Nishitani's being embarrassed at the label of "Buddhist" (1992, 131). ➤ On forgetting everything in meditation, even being a Buddhist or a Christian, see NISHITANI 1985C, 4–5. In this same regard, we may note a criticism he raises against those worried about the possibility of the emperor's son marrying a Catholic. His own view is that the emperor should be free of all such religious restrictions, and that by the same token Catholic "exclusivism" should also be avoided (1961B, 57).

NISHITANI's brief remark on inculturation, the only one I was able to locate in his writings and discussions, appeared in 1961B, 365. ➤ Regarding his thoughts on the aims and difficulties of interreligious dialogue, see VAN BRAGT 1992, 46–50. ➤ Regarding the self-enclosure of Nishitani's thinking, see the blunt—if not always well-informed—criticism of PHILLIPS (1987), who reviews the arguments of *Religion and Nothingness* to criticize Nishitani on a number of counts, among them a certain uncritical attachment to Zen and to eastern Buddhism in general, a flouting of reason by gratuitous appeals to privileged experience, and a distance from the variety of ways people can effectively question the meaning of their lives and make their choices.

Regarding the sign over his door, it was certainly more than a treasured gift from D. T. Suzuki. It is the starting point and the goal of the philosopher's discipline for him. In a special message prepared for an international conference in 1984 on *Religion and Nothingness,* Nishitani wrote that his philosophical goal was the return to daily life by "making philosophy work as the thinking of basic non-thinking" (1989C, 4).

Other citations: MORI Tetsurō 1997, 1; NISHITANI 1960D, 20–4; 1961B, 341; 1968A, 109; 1981B, 140; 1986D, 149; 1991B, 4; NKC 17: 121, 124–5, 128.

Bibliography

Bibliographical details regarding translations of the writings of Nishida, Nishitani, and Tanabe include a reference, in square brackets, to the source in their respective collected works. ➤ Individual volumes of their collected works typically contain an afterword, usually written by one of the editors, as well as a publisher's leaflet that often contains useful historical information. These are cited as such in the notes, with the name of the author, but have been omitted from the bibliography. ➤ All of their collected works suffer from a lack of proper indexing, though a companion volume to a selection of Nishida's writings (FUJITA Masakatsu, 1998A) partially fills the gap for Nishida. An unpublished catalogue of foreign words culled from Nishida's works by Agustín Jacinto is available through the Centro de Estudios de las Tradiciones in the Colegio de Michoacán, Mexico. ➤ No complete bibliography of secondary sources on any of the three philosophers exists, as far as I know, and no annotated list in any form. Meantime one may consult the following: special editions of *The Eastern Buddhist* on Nishida (1985) and Nishitani (1992); a sizable listing of Japanese and western works on Nishida in the FUJITA volume mentioned above (542–92); and a rather good but dated list in ŌHASHI 1990, 507–40.

Abbreviations

NKZ 『西田幾多郎全集』. *Complete works of Nishida Kitarō.* Tokyo: Iwanami Shoten, 1978. 19 vols.

THZ 『田辺元全集』. *Complete works of Tanabe Hajime.* Tokyo: Chikuma Shobō, 1963–1964. 15 vols.

NKC 『西谷啓治著作集』. *Collected works of Nishitani Keiji.* Tokyo: Sōbunsha, 1986–1995. 26 vols.

Abe Masao 阿部正雄

1989 Nishitani's Challenge to Western Philosophy and Theology. UNNO 1989, 13–45.

1990 Introduction. NISHIDA 1990C, VII–XXVI.

1995 The Logic of Absolute Nothingness, as Expounded by Nishida Kitarō. *The Eastern Buddhist* 28/2: 167–74.

1997 Buddhism in Japan. CARR and MAHALINGAM 1997, 746–91.

Abe Nobuhiko 阿部信彦
1993 *Semiotics of Self in Theology: A Comparative Study of James and Nishida.* Ph.D. dissertation, Harvard University. Ann Arbor: University Microfilms.
Abe Yoshishige 安倍能成
1951 田辺元君と私 [Tanabe Hajime and I]. KŌBUNDŌ 1951, 249–56.
Aihara Shinsaku 相原信作
1951 田辺先生について [On Professor Tanabe]. KŌBUNDŌ 1951, 262–70.
Akizawa Shūji 秋沢修二
1941 田辺哲学と全体主義 [Tanabe's philosophy and totalitarianism]. *Science Magazine,* 6: 87–93.
Akizuki Ryōmin 秋月龍珉
1996 『絶対無と場所: 鈴木禅学と西田哲学』 *[Absolute nothingness and locus: Suzuki's Zen and Nishida's philosophy].* Tokyo: Seidosha.
Altizer, Thomas J. J.
1989 Emptiness and God. UNNO 1989, 70–81.
Arima Tatsuo 有馬達郎
1969 *The Failure of Freedom: A Portrait of Modern Japanese Intellectuals.* Cambridge: Harvard University Press.
Arisaka Yōko 有坂陽子
1996A The Nishida Enigma: "The Principle of the New World Order." *Monumenta Nipponica* 51/1: 81–99.
1996B *Space and History: Philosophy and Imperialism in Nishida and Watsuji.* Ph.D. dissertation, University of California, Riverside. Ann Arbor: University Microfilms.
Berque, Augustin, ed.
2000 *Logique du Lieu et dépassemente de la modernité.* Vol. 1, *Nishida: La mouvance philosophique.* Paris: Éditions OUSIA.
Bowers, Russell H., Jr.
1995 *Someone or Nothing: Nishitani's "Religion and Nothingness" as a Foundation for Christian-Buddhist Dialogue.* New York: Peter Lang.
Brüll, Lydia
1989 *Die Japanische Philosophie: Eine Einführung.* Darmstadt: Wissenschaftliche Buchgesellschaft. 2nd edition, 1993.
Buri, Fritz
1972 The Fate of the Concept of God in the Philosophy of Religion of Keiji Nishitani. *Northeast Asia Journal of Theology* 8: 49–56.
1997 *The Buddha-Christ as the Lord of the True Self: The Religious Philosophy of the Kyoto School and Christianity.* Macon: Mercer University Press.
Carr, Brian, and Indira Mahalingam, eds.
1997 *Companion Encyclopedia of Asian Philosophy.* London: Routledge.
Carter, Robert E.
1997 *The Nothingness beyond God: An Introduction to the Philosophy of Nishida Kitarō.* St. Paul: Paragon House.
Cestari, Matteo, ed.
1998 The Knowing Body: Nishida's Philosophy of Active Intuition. *The Eastern Buddhist* 31/2: 179–208.
2001 *Il corpo e la conoscenza.* Venice: Cafoscarina.

Chun, Paul San-wan

1979 *The Christian Concept of God and Zen "Nothingness" as Embodied in the Works of Tillich and Nishida.* Ph.D. dissertation, Temple University. Ann Arbor: University Microfilms.

Dallmayr, Fred

1992 Nothingness and "Sunyata": A Comparison of Heidegger and Nishitani. *Philosophy East and West* 42/1: 37–48.

Dilworth, David A.

1969 The Initial Formations of "Pure Experience" in Nishida Kitarō and William James. *Monumenta Nipponica* 24/1–2: 93–111.

1970 Nishida's Early Pantheistic Voluntarism. *Philosophy East and West* 20/1: 35–49.

1979 The Concrete World of Action in Nishida's Later Thought. NITTA and TATEMATSU 1979, 249–69.

1987 Introduction: Nishida's Critique of the Religious Consciousness. Postscript: Nishida's Philosophy of the East. NISHIDA 1987B, 1–45, 127–49.

Dilworth, David A., and Valdo H. Viglielmo, eds.

1998 (with Agustín Jacinto Zavala). *Sourcebook for Modern Japanese Philosophy: Selected Documents.* Westport: Greenwood Press.

Doak, Kenneth

1995 Nationalism as Dialectics: Ethnicity, Moralism, and the State in Early Twentieth-Century Japan. HEISIG and MARALDO 1995, 174–96.

Eberfeld, Rolf, ed.

1999 *Logik des Ortes: Der Anfang der modernen Philosophie in Japan.* Darmstadt: Wissenschaftliche Buchgesellschaft.

Enns, Amelie

1988 The Subject-Object Dichotomy in Heidegger's *A Dialogue on Language* and Nishitani's *Religion and Nothingness. Japanese Religions* 15/1: 38–48.

Feenberg, Andrew

1999 Experience and Culture: Nishida's Path "To the Things Themselves." *Philosophy East and West* 49/1: 28–44.

Franck, Frederick, ed.

1982 *The Buddha Eye: An Anthology of the Kyoto School.* New York: Crossroad.

Fredericks, James

1988 *Alterity in the Thought of Tanabe Hajime and Karl Rahner.* Ph.D. dissertation, University of Chicago. Ann Arbor: University Microfilms.

1989 Cosmology and Metanoia: Buddhist Path to Process Thought for the West. *The Eastern Buddhist* 22/1: 111–27.

1990A *Philosophy as Metanoetics:* An Analysis. UNNO and HEISIG 1990, 43–71.

1990B The Metanoetics of Inter-Religious Encounter. UNNO and HEISIG 1990, 163–78.

Fujita Kenji 藤田健治

1993 『西田幾多郎: その軌跡と系譜』 *[Nishida Kitarō: His place and geneaology].* Tokyo: Hōsei University Press.

Fujita Masakatsu 藤田正勝

1998A (ed.) 『西田哲学研究の歴史』 *[A history of studies in Nishida's philosophy].* 『西田哲学 選集』 *[Selected writings of Nishida's philosophy]*, supplementary vol. 2. Kyoto: Tōeisha).

1998B Questions Posed by Nishida's Philosophy. *Zen Buddhism Today* 15: 51–64.

Funayama Shin'ichi 船山信一

1965 『大正哲学史研究』*[Studies in the history of Taishō philosophy]*. Kyoto: Hōritsu Bunkasha.

1984 『ヘーゲル哲学と西田哲学』*[The philosophies of Hegel and Nishida]*. Tokyo: Miraisha.

Furuta Hikaru 古田 光

1956 日本的観念論哲学の成立 [The emergence of Japanese philosophical idealism]. Tōyama Shigeki 遠山茂樹 et al., eds.,『近代日本思想史』*[A history of modern Japanese thought]*. Vol. 2. Tokyo: Aoki Shoten, 417–87.

1959 十五年戦争下の思想と哲学 [Thought and philosophy during the fifteen-year war] in vol. 4 of『近代日本社会思想史』*[The history of social thought in modern Japan]*, Furuta Hikaru 古田 光 et al., eds. Tokyo: Chikuma Shobō.

1983 歴史と実存の省察: 西田幾多郎と田辺元 [Reflections on history and Existenz: Nishida Kitarō and Tanabe Hajime], Furuta Hikaru 古田 光 and 鈴木 正 Suzuki Masashi, eds.『近代日本の哲学』*[Modern Japanese philosophy]*. Tokyo: Hokuju Shuppan, 143–60.

Gilkey, Langdon

1990 Tanabe's Contribution to East-West Dialogue. Unno and Heisig 1990, 72–85.

González Valles, Jesús

2000 *Historia de la filosofía japonesa*. Madrid: Tecnos.

Hamada Junko 浜田恂子

1994 *Japanische Philosophie nach 1868*. Leiden: E. J. Brill.

Hanaoka (Kawamura) Eiko 花岡(川村)永子

1988 『キリスト教と西田哲学』*[Christianity and Nishida's philosophy]*. Tokyo: Shinkyō Shuppansha.

1990 The Logic of the Species and the Pursuit of True Reality. Unno and Heisig 1990, 223–34.

1995 田辺哲学と有機体の哲学: 場所の論理を介して [Tanabe's philosophy and the philosophy of organism: A view from the logic of locus].『求真』2: 2–16.

Hanazawa Hidefumi 花澤秀文

1999 『高山岩男: 京都学派哲学の基礎的研究』*[Kōyama Iwao: Basic studies on the Kyoto school]*. Kyoto: Jinbun Shoin.

Hase Shōtō 長谷正當

1990 The Structure of Faith: Nothingness-qua-Love. Unno and Heisig 1990, 89–116.

1994 田辺哲学と E. レヴィナスの哲学: 哲学の立脚点としての存在論と倫理について [The philosophies of Tanabe and Levinas: Ontology and ethics as philosophical positions].『求真』1: 2–22.

1997 Emptiness Thought and the Concept of the Pure Land in Nishitani: In the light of Imagination and the Body. *Zen Buddhism Today* 14: 65–80.

1998A 死と実存協同: 田辺の晩年の思想をめぐって [Death and existential collaboration: Tanabe's late thought].『哲学研究』565: 1–26.

1998B The Problem of the Other in Self-Awareness. *Zen Buddhism Today* 15: 119–38.

1999 Nihilism, Science, and Emptiness in Nishitani. *Buddhist-Christian Studies* 19: 139–54.

Hashi Hisaki 橋 柃

1997 絶対無の場所における自己の問題 [The problem of the self in the locus of absolute nothingness: A point of contact between Nishida's philosophy and Zen studies]. Kawanami Akira 河波 昌,『場所論の種々相: 西田哲学を中心に

して』[*The many faces of locus theory: A focus on Nishida's philosophy*]. Tokyo: Hokuju Shuppan.

Heine, Steven

1990 Philosophy for an "Age of death": The Critique of Science and Technology in Heidegger and Nishitani. *Philosophy East and West* 40/2: 175–93.

1991 "The Buddha or the Bomb": Ethical Implications in Nishitani Keiji's Zen View of Science. *Buddhist Ethics and Modern Society*, ed. by Charles Wei-hsun Fu and S. A. Warrytko (New York: Greenwood, 1991), 281–95.

1994 History, Transhistory, and Narrative History: A Postmodern View of Nishitani's Philosophy of Zen. *Philosophy East and West* 44/2: 251–78.

Heisig, James W.

1983 Translator's Introduction. TAKEUCHI Yoshinori 1983, XIII–XXII.

1986 Śūnyatā and Kénosis. *Academia* 43: 1–29. Reprinted: *Spirituality Today* 39/2 (1987), 132–42; 39/3: 211–24.

1986 Foreword. TANABE 1986, VII–XXX.

1990A The Religious Philosophy of the Kyoto School. UNNO and HEISIG 1990, 12–45.

1990B The "Self that is Not-a-Self": Tanabe's Dialectics of Self-Awareness. UNNO and HEISIG 1990, 277–90.

1991 真の自己の探求 [The quest of the true self],『宗教学会報』6: 32–50.

1992A 一歩ならぬ一歩 [A step that is not a step]『溪聲西谷啓治』. Kyoto, Tōeisha, vol. 1, 265–9.

1992B Dirty Water, Clear Thinking. *The Eastern Buddhist* 25/1: 85–91.

1995A Tanabe's Logic of the Specific and the Spirit of Nationalism. HEISIG and MARALDO 1995, 255–88.

1995B Tanabe's Logic of the Specific and the Critique of the Global Village. *The Eastern Buddhist* 28/2: 198–224.

1996 西谷の外国における評価について [Nishitani's reception abroad].『大乗禅』871: 12–16.

1997 The Quest of the True Self: Jung's Rediscovery of a Modern Invention. *Journal of Religion* 77/2: 252–67.

1998 The Kyoto School. *Routledge Encyclopedia of Philosophy*. London: Routledge, 5: 323–30.

1999A Philosophy as Spirituality: The Way of the Kyoto School. Takeuchi Yoshinori, ed., *Buddhist Spirituality. Volume 2: Later China, Korea, Japan, and the Modern World*, New York: Crossroad, 367–88.

1999B Introducción. NISHITANI 1999A, 9–25.

2000 Non-I and Thou: Nishida, Buber, and the Moral Consequences of Self-Actualization. *Philosophy East and West* 50/2: 179–207.

Heisig, James W., and John Maraldo, eds.

1995 *Rude Awakenings: Zen, the Kyoto School, and the Question of Nationalism*. Honolulu: University of Hawai'i Press.

Higashi Sen'ichirō 東 専一郎

1985 西田哲学と道元 [Nishida's philosophy and Dōgen]. TAKEUCHI Yoshinori and ŌSHIMA 1985, 149–74.

1992 情意のうちの空 [Emptiness within feeling-will]. UEDA Shizuteru 1992B, 71–97.

Himi Kiyoshi 氷見 潔

1990A『田辺哲学研究: 宗教哲学の観点から』[*Studies in the philosophy of Tanabe Hajime: A view from the philosophy of religion*]. Tokyo: Hokuju Shuppan.

1990B Tanabe's Theory of the State. UNNO and HEISIG 1990, 303–15.

Hirokawa Kazuo 廣川和夫
1999 「私と汝」の問題: 中期西田哲学に動いているもの [The problem of "I and you": Elements at work in the middle years of Nisahida's philosophy].『宗教研究』325: 27–51.
Hiromatsu Wataru 廣松 渉
1980 『〈近代の超克〉論: 昭和思想史への一視角』*[The "Overcoming modernity" debate: A perspective on the intellectual history of the Shōwa period]*. Tokyo: Kōdansha, 1980.
Hisamatsu Shin'ichi 久松真一
1985 西田哲学と禅 *[Nishida's philosophy and Zen]*. SHIMOMURA 1985A, 43–69.
Horio Tsutomu 堀尾 孟
1992 The Zen Practice of Nishitani Keiji. *The Eastern Buddhist* 25/1: 92–7.
1993 西谷先生に於ける「宗教的探求」 [The "religious quest" in Professor Nishitani]. KYOTO SOCIETY 1993, 108–40.
1995 The *Chūōkōron* Discussions, Their Background and Meaning. HEISIG and MARALDO 1995, 289–315.
1997A Nishitani's Philosophy: The Later Period. *Zen Buddhism Today* 14: 19–32.
1997B ニヒリズムを通してニヒリズムの超克: 西谷啓治 [Overcoming nihilism through nihilism: Nishitani Keiji]. Fujita Masakatsu 藤田正勝, ed.,『日本近代思想を学ぶ人のために』*[For students of modern Japanese thought]* (Kyoto: Sekai-shisō-sha, 1997), 285–307.
1998 *Gyakutaiō* and *Gyakuen:* Nishida's philosophy, Nishitani's Philosophy, and Zen. *Zen Buddhism Today* 15: 155–68.
Horio Tsutomu 堀尾 孟 and Ueda Shizuteru 上田閑照, eds.
1997 『禅と現代世界』*[Zen and the contemporary world]*. Kyoto: Zen Bunka Kenkyūjo.
Hosoya Masashi 細谷昌志
1998 最後の田辺哲学: 絶筆『マラルメ覚書』について [Tanabe's final philosophy: His last essay, "A Memorandum on Mallarmé"].『求真』5: 2–27.
Hubbard, Jamie, and Paul L. Swanson, eds.
1997 *Pruning the Bodhi Tree: The Storm over Critical Buddhism.* Honolulu: University of Hawai'i Press.
Huh Woo-sung
1988 *A Critical Exposition of Nishida's Philosophy.* Ph.D. dissertation, University of Hawai'i. Ann Arbor: University Microfilms.
Ienaga Saburō 家永三郎
1988 『田辺元の思想史的研究: 戦争と哲学者』*[Studies in the history of Tanabe Hajime's thought: War and the philosopher]*. Tokyo: Hōsei University Press.
Ishida Yoshikazu 石田慶和
1993 『日本の宗教哲学』*[Japanese philosophy of religion]*. Tokyo: Sōbunsha.
Ishizawa Kaname 石沢 要
1996 田辺山荘について [Tanabe's villa].『求真』3: 33–35.
Ives, Christopher
1989 Non-dualism and Soteriology in Whitehead, Nishida and Tanabe: A Response to James Fredericks. *The Eastern Buddhist* 29/1: 128–38.
1995 (ed.) *Divine Emptiness and Historical Fullness.* Valley Forge: Trinity Press International.

Jacinto Zavala, Agustín

1984 *Zen y personalidad.* Michoacán: El Colegio de Michoacán.

1985 *Estado y filosofía.* Michoacán: El Colegio de Michoacán.

1989 *Filosofía de la transformación del mundo: Introducción a la filosofía tardía de Nishida Kitarō.* Michoacán: El Colegio de Michoacán.

1993 *La derecha en la escuela de Kioto. Avances de Investigación* (El Colegio de Michoacán), serie 1, no. 4.

1994 *La filosofía social de Nishida Kitarō.* Michoacán: El Colegio de Michoacán.

1995 (ed.) *Textos de la filosofía japonesa moderna.* Michoacán: El Colegio de Michoacán.

1997 *La otra filosofía japonesa.* Michoacán: El Colegio de Michoacán.

1998 The Bodily Manifestation of Religious Experience and Late Nishida Philosophy. *Zen Buddhism Today* 15: 33–50.

James, George A.

1991 Religion, Nothingness, and the Challenge of Post-Modern Thought: An Introduction to the Philosophy of Keiji Nishitani. *International Philosophical Quarterly* 31/3: 295–308.

Kadowaki Ken 門脇 健

1997 The Circle Play: Nïshitani and Hegel. *Zen Buddhism Today* 14: 57–64.

Kajitani Sūnin 梶谷宗認

1992 Layman Keisei Nishitani. *The Eastern Buddhist* 25/1: 97–8.

Kasulis, Thomas P.

1982 The Kyoto School and the West: Review and Evaluation. *The Eastern Buddhist* 15/2: 125–44.

1989 Whence and Whither: Philosophical Reflections on Nishitani's View of History. UNNO 1989, 259–78.

1995 Sushi, Science, and Spirituality: Modern Japanese Philosophy and its Views of Western Science. *Philosophy East and West* 46/2: 227–48.

Katō Shūichi 加藤周一

1959 戦争と知識人 [War and the intellectuals], Furuta Hikaru et al., eds.,『知識人の生成と役割』*[The emergence and role of the intellectual].* Tokyo: Chikuma Shobō, ch. 5.

Kawashima Gaizō 川島炫三

1997 田辺元が群馬に遺したメッセージ [Tanabe's final message to Gunma].『求真』4: 59–66.

1998A 初期の田辺哲学: 自然科学的形而上学批判 [Tanabe's early philosophy: A scientific critique of metaphysics].『求真』5: 42–53.

1998B『徳の戦い』*[Struggles of virtue].* Tsuyama: Koneko Imai Shoten.

1999 初期の田辺哲学:「種の論理」への助走 [Tanabe's early philosophy: Approaching the logic of the specific].『求真』6: 52–71.

Keta Masako 氣田雅子

1985 西田哲学と禅 [Nishida's philosophy and Zen].『理想』621: 163–73.

1999『ニヒリズムの思索』*[Nihilistic thinking].* Tokyo: Sōbunsha.

2000 すべてがそこからそこへ [The whence and whither of it all]. NANZAN INSTITUTE 2000, 226–43.

Knauth, Lothar

1965 Life is Tragic: The Diary of Nishida Kitarō. *Monumenta Nipponica* 20/3–4: 334–58.

Kobayashi Hideo 小林秀雄
1968 『小林秀雄全集』 *[Complete works of Kobayashi Hideo]*. Tokyo: Shinchōsha.
Kobayashi Toshiaki 小林敏明
1997 『西田幾多郎: 他性の文体』 *[Nishita Kitarō: A different kind of style]*. Tokyo: Ōta Shuppan.
Kōbundō 弘文堂, ed.
1951 『田辺哲学』 *[Tanabe's philosophy]*. Tokyo: Kōbundō.
Koch, Hans-Joachim
1990 *Amor Fati bei Friedrick Nietzsche und Hajime Tanabe*. Essen: Hinder u. Deelman.
Kopf, Gereon
1999 Alterity and Nothingness: An Exploration of Nishida's I and Thou. *Journal of the Faculty of Religious Studies* 27: 109–22.
Kosaka Kunitsugu 小坂国継
1991 『西田哲学の研究: 場所の論理の生成と構造』 *[Studies in Nishida's philosophy: The formation and structure of the logic of locus]*. Kyoto: Minerva Shobō.
1994 『西田哲学と宗教』 *[Religion and the philosophy of Nishida]*. Tokyo: Daitō Shuppansha.
1997 『西田幾多郎をめぐる哲学者群像: 近代日本哲学と宗教』 *[Portraits of philosophers in Nishida's circle: Modern Japanese philosophy and religion]*. Kyoto: Minerva Shobō.
Kōsaka Masaaki 高坂正顕
1935 『西田哲学』 *[Nishida's philosophy]*. Tokyo: Iwanami Shoten.
1940 『続西田哲学』 *[Nishida's philosophy II]*. Tokyo: Iwanami Shoten.
1961 『西田幾多郎の生涯と思想』 *[The life and thought of Nishida Kitarō]*. Tokyo: Kokusai Nihon Kenkyūjo.
1965 『西田哲学と田辺哲学』 *[The philosophies of Nishida and Tanabe]*. Reprinted in vol. 8 of 『高坂正顕著作集』 *[Collected works of Kōsaka Masaaki]*. Tokyo: Risōsha, 1965, 235–372.
1978 『西田幾多郎と和辻哲郎』 *[The philosophies of Nishida and Watsuji]*. Tokyo: Shinchōsha.
Kōyama Iwao 高山岩男
1943 『世界史の哲学』 *[Philosophy of world history]*. Tokyo: Iwanami Shoten.
1949 西田先生の思ひ出 [Recollections of Professor Nishida]. Kōyama Iwao, Shimatani Shunzō 島谷俊三, eds.,『西田寸心先生片影』 *[Traces of Professor Nishida Sunshin]*. Tokyo: Reimei Shobō.
1951 田辺哲学の史的意識と特色 [The historical consciousness and special traits of Tanabe's philosophy]. Kōbundō 1951, 3–22.
1964 田辺先生の想い出 [Reminiscing on Professor Tanabe] 『哲学研究』 489, 42/7: 679–82.
Kracht, Klaus
1984 Nishida Kitarō (1870–1945) as a Philosopher of the State. Gordon Daniels, ed., *Europe Interprets Japan*. Tenterden, Kent: Paul Norbury Publications, 198–203.
Kristiansen, Roald
1987 *Creation and Emptiness: Transforming the Doctrine of Creation in Dialogue with the Kyoto School of Philosophy*. Ph.D. dissertation, Emory University. Ann Arbor: University Microfilms.
1989 Den Tomme Gud: Kristen Gudstro Og Buddhistisk Tomhetslaere. *Norsk Teologisk Tidsskrift* 90: 19–30.

Kume Yasuhiro 粂 康弘
1999 『西田哲学: その成立と陥穽』 *[Nishida's philosophy: Its emergence and pitfalls]*. Tokyo: Nōbunkyō.

Kyoto Society for Religious Philosophy 京都宗教哲学会
1993 『溪聲西谷啓治』 *[Keisei Nishitani Keiji]*. 2 vols. Kyoto: Tōeisha.

Lai, Whalen
1990 Tanabe and the Dialectics of Mediation: A Critique. Unno and Heisig 1990, 256–76.

Laube, Johannes
1981 Die Interpretation des Kyōgyōshinshō Shinrans durch Hajime Tanabe. *Zeitschrift für Missionswissenschaft* 65/4: 277–93.
1984 *Dialektik der absoluten Vermittlung: Hajime Tanabes Religionsphilosophie als Beitrag zum "Wettstreit der Liebe" zwischen Buddhismus und Christentum.* Freiburg: Herder.
1990 The Way of Metanoia and the Way of the Bodhisattva. Unno and Heisig 1990, 316–39.
1994 Sur la personne et l'ouevre de Hajime Tanabe. *Revue philosophique de Louvain* 9/4: 423–9.

Lavelle, Pierre
1994A Nishida Kitarō, l'école de Kyōto et l'ultra-nationalisme. *Revue philosophique de Louvain* 4/92: 430–58.
1994B The Political Thought of Nishida Kitarō. *Monumenta Nipponica* 49/2: 139–65.

Little, David
1989 The Problem of Ethics in *Religion and Nothingness.* Unno 1989A, 181–7.

Lüth, Paul
1944 *Die japanische Philosophie.* Tübingen: J. C. B. Mohr.

Mafli, Paul
1996 *Nishida Kitarō's Denkweg.* Munich: Judicium.

Maraldo, John C.
1988 Nishida and the Individualization of Religion. *Zen Buddhism Today* 6: 70–87.
1989 Translating Nishida. *Philosophy East and West* 39/4 : 465–95.
1990 Metanoetics and the Crisis of Reason. Unno and Heisig 1990, 235–55.
1992 Practice, Samādhi, Realization: Three Innovative Interpretations by Nishitani Keiji. *The Eastern Buddhist* 25/1: 8–20.
1995 Questioning Nationalism Now and Then: A Critical Approach to Zen and the Kyoto School. Heisig and Maraldo 1995, 333–62.
1997 Contemporary Japanese Philosophy. Carr and Mahalingam 1997, 810–35.
1998A Nishida Kitarō. *Routledge Encyclopedia of Philosophy.* London: Routledge, 13–16.
1998B Emptiness, History, Accountability: A Critical Examination of Nishitani Keiji's Standpoint. *Zen Buddhism Today* 15: 97–118.

Marchianò, Grazia, ed.
1996 *La scuola di Kyōto: Kyōto-ha.* Messina: Rubbettino.

Masía Clavel, Juan
1992 Filosofía del absoluto en K. Nishida: Apropiación crítica de lo budista y lo cristiano por un filósofo japonés. José Gómez Caffarena and José María Mardones, eds., *Cuestiones epistemológicas: Materiales para el estudio de la religión.* Madrid: Anthropos, vol. 1, 137–47.

Matsuda Fukumatsu 松田福松

1933 科学的精神と新スコラスティク打破: 田辺博士の所論に因みて [The spirit of science and the overthrow of neo-scholasticism in connection with the theory of Dr. Tanabe]. 『原理日本』 November.

Matsumaru Hisao 松丸壽雄

1997A Nishitani's *Religionsphilosophie:* Religion and the Standpoint of *Śūnyatā. Zen Buddhism Today* 14: 97–114.

1997B 「中」の立場の探求: 西谷の宗教哲学 [The quest of the "middle" standpoint: The religious philosophy of Nishitani]. HORIO and UEDA 1997, 500–37.

Miki Kiyoshi 三木 清

1986 『三木清全集』 *[Complete works of Miki Kiyoshi]*. 20 vols. Tokyo: Iwanami Shoten.

Minamoto Ryōen 源 了圓

1995 The Symposium on "Overcoming Modernity." HEISIG and MARALDO 1995, 197–229.

Minoda Muneki 蓑田胸喜

1933 田辺元氏の科学政策論の学術的誤謬を分析す [An analysis of the academic fallacy in Tanabe Hajime's idea of scientific policy] 『原理日本』 November.

Miyakawa Tōru 宮川 透

1956 『近代日本思想の構造』 *[The structure of modern Japanese thinking]*. Tokyo: Tokyo University Press.

Mori Kiyoshi 森 清

1991 『大拙と幾多郎』 *[Daisetsu and Kitarō]*. Tokyo: Shinchōsha.

Mori Tetsurō 森 哲郎

1995 Nishitani Keiji and the Question of Nationalism. HEISIG and MARALDO 1995, 233–54.

1997 Religion in the Early Thought of Nishitani Keiji: The Bottomlessness of Nature. *Zen Buddhism Today* 14: 1–18.

Mutō Kazuo 武藤一雄

1951 政治・社会: 田辺博士の社会民主主義の哲学 [Politics and society: Professor Tanabe's philosophy of social democracy]. KŌBUNDŌ 1951, 138–53.

1986 『神学的・宗教哲学的論集』 *[Essays on theology and the philosophy of religion]*, 3 vols. Tokyo: Sōbunsha.

1992 A Man of the Universe. *The Eastern Buddhist* 25/1: 99–100.

Nakagawa Hisasyasu 中川久定

1994 西田幾多郎の哲学と文体 [The philosophy and literary style of Nishida Kitarō]. 『創文』 9.

Nakamura Yūjirō 中村雄二郎

1983 『西田幾多郎』 *[Nishida Kitarō]*. Tokyo: Iwanami Shoten.

1984 『西田哲学』 *[Nishida's philosophy]*. Tokyo: Iwanami Shoten.

1987 『西田哲学の脱構築』 *[The deconstruction of Nishida's philosophy]*. Tokyo: Iwanami Shoten.

1988 『場所: トポス』 *[Locus: Topos]*. Tokyo: Kōbundō.

Nakano Hajimu 中埜 肇

1975 『田辺元集』 *[A Tanabe Hajime collection]*. Tokyo: Chikuma Shobō.

Nakaoka Narifumi 中岡成文

1999 『私と出会うための西田幾多郎』 *[A Nishida for me to encounter]*. Tokyo: Demadosha.

Nakayama Enji 中山延二

1979 『仏教と西田·田辺哲学』 *[Buddhism and the philosophies of Nishida and Tanabe]*. Kyoto: Hyakkaen.

Nanbara Shigeru 南原 繁

1972 国家と宗教 [State and religion], 『南原繁著作集』 *[Collected works of Nanbara Shigeru]*. Tokyo: Iwanami Shoten, vol. 1.

Nanzan Institute for Religion and Culture 南山宗教文化研究所, ed.

1981 『絶対無と神』 *[Absolute nothingness and God]*. Tokyo: Shunjūsha.

1999 『キリスト教は仏教から何を学べるか』 *[What does Christianity have to learn from Buddhism?]*. Kyoto: Hōzōkan.

2000 『宗教と宗教の〈あいだ〉』 *[The "between" of religion and religion]*. Nagoya: Fūbaisha.

Ng Yu-kwan 呉 汝鈞

1995 『京都學派哲學: 久松真一』 *[The ; hilosophy of the Kyoto school: Hisamatsu Shin'ichi]*. Taipei: Wenjin.

1998 『絶対無的哲學: 京都學派哲學導論』 *[The philosophy of absolute nothingness: An introduction to the philosophy of the Kyoto school]*. Taipei: Taiwan Commercial Press.

Nishida Kitarō 西田幾多郎

1936A Brief an den Schriftleiter der Zeitschrift *Risō*. Trans. by R. Ōki. *Cultural Nippon* 4/2: 123–8. [13: 137–41]

1936B Logik und Leben. *Cultural Nippon* 4/4: 365–70. [8: 273–395, partial]

1939 Dir morgenländische und abendländische Kulturformen in alter Zeit vom metaphysischen Standpunkt ausgesehen. Trans. by F. Takahashi. *Abhandlungen der Preußischen Akademie der Wissenschaft*, Einzelausgabe, 3–19. [7: 429–53]

1940 Dir Einheit des Wahren, des Schönen und des Guten. Trans. by F. Takahashi. *Journal of the Sendai International Society*, 116–66. [3: 350–91]

1958A The Intelligible World. SCHINZINGER 1958, 68–141. [5: 123–85]

1958B Goethe's Metaphysical Background. SCHINZINGER 1958, 143–59. [12: 138–49]

1958C The Unity of Opposites. SCHINZINGER 1958, 161–241. [9: 147–222]

1958D The Problem of Japanese Culture. Wm. Theodore De Bary, ed., *Sources of Japanese Tradition*. New York: Columbia University Press. Vol. 2, 350–65. [12: 275–394, partial]

1963 *Ensayo sobre el bien*. Trans. by Anselmo Mataix and José M. de Vera. Madrid: Revista de Occidente. [1: 1–200]

1970A Towards a Philosophy of Religion with the Concept of Preestablished Harmony as a Guide. Trans. by David Dilworth. *The Eastern Buddhist* 3/1: 19–46. [11: 114–46]

1970B *Fundamental Problems of Philosophy*. Trans. by David Dilworth. Tokyo: Sophia University. [7: 1–454]

1970C Religious Consciousness and the Logic of the Prajñāparamitā Sūtra. Trans. by David Dilworth. *Monumenta Nipponica* 25: 203–16. [11: 392–412]

1972 General Summary of The System of Self-Consciousness of the Universal. WARGO 1972, 362–422. [5: 419–81]

1973A *Art and Morality*. Trans. by David A. Dilworth and Valdo H. Viglielmo. Honolulu: University of Hawai'i Press. [3: 237–545]

1973B Was liegt dem Selbstsein zugrunde? Trans. by Yagi Seiichi. S. Yagi and Ulrich Luz, eds., *Gott in Japan: Anstöße zum Gespräch mit japanischen Philosophen, Theologen und Schriftstellern.* Munich: Kaiser, 94–112. [11: 392–412]

1979 Affective Feeling. Trans. by David Dilworth and Valdo Viglielmo. NITTA and TATEMATSU 1979, 223–47. [3: 51–77]

1984 On the Doubt in our Heart. Trans. by Jeff Shore and Fusako Nakazawa. *The Eastern Buddhist* 17/2: 7–11. [13: 85–9]

1985A La crisis de la cultura japonesa. JACINTO 1985, 41–134. [12: 275–394]

1985B El problema de la razón de estado. JACINTO 1985, 135–93. [10: 265–333]

1985C Teoría del *kokutai.* JACINTO 1985, 195–228. [12: 397–434]

1986 The Logic of *Topos* and the Religious Worldview. Trans. by Yusa Michiko. *The Eastern Buddhist* 19/2: 1–29, 20/1: 81–119. [11: 371–464]

1987A *Intuition and Reflection in Self-Consciousness.* Trans. by Valdo H. Viglielmo with Takeuchi Yoshinori and Joseph S. O'Leary. Albany: SUNY Press. [2: 1–350]

1987B *Last writings: Nothingness and the Religious Worldview.* Trans. by David Dilworth. Honolulu: University of Hawai'i Press. [11: 371–464]

1987C An Explanation of Beauty: Nishida Kitarō's *Bi no Setsumei.* Trans. by Steve Odin. 42: 211–17. [13: 78–80]

1988 *A Study of Good.* Trans. by Valdo Viglielmo. Westport: Greenwood Press. [1: 1–200]

1989 *Über das Gute.* Trans. by Peter Pörtner. Frankfurt: Insel. [1: 1–200]

1990A Selbstidentität und Kontinuität der Welt. Trans. by Elmar Weinmayr. ŌHASHI 1990, 54–118. [8: 7–189]

1990B Die künsterlische Schaffen als Gestaltungsakt der Geschichte. Trans. by Elmar Weinmayr. ŌHASHI 1990, 119–37. [10: 223–41]

1990C *An Inquiry into the Good.* Trans. by Masao Abe and Christopher Ives. New Haven: Yale University Press. [1: 1–200]

1990D Die Welt als dialektisches Allgemeines: Eine Einführung in die Spätphilosophie von Kitarō Nishida. Trans. by Matsudo Yukio. Berlin: Vista, 115–246.

1991 *La culture japonaise en question.* Trans. by Pierre Lavelle. Paris: Publications Orientalistes de France. [12: 275–394]

1995A *Indagación del bien.* Trans. by Albert Luis Bixio. Barcelona: Gedisa. [1: 1–200]

1995B The Retirement Speech of a Certain Professor. Trans. by Wayne Yokoyama. *The Eastern Buddhist* 28/2: 245–7. [12: 168–71]

1995C Gutoku Shinran. *The Eastern Buddhist* 28/2: 242–4. [1: 407–9]

1995D La experiencia pura. JACINTO 1995, 67–74. [1: 9–18]

1995E Problemas de la cultura japonesa. JACINTO 1995, 75–102. [14: 389–417]

1995F Discurso ente el Tennō: Sobre la filosofía de la historia. JACINTO 1995, 103–7. [12: 267–72]

1995G Fundamentación filosófica de las matemáticas. JACINTO 1995, 109–52. [11: 237–85]

1995H Lógica del topos y cosmovisión religiosa. JACINTO 1995, 153–233. [11: 371–464]

1996A The Principle of the New World Order. ARISAKA 1996A, 100–5. Also translated in DILWORTH and VIGLIELMO 1998, 73–7. [12: 426–34]

1996B L'Essence nationale du Japon. Trans. by Pierre Lavelle. Yves-Marie Allioux, ed., *Cent ans de pensée au Japon.* Paris: Editions Philippe Picquier, 81–114. [10: 265–333]

1996C *L'io e il tu.* Trans. by R. Andolfato. Padova: Ungarese. [6: 321–427]

1996D Foreword to Tanabe Ryūji, *Koizumi Yakumo*. Trans. by Yusa Michiko, *Monumenta Nipponica* 51: 313–16. [1: 410–13]
1997A *Essai sur le bien, chapitre I & II*. Trans. by Ōshima Hitoshi. Paris: Éditions Osiris. [1: 3–101]
1997B Coincidentia Oppositorum and Love. Trans. by Wayne Yokoyama. *The Eastern Buddhist* 30/1: 7–12. [14: 301–9]
1998A The Historical Body. DILWORTH and VIGLIELMO 1998, 37–53. [14: 265–91]
1998B The World as Identity of Absolute Contradiction. DILWORTH and VIGLIELMO 1998, 54–72. [9: 305–35]
1998C On National Polity. DILWORTH and VIGLIELMO 1998, 78–95. [12: 397–416]
1999A Ort. EBERFELD 1999, 72–139. [4: 208–89]
1999B Ich und Du. EBERFELD 1999, 140–203. [6: 321–427]
1999C Ortlogic und religiöse Weltanschauung. EBERFELD 1999, 204–84. [11: 371–464]
1999D *Logique du lieu et vision religieuse du monde*. Trans. by Sugimura Yasuhiko and Sylvain Cardonnel. Paris: Editions Osiris. [11: 371–464]
1999E *Un étude sur le bien* (prefaces and chap. 1). Trans. by Bernard Stevens. *Revue philosophique de Louvain* 1: 19–29. [1: 3–17]
1999F Logique prédicative. Trans. by Jacynthe Tremblay. *Revue philosophique de Louvain* 1: 57–95. Reprinted: TREMBLAY 2000A, 159–88. [5: 58–97]
1999G Logique de lieu et vision religieuse du monde (chap. 2). Trans. by Sugimura Yasuhiko and Sylvain Cardonnel. *Revue philosophique de Louvain* 1: 96–112. [11: 391–412]
2000A Le monde intelligible. TREMBLAY 2000A, 189–228 [5: 123–85]
2000B La position de l'individuel dans le monde historique. TREMBLAY 2000A, 229–74. [9: 69–146]
2001A L'intuizione attiva. CESTARI 2001. [8: 541–71]
2001B Saggio su Descartes. CESTARI 2001. [11: 141–75]

Nishitani Keiji 西谷啓治
1943 (roundtable discussion with Kōsaka Masaaki, Kōyama Iwao, and Suzuki Shigetaka 鈴木成高.) 『世界史的立場と日本』 *[The World-Historical Standpoint and Japan]*. Tokyo: Chūōkōron-sha.
1959 The Problem of Myth. *Religious Studies in Japan*. Tokyo: Maruzen, 50–60. [6: 287–301]
1960A Der Buddhismus und das Christentum. *Zeitschrift für Kultur und Geschichte Ostasiens* 88: 5–32. [6: 257–86]
1960B Der Buddhismus und das Christentum. *Nachrichten der Gesellschaft für Natur- und Völkerkunde Ostasiens* 88: 5–32. [6: 257–86]
1960C Die religiös-philosophische Existenz im Buddhismus. Richard Wisser, ed. *Sinn und Sein: Ein philosophisches Symposion*. Tübingen: Max Niemeyer Verlag, 381–98. [17: 89–112]
1960D The Religious Situation in Present-Day Japan. *Contemporary Religions in Japan*. 1: 7–24. [19: 3–20]
1961A Eine buddhistische Stimme zum Thema Entmythologisierung. *Zeitschrift für Religions- und Geistesgeschichte* 13/3–4: 244–62, 345–56.
1961B (roundtable discussion with Kōsaka Masaaki, Mutō Kazuo, Kuyama Yasushi 久山 康, Endō Shūsaku 遠藤周作, et al.) 『戦後日本精神史』 *[Postwar Japanese Intellectual History]*. Tokyo: Sōbunsha.
1964A Rationale of the International Institute for Japan Studies. *Japan Studies* 1/1: 1–8.
1964B Japan in the World. *Japan Studies* 1: 2–9.

1965 Harmony of Religion and Science. *Japan Studies* 9, 7–8.
1967 はしがき [Preface]. Nishitani Keiji, ed.,『現代日本と哲学』*[Contemporary Japan and philosophy]*. Tokyo: Yukonsha, 1–5.
1968A A Buddhist Philosopher Looks at the Future of Christianity. *Japanese Christian Yearbook*. Tokyo: Kyōbunkwan, 108–11.
1968B Japan in the Contemporary World. *Japan Studies* 13: 1–6.
1968C Kami and Fundamental Experience. *The Concept of Kami*. Tokyo: Shinto Studies, 27–9.
1969 On Modernization and Tradition in Japan. Trans. by Kuyama Yasushi and Kobayashi Nobuo. *Modernization and Tradition in Japan*. Nishinomiya: International Institute for Japan Studies, 69–96. [25: 47–76]
1975A The Significance of Zen in Modern Society. *Japanese Religions* 8/3: 18–24.
1975B (roundtable discussion with Tsukamoto Zenryū and Shibayama Zenkei.) Chinese Zen. *The Eastern Buddhist* 8/2: 66–93.
1976 Zum Geleit. WALDENFELS 1976, 3–4.
1978 The Problem of Time in Shinran. Trans. by Dennis Hirota. *The Eastern Buddhist* 11/1: 13–26. [18: 211–23]
1979 (symposium with Kobayashi Hideo 小林秀雄, Kawakami Tetsutarō 河上徹太郎, et al.)『近代の超克』*[Overcoming modernity]*. Tokyo: Fusanabō.
1981A Ontology and Utterance. *Philosophy East and West* 31/1: 29–43.
1981B Postwar Japanese Thought: 1945–1960. *Japan Christian Quarterly* 47/3: 132–78. Translation of most of chapter 2 of 1961B.
1982A *Religion and Nothingness*. Trans. by Jan Van Bragt. Berkeley: University of California Press. [10: 3–319]
1982B The I-Thou Relation in Zen Buddhism. Trans. by Norman Waddell. FRANCK 1982, 47–60. [12: 276–89]
1982C Science and Zen. Trans. by Richard DeMartino. FRANCK 1982, 111–37. [11: 227–61]
1982D The Awakening of Self in Buddhism. Trans. by Bandō Shōjun. FRANCK 1982, 22–30. [17: 79–87]
1983 Zen and the Modern World. *Zen Buddhism Today* 1: 19–25. [11: 161–205]
1984A The Standpoint of Zen. Trans. by John C. Maraldo. *The Eastern Buddhist* 17/1: 1–26. [10: 135–87]
1984B Was bedeutet eigentlich...? *Zen Buddhism Today* 2: 185–7.
1985A All-Einheit als eine Frage. *All-Einheit: Wege eines Gedankens in Ost und West*. Ed. by Dieter Henrich. Stuttgart: Klett-Cotta, 12–21. [6: 257–86]
1985B Encountering No-Religion. Trans. by Livia Knaul. *Zen Buddhism Today* 3: 141–4.
1985C An Interview with Keiji Nishitani. *FAS Society Journal* (Summer), 3–9.
1985D The Days of My Youth: An Autobiographical Sketch. Trans. by Jess Shore. *FAS Society Journal* (Winter), 25–30. [20: 175–84]
1986A The Starting Point of My Philosophy. Trans. by Jeff Shore. *FAS Society Journal* (Autumn), 24–9. [20: 185–95]
1986B Three Worlds—No Dharma: Where to Seek the Mind? *Zen Buddhism Today* 4: 119–25. [19: 3–10]
1986C *Was ist Religion?* Trans. by Dora-Fischer-Barnicol. Frankfurt: Insel Verlag. [10: 3–319]
1986D Remembering Dr. Daisetz T. Suzuki. Masao Abe, ed., *A Zen Life: D. T. Suzuki Remembered*. Tokyo: Weatherhill, 1986, 148–59. [21: 115–26]
1986E (interview) Walking on the Waves. *Parabola* 11/4: 18–27.

1986F Modernisierung und Tradition in Japan. Constantin v. Barloewen and Kai Werhahn-Mees, eds., *Japan und der Westen.* Frankfurt: Fischer Verlag, 183–204. [25: 47–76]

1987A Reflections on Two Addresses by Martin Heidegger. PARKES 1987, 145–54. [14: 53–69]

1987B Kōan Zen. *FAS Society Journal* (Fall), 8–11.

1988 (discussion with Kawai Hayao and David Miller.) The Divine in the Contemporary World. Trans. by Mark Unno. *Kyoto Journal* (Fall), 16–22.

1989A Vorbereitende Bemerkungen zu zwei Meßkircher Ansprachen von M. Heidegger. *Japan und Heidegger,* ed. by Hartmut Buchner. Sigmaringen: Jan Thorbecke Verlag, 147–58.

1989B Ein tiefes Gefühl für die Krise der modernen Zivilisation: Nachruf auf M. Heidegger. Ibid., 193–4.

1989C Encounter with Emptiness. UNNO 1989, 1–4.

1989D (discussion with Yagi Seiichi 八木誠一.)『直接経験: 西洋精神史と宗教』*[Immediate experience: Religion and the intellectual history of the west].* Tokyo: Shunjūsha.

1989E The Japanese Art of Arranged Flowers. Trans. by Jeff Shore. *Chanoyu Quarterly* 60: 7–16.

1990A Vom Wesen der Begegnung. Trans. by Ōhashi Ryūsuke and Hartmut Buchner. ŌHASHI 1990, 258–74. [11: 342–52]

1990B Die "Verrüktheit" beim Dichter Bashō. Trans. by Engelbert Jorißen. ŌHASHI 1990, 275–99. [20: 135–49]

1990C *The Self-Overcoming of Nihilism.* Trans. by Graham Parkes and Setsuko Aihara. Albany: SUNY Press. [8: 3–290]

1990D (discussion with Sasaki Tōru 佐々木 徹.)『西谷啓治随聞』*[Nishitani Keiji: At random].* Tokyo: Hōzōkan.

1990E Religious-Philosophical Existence in Buddhism. Trans. by Paul Shepherd. *The Eastern Buddhist* 23/2: 1–17. [17: 89–113]

1991A *Nishida Kitarō.* Trans. by J. W. Heisig and Yamamoto Seisaku. Berkeley: University of California Press. [9:5–327]

1991B A Buddhist Voice in the Demythologizing Debate. Trans. by Richard F. Szippl. *The Eastern Buddhist* 24/1: 1–27.

1995 El nihilismo como existencia. JACINTO 1995, 315–27. [8: 3–16]

1996 The Problem of *Anjin* in Zen (I). Trans. by Mark L. Blum. *The Eastern Buddhist* 29/1: 1–32. [11: 33–61]

1998A The Contemporary Era as a Turning Point in World History. DILWORTH and VIGLIELMO 1998, 381–4. [4: 295–301]

1998B Concerning the Worldview of the New Japan. DILWORTH and VIGLIELMO 1998, 385–91. [4: 347–55]

1998C The Nation and Religion. DILWORTH and VIGLIELMO 1998, 392–401. [4: 368–80]

1999A *La religión y la nada.* Trans. by Raquel Bouso García. Madrid: Ediciones Siruela. [10: 3–319]

1999B Emptiness and Sameness. Michele Marra, *Modern Japanese Aesthetics.* Honolulu: University of Hawai'i Press, 1999, 179–217. [13: 111–60]

2000 (discussion with Abe Masao.) 世界悪とニヒリズム [A dialogue on global evil and nihilism]. Abe Masao,『虚偽と虚無』*[Fiction and nihility].* Kyoto: Hōzōkan, 173–205.

Nitta Yoshihiro 新田義弘 and Tatematsu Hirotaka 立松弘孝
1979 *Japanese Phenomenology*. Analecta Husserliana 8. Boston: Reidel.
Nitta Yoshihiro, Tatematsu Hirotaka, and Shimomisse Eiichi 下店栄一
1979 Phenomenology and Philosophy in Japan. NITTA and TATEMATSU 1979, 3–17.
Noda Matao 野田又夫
1955 East-West Synthesis in Nishida Kitarō. *Philosophy East and West* 4/4: 345–59.
1984 『哲学の三つの伝統』 *[Three philosophical traditions]*. Tokyo: Kinokuniya Shoten.
Noguchi Tsuneki 野口恒樹
1982 『西田哲学から我汝哲学へ』 *[From Nishida's philosophy to a philosophy of I and you]*. Ise: Shōhakusanbō.
Numata Shigeo 沼田滋夫
1984 『西田哲学への旅』 *[A journey to Nishida's philosophy]*. Tokyo: Hokuju Shuppan.
Ogawa Tadashi 小川 侃
1979 The Kyoto School of Philosophy and Phenomenology. NITTA and TATEMATSU 1979, 207–21.
Ōhashi Ryōsuke 大橋良介
1990 *Die Philosophie der Kyōto Schule*. Freiburg: Karl Alber.
1991 「種の論理」再考 [Rethinking the logic of the specific]. TAKEUCHI Yoshinori, MUTŌ and TSUJIMURA, 1991, 104–30.
Okamura Mihoko 岡村美穂子 and Ueda Shizuteru 上田閑照
1999 『大拙の風景：鈴木大拙とは誰か』 *[Daisetsu's landscape: Who was Suzuki Daisetsu?]*. Kyoto: Tōeisha.
O'Leary, Joseph S.
1987 Foreword. NISHIDA 1987A, VII–XXIII.
Ōmine Akira 大峯 顯
1990 悲哀と意識：西田哲学における情意なものについて [Sadness and consciousness: Feeling-will in Nishida's philosophy]. UEDA Shizuteru 1990, 101–37.
1995 西田幾多郎と夏目漱石：エリオットの詩的世界との出会い [Nishida Kitarō and Natsume Sōseki: Encounters with the poetic world of T. S. Eliot.] 『思想』 857: 181–98.
Onodera Isao 小野寺 功
1992 『大地の神学』 *[A theology of the earth]*. Kyoto: Kōrosha.
Ōshima Yasumasa 大島康正
1951 教師としての田辺先生 [Professor Tanabe as a teacher]. KŌBUNDŌ 1951, 273–84.
1965 大東亜戦争と京都学派—知識人の政治参加について [The great Asian war and the Kyoto school: The political participation of the intellectuals]. 『中央公論』 8: 125–43.
Ozaki Makoto 尾崎 誠
1990 *Introduction to the Philosophy of Tanabe: According to the English Translation of the Seventh Chapter of "The Demonstratio of Christianity."* Amsterdam: Editions Rodopi.
Parkes, Graham
1987 (ed.) *Heidegger and Asian Thought*. Honolulu: University of Hawai'i Press.
1990 Introduction. NISHITANI 1990C, XV–XXVIII.
1993 Nietzsche and Nishitani on the Self-Overcoming of Nihilism. *International Studies in Philosophy*, 25/2: 51–60.

1997 The Putative Fascism of the Kyoto School and the Political Correctness of the Modern Academy. *Philosophy East and West* 47/3: 305–36.

Paslick, Robert H.

1997 From Nothingness to Nothingness: The Nature and Destiny of the Self in Boehme and Nishitani. *The Eastern Buddhist* 30/1: 13–31.

Paul, Gregor

1986 *Zur Geschichte der Philosophie in Japan und zu ihrer Darstellung*. Tokyo: Deutsche Gesellschaft für Natur– und Völkerkunde Ostasiens.

1993 *Philosophie in Japan: Von den Anfängen bis zur Heian-Zeit*. Munich: Judicium.

Phillips, Stephen H.

1987 Nishitani's Buddhist Response to "Nihilism." *Journal of the American Academy of Religion* 55/1: 75–104.

Piovesana, Gino K.

1963 *Recent Japanese Philosophical Thought, 1862–1962: A Survey*. Tokyo: Enderle. Revised and reprinted: *Recent Japanese Philosophical Thought, 1862–1996: A Survey*. Curzon, Richmond, Surrey, 1994.

Piper, R. F.

1936 Nishida, Notable Japanese Personalist. *The Personalist* 17/1: 21–31.

Prieto, Félix, ed. and trans.

1989 *Dogen, La naturaleza de Buda (Shobogenzo)*. Barcelona: Ediciones Obelisco.

Robinson, Cora-Jean Eaton

1989 The Conflict of Science and Religion in Dynamic *Śūnyatā*. UNNO 1989A, 101–13.

Rodante, Angelo

1995 *Sunyata buddhista e kenosi cristologica in Masao Abe*. Roma: Città Nuova.

Sasaki Tōru 佐々木 徹

1977 『西田幾多郎の世界』 *[The world of Nishida Kitarō]*. Tokyo: Keisō Shobō.

1986 『西谷啓治: その思索への道標』 *[Nishitani Keiji: Signposts to his thought]*. Tokyo: Hozōkan.

Scheiffele, Eberhard

1984 Bemerkungen zur deutschen Übersetzung von Keiji Nishitanis *Shūkyō to wa nanika. Zen Buddhism Today* 2: 78–89.

Schinzinger, Robert

1940 Über Kitaro Nishidas Philosophie. *Monumenta Nipponica* 3: 28–39.

1958 *Intelligibility and the Philosophy of Nothingness*. Tokyo: Maruzen.

1983 *Japanisches Denken: Der weltanschauliche Hintergrund des heutigen Japan*. Berlin: Eric Schmidt Verlag.

Shaner, David Edward

1987 Beneath Nihilism: The Phenomenological Foundations of Meaning. *Personalist Forum* 3: 113–39.

Shibayama Futoshi 柴山 太

1994 *Coping with the Anglo-American World Order: Japanese Intellectuals and the Cultural Crises of 1913–1953*. Ph.D. dissertation, Yale University. Ann Arbor: University Microfilms.

Shimomura Toratarō 下村寅太郎

1947 『若き西田幾多郎先生』 *[Young Professor Nishida Kitarō]*. Kyoto: Jinbunshoin.

1966 The Modernization of Japan, with Special Reference to Philosophy. *The Modernization of Japan* (Tokyo: Japan Society for the Promotion of Science), 1–28.

1977 『西田幾多郎: 同時代の記録』 *[Nishida Kitarō: A contemporary record]*. Tokyo: Iwanami Shoten.

1985A (ed.) 『西田幾多郎とその哲学』 *[Nishida Kitarō and his philosophy]*. Kyoto: Tōeisha.

1985B 西田先生と数学のこと [Professor Nishida and mathematics]. SHIMOMURA 1985A, 141–51.

1988 Nishida Kitarō and Some Aspects of his Philosophical Thought. NISHIDA 1988, 191–217.

1990 『西田哲学と日本の思想』 *[Nishida's philosophy and Japanese thought]*. 『下村寅太郎著作集』 *[Collected works of Shimomura Toratarō]*. Tokyo: Misuzu Shobō, vol. 12.

1992 Anecdotes That Now Seem Ancient. *The Eastern Buddhist* 25/1: 125–8.

Stevens, Bernard

1996 Histoire de l'être et nihilisme dans la perspective de l'école de Kyōto. *Heidegger Studies* 12: 83–94.

1997 Political Engagement and Political Judgment in the Thought of Nishitani Keiji. *Zen Buddhism Today* 14: 33–56.

1998 Reflections on the Notion of Reality in the Thought of Nishida and Nishitani. *Zen Buddhism Today* 15: 1–14.

2000 *Topologie du néant: Une approche de l'école de Kyōto*. Paris: Éditions Peeters.

Streng, Frederick

1982 Three Approaches to Authentic Existence: Christian, Confucian, and Buddhist. *Philosophy East and West* 32: 371–92.

Strolz, Walter

1984 Zen-Buddhismus und christlicher Glaube: Zum Buch von Keiji Nishitani *Was ist Religion? Zen Buddhism Today* 2: 60–77.

Sueki Takehiro 末木剛博

1988 『西田幾多郎: その哲学体系』 *[Nishida Kitarō: His philosophical system]*. 4 vols. Tokyo: Shinjūsha, 1983–1988.

Suzuki Sadami 鈴木貞美

2000 La philosophie vitaliste de Nishida Kitarō: Ses limites et ses possibilités dans le courant de pensée du "dépassement de la modernité" au Japon. BERQUE 2000, 117–41.

Swanson, Paul L.

1996 Absolute Nothingness and Emptiness in Nishitani Keiji: An Essay from the Perspective of Classical Buddhist Thought. *The Eastern Buddhist* 29/1: 99–108.

Takahashi Satomi 高橋里美

1962 田辺元君の死を悼む [In memoriam: Tanabe Hajime]. 『思想』 459: 1258–9.

1973A 『フッセルの現象学および現代日本の体系哲学について』 *[Husserl's phenomenology and systematic philosophy in Japan today]*. 『高橋里美全集』 *[Complete works of Takahashi Satomi]*, vol. 4. Tokyo: Fukumura.

1973B 学者を怒らせた話 [A talk that angered the scholar]. *Complete Works of Takahashi Satomi*, ut supra, vol. 7.

Takeda Ryūsei 武田龍精

1991 『親鸞浄土教と西田哲学』 *[Shinran's Pure Land Buddhism and Nishida's philosophy]*. Kyoto: Nagata Bunshōdō.

1996 宗教·哲学·科学 [Religion, philosophy, science] 『大乗禅』 871: 59–69.

Takemura Makio 竹村牧男

1997 「即非の論理」の宗教哲学: 大拙と寸心の魂の交流をめぐって [Religious philosophy based on "the logic of *soku-hi*": The soul-exchange of Suzuki and Nishida].『哲学·思想論集』22: 1–28.

Takeuchi Seiichi 竹内整一, Satō Masao 佐藤雅男, Deoka Hiroshi 出岡 宏, Takeuchi Yoshimi 竹内 好, and Nagano Mika 長野美香

1996 『《善の研究》用語索引』 *[Glossary of technical terms in "An Inquiry into the Good"].* Tokyo: Perikansha.

Takeuchi Yoshimi 竹内 好

1979 近代の超克 [Overcoming modernity]. See NISHITANI 1979, 273–341.

Takeuchi Yoshinori 武内義範

1959 Buddhism and Existentialism: The Dialogue between Oriental and Occidental Thought. *Religion and Culture: Essays in Honor of Paul Tillich,* ed. by W. Leibrecht. New York: Harper, 291–318.

1981 田辺哲学と絶対無 [Tanabe's philosophy and absolute nothingness]. NANZAN INSTITUTE 1981, 196–220.

1982 The Philosophy of Nishida: An Interpretation. FRANCK 1982, 179–202.

1983 *The Heart of Buddhism: In Search of the Timeless Spirit of Primitive Buddhism.* Trans. by J. W. Heisig. New York: Crossroad. Italian edition: *Il cuore del Buddhismo: Alla ricerca dei valori originari e perenni del Buddhismo.* Trans. by Maria De Giorgi (Bologna: Editrice Missionaria Italiana, 1999).

1986 Translator's Introduction. TANABE 1986, XXXI–XLVII.

1990 Recollections of Professor Tanabe. UNNO and HEISIG 1990, 1–11.

1992 The Spirit of Poverty. *The Eastern Buddhist* 25/1: 128–30.

1999 『武内義範著作集』 *[Collected works of Takeuchi Yoshinori],* 5 vols. Kyoto: Hōzōkan.

Takeuchi Yoshinori, Mutō Kazuo, and Tsujimura Kōichi 辻村公一, eds.

1991 『田辺元: 思想と回想』 *[Tanabe Hajime: Thoughts and reminiscences].* Tokyo: Chikuma Shobō.

Takeuchi Yoshinori, Ōshima Yasumasa, et al., eds.

1985 『哲学の世界』 *[The world of philosophy].* Tokyo: Sōbunsha.

Takeuchi Yoshitomo 竹内良知

1970 『西田幾多郎』 *[Nishida Kitarō].* Tokyo: Tokyo University Press.

1978 『西田幾多郎と現在』 *[Nishida Kitarō and the present].* Tokyo: Daisanbunmeisha.

1992 『西田哲学の〈行為的直観〉』 *["Active intuition" in Nishida's philosophy].* Tokyo: Nōbunkyō.

Takizawa Katsumi 滝沢克巳

1972 『滝沢克巳全集』 *[Complete works of Takizawa Katsumi].* Kyoto: Hōzōkan.

Tanabe Hajime 田辺 元

1959A Todesdialektik. *Festschrift Martin Heidegger zum 70. Geburtstag,* ed. by Günther Neske. Pfullingen, 1959, 93–133. [13: 252–76]

1959B Memento Mori. *Philosophical Studies of Japan* 1: 1–12. [13: 165–75]

1969 The Logic of the Species as Dialectics. Trans. by David Dilworth and Satō Taira. *Monumenta Nipponica* 24/3: 273–88. [7: 257–69]

1971 Zu Hegels Lehre vom Urteil. *Hegel-Studien* 6: 211–29. [3: 136–51]

1973 Memento Mori (German translation). Yagi Seiichi and Ulrich Luz, eds., *Gott in Japan.* Munich: Ch. Kaiser, 113–26. [13: 165–75]

1986 *Philosophy as Metanoetics.* Trans. by Takeuchi Yoshinori, Valdo Viglielmo, and J. W. Heisig. Berkeley: University of California Press. [9: 1–269]

1990A Versuch, die Bedeutung der Logik der Spezies du klären. Trans. by Johannes Laube. Ōhashi 1990, 145–95. [6: 466–502]

1990B Die Grenze des Gedichts "Die junge Parze" und ihre Überwindung. Trans. by Johannes Laube. Ōhashi 1990, 196–224. [13:92–109]

1990C Religion, Theology, and Philosophy. Conclusion: Love, Struggle, and Freedom. Ozaki 1990, 127–69. [10: 235–69]

1995A La diálectica de la lógica de la especie. Jacinto 1995, 247–50. [7: 253–69]

1995B La especie como base de la estructura práxica de la lógica. Jacinto 1995, 251–81. [7: 345–54]

1995C El carácter religioso de la práctica. Jacinto 1995, 283–305. [7: 345–72]

1998A A New Stage in Historical Reality. Dilworth and Viglielmo 1998, 106–14.

1998B Christianity, Marxism, and Japanese Buddhism: In Anticipation of a Second Religious Reformation. Dilworth and Viglielmo 1998, 115–58. [10: 271–324]

1998C Religion, Theology, and Philosophy: A Concluding Word on Love, Struggle, and Freedom. Dilworth and Viglielmo 1998, 159–89. [10: 235–69]

Thelle, Notte

1992 The Flower Blooms on the Cliff's Edge: Nishitani Keiji, a Thinker between East and West. *The Eastern Buddhist* 25/1: 130–7.

Thompson, Evan

1986 Planetary Thinking/Planetary Building: An Essay on Martin Heidegger and Nishitani Keiji. *Philosophy East and West* 36/3: 235–52.

Tosaka Jun 戸坂 潤

1970 『戸坂潤全集』 *[Complete works of Tosaka Jun].* Tokyo: Keisei Shobō.

Tremblay, Jacynthe

2000A *Nishida Kitarō: Le jeu de l'individuel et de l'universel.* Paris: CNRS Editions.

2000B *La néantisation du soi dans la logique du basho.* Berque 2000, 87–116.

Tsujimura Kōichi 辻村公一

1965A (ed.)『田辺元』. *[Tanabe Hajime].* Tokyo: Chikuma Shobō.

1965B 田辺哲学について [Tanabe's philosophy]. Tsujimura 1965, 7–62.

1991 田辺哲学とハイデッガーの思索 [Tanabe's philosophy and Heidegger's thought]. Takeuchi, Mutō, and Tsujimura 1991, 131–67.

Tsunoda Yukihiko 角田幸彦

1994 『西田幾多郎との対話: 宗教と哲学をめぐって』 *[In dialogue with Nishida Kitarō: Religion and philosophy].* Tokyo: Hokuju Shuppan.

Ueda Hisashi 上田久

1978 『祖父西田幾多郎』 *[My grandfather, Nishida Kitarō].* Tokyo: Nansōsha.

Ueda Shizuteru 上田閑照

1981 西田哲学における宗教理解について [The understanding of religion in Nishida's philosophy]. Nanzan Institute 1981, 56–81.

1990 (ed.)『西田哲学への問い』 *[Questioning Nishida's philosophy].* Tokyo: Iwanami Shoten.

1991 『西田幾多郎を読む』 *[Reading Nishida Kitarō].* Tokyo: Iwanami Shoten.

1992A My Teacher. *The Eastern Buddhist* 25/1: 1–7.

1992B (ed.)『情意における空』 *[Emptiness in feeling-will].* Tokyo: Sōbunsha.

1995A 『西田幾多郎: 人間の生涯ということ』 *[Nishida Kitarō: This thing we call a person's life].* Tokyo: Iwanami Shoten.

1995B Nishida's Thought. Trans. by Jan Van Bragt. *The Eastern Buddhist* 28/1: 29–47.

1995C The Difficulty of Understanding Nishida's Philosophy. *The Eastern Buddhist* 28/2: 175–82.

1995D Nishida, Nationalism, and the War in Question. HEISIG and MARALDO 1995, 77–106.

1997 『宗教への思索』 *[Explorations in religion]*. Tokyo: Sōbunsha.

1998A 西田幾多郎:「あの戦争」と『日本文化の問題』 [Nishida Kitarō: "That war" and *The Question of Japanese Culture*]. FUJITA Masakatsu 1998A, 462–509.

1998B 『西田哲学への導き: 経験と自覚』 *[A guide to Nishida's philosophy: Experience and awareness]*. Tokyo: Iwanami Shoten.

Ueda Yasuharu 上田泰治

1985 田辺哲学における生物学 [Biology in Tanabe's philosophy]. TAKEUCHI Yoshinori and ŌSHIMA 1989, 205–27.

Ueda Yoshifumi 上田義文

1990 Tanabe's Metanoetics and Shinran's Thought. UNNO and HEISIG 1990, 134–49.

Uesugi Tomoyuki 上杉和行

1982 『雪門禅師と西田幾多郎』 *[Zen Master Setsumon and Nishida Kitarō]*. Kanazawa: Nōtō Printers.

1988 『西田幾多郎の生涯』 *[The life of Nishida Kitarō]*. Kyoto: Tōeisha.

Ueyama Shunpei 上山春平

1971 『日本の思想』 *[Japanese thought]*. Tokyo: Simul Shuppansha.

Umehara Takeshi 梅原 猛

1959 京都学派との交渉私史: 天ぷらと哲学 [A personal history of dealings with the Kyoto school: Tempura and philosophy]. 『思想の科学』 8: 31–8.

Unno, Taitetsu

1989A (ed.) *The Religious Philosophy of Nishitani Keiji: The Encounter with Emptiness.* Berkeley: Asian Humanities Press.

1989B Emptiness and Reality in Mahāyāna Buddhism. UNNO 1989A, 307–20.

1990 Shin Buddhism and Metanoetics. UNNO and HEISIG 1990, 117–33.

Unno, Taitetsu and James W. Heisig, eds.

1990 *The Religious Philosophy of Tanabe Hajime: The Metanoetic Imperative.* Berkeley: Asian Humanities Press.

Van Bragt, Jan

1966 Notulae on Emptiness and Dialogue: Reading Professor Nishitani's "What is Religion?" *Japanese Religions* 4/4: 50–78.

1971 Nishitani on Japanese Religiosity. J. Spae, ed., *Japanese Religiosity*. Tokyo: Oriens, 271–84.

1982 Translator's Introduction. NISHITANI 1982A, XXIII–XLV.

1987 Religion and Science in Keiji Nishitani. *Zen Buddhism Today* 5: 161–74.

1989 Translating *Shūkyō to wa nani ka* into *Religion and Nothingness.* UNNO 1989A, 5–12.

1991 The Challenge to Christian Theology from Kyoto-School Buddhist Philosophy. *Studies in Interreligious Dialogue* 1: 41–57.

1992 Nishitani the Prophet. *The Eastern Buddhist* 25/1: 28–50.

1995 Kyoto Philosophy: Intrinsically Nationalistic? HEISIG and MARALDO, 1995, 233–54.

1998 Nishitani Revisited. *Zen Buddhism Today* 15: 77–96.

Vianello, Giancarlo

1996 La scuola di Kyōto attraverso il novecento. MARCHIANÒ 1996, 25–65.

Viglielmo, Valdo

1971 Nishida Kitarō: The Early Years. Donald H. Shively, ed., *Tradition and Modernization in Japanese Culture.* Princeton: Princeton University Press.

Vroom, Hendrik M.

1986 Aan het Nihilisme voorbij: De Godsdienstfilosofie van Nishitani. *Nederlands Theologisch Tijdschrift* 40: 143–59.

Waldenfels, Hans

1976 *Absolutes Nichts: Zur Grundlegung des Dialoges zwischen Buddhismus und Christentum.* Freiburg: Herder. English translation: *Absolute Nothingness: Foundations for a Buddhist-Christian Dialogue.* Trans. by J. W. Heisig. New York: Paulist, 1980.

1995 God's Kenosis and Buddhist Sunyata in the World of Today. IVES 1995, 150–64.

Wargo, Robert J. J.

1972 *The Logic of Basho and the Concept of Nothingness in the Philosophy of Nishida Kitarō.* Ph.D. dissertation, University of Michigan. Ann Arbor: University Microfilms.

Wattles, Jeffrey

1990 Dialectic and Religious Experience in *Philosophy as Metanoetics.* UNNO and HEISIG 1990, 340–59.

Yagi Seiichi 八木誠一

1998 The Language of the Kyoto School of Philosophy. *Zen Buddhism Today* 15: 65–76.

Yamada Munemutsu 山田宗睦

1975 『昭和の精神史: 京都学派の哲学』 *[Intellectual history of the Shōwa period: The philosophy of the Kyoto school].* Kyoto: Jinbun Shoin.

1978 『西田幾多郎の哲学』 *[The philosophy of Nishida Kitarō].* Tokyo: San'ichi Shobō.

Yamamoto Seisaku 山本誠作

1987 『無とプロセス: 西田思想の展開をめぐって』 *[Nothingness and process: The development of Nishida's thought].* Kyoto: Kōrosha.

Yamashita Tadanori 山下忠規

1990 Metanoetics and Christian Theology. UNNO and HEISIG 1990, 201–20.

Yoo Chul Ok

1976 *Nishida Kitarō's Concept of Absolute Nothingness in its Relation to Japanese Culture.* Ph.D. dissertation, Boston University. Ann Arbor: University Microfilms.

Yoshioka Kenjirō 吉岡健二郎

1996 La visione artistica di Nishida Kitarō. MARCHIANÒ 1996, 105–50.

Yuasa Yasuo 湯浅泰雄

1987A Modern Japanese Philosophy and Heidegger. PARKES 1987, 155–74.

1987B *The Body.* Trans. by T. P. Kasulis and Nagatomo Shigenori. Albany: SUNY.

Yusa Michiko 遊佐道子

1989 Fashion and *A-lētheia:* Philosophical Integrity and War-Time Thought Control. 『比較思想研究』 281–94.

1992 The Eternal is the Transient is the Eternal: "A flower blooms and the whole world arises." *The Eastern Buddhist* 25/1: 149–54.

1995A Reflections on Nishida Studies. *The Eastern Buddhist* 28/2: 287–96.

1995B アメリカにおける西田研究を考える [Thoughts on Nishida studies in the United States].『思想』857: 221–35.
1995C Nishida and Totalitarianism: A Philosopher's Resistance. HEISIG and MARALDO 1995, 107–31.
1998A『伝記西田幾多郎』*[A biography of Nishida Kitarō]*.『西田哲学選集』, supplementary vol. 1. Kyoto: Tōeisha).
1998B Nishida's Philosophy of Religion: A Religious Philosophy. *Zen Buddhism Today* 15: 15–32.
1998C Philosophy and Inflation: Miki Kiyoshi in Weimar Germany, 1922–1924. *Monumenta Nipponica* 53/1: 45–71.

Special editions of journals

The Eastern Buddhist
1992 In Memoriam Nishitani Keiji, 1900–1990. 25/1.
1995 Nishida Kitarō Memorial Issue. 28/2.
Études phénoménologiques
1993 L'École de Kyōto. 18.
Ideals『理想』
1963 田辺元の哲学 [The philosophy of Tanabe Hajime]. 357.
Mahāyāna Zen『大乗禅』
1992 西田哲学と対話 [Nishida's philosophy and dialogue], 827, 828.
1996 西谷啓治研究 [Studies on Nishitani Keiji], 859. Partially translated in *Buddhist-Christian Studies* 19 (1999), 137–72.
1997 西谷啓治研究 [Studies on Nishitani Keiji]. 871.
Philosophical Studies『哲学研究』
1964 田辺元博士追悼号 [In memoriam: Dr. Tanabe Hajime]. 489.
Revue philosophique de Louvain
1994 La reception européenne de l'école de Kyōto. 4 (Novembre).
1999 Nishida. 1 (Fevrier).
Science Magazine『科学ペン』
1941 田辺哲学 [The philosophy of Tanabe]. 6.
Thought『思想』
1936 特輯, 西田哲学 [Special issue: Nishita Kitarō]. 164.
1995 西田幾多郎: 歿後50年 [Nishida Kitarō: Fifty years after his death]. 857.
Zen Buddhism Today
1997 Religion and the Contemporary World in Light of Nishitani Keiji's Thought. 14.
1998 Nishida's Philosophy, Nishitani's Philosophy, and Zen. 15.

Index

CPSIA information can be obtained
at www.ICGtesting.com
Printed in the USA
BVHW080525221218
536219BV00001B/24/P